Religion, Metaphysics, and th

MW00626517

CHRISTOPHER BEN SIMPSON

# Religion, Metaphysics, and the Postmodern

## William Desmond and John D. Caputo

WIPF & STOCK · Eugene, Oregon

Wipf and Stock Publishers
199 W 8th Ave, Suite 3
Eugene, OR 97401

Religion, Metaphysics, and the Postmodern
By Simpson, Christopher Ben
Copyright©2009 by Simpson, Christopher Ben
ISBN 13: 978-1-5326-0509-3
Publication date 8/5/2016
Previously published by Indiana University Press, 2009

# Contents

# Acknowledgments

The U.S. Fulbright Program made possible the research for this work in 2003–2004 at the Institute of Philosophy at Katholeike Universiteit Leuven. I wish to thank Tom Tanner, Karen Diefendorf, and Lincoln Christian University for enabling the completion of my work at the University of Nottingham, and Steven Cone, Renee Ryan, Michelle Knight, and Jonathan Harrison for their time and their valuable comments on sundry draft chapters. I wish to thank John Milbank for believing in me and my project—for his guidance and insightful suggestions in the latter's completion. I am grateful to Conor Cunningham and Graham Ward for their attentive reading and the lively and pleasant exchange that helped me put the project in its finished form. I thank John Caputo for his help with this work and beyond. William Desmond has been an inspiring model, mentor, and friend. I thank him for his warm hospitality both in person and at a distance—for his constancy, his help, and his advice. For his continual generosity, I have only the deepest gratitude.

I dedicate this work to my wife, Kaysha, to our son, David—who was born as I began this work—and to our daughter, Lydia—who was born as I was finishing it. Their abiding love and warm companionship has sustained me in the hard years that have passed in its writing.

# Abbreviations

## William Desmond's Works

| | |
|---|---|
| *AOO* | *Art, Origins, Otherness.* Albany: SUNY Press, 2003. |
| AT | "Autonomia Turannos." *Ethical Perspectives* 5:4 (1998). |
| *BB* | *Being and the Between.* Albany: SUNY Press, 1995. |
| BDD | "Being, Determination, and Dialectic." *Review of Metaphysics* 48 (June 1995). |
| *BHD* | *Beyond Hegel and Dialectic.* Albany: SUNY Press, 1992. |
| BR | "On the Betrayals of Reverence." *Irish Theological Quarterly* 65 (2000). |
| CWSC | "Caesar With the Soul of Christ." *Tijdschrift voor Filosofie* 61 (1999). |
| *DDO* | *Desire, Dialectic and Otherness.* New Haven, Conn.: Yale University Press, 1987. |
| *EB* | *Ethics and the Between.* Albany: SUNY Press, 2001. |
| En | "Enemies." *Tijdschrift voor Filosofie* 63 (2001). |
| *GB* | *God and the Between.* Oxford: Blackwell, 2008. |
| GEW | "God, Ethos, Ways." *International Journal of the Philosophy of Religion* 45 (1999). |
| *HG* | *Hegel's God.* Aldershot: Ashgate, 2003. |
| HT | "Hyperbolic Thoughts." In *Framing a Vision of the World,* ed. André Cloots and Santiago Sia. Leuven: Leuven University Press, 1999. |
| MC | "Is There Metaphysics After Critique?" (2004) [unpublished]. |
| NDR | "Neither Deconstruction nor Reconstruction." *International Philosophical Quarterly* 40:1:157 (March 2000). |
| *PO* | *Philosophy and Its Others.* Albany: SUNY Press, 1990. |
| PR | "Philosophy of Religion." In *The Examined Life,* ed. Stanley Rosen. Quality Paperback Book Club, 2000. |
| *PU* | *Perplexity and Ultimacy.* Albany: SUNY Press, 1995. |

## John D. Caputo's Works

| | |
|---|---|
| *ADG* | *After the Death of God.* Ed. Jeffery Robbins. New York: Columbia University Press, 2007. |
| *AE* | *Against Ethics: Contributions to a Poetics of Obligation with Constant Reference to Deconstruction.* Bloomington: Indiana University Press, 1993. |
| BA | "Beyond Aestheticism: Derrida's Responsible Anarchy." *Research in Phenomenology* 18 (1988). |

| | |
|---|---|
| *DH* | *Demythologizing Heidegger.* Bloomington: Indiana University Press, 1993. |
| GA | "God and Anonymity: Prolegomena to an Ankhoral Religion." In *A Passion for the Impossible: John D. Caputo in Focus,* ed. Mark Dooley. Albany: SUNY Press, 2003. |
| GNA | "The Good News About Alterity: Derrida and Theology." *Faith and Philosophy* 10 (1993). |
| HKFM | "Heidegger, Kierkegaard and the Foundering of Metaphysics," *International Kierkegaard Commentary,* Vol. 6: "Fear and Trembling" and "Repetition," ed. Robert Perkins. Macon, Ga.: Mercer University Press, 1993. |
| *MD* | *Modernity and Its Discontents.* New York: Fordham University Press, 1992. |
| Meta | "Metanoetics: Elements of a Postmodern Christian Philosophy." *Christian Philosophy Today.* New York: Fordham University Press, 1999. |
| MMD | "On Mystics, Magi, and Deconstructionists." In *Portraits of American Continental Philosophers,* ed. James Watson. Bloomington: Indiana University Press, 1999. |
| *MRH* | *More Radical Hermeneutics: On Not Knowing Who We Are.* Bloomington: Indiana University Press, 2000. |
| *OR* | *On Religion.* London and New York: Routledge, March 2001. |
| *PhTh* | *Philosophy and Theology.* Nashville, Tenn.: Abingdon, 2006. |
| PMDG | "Postmodernism and the Desire for God: An Email Conversation with Edith Wyschogrod." *Cross-Currents* 48:3 (Fall 1998). |
| *PT* | *The Prayers and Tears of Jacques Derrida: Religion without Religion.* Bloomington: Indiana University Press, 1997. |
| *Rel* | *Blackwell Readings in Continental Philosophy: The Religious.* Ed. John D. Caputo. Oxford: Blackwell, 2001. |
| *RH* | *Radical Hermeneutics: Repetition, Deconstruction and the Hermeneutic Project.* Bloomington: Indiana University Press, 1987. |
| *WoG* | *The Weakness of God: A Theology of the Event.* Bloomington: Indiana University Press, 2006. |
| WSWB | "Without Sovereignty, Without Being: Unconditionality, the Coming God, and Derrida's Democracy to Come." *JCRT* 4.3 (August 2003). |

Religion, Metaphysics, and the Postmodern

# Introduction

I encountered William Desmond's work as a young would-be Derridean. It found me preoccupied, tracing the question—from Derrida to Levinas, Heidegger, Nietzsche—of how metaphysics became such a pervasive and malevolent force from which thought is to be freed with strange stratagems. Desmond's writing struck me as loosening the fetters and blinders—the assumed answers and latent liturgies—of these supposed liberations, and thus it presented me with an engaging and surprising (curious, perplexing, astonishing) vision . . . opening another way to see.

This work is intended to be an orienting opening into this other way—at once a systematic presentation of William Desmond's philosophical system and an argument for its viability and superiority relative to dominant alternate visions, here represented by those of John D. Caputo. The broad issue addressed is the status of religion and/or God-talk in the context of "postmodernity." It attends to the question: How should we think of religion and God today? How now—in the context of recent continental ("postmodern") philosophy—God? Within the broad outlines of this question, I wish to address the more particular issue of the relationship between religion and metaphysics—and, secondarily, ethics.

With regard to this relationship, there is a broad consensus within contemporary continental philosophy that is sometimes called "postmodern." There is a kind of post-metaphysical orthodoxy. The issue of the relevance of metaphysics for talk of God and religion is more often than not a non-issue. It is taken as given that "metaphysics" is no longer a live option for serious thinkers today, and that the task of thinking about religion relative to metaphysics is to learn to think God and/or do religion without or "after" it. Indeed, "metaphysics" seems to have become, in many quarters of contemporary continental thought, a pejorative term—a dirty word—meaning something like "what's been wrong with philosophy hitherto."

To put it more precisely, within the context of much contemporary continental philosophy, the *issue* of the nature of religion and God-talk has been treated in a post- or anti-metaphysical *manner*, informed by a certain "postmodern" philosophical *framework*. This particular treatment of this issue is worth addressing for several reasons. First, the question of the relation of metaphysics to religion in the context of postmodernity merits examination because of the perennial significance of the *issue* of the nature of religion and God-talk itself. Second, it is worth addressing because of the prevalence of a post- or anti-metaphysical *treatment* of or perspective on religion, as is evidenced in various ongoing conferences and publications in this vein (along with those going against the flow, as it were). Third, it is worth addressing because of the prevalence of the informing philosophical *framework* of "postmodern" continental philosophy on the contemporary philosophical scene.

It could be said that the vast majority of contemporary so-called postmodern continental philosophy of religion is post- or anti-metaphysical. Beyond this, the more explicitly deconstructive form of "postmodern" philosophy of religion is likewise more explicitly and stridently anti-metaphysical. Thus, any metaphysical alternative that wishes to break into the discourse with any kind of plausibility should be able to deal with the strongest objections and critiques leveled against metaphysics from something like this most skeptical of quarters—from deconstruction. Thinkers that might fit in this dominant, hitherto anti-metaphysical frame would include the likes of Mark C. Taylor, Gianni Vattimo, Jean-Luc Marion, and John D. Caputo, who largely take their point of departure from Nietzsche, Heidegger, Levinas, and Derrida. For the purposes of this study, I will be for the most part limiting the scope of the discussion of such a post- or anti-metaphysical treatment of religion and God-talk to the particular work of John D. Caputo as a representative of the broader post- or anti-metaphysical trend in contemporary continental philosophy of religion as well as its more strident deconstructive form, incorporating and presenting clearly the anti-metaphysical religious ramifications of, say, Heidegger or Derrida (though the readings of such are, of course, a matter of contention).

Caputo treats the *issue* of the nature of religion and God-talk in a post- or anti-metaphysical *manner,* being so informed by a postmodern philosophical *framework.* Why Caputo? Caputo is a prime representative of the religion and postmodernism discourse in that he has hosted the Villanova "Religion and Postmodernism" conferences and edited the collections of essays that have come from them. He is also a prolific and broadly read thinker who has edited a reader on religion and postmodernism (*The Religious*) and has written works popularizing this position (*On Religion* and *Deconstruction in a Nutshell*). He has also written numerous scholarly works, such as *Radical Hermeneutics, Against Ethics,* and *The Prayers and Tears of Jacques Derrida.* Furthermore, Caputo has a position of prominence in the Anglo-American continental philosophical arena as the representative of Derrida—especially bringing Derrida's thought into the field of religious studies and/or philosophy of religion.

Caputo can be seen as representing one currently prevalent way of answering the question of how to think about God and religion in contemporary continental philosophy—a way, in particular, that uses deconstructive thought as a framework. He eloquently represents a "religious turn" in some postmodern philosophy. This prevalent way of thinking turns on two points, one negative and one positive. First (on the more Nietzschean side), there is the *rejection* of metaphysics and of any metaphysical notion of God as expressed in the pronounced death of the metaphysical God, and the critique of "onto-theology"—that is, use or instrumentalization of the idea of God to function as an univocal explanation/foundation that is primarily a projection of our power, a means of securing ourselves in the world. All metaphysics are considered to be one form or another of "onto-theology." Second (on the more Levinasian side), there is an affirmation of religion and God-talk inasmuch as there is *reduction* of religion/God-talk to one's (largely contentless) ethical obligation to the other. Taken together, these two points represent a particular configuration of the relations between metaphysics, ethics, and religion/God-talk in which religion/God-talk is divorced from metaphysics (rejection) and fused—without remainder—with ethics (reduction) to produce a kind of "LeviNietzschean" religiousness.

That much said, in this work I will present a position that stands in contrast to this kind of broad post- or anti-metaphysical position in general and to Caputo's position in particular. I will lay out a dissident metaphysical position on how to talk about religion and God today. Toward this end, I will examine the work of contemporary philosopher William Desmond. I will represent Desmond as providing a significantly different perspective—a dissident voice—in the contemporary continental discussion regarding God and religion. More specifically, Desmond treats the *issue* of religion/God-talk in a different, metaphysical *manner,* being informed by his own particular philosophical *framework.* The result is an alternative configuration of the relations between metaphysics, ethics, and religion/God-talk—an alternative whose difference is owed to a different, more positive (yet different than other metaphysical thinkers like Deleuze or Badiou) view of metaphysics than that of much of continental philosophy today and of John D. Caputo in particular.

The thesis of this work is that William Desmond's approach to thinking about religion and God in relation to the domains of metaphysics and ethics provides a viable and preferable alternative to the like position represented in the work of John D. Caputo. To speak of the position represented in Desmond's work as "alternative" implies a way for one today (in the midst of postmodernity) to look at the same thing (religion and God) differently (metaphysically—or at least post-post-metaphysically). Beyond this main thesis—of the superiority of a theistic metaphysical frame (such as Desmond's) over the kind of late-twentieth-century postmodern anti-metaphysical frame represented by Caputo—I suggest that Desmond's work can be seen as part of a larger emerging scholarly movement advocating such a theistic metaphysical frame.

Indeed, it must be recognized that, as Caputo represents a broader field of work, Desmond's work stands in the midst (though being quite independent of) an emerging, though diverse, metaphysical field of thinkers. This field divides into (1) very explicitly theistic thinkers, such as Desmond and those who, under the (bold) banner of Radical Orthodoxy, all draw principally from the Christian, Platonic, and Thomistic traditions (though they are quite eclectic); and (2) very explicitly atheistic thinkers such as Gilles Deleuze and Alain Badiou, who largely take their point of departure from Marx and Nietzsche (though they too are intensively and extensively eclectic). Mindful of this, I address throughout the following the resonances (and possible dissonances) between Desmond's thought and its parallels in that of Milbank, Pickstock, and others. Such subsidiary discussions suggest the fecundity and relevance of Desmond's thought for thinking about God, metaphysics, and ethics in this early twenty-first century. Part of the parallel here between Desmond and Radical Orthodoxy is a retrieval of certain pre-modern and counter-modern voices.[1] Beyond this, I consider briefly (in an admittedly minimal and initial manner) other presently ascendant (and either metaphysical or theistic) theorists such as Marion (a confessional anti-metaphysical thinker), Badiou, and Deleuze. Through these largely endnoted excursus, I occasionally locate Desmond's distinctive metaphysical perspective relative to these other projects.

The general strategy of the central argument of this work is as follows: Caputo, again as representing a kind of "postmodern" orthodoxy, is motivated by certain concerns such as wanting to avoid false totalities/absolutes (closure) and wanting to be honest to the way things are and to affirm concrete actuality/ reality/existence and genuine otherness (openness). Caputo critiques metaphysics, ethics, and religion insofar as metaphysics, in his understanding, stands in opposition to his motivating concerns, and thus should be rejected and extricated from ethics and religion. Caputo provides an alternative, postmodern "LeviNietzschean" vision (a Levinasian ethical religiosity grafted onto a Nietzschean negation of any robust metaphysical belief issuing in a radical hermeneutics, an ethics without ethics, and a religion without religion) that he sees as addressing his concerns. *Desmond, I argue, provides a viable and preferable alternative to—and an alternative narrating of—this LeviNietzschean vision.* Desmond's vision is *viable* in that it answers Caputo's critiques—showing that they need not be the case. Here Desmond shows how metaphysics (and ethics and religion informed by metaphysics) *escapes* Caputo's narration/location. Desmond defeats Caputo's defeaters, as it were—negates Caputo's negations in order to make Desmond's vision a possible position. On a deeper level, Desmond's vision is arguably *preferable* inasmuch as it can be used to critique Caputo's vision— largely in that it (Desmond's vision) can be seen to fulfill Caputo's motivating concerns in a more satisfying manner than Caputo's own LeviNietzschean vision. It does this in two ways. First, from Desmond's vision one can see how the LeviNietzschean vision tends to, in fact, betray its motivating concerns. Second, Desmond's position shows how a metaphysical vision/stance/picture (like Desmond's) is, in fact, necessary for one to fulfill these concerns—or simply necessary, as such. In this manner, Desmond out-narrates the "postmodern" LeviNietzschean position, showing Desmond's as a preferable position—as possessing a broader explanatory reach.

Central to this discussion is an understanding of what metaphysics is or may be. My contention is that Desmond has a more helpful, more complex understanding of the domain (and history and possibilities) of metaphysics, whereas Caputo's understanding of metaphysics closes off some possibilities that would fit well with other fundamental elements or impulses in his own work (as I show). A broader understanding of metaphysics that can provide a ground for comparison between Desmond and Caputo (though they fill it out in very different ways and to different rhetorical ends) is that of an endeavor to think and come to some kind of knowledge of reality, of what is beyond or behind or revealed within the phenomena of experience. The traditional topoi of this philosophical sounding include, most significantly, the self or the soul, the world, and God.

This work is intended to contribute to the present ongoing scholarly discussion by presenting the potential significance of Desmond's work as providing a theistic metaphysical alternative to (indeed, a kind of test case for putting into question the post- or anti-metaphysical postmodern orthodoxy of) a major strain in contemporary continental philosophy of religion. Developing out of this more general point, the specific contribution of this work is first and foremost its more systematic and unified presentation of Desmond's thought. Desmond's work can be complex, dense, meditative, and full of neologisms; and as such, it can sometimes be difficult to penetrate and understand fully. Thus, the present work operates on a dual level of presentation, as it were: first, there is my own synthetic and systematic presentation of Desmond's thought; and second, this is accompanied by representative selections of Desmond's own beautiful if sometimes enigmatic idiom in the copious endnotes. In addition, there are numerous references (included as parenthetical notations) to locations in Desmond's corpus where the ideas presented can be explored more in depth in their original context. As such, the systematic portions of chapters 2, 3, and 4 (which can stand on their own apart from the engagement with Caputo) are, at once, a digest of Desmond's ideas and a series of doorways into Desmond's texts. Secondarily, this work makes the original contribution of the specific confrontation of Desmond and Caputo as presenting two emergent (increasingly popular) yet conflicting voices in Anglo-American contemporary continental philosophy that are writing about the same kinds of things—as in the relations between metaphysics, ethics, and religion.

Regarding a preliminary assessment of this project's broader contribution to scholarship, this project will contribute to several different discussions. It will contribute to the current religion and postmodernism discourse within the broader field of contemporary continental philosophy. Within the context of this discussion, Desmond advocates what has been (up until recently) the largely unentertained option of a metaphysical way of thinking about religion and God that yet resonates with certain basic postmodern concerns. This project will also introduce and recommend Desmond's work as fruitful resource (beyond the relative ghetto of Hegel studies where he is more well known). Finally, this project has the potential to contribute to the fields of religious studies and systematic theology (more particularly to what is called "foundations" or "fundamental theology" or "prolegomena" or "philosophical theology"), inasmuch as its subject matter relates to the proper way—the ground rules, so to speak—to talk about God today.

More concretely, I use the following methodological path in outline. In the first chapter, I systematically examine John D. Caputo's work to make clear his positions regarding metaphysics, ethics, religion/God, and their interrelation. I also analyze Caputo's position relative to his critiques (of metaphysics, ethics, and religion), his motivating concerns, and his strong conclusions. In the second chapter, I systematically lay out William Desmond's metaphysics in part one, and show, in part two, how Desmond's thought can answer Caputo's critiques, address his motivating concerns, and critique his strong conclusions. In the third chapter, I give a similar treatment of Desmond's understanding of ethics and then relate this to Caputo's work on (or "against") ethics. In the fourth chapter, I treat, somewhat more extensively, Desmond's understanding of religion and God—again, in the second part of this chapter, comparing and contrasting this to Caputo's presentation. I conclude this work by drawing together the preceding results and briefly considering the significance of Desmond's alternate "divine hyperbolics" relative to the question of how to think of religion and God in the wake of postmodernity—indeed in the wake of its passing.[2]

# 1   Caputo

John D. Caputo's philosophical work over the last two decades can be organized around the task of exorcising a "faithless" metaphysics from our thinking. For Caputo, such a metaphysics is not faithful to life—to the factical reality of human existence—losing the task of living in the labyrinth of speculative thought. It is not faithful to the human other—losing the particular person in the matrices of universal laws. It is not faithful to "faith"—losing a properly religious faith and relation to "God" in its fixation on crafting properly proportioned propositions about the divine as a "thing" to be examined. This entanglement with the dishonesty and "bad faith" of such a "faithless" metaphysics—as it worms its way from metaphysics to ethics to religion—is the nemesis against which a new and postmodern way of thinking and being struggles. This way, for Caputo, is a truly honest, ethical, and (most of all) religious faithfulness without metaphysics.

## Caputo's Critique of Metaphysics

For Caputo, the problem with metaphysics can be summarized as follows: Metaphysics is not faithful to life insofar as it is an abstract system that privileges static unity in order to provide a stable foundation for life. Metaphysics endeavors to lift one above (*meta*) the flux (*physis*) of actuality—providing one with "a fast way out of the back door of the flux" (*RH* 3, 1). Such a metaphysics involves the elevation of knowledge of reality to a kind of absolute knowledge—a privileged access to the real. Caputo sees this metaphysical self-elevation as a fundamental tendency of philosophy as such.[1] Metaphysics is fundamentally a metaphysics of presence, bent on giving "elegant assurances about Being and presence even as factical existence [is] being tossed about by *physis* and *kinesis*" (*RH* 1).

Metaphysics, for Caputo, is *not faithful to life* in that its pretentious self-elevation supplants factical existence. Metaphysics claims a privileged access—a capitalized "Knowledge" of the fundament of reality, or ourselves, or whatever—of the capitalized Secret.[2] Caputo describes such metaphysics as an "essentialism"—as "the various claims to be *in on* The Secret and thereby to have surpassed the limits of offering a mere mortal interpretation" (*MRH* 3). This pretentious claim, for Caputo, is unjustified and ultimately dishonest to our severely finite human situation. In fact, metaphysics is a kind of code word for Caputo for just this arrogant philosophical posturing.[3] "The secret," Caputo rejoins, "is that there is no Secret, no capitalized Know-it-all Breakthrough

Principle or Revelation that lays things out the way they Really Are" (*OR* 21).[4] We humans have to deal with existing in a situation of "disaster"—of the loss of "one's star (*dis-astrum*)," of being "cut loose from one's lucky or guiding light" (*AE* 6).

Metaphysics' pretension and concomitant lack of fidelity to life, for Caputo, largely arises out of its abstraction. For Caputo, metaphysics is an essentially abstract enterprise seeking to achieve understanding through disinterested speculation. Taking (Platonic) recollection and (Hegelian) mediation as the basic forms of metaphysical thinking, Caputo sees them both as a turn toward abstraction—"to pure thought and disengaged speculation" (*RH* 32). This, however, is metaphysics' downfall: "The great mistake of metaphysics," Caputo writes, is "to think that we can come up with a pure, interest-free rationality" (*RH* 262). Thus, the Western metaphysical tradition, from its opening gesture to its consummation, is a grand "intellectual illusion" (*RH* 19).

Metaphysics, for Caputo, is an abstract system that, as such, entails a certain fixation on universality. For Caputo, a philosophical system entails a fixed set of universal rules.[5] Such universals obtain to reality in a necessary way that cannot be otherwise—following "the rule of essence and necessity" (*RH* 32).[6] A system of necessary and universal propositions presents, for Caputo, a violent hierarchy—a set of structures "that flatten out, and level off, and exclude, and marginalize, and silence." (Meta 223). What is "flattened out" and "leveled off" in the system is the particularity, singularity, and individuality that pervade and complicate concrete existence. Such "ineffable" singularities constitute "a breach in the surface of philosophy" (*AE* 73).[7] Thus, metaphysical systems seek to "contain what they cannot contain"—that is, the singular, the individual, the fragment.[8]

Such an abstract metaphysical system, fixated on universality, functions in such as way that it *privileges static unity*. Caputo claims that philosophy, as metaphysics, from its beginning has sought intelligibility at the expense of movement and difference.[9] Metaphysics is the "metaphysics of presence" that defines reality in stark terms as pure, present being and its negation. Insomuch as any movement would call this binary opposition into question, movement as such is suppressed (*RH* 20, 34).[10] With the suppression of movement, metaphysics can impose an order that escapes and/or arrests the chaotic flux of existence (*RH* 1).[11] Both recollection and mediation are examples of this movement against movement: recollection is a spurious "backwards" movement (*RH* 14), while mediation is a more cunning yet ultimately illusory movement in that it mimics movement under the guiding hand of a necessary logic (*RH* 17–19; HKFM 210-11). This privileging of static unity culminates in philosophy-as-metaphysics' drive toward an abstract static system in which knowledge of reality is elevated to absolute knowledge—a unified totality and a totalizing unity.

Finally, metaphysics, presenting such a total knowledge of reality, gives an absolutely *stable foundation for life*. Because of this, Caputo charges that metaphysics effectively makes light of the difficulty of existence—it allays our fears with the "assurances of the same" (*RH* 1; *PT* 5).[12] Instead, Caputo engages in the *deconstruction* of such metaphysical stabilizers—disabling them by showing "how the sausage is made"—that they are constructed, all-too-human products that are not eternal or self-evident or rationally necessary but are shot through with the certain arbitrariness and instability that attends any determination. Deconstruction hears the subterranean equivocal and indeterminate echoes in any univocal determination—and especially those that would serve as policing foundations that would arrest and fix the flux of existence and the play of meaning.

The motivating concerns behind Caputo's critique of metaphysics and his seeking an alternative are twofold. First, seeking a properly humble way of thinking that is appropriate to where we in fact find ourselves, Caputo wants a way of thinking that avoids elevating knowledge of reality to a falsely absolute status. Second, wanting to be true to life and to enjoin an active engagement in life, he seeks to avoid any way of thinking that ultimately supplants the living of life (in the midst of the flux of actuality) with the knowledge of reality (so falsely elevated—against the first concern). In Caputo's understanding, metaphysics fails on both scores.

## Caputo's Radical Hermeneutics: Metaphysics without Metaphysics

Against such a metaphysics (and, for him, metaphysics as such), Caputo presents a radical hermeneutics as an alternative way to think about reality and our place therein. Radical hermeneutics is a way of thinking about reality—a kind of "metaphysics"—that intends to be otherwise than traditional Western metaphysics—"without metaphysics." As such an alternative to metaphysics (or perhaps an alternative kind of metaphysics), radical hermeneutics is faithful to life insofar as it is a way of thinking that is involved in (interested in, in the midst of) life in its particularity and difference toward the end of directing one toward the difficulty of one's existence.

The task of radical hermeneutics is to reexamine and rethink the situation (and situatedness) of human existence—"to reconstitute a more radicalized notion of this being 'which we ourselves are'"—to get a fix on "the radicality of the fix in which we poor existing individuals find ourselves" (*RH* 289; *MRH* 12). This reappraisal of human existence focuses on the necessity, the inescapability, of interpretation (*MRH* 3; *OR* 21). Furthermore, Caputo describes radical hermeneutics as "a hermeneutic more deeply construed" in that it provides no grounding or foundation for interpretation to guide it and ensure its stability and fidelity.[13] But, on the telling of radical hermeneutics, this precisely is the fidelity of radical hermeneutics—for we have no access to a reality outside of interpretation. Thus, radical hermeneutics stands as a kind of strange bulwark—a foundationless, slippery thing—against the assurances of traditional metaphysics that are betrayals of factical human existence.[14]

Caputo's radical hermeneutics takes its bearings from Heidegger and

Derrida—with continual reference to Nietzsche. The "hermeneutics" of radical hermeneutics largely takes its meaning from Heidegger as an examination of human facticity and the "the groundless play of Being's comings and goings."[15] However, the increasingly dominant resource for Caputo's work is Jacques Derrida. For Caputo, Derrida is "the philosopher of the flux par excellence" (*RH* 116). With Derrida, "radical" hermeneutics takes on a Nietzschean affirmation of flux and becoming, of the endless play of signs and texts, that stands against metaphysics' stabilizing the flux and stopping the play (*RH* 116–18). It is thus that radical hermeneutics "situates itself in the space that is opened up by the exchange between Heidegger and Derrida" (*RH* 5).

For Caputo, radical hermeneutics provides a *minimalist* understanding of human existence. Recognizing that one cannot fully do away with metaphysics altogether, Caputo seeks a "minimalist metaphysics"—for it is best "to hold metaphysics to a minimum" (*AE* 93). A minimalist metaphysics does not over-estimate the status and scope of its knowledge (*GA* 1–2). It is concerned with staying with modest "finite facts" as they appear, if indefinitely, on the surface of experience—not speculating about founding depths (*GA* 1, 3; *AE* 38). In order to accommodate this restrained posture, the minimalist seeks a minimally restrictive or constraining idiom (*AE* 71).[16] This minimalist metaphysics follows "the logic of the *sans*" that Caputo appropriates from Blanchot and Derrida.[17] Thus, radical hermeneutics seeks to present a "metaphysics without metaphysics"—the minimalist metaphysics of a "postmetaphysical rationality" that acknowledges (contrary to traditional metaphysics) "the uncircumvent-able futility involved in trying to nail things down" (*RH* 211). This minimalist metaphysics without metaphysics favors such constitutionally inadequate basic metaphorics as flux, fluidity, movement, free play, instability, events, and happenings as providing the best vocabulary for talking about reality—if we must (*RH* 257, 262; *MD* 140; *MMD* 28).

Whereas, for Caputo, the representative philosophical (non-)movements of metaphysics are recollection and mediation, the representative movement (and movement indeed) of radical hermeneutics is *repetition*. Recollection, taken as the exemplary movement of traditional metaphysics, seeks an original and pure presence that is uncontaminated by the arbitrariness of our all-too-fluid human existence. Repetition, however, sees every "presence"—rather than as something "prior" to lesser, shadowy copies or repetitions thereof that one must trace back to their pure source—as an effect of "repetition."[18] Following Derrida and Heidegger (against Husserl), Caputo sees the "essences" to be found in consciousness—as, in fact, constructed through an always-different linguistic and historical process. This is a break with metaphysics' drive toward a static unity insulated from the vagaries of life and an embracing of a creative and productive movement *into* the difficulties of life (*RH* 3; *HKFM* 206, 210n). Repetition points to the fact that any unity, identity, or actuality in life is one that is *produced* and not *found* (*RH* 17). With repetition there is the possibility (contrary to metaphysics) of novelty and movement (*HKFM* 12). Repetition is a movement that makes its way in and through and not out of the flux. As occupying the core of a radical hermeneutics, repetition entails coping with the flux of life without metaphysical "certification" and facing up to the difficulty of life (*RH* 239; MMD 28).

A radical hermeneutics seeks to be *faithful to life*—to be honest about the situation in which we find ourselves. As such, radical hermeneutics is a "work of dis-illusionment" that frees one from illusory comforts and leaves one exposed to the hard (difficult) truth that there is no hard (solid) truth—"the cold, hermeneutic truth, the truth that there is no truth, no master name which holds things captive" (*RH* 146, 192). Before such a realization of our "poverty" as individuals within the limits of existence, radical hermeneutics provides a "lesson in humility" regarding the kind of finish we can put on our ideas—not to put "too high a polish" or "a more sanguine gloss" on our grasp of reality that we ought—for it "understands the power of the flux to wash away the best-laid schemes of metaphysics" (*MRH* 2, 12; *RH* 258; *AE* 224–25). The modesty of this "ascetic ideal" that is faithful to life revolves around a basic "non-knowing" or "structural blindness"—a lack (want) that gives rise to desire (want)—that gives rise to a passion driven by not knowing who we are or where we are going (*AE* 225, 230; *MRH* 2, 5).[19]

The faithfulness of radical hermeneutics to our existence counters metaphysics' abstraction, seeking to get above the flux with a basic *interestedness* in the midst of the rush of things. "The existing spirit," Caputo writes, "exists (*esse*) in the midst (*inter*) of time ... in the midst of the flux. Its *esse* is *inter-esse;* its being is being-between, being-in-the-midst-of" (HKFM 220). The repetition at the heart of radical hermeneutics embraces this basic locatedness in the midst of temporal becoming (this passive *inter,* being-in-the-midst) and takes up the proper task of forging ahead in this situation as an active *being, esse* in the context of the between (*RH* 33). This repetition as interestedness is "the way of the existing individual" (HKFM 208). As aware of our being-between, radical hermeneutics brings a new emphasis on difference and otherness as occupying a space of priority—as that of which we find ourselves in the midst.

Radical hermeneutics counters metaphysics' urge to subsume everything within a singular, universal system with the awareness of abiding *difference*—it is "a philosophy of 'alterity,'" with "a relentless attentiveness and sensitivity to the 'other'" (GNA 453). Caputo describes radical hermeneutics as a philosophy of difference in terms of its being a "heterology." This heterology takes two forms: the heteronomic and the heteromorphic. Heterology in the sense of *heteronomism* views difference in terms of the particular and singular other that stands against metaphysics' universal system of sameness—it is the serious "Rabbi" vigilantly on the lookout for the singular other (*AE* 42–43, 59). Here, humility takes the form of restraint toward the singular. Heteronomic heterology continues the minimalist project of radical hermeneutics as seeing reality as being made up of particulars and indigestible singularities.[20] Such a singular is "marked by its idiosyncrasy, its idiomaticity, its uniqueness, its anomaly, its unclassifiability, its unrepeatability" (*MRH* 179). Reality is to be seen in terms of concrete, singular, idiosyncratic events happening to particular individuals (as the subjects of particular events) without there being any deeper structure (*AE* 94–95).[21]

Heterology in the sense of *heteromorphism* views difference in terms of the plural, the multiple, the diverse that stands against metaphysics' unity—it is the exuberant "Dionysiac" celebrating alteration and the many (*AE* 42–43, 59). Heteromorphic heterology continues the minimalist project of radical hermeneutics as seeing reality in terms of "a kind of felicitous nominalism" that keeps things open-ended, celebrates diversity and alteration, and happily greets unanticipated pluralities—it is a "minimalism" that seeks to "maximize the possibilities and keep the door open to results that have not come in yet" (*MRH* 6; *RH* 206). Here, humility takes the form of caution so as "to keep as many options open as possible" (*RH* 258). Radical hermeneutics as heteromorphic heterology is liberating—for oneself as freeing one to a multiplicity of options[22] and for the other as keeping the free-play of diverse and changing reality free of the closure of metaphysics' urge to static unity (*RH* 262). As a fundamentally "otherwise" way of speaking, radical hermeneutics as heterology in both its heteronomic, "Rabbinic" mode and its heteromorphic, "Dionysian" mode, is what Caputo calls a "jewgreek" metaphysics without metaphysics.[23]

Radical hermeneutics' awareness of difference leads away from metaphysics' stabilizing function toward a proper understanding of *the difficulty of life*. Factical life—anxious because of its lack of hard truths—is difficult, not made safe by a metaphysical canopy (*RH* 1, 189; *MRH* 4; *AE* 4). Life is difficult, for we poor existing individuals have to make judgments, but such judgments or decisions are made against the backdrop of "undecidability." Undecidability— signaling the inescapability of the flux—is the condition of the possibility of real decision (*AE* 63, 99). Real decision is difficult precisely because we do not know the right answer in advance.[24] Living life and making decisions in the face of the flux and undecidability brings us back to radical hermeneutics' central (quasi-)concept of repetition, which moves from thought to existence—to the task of moving ahead as an existing individual (*HKFM* 208) and forging a self—of seeing one's self not as a thing to know (via metaphysics) but as a task (*RH* 21, 29).

Radical hermeneutics as a thinking about reality after metaphysics, a metaphysics without metaphysics, moves in the opposite direction from metaphysics— from an abstract escape from the vagaries of existence to an interested involvement in the living of life. As such, radical hermeneutics as an awareness of the difficulty of life leads one from metaphysics (as thinking about reality) to ethics (as regarding how one is to relate to others)—from "what" to "how" (*RH* 257). This much is evident in the strong conclusions of Caputo's radical hermeneutics. The first conclusion is the denial of the possibility (and/or propriety) of any robust knowledge of reality (or metaphysics) because such is a mask for absolute knowledge of reality—that the only acceptable "metaphysics" is one that recognizes that we do not (and cannot) know who we are or what is going on or what is true—in short, "without metaphysics." The second conclusion is the denial of the importance of such a robust knowledge (metaphysics) for life—that metaphysics stands in a position of fundamental opposition to our living of life as it truly is, in all of its ambiguity and difficulty, and we can and should (and ultimately cannot but) make our ways without it.

## Caputo's Critique of Ethics

While radical hermeneutics presses powerfully toward ethics as its goal and consummation, Caputo admits that he has serious problems with ethics as well—so serious that he could be said to be "against ethics." The basic problem with ethics for Caputo is that it is based on metaphysics and functions toward the same end—to give (false) stability to life. In brief, Caputo contends that not being faithful to life leads to not being faithful to the human other.

For Caputo, ethics is fundamentally *dependent on metaphysics*. Ethics is "a certain *episteme*"—"a (certain) metaphysics (of morals), a metaphysics charged with making obligation safe" (*RH* 5, 73). Ethics—the kind of ethical theory based on metaphysics—seeks to elevate knowledge of its subject matter through metaphysics. Caputo sees the situation now as the "end of ethics."[25] Ethics as depending on failed metaphysics for its grounds ends up being groundless—as being "without why" (*AE* 24–25, 237).

Just as traditional metaphysics is not faithful to life for Caputo, so ethics—as building upon and complicit in such a faithless metaphysics—is not faithful to the other. Ethics, like metaphysics, ends up supplanting (ethical) existence with a kind of abstract knowledge. Caputo contends that life and one's relation to the other is more difficult and risky than ethics would allow (*AE* 4). Regarding the difficulty of ethical existence, he writes that "we always proceed in the blind, divested of the sure guidance [that] theoretical seeing feigns to lend in advance as we negotiate the ups and downs of existence" (*MRH* 173). As with metaphysics, ethics' abstraction from ethical existence entails a preoccupation with unity, sameness, and universality.

Ethics, for Caputo, seeks to be a *system of universal rules*. The "mainstream metaphysics of morals" must "invoke universal, rational, or natural laws" (*BA* 66–67). Ethical systems, like and as metaphysics, privilege a kind of static unity to make their knowledge absolute—and this by finding a fixed point of reference to absolve ethical reflection from the arbitrariness of existence. Yet this belief "that what we do . . . admits of formulation in hard and irrevocable rules" is an obstacle to understanding truly ethical living (*RH* 212). The problem with ethical laws and principles is that they have to say something about individuals making particular choices in particular situations (*AE* 73); but such ethical rules (1) do not directly apply to singular situations (i.e., they must be interpreted), (2) do not get away from the internal instability that shadows any universal structure, and (3) are not available as fully understood and fully justified in time for the individual to use them.[26] Ethical existence is instead entangled in groundlessness, singularity, particularity, novelty, transcendence, and incomprehensibility that resist any kind of universal ethical rules (*AE* 14; *MRH* 173). This focus on unity, sameness, and universality intends but fails to provide a sure footing for ethical relations.

Ethics, like and as metaphysics, seeks *to provide a stable foundation for life* but ends up making light of life's difficulty. Ethics seeks to make ethical relations "safe."[27] "But judgment," Caputo contends, "is not safe" (*AE* 97). Life (and obligation) is more difficult and risky than ethics would allow—"a film of undecidability creeps quietly over the clarity of decisions" (*AE* 4).

For Caputo, the (metaphysical) knowledge of ethical norms supplants the difficulty of ethical living. Thus, the conclusion of Caputo's critique of ethics and the motivating concerns behind his seeking an alternative can be understood in terms of the following: first, he wants a humble and realistic approach to ethics that avoids elevating the knowledge of ethical guides to a falsely absolute status; and second, he wants an honesty and an engagement that avoids supplanting genuine ethical existence in all its difficulty with the knowledge of ethical guides (so falsely elevated). Metaphysically buttressed ethics fail with regard to both of these concerns.

## Caputo's Post-Metaphysical Ethics: Ethics without Ethics

For Caputo, a post-metaphysical ethics—as an ethics (a way of thinking about relating to the other) without ethics (without any metaphysical ethical system)—is faithful to the other insofar as it is a way of thinking that is involved in the relation to the other in its particularity and difference toward the end of directing one toward the difficulty of such a relation.

A post-metaphysical ethics proceeds from the foundationless foundation of radical hermeneutics—it takes place in the withdrawal of foundations, of any deeper grounding, of any metaphysical certification (*AE* 37; *RH* 236, 239). Following radical hermeneutics, a post-metaphysical ethics is ethical repetition—the task of constituting, producing, forging, becoming oneself as an ethical self in the midst of the flux of existence without the knowledge of any prior guide or foundation (*RH* 17, 21, 28–30, 58; HKFM 207, 209–10). The ethical self that is forged is a self in relation to the other without metaphysics. With the end of metaphysics comes "the end of ethics," which "clears the way for a more ethical ethics, allowing the ethicalness of ethics to break out, while insisting that most of what passes itself off as ethics is an idol" (*MRH* 174). Such an ethics after the end of ethics—"a morals without a metaphysics of morals"—is, as following the project of radical hermeneutics, a minimalism—seeking a maximally "open and undetermined" and "weak and nonconstraining" notion of the Good (*RH* 257; *AE* 33, 41). Such a post-metaphysical ethics succeeds in being more faithful to the other than its metaphysical counterpart.

Post-metaphysical ethics seeks to be *faithful to the other*. The project of radical hermeneutics, of seeing the fundamental instability of life, calls on the virtue—not only of humility regarding our knowledge of reality, of a "generalized *Gelassenheit*" that lets "all things be what and how they are" (*RH* 288)—but also the virtue of compassion arising from our common, comfortless fate with others (*RH* 259). This compassion fundamentally entails a sensitivity—"a hyperbolic sensitivity or hypersensitivity"—to the other (GNA 266). This sensitivity to and interestedness in the other entails a deeper awareness of difference—of the other as other.

An "otherwise" ethics, a post-metaphysical ethics is, for Caputo, a *heterology*. Caputo summarizes such a heterological ethics using Augustine's dictum: "*Dilige, et quod vis fac*"—"Love, and do what you will" (*AE* 41, 121–22).[28] This dictum—as a kind of "principle without principle" proposing "a maximally weak and nonconstraining notion of the Good"—follows the dual trajectory of the heterology of the project of radical hermeneutics, that of heteronomism (*dilige*) and heteromorphism (*et quod vis fac*) (*AE* 41, 121).

The first kind of difference, of *heteronomism,* is the sober, self-effacing, "Rabbinical" posture of being responsive to the call of the other and the call to love (*dilige*) the other—of placing one in the position of a "*noncoercive heteronomy*" (*AE* 42–43, 55, 61; *MRH* 186). For Caputo, this ethical heteronomism—displaying heavily Levinasian overtones—takes the form of *obligation.* Obligation "happens to" one inasmuch as something—some transcendent alterity—seizes and disrupts one from without and demands one's response (*AE* 7, 8, 14).[29]

Caputo reiterates the *minimalism* of radical hermeneutics in the "event" or "happening" of obligation. "Obligation," Caputo writes, "happens"—and this happening is groundless, in a void, without any evident further "why" (*AE* 6, 14, 25, 192, 225, 237). Obligation is a "responsible anarchy"—a "perspective" or "*hermeneia*" that grapples with the abyss (being without any first principle or *arche*) in seeing or hearing in it the call of the other upon one (BA 60; *AE* 85, 190, 238). Beyond this, we cannot—or, at least, Caputo admits that he does not—know what obligation "is" (*AE* 192). On this minimalist account of obligation, the locus of the event or happening of obligation is simply the vulnerable and suffering "flesh" of the other (*AE* 196, 209, 214).[30]

This first kind of difference, of *heteronomic* obligation, finds expression in a radical partiality to the singular, individual other that is before one (*AE* 191, 225). Caputo, following Derrida, speaks of this obligation to the singular other in terms of "the undeconstructibility of justice"—that the ideal of justice is to respond to the needs of the radical singularity of the particular other (GNA 465; *DH* 200).[31] This ethical privileging of radical, ineffable, unanticipated singularity in obligation is represented by Caputo, following Derrida, in the "hyperbolic" statement: *tout autre est tout autre*—"every other is wholly other" (*MRH* 175, 179; *AE* 74–75; *DH* 196–206).[32]

A post-metaphysical ethics is an ethics of obligation. "Obligation," Caputo argues, "is what is important about ethics, what ethics contains without being able to contain" (*AE* 18). Obligation is the core of ethics that metaphysical ethics is based upon and betrays, that scandalizes metaphysical ethics, and to which post-metaphysical ethics seeks to be faithful (*AE* 5).

The second kind of difference or heterology, that of *heteromorphism,* is the exuberant, carnivalistic, Dionysiac posture of celebrating difference (*et quod vis fac*) as multiplicity and diversity (*AE* 42–43, 61, 121–22). Such an ethical heteromorphism is an "ethics of *Gelassenheit*" that enjoins humility and caution before the play of things—a "letting be" that is maximally nonconstraining and proceeds "in such a way as to keep as many options open as possible" (*RH* 258–59, 264; *AE* 41, 121). This "ethics of *Gelassenheit*" (from the Heideggerian side of radical hermeneutics) also opens toward an equally heteromorphic "ethics of dissemination" (from the Derridean side). The humble letting-be makes one a more active advocate for toleration of plurality—of nonexclusionary egalitarianism that seeks "to let many flowers bloom" (*OR* 62; *RH* 254–55, 260, 288; *AE* 39).[33]

For Caputo, such a heterological, post-metaphysical ethics—an ethics without ethics that follows radical hermeneutics' metaphysics without metaphysics—functions to place an accent on the *difficulty* of ethical relation. Post-metaphysical ethics sees that we act lacking unshakable metaphysical foundations, and thus with a heightened awareness of our insecurity—of our "fear and trembling" (*RH* 239; *AE* 191). We are, again, in a situation of undecidability, in which we have to make ethical decisions and judgments without any sure guidelines that would answer our questions ahead of time (*AE* 3, 63).

Caputo's post-metaphysical ethics effectively re-inscribes ethics within the "repetition" of radical hermeneutics. In ethical repetition the individual seeks to constitute, to produce the self (whose existence precedes its essence) (*RH* 30, 58; HKFM 207). However, in seeking to constitute the self *as ethical,* ethical repetition presses toward a privilege for the other that is also a de-centering of the self. Ethical repetition is in need of—focused/centered around—the other.[34] Thus, ethical repetition deconstructs its own project, in that in order to achieve itself, it has to become something else. To put it another way, if the other is only a function of a project of self-becoming, it is not truly other—ethics is not ultimately about self-becoming (even this constructed stability is too stable). This "something else" is a "hyperbolic" ethics—a religious ethics—that is even further purified of metaphysics. It is thus that an awareness of the difficulty of ethical life leads one to the use of religious language. Disentangling oneself from a faithless metaphysics in order to be faithful to life and to the other brings one more and more into the realm of "faith"—the domain of properly religious faith.

This further disentanglement of ethics from metaphysics can be seen in the strong conclusions of Caputo's post-metaphysical ethics (without ethics). The first strong conclusion is the denial of ethics inasmuch as it entails a metaphysical knowledge of ethical guides—the only acceptable ethics is one that operates without metaphysics—that is, without the aforementioned "ethics." Following closely is the second strong conclusion of Caputo's post-metaphysical ethics—echoing that of his radical hermeneutics—which is the denial of the significance of metaphysical knowledge for truly ethical living.

## Caputo's Critique of Religion

Religion, for Caputo, is also susceptible to metaphysical faithlessness. Such metaphysical religion is detrimental to a properly religious faith insofar as it is an abstract system of certain propositions that privileges static unity in order to provide a stable foundation for life that undercuts a properly religious faith.

Metaphysical religion elevates the knowledge of God or the divine or the absolute to an absolute level. Such metaphysical religion inscribes God into an onto-theo-logical (metaphysical) framework in which God functions as a highest being and first cause. It forgets that religion is a human practice and that all such onto-theo-logical frameworks are never more absolute than their finite makers (*Rel* 2).[35] This metaphysical religion is detrimental to a properly religious faith in that it supplants religious existence with a metaphysical knowledge fixated on abstract propositions—confusing "religious life with assenting to certain propositions" (*Rel* 2-3).

Metaphysical religion's fixation on abstract propositions entails talking of God in terms of a systematic universality and sameness. Metaphysical religion absolutizes propositions about God that are but contingent human artifacts—it confuses the infinite transcendence of God with human religion, elevating the latter to the status of the former (*MRH* 255; *OR* 93-94). Such religious systems present themselves as attaining a rigorous and certain status that is, in fact, beyond human capacities.[36] This kind of theological system presents God as an ultimate static unity—as a "God of the same"—that is subordinated to Greek ontology (HKFM 223; *PT* 113).[37] For Caputo, such a systematically constructed "God of the same" functions to privilege an exclusivist hierarchy (*AE* 34; *OR* 110).

Metaphysical religion's fixation on conceiving of God in terms of unity, sameness, and universality functions to give life a stable foundation that makes light of and thus undercuts the difficulty of a properly religious faith. Metaphysical religion seeks a "Secret" or a "heavenly hook" to "bail us out and lift us above the flux of undecidability" (*MRH* 193; *PT* 334). The radically finite situation of human life in the midst of the flux that is recognized in the radically hermeneutical concept of repetition severely limits the kind of claims theology can make (HKFM 222-23).

For Caputo, the metaphysical knowledge of God supplants religious life—living religious faith. Thus, the conclusion of Caputo's critique of religion can be summarized in that metaphysical religion (1) elevates the knowledge of God to a falsely absolute status, and (2) ultimately supplants a properly religious faith. The motivating concerns behind his seeking an alternative to this kind of religion are (as with metaphysics and ethics), first, a desire for a properly/

realistically humble regard for our knowledge of God and, second, an interest in preserving the properly existential/lived character of religious faith.

## Caputo's Post-Metaphysical Religion: Religion without Religion

For Caputo, post-metaphysical religion, or "religion without religion," is faithful to "God"—is a properly religious faith—insofar as it denies the knowledge of God and the significance of such knowledge for religious faith and thus opens the way for a passionate love of God that is embodied in the love of the other. Post-metaphysical religion, as a "more chastened" notion of religious faith, begins with the death of the God of metaphysics—of onto-theo-logy— the God that is tailored to fit knowledge (*RH* 271; *Rel* 2; *MRH* 174). This post-metaphysical religion consists of a properly religious faith that is free from faithless (to life, to the other, to faith) metaphysics. Such religion is a "religion without religion" in that here one can "be deeply and abidingly 'religious' with or without theology, with or without the religions"—that is, with or without any particular or determinate claims to religious knowledge (*OR* 3).

### Experience and the Love of God

Properly religious faith is fundamentally concerned with passion—or, more specifically, a "passion of non-knowing" (*MRH* 5)—a passion for the impossible that constitutes a (if not the) structure of experience. This structure of experience is a passion for and affirmation of the *tout autre,* of a wholly other that breaks open the present horizon of possibility—that looks forward to something new and unlooked for, to the impossible (*PT* xxiv, 202; *MRH* 258). Caputo goes so far as to say that the religious is what constitutes experience as experience—in that only with the impossible does one truly experience something new (*OR* 9, 11). This "religious edge to experience," Caputo writes, "that notion of life at the limit of the possible, on the verge of the impossible, constitutes a religious structure, the religious side of every one of us" (*OR* 11). We can thus see a similar movement in Caputo's treatment of repetition as a fundamental structure of experience that is religious insomuch as genuine repetition only occurs when one sees that repetition is not possible for one to achieve—when one sees that repetition is impossible—and then opens to that beyond the self for the transformation of the self (*RH* 30; *HKFM* 217).[38] Following Derrida, Caputo names this fundamental passion for the impossible in human experience as "the love of God"—which is religion (*OR* 1, 113; *PT* 332). For Derrida and Caputo, "the name of God" is "the name of what we desire and love without question, *sans voir, sans avoir, sans savoir*"—"God" is the impossible (without seeing, possessing, or knowing) that we passionately desire.[39] Thus, the passion of life leads us to the love of God.

The passion of life that is the love of God entails a deep attunement and directedness toward "the other." God, as "the impossible," is "the coming (*l'invention*) of the other" (*PT* 71–76). For Caputo, post-metaphysical religion is to be (with radical hermeneutics and post-metaphysical ethics) heterological. The heteronomism of post-metaphysical religion is evident in that the God of properly religious faith is "an absolute heterogeneity that unsettles all the assurances of the same within which we comfortably ensconce our selves"—in short, "the God of the other" (*PT* 5).[40]

At the heart of Caputo's reflections on "God" and "the other" is the close relationship between religion and obligation. In both there is a bond between the singular individual and the singular other. Following Levinas and Derrida, Caputo recognizes a structural identity between religion and obligation. Religion is obligation to a singularity that is higher than the universal.[41] Religion is

> the *re-ligare,* which means the one-on-one bond of the existing individual with the Absolute, the absolute relation to the Absolute. The *re-ligare* is the *ob-ligare,* the absolute bond, the obligation, but without the shelter afforded by the universal. (*AE* 18)[42]

In obligation and religion, one is subject to a call, an unconditional solicitation. As religion reflects obligation, so does obligation reflect religion, in that with obligation we experience an *other* that commands respect and has a mysterious depth to it.[43] In both, one is structurally "on the receiving end" (*AE* 11). The "power" in both obligation and religion is that of the call, the appeal, not that of the ontological (metaphysical) status of the caller. Thus, in both obligation and religion "something unconditional happens, without sovereignty and without being, without force and without power"—"whose only power is the power of a powerless but unconditional appeal" (*WSWB* 9, 26). Caputo's religious project can thus be seen as an effort to conceive of a God "without sovereignty" in terms of obligation to the other (*WSWB* 12).

At the core of Caputo's conception of the relation between religion and obligation is the Derridean understanding of the *tout autre*. "*Tout autre,*" Derrida says, "*est tout autre.*"[44] In other (English) words, every other is wholly other. The relation that is obligation—that we have with every singular, human "other"—is identical with the relation that is religion—that we have with a singular, "absolute," wholly "Other."[45] Caputo writes approvingly that for Derrida "it is enough for 'God' to be the name of the absolutely other, a place holder for the *tout autre*"—this is "the work done by the name of God, the value of religious discourse and religious stories" (*PT* 101, 102).[46]

Thus, religion—the kind of relation one has with God—is a *hyperbolic* way of speaking of obligation—of one's "hypersensitivity" to the demands of the other (*GNA* 466). This is Caputo's understanding of Levinas' "unlikely story" of the other and absolute alterity.[47] The absolutely Other is "a poetic and hyperbolic name for the fact, as it were, of obligation, of heteronomy . . . a way of saying: obligation happens, *emphatice!*" It is a way of speaking of "an extreme of responsibility, of responsiveness and sensibility to the demands of singularity" (*AE* 83; *DH* 200).

### God or Love?

On the more heteromorphic side of this post-metaphysical, heterological religion, Caputo sees religious faith as an essentially (even radically) hermeneutical enterprise that deals with certain basic undecidable situations. Religious faith, for Caputo, is a kind of hermeneutics (*MRH* 236). As such, faith operates under the "disconcerting conditions" of undecidability—with the reading of ambiguous traces that cannot be absolutely tracked down—with making its way in the dark flux of existence (*RH* 281; *MRH* 200, 210; *PT* 57–61). Religious faith has to deal with the tragic sense of life—the persistence of the abyss—that perpetually throws it into question. Religion is anxiously "co-constituted" with its non-religious other that sees an abysmal, anonymous nothing behind life—that sees life and its suffering as an innocent and meaningless becoming (*OR* 120, 124; *AE* 245; *RH* 282, 288; *GA* 16). The tragic view, in which flux rules all, cannot be excluded or silenced. Faith must own up to it—include it in itself. Whereas Caputo, in his earlier work (i.e., up to *Radical Hermeneutics*) could resolve the tension, in a sense, by conceiving of religious faith as a (quasi-Heideggerian) mystical experience of the flux, the abyss itself, he prefers a fundamental and persistent (Derridean) undecidability between the religious and the Nietzschean tragic view in his subsequent work (*RH* 269, MMD 28–29). Thus, the love of and obligation to the other that constitute the heart of a post-metaphysical religion are themselves construals—seeing compassion as meaningful—on the face of an anonymous and loveless force/flux/nothing/abyss (*OR* 118; *AE* 244–45).

The other and, in his more recent work, more prominent undecidability inherent in properly religious faith is that obtaining between "God" and "love." We ultimately do not and cannot know whether "love" is an example of, a way of telling us something about, God or if "God" is an example of, a way of telling us something about, love.[48] This reflects the undecidability intimated above between the other and God to whom we are absolutely obligated.[49] Properly religious faith exists in the "endless substitutability and translatability" between "God" and "love" (*PT* 52; *OR* 126).[50]

### "God"/"Love"

A key point to which Caputo repeatedly returns is that undecidability is not a recipe for indecision and inaction, for the abolition of faith and deeds, but the condition for the possibility of faith (*MD* 192; *AE* 244; *RH* 281, 288; *MRH* 220–21). The "post-metaphysical" non-knowing that puts our knowledge of reality in a permanent state of undecidability is what makes post-metaphysical religious faith other to (all-too-metaphysical) knowledge. For Caputo, faith, as a decision in the face of undecidability, is fundamentally tied up with action.

In the end, the basic and inescapable undecidability between God and love functions to elicit loving action and deed. Ultimately, it does not matter what exemplifies what: it does not matter which is ultimate (*PT* 138). What does matter—what follows, regardless of which is which—is action. Either or both call us to become different, actively loving people.[51] In fact, Caputo goes so far as to say that "God" is less a name of a "what" than a "how," an invitation to action, "the name of a deed"—whose force is more pragmatic than semantic (*OR* 115, 135, 141; PMDG 304). Thus, in the end, it does not matter if a properly religious faith is "religious" (talking about God) or not, as long as it is loving.[52] Properly religious faith is reducible to loving obligation to the other, without remainder. It is thus that one can "be deeply and abidingly 'religious' with or without theology, with or without the religions" (*OR* 3).

In sum, Caputo's religion without religion is marked by certain strong conclusions. The first strong conclusion is the denial of metaphysical knowledge of the absolute or God, in that such is a mask for absolute knowledge. What is emphasized instead is one's fundamental position of non-knowing. The second strong conclusion is the denial of the significance of metaphysical knowledge for religious life. What is important is the passion. A genuine religious faith (or love) that is dragged down by or hoisted up into a "faithless" metaphysics is thus betrayed.

## "Faithless" Metaphysics or Genuine Religious Faith

In Caputo's work, one is ultimately faced with a choice between a "faithless" metaphysics and genuine religious faith—true religion. This "bad faith" metaphysics is not faithful or honest to life (to "who we are"), and as such it leads to bad faith in relating to others and to God. On the other side, metaphysics without metaphysics, ethics without ethics, and religion without religion coincide in a single way of being that is faithful to existence in the flux and is faithful in obligation to the singular other, which is the same as being faithful to "God."

This progression from metaphysics to its/the other is manifest in how Caputo presents several positions—or rather, "denials"—regarding metaphysics, ethics, and religion. Regarding metaphysics, Caputo—motivated by concern about metaphysics' elevation of knowledge of reality to a falsely absolute status and supplanting the living of life (in the midst of the flux of actuality) with the knowledge of reality (so falsely elevated)—denies any robust knowledge of reality (or metaphysics) as well as the significance of any such robust knowledge (metaphysics) for life. Regarding ethics, Caputo—motivated by concern about ethics' elevation of the knowledge of ethical guides to a falsely absolute status and supplanting genuine ethical existence in all its difficulty with the knowledge of ethical guides (so falsely elevated)—denies any ethics that entails (metaphysical) knowledge of ethical guides and the significance of any such ethical knowledge for truly ethical living. Regarding religion, Caputo—motivated by concern about metaphysical religion's elevation of the knowledge of God to a falsely absolute status and supplanting a properly religious faith—denies any metaphysical knowledge of the absolute or God and the significance of metaphysical knowledge for genuine religious faith.

# 2   Metaphysics

The aim of this chapter is to lay out Desmond's understanding of metaphysics (in part one) and to then examine it in relation to Caputo's (in part two). In part one, we will explicate Desmond's thoughts on the nature of metaphysics and its place in modern thought (section I), the fourfold "logic" of being and our relation to it (section II), the progression of how being manifests itself to thought (section III), and the picture of being that this logic and this progression yield in terms of the multiple "transcendences" within the "metaxological community of being" (section IV). In part two, this vision of metaphysics is compared to that of Caputo; in so doing, Desmond's metaxological metaphysics is presented as a viable and indeed preferable alternative to LeviNietzschean "radical hermeneutics."

## Part One: A Presentation of William Desmond's Metaphysics

### Section I: Of Metaphysics in the Present Age

#### §1. "Metaphysics"

Metaphysics asks the question of being. It inquires into the meaning of being—the significance of the "to be" (*BB* 3; *MC* 9). Metaphysics also asks the ultimate "why" of being: why being and not nothing? (*BB* 4; *HG* 3). William Desmond understands the "meta" of metaphysics as double, as referring to how it is to meditate on both the "beyond" (implicit in the question of the "why" of being) and the "in the midst" of being as intimately related—an "interpretive fidelity" to the emergent happenings in the middle that refer one to otherness and transcendence (*BB* xiii).[1] Part of the being "in the midst" that Desmond considers to be good meta-physics is its awareness that it always starts too late—*in medias res*—in the middle of things (*BB* 5; *AOO* 3).[2] In this middle, the metaphysician encounters and struggles with an excess of being—not merely indeterminate but plural and "overdeterminate"(BDD 761)[3]—that gives rise to the astonishment and perplexity that constitute the abiding engine of metaphysical thought (*BB* 52, 204).[4] This excessive or gratuitous surplus of given being calls at once for a metaphysical thinking that is an act of gratitude for such gratuity (*BB* 230–31) and for a mindfulness that is itself generous toward its objects, its others (*BHD* 267). Such a generous endeavor to mindfully interpret the plenitude of being must, for Desmond, be itself plural—plurivocal. It must take up Aristotle's observation: *to on legetai pollachōs* ("being is said in many ways," *BB* xiii, 34). As seeking to do justice to this fullness, metaphysics requires a finesse that recognizes that being—and our best intelligent understanding of being—extends beyond the horizons of *determinate* intelligibility and so disquiets our thinking and strains our language (*BB* 45; BDD 764).[5] Given his view of the complex and difficult (if not daunting) task of being true to the fullness of being, Desmond sees metaphysical thinking as entailing an awareness of inevitable failure (*BB* xii), that it is an uncertain venture—a wager and a promise (*BB* 46)—and as such calls for humility (*BB* 192). Metaphysics never truly leaves behind the singularity of the thinker for the anonymity of a system, for metaphysics is always undertaken in a particular between (it "starts too late") and bears the singular existential burden of its uncertain wager (*BB* 13, 45, 188).[6]

Granting his view of metaphysics, it is not difficult to see Desmond's rejection of the post-metaphysical perspective. He sees such a perspective as unfairly totalizing metaphysics in terms of a rigid, totalizing univocity—a fascism of concepts (*BHD* 45; *BB* 344; *PU* 24, 217).[7] There is no completion or realization or consummation or end of metaphysics that brings it to a close and to an end, for the sources and tasks (ends) of metaphysical thinking are perennial and exceed complete determinate objectification (*BB* xvi, 15).[8] Metaphysics is not something to be overcome. Indeed, for Desmond, it cannot be; it is inescapable—for all reflection is dependent on and complicit in the question of the meaning of the "to be" that moves us to wonder and perplexity (*BHD* 341; BDD 758).[9] Metaphysics proceeds from an inherent exigence—from our need to think it (NDR 48; MC 5).[10]

## §2. A Heterological Speculum

This conception of metaphysics lies at the core of Desmond's vision of a different kind of practice of speculative philosophy—"a speculative philosophy of non-identity" in which thought thinking itself is not the destination (removed into itself in contemplation of its union with the universal) but a way station on thought's way to thinking what is irreducibly other to thought.[11] One need not be a Hegelian to be a speculative philosopher (*BHD* 45). Such a suggestion of a speculative philosophy of non-identity, however, appears against the backdrop of what Desmond recognizes as a certain ambiguity— if not ambivalence—within the western philosophical tradition that is at least partially responsible for the contemporary phenomenon of philosophy's becoming a problem to itself—for its "unsureness about its own enterprise" (*PO* 16–18). The philosophical tradition is not simple and unilinear—leading toward some consummation, completion, and/or exhaustion (*DDO* 4). The tradition is mixed with such a speculative philosophy of non-identity as Desmond proposes and a certain reductive *tendency*. This tendency privileges thought thinking itself over thought thinking its other, the abstract over the concrete and elemental, universal philosophy over the singular philosopher's philosophizing, the static over the dynamic (*PO* 6; *PO* 272; *PU* 32; *DDO* 90). Such a tendency yields an excessively narrow view of reason as "determinate cognition of the determinate"—falling in the direction of scientism or positivism (*BHD* 271; *PU* 45; BDD 748).

Taking speculative philosophy in a different direction from this tendency, Desmond suggests philosophy as a mindfulness of what is at work in the middle of our existence—of our inescapable being in relation to what is other in terms of determinate or indeterminate intelligible mediation (or intermediation) (*PO* 11, 18; *PU* 22; *AOO* 4).[12] This speculative mind would be a watching of the play of life that is more akin to ancient *theoria* that "contemplatively enjoys being as it is" and in which one is open to being in its otherness (*DDO* 216; *PO* 163; *BHD* 43).[13] True speculative philosophy for Desmond is a receptive contemplation that "introduces a rupture into habitual seeing"—that reawakens astonishment before this otherness of being (*PO* 235–36, 242).

As such an otherwise speculation—reflecting with and upon a heterological speculum—philosophy has a double exigency (or imperative or requirement or desideratum) (*BHD* 8, 129, 248). The first exigency stresses thought remaining true to its own form of mindfulness with coherence and consistency—the self-mediation of thought thinking itself (*PO* 6–7; *BHD* 8, 128–29). The second exigency stresses thought beyond self-mediation that is open to the otherness of being—open to finding "its self-mediations ruptured by forms of otherness that its categories cannot completely master"—the intermediation of thought thinking its other (*PU* 16; *PO* 6–7; *BHD* 9, 128–29).[14] In Desmond's thought, speculative philosophy, having a tendency to privilege and fixate upon the first exigency, progresses from the first to the second—in that thought thinking itself leads to thought thinking its other (*PO* 6; *BHD* 249).

Here, Desmond is presenting an alternative alterity: neither the LeviNietzschean other, whose absolute otherness absolves and dissolves any possibility of relation; nor Deleuze's difference within the univocal plane of immanence; nor Badiou's pure (empty) multiplicity; nor Marion's given and giving otherness with an allergy to mediation. As we will see later, the question of the other, of difference (ultimately, of community) and the question of love, desire, eros, agape—of *relation* to the other—are closely interrelated and together constitute, perhaps, the central philosophical issue for this turn of the century. This issue, as Desmond recognizes, is thoroughly metaphysical.

For Desmond, the progression of speculative thought beyond itself is a process of breaking down and breaking through. Speculative philosophy not only entertains but mindfully safeguards irreducible perplexities that constitute a breakdown—a self-debunking—of thought's claims of self-sufficiency and absolute self-certain knowing (*PO* 242; *BHD* 43, 243; *AOO* 4).[15] It concerns itself with the limits, the extremities of thought (*BHD* 42–43). This kind of speculative philosophy, as Desmond presents it, can then come to find a new kind of affirmation breaking through its own breakdown—a festivity of mind, a speculative "yes" that makes mind "agapeic" (*BHD* 17, 137, 302, 341).[16]

§3. The (First) Ethos—The Between

The kind of metaphysics that Desmond proposes is a reflective mindfulness of the community of being. This community of being—as a plurivocal community that sustains otherness in relation—is called "the ethos" or "the ontological ethos" or "the between" in Desmond's work (*PU* 12).[17] "The between"—"the middle"—is our given place in being as between being and non-being (*PO* 18).[18] It is the primal, primordial, and elemental ethos that is the matrix or milieu of all our subsequent (if always already present) constructions (GEW 23–25; AT 235; En 130; *EB* 17, 37). Our dwelling in this most basic given ontological ethos is not neutral; the ethos manifests the worth of being, the value inherent in the given, its hospitality to the good (*EB* 23, 177; *AOO* 292). The ethos is charged with value.[19]

This charged ethos is the ontological context for all our self-mediations and intermediations—for all of our participation in and reconfiguration of the ethos in terms of our more specific presuppositions (GEW 23, 25; En 130; *EB* 17). It is the overdetermined matrix from and within which we make our more determinate judgments and valuations. It is because of a more excessive preexisting goodness or worth in being that we can think of goodness or value or worth at all. We think and value determinately from the overdeterminate resources of the ontological ethos (*EB* 17, 23).[20] The ethos/between is a prior happening (*EB* 21; MC 16) and givenness that is always already given and that, as such, contains the promise/potentiality/possibility of the fulfillment/realization/actualization of beings (GEW 25; MC 6, 9). As so overdetermined, the ethos is equivocal— lacking precisely (and so not precisely lacking) in its fullness—not reducible to simple univocal determinations (AT 250; *EB* 79, 123; BR 222). The enabling resource then comes to look more ambiguous; it is a chiaroscuro—an ambivalent play of light and shadow, of the clear and the obscure—that makes us uneasy about the meagerness of our knowing and valuing and demands a more finessed, more artful dwelling (*EB* 123, 166, 169, 276).[21]

Metaphysics, for Desmond, is to be just such a dwelling. One of metaphysics' great tasks is mindfulness of this primal ethos—tracing the contours of the between—the community of being that enables our thinking and being.[22] Furthermore, when metaphysics tries to reflect upon the ethos, it tries to reflect on its own source. Here the between is the ethos of the intimate strangeness of being—as intimately present yet overdeterminate, thus enigmatic—that occasions our astonishment and perplexity and awakens us to mindfulness as such (NDR 47; *EB* 21).

### §4. The Second Ethos—The Present Age—(Post)Modernity

Desmond presents a further complication of this picture of the ethos. Within the matrix of the first, primal ethos there is constructed a second, reconfigured ethos. This reconfigured ethos is made up of the more determinate judgments and valuations that we come up with to get a handle on the fullness of the between. This process (call it hermeneutics?) naturally causes certain aspects of the community of being to come into focus while it throws others into recess. The problem, as Desmond sees it, is that the dominant reconfigured ethos in the last several centuries—the present age, modernity—has functioned to cut off mindfulness from some of the deeper, overdeterminate resources of the primal ethos, or the between, such that "the constructed ethos tries to absorb the giving ethos" without remainder (*EB* 44–45; GEW 23; MC 9).[23]

The modern ethos, as Desmond understands it, is pervasively instrumental and pragmatic—seeking to have determinate knowledge and thus control over beings.[24] This impulse comes to manifestation in the twofold process of the *objectification of being* and the *subjectification of value* that Desmond describes as the "*double face* of modernity" (*EB* 41; *HG* 21–22; *AOO* 292; MC 3). Being is objectified in that it is neutralized or devalued or evacuated—emptied of any value or worth or goodness in itself—and made into a "merely empirical" mechanism (AT 235–37; NDR 46; *EB* 99; *HG* 21–22). The subjectification of value comes about as there is a "revaluation" of value in terms of human self-determination (AT 235–37)[25] that comes to see the supreme value as freedom understood in terms of human autonomy—ultimately flowering to reveal its core in the will to power (AT 233; *EB* 35). The objectification of being serves the purposes of the subjectification of value (for there is no other value but that imposed upon the world by human power), while the subjectification of value drives the objectification of being (for humans cannot be truly autonomous if there is any value or good other than that which they create). The end result is an instrumentalized ethos in which being has value only insofar as it serves human will to power— the *autonomia turannos*.[26] The result of this twofold process and its instrumentalization of the ethos is a trajectory toward distrust, hostility, and ultimately a kind of nihilism. The objectification of being makes the ethos into a "neutral medium of valueless happening," yielding a "devalued soil of otherness" (AT 237; *EB* 19, 27). Where the primal ethos does not "fit" the purposes of autonomous humanity—when its equivocity resists determinate intelligibility— the modern ethos distrusts this equivocal intransigence and seeks to secure itself against it (*EB* 23, 26, 41, 169).[27] With this distrust of the equivocity of the ethos comes the modern mind's methodical doubt and suspicion of being other than itself, leading to a hostile, oppositional stance toward the ethos of being (*EB* 24). This hostility of autonomous, value-creating humanity toward the valueless ethos moves toward nihilism in that the same humans who claim to create value participate themselves in the valueless whole (MC 14). The end result is that the only value in the universe is the product of worthless humanity's inherently valueless valuations. In this nihilism is made manifest the loss of the fullness and the intimate strangeness (or strange intimacy) of the ethos in the modern ethos (NDR 47; *EB* 167).

From this perspective, Desmond sees so-called postmodern thought as (at least partially) diagnosing certain problems with modernity—such as its fixation on excessively dualistic thinking and on univocal determinate intelligibility (*BHD* 287; NDR 41–42). Nonetheless, Desmond sees the postmodern as partaking of the same modern ethos. Postmodernism is perhaps more a kind of "hypermodernism"—a self-determination become self-laceration (NDR 41; *EB*

169–70; *AOO* 276).[28] Postmodernism, for Desmond, is modernism—a denizen of the same modern, reconfigured ethos[29]—but taken to an extreme of deconstructing the sole constructions of value (human constructions) allowed by the modern ethos. One can see how Desmond rejects postmodern talk about metaphysics as culminating in nothing more than disguised totalizing instrumental reason as itself a totalization operating from within just such an instrumental framework. At the same time, Desmond does recognize a totalizing tendency of some (especially modern) metaphysics and criticizes it himself (*PO* 237, 357; *BB* xvi, 17; *AOO* 4).[30]

### Section II: The Fourfold Sense of Being (The Fourfold)

Desmond begins his metaphysics with the "how" of metaphysics—how it proceeds—how to go about talking about being. This "how" of metaphysics or being takes the form of a "logic" reminiscent of—and indeed related to—that of Hegelian dialectic but with important differences—regarding the nature and the importance of difference. This "logic" (though Desmond does not call it such) intends to lay out a plurality of ways of talking about and relating to being, taking a clue from Aristotle's "*to on legetai pollachōs*"—"being is said in many ways" (*PO* 4–6). Desmond's name for this plurality is "the fourfold sense of being."[31] This fourfold sense of being proposes a way to think about metaphysics, and our relation to what is other to thought, that is plurivocal and thus appropriate to the plural fullness or overdetermination of given being (*DDO* 5; BDD 762). Desmond writes:

> My claim is that the fourfold sense of being offers a flexible systematic framework that allows us complexly and very comprehensively to interpret the variety of possible relations, and the very ontological richness of what is at stake in each of the perplexities. (*BB* xiii)

Such a plural and flexible framework is necessary in order to deal with the complex interplay of many elements—unity and multiplicity, sameness and difference/otherness, immediacy and mediation, determinacy and indeterminacy, immanence and transcendence—that is entailed in our understanding of being and in being itself (BDD 762). One moves through the fourfold sense of being, propelled by a *dunamis,* an immanent exigency, an *eros* whose orientation toward/desire for wholeness and otherness drives thought through the breakdown of less whole, less true understandings of being until all of the senses are teleologically suspended in the open whole of the metaxological community of being, which is the true. This fourfold sense of being is the basis for Desmond's understanding of selves or ethical selvings (how we relate to our selves), of human ethical communities (how we relate to others) and of God and religion (how God relates to humans and the world in general and how we relate to God).

## §1. The Univocal

The first of the fourfold sense of being is the univocal sense of being. The univocal sense stresses immediate unity and simple sameness over multiplicity, mediation, and difference (*DDO* 6; *BHD* 6; *BB* xii; *PU* 12; BDD 762). There is a unity, sometimes an immediate unity, between mind and being or between self and other. In this univocal relation, there is a heavy emphasis on determinacy such that all being is seen to be determinately intelligible— "that to be is to be intelligible, and that to be intelligible is to be determinate" (BDD 734, 762; *PU* 12). Thus, mind can, in principle, know being fully and without remainder.[32] So the univocal sense can be understood as a kind of "naïve realist" position that holds forth an ideal of "objective mind" (*DDO* 142; *PU* 105).

The univocal sense of being is at once true and untrue to being—bearing an indispensable role but intimating senses beyond itself. Desmond sees the univocal sense as true to being—indeed, as necessary to talk about being—in that we need determination to identify and distinguish in the happening of the between (*BB* 48; *PU* 12). Yet it is when univocity is made the exclusive sense of being that one encounters problems, namely, that it cannot account for the complexity either in the external object/other/being or in the internal subject/self/mind or in their relation to each other (*DDO* 6; *BHD* 6).[33] Univocity, in trying to fix truth determinately—in seeking to attain comprehensive consistency and coherence—runs against limits that undermine its claims to absoluteness (*BB* xiv–xv, 73, 81–82). Univocity, pressed to the extreme of making such absolute claims, subverts itself in two principle ways. First (on the side of the object/other), univocity abstracts itself from the chiaroscuro, the ambiguity of being, and ignores what does not fit into its determinate framework—thus equivocally contradicting itself by actually ignoring that to which it intends to attend.[34] Second (on the side of the subject/self), the univocal sense of being cannot univocally account for the will to univocity—the desire to account for all of being in terms of determinate intelligibility—itself (*BB* 81–82).[35]

## §2. The Equivocal

The second of the fourfold sense of being is the equivocal. The equivocal sense stresses manyness over unity, difference over sameness, ambiguity over clarity (*DDO* 6; *BHD* 6; BDD 762).[36] It calls attention to unmediated (even un-mediat-able) difference—seeing a sheer plurality and a fragmented dispersal that cannot be brought into any kind of a unity (*PU* 12–23). There is such a stress on immediate difference that there is little if any relation between mind and being—there is no mediation between self and other. Otherness recedes into unintelligibility. Thus, the equivocal sense of being stresses indeterminacy in our relation to being—a doubling of voices that cannot be brought to a unity (*BB* 87). This reflects a kind of "subjective mind" that sees no community between mind and being (and any supposed community in being but as a subjective projection) that one finds in a strong empiricism or skepticism (*PU* 105).

The equivocal sense, like the univocal, is at once true and untrue to being—bearing an indispensable role but intimating senses beyond itself. The equivocal sense of being, for Desmond, is truthful in that it points to the equivocity in being itself—in being's becoming. The equivocal sense calls attention to being as an ongoing process (a "universal impermanence") in which there is often an intermingling of opposites and in which univocal determinate labels thus have limited staying power (*EB* 123).[37] However, the equivocal sense, taken on its own, advocates a sheer plurality that is merely fragmenting. Here being and mind are set in opposition to one another such that there is no relation but only unmediated difference (*BHD* 6; *BB* xii; *PU* 12–13). Like univocity, equivocity is a privative relation in which there is only a negative sense of separation. The univocal and the equivocal senses "are two sides of the same orientation to the immediate" that sees all relation in such either/ors as total presence/absence, total union/difference, total determinate-clarity/indeterminate-ambiguity (*DDO* 6, 237). The equivocal sense, again like the univocal, subverts itself in that remaining with sheer equivocity means not only the dispersal of being but the dissolution of mindfulness itself. There is no reason the absolute claim of equivocity should stand when all other absolute claims cannot. For Desmond, the inherent drive of mindfulness cannot stop with equivocity's mere fragments; it calls for a deeper understanding of the differences, othernesses, and ambiguities in the flux of being (*BB* 132, 142).[38] This calls for the mediating work of the dialectical sense of being.

## §3. The Dialectical

The dialectical is the third of the fourfold sense of being. The dialectical sense, unlike the univocal and equivocal, stresses neither simple sameness nor simple difference. Ultimately, the dialectical stresses a unity of the same and the different—a unity produced from the side of the self to encompass the difference of otherness (*DDO* 6). The dialectical seeks to recover or return to the promise of the univocal sense beyond the difference and dispersal of the equivocal (*BB* 143, 175, 178). The dialectical sees the contradiction of the equivocal, not as a dead end for thought, but as a source to drive thinking on to seek a better determination of the significance of such contradiction and ultimately of the meaning of being (*BB* 144). The dialectic dwells with otherness by placing it in the context of—by subsuming it within—a deeper togetherness, a larger whole, a more embracing totality (*EB* 120).[39] This greater unity is thought itself—thought that thinks itself in thinking its other (*BB* 175, 446).

The dialectical sense of being seeks to attain unity through mediation. The mediation of difference is an expression of the self-transcending dynamism of thought which is itself internally differentiated and complex—itself a process of finding unity in difference (*DDO* 6; *BB* xii).[40] Mediation endeavors to think through the immediate equivocity, difference, and ambiguity of being (*BB* 131; *PU* 14). Dialectical mediation tends to see all mediation in terms of self-mediation—difference and otherness is ultimately but an occasion for the self to come understand itself—to return to itself—to attain greater self-consciousness (*BHD* 6–7; *BB* xiv–xv).[41] With regard to determinacy, the dialectical sense sees self-mediation as proceeding through a process of self-determination. The dialectical sense agrees with the univocal in taking all being to be determinately intelligible, but it also sees this as the fruit of a process in which the indeterminate is shown—or made—to be determinate by the thinking self (*EB* 117).[42] This self-mediation and self-determining dialectical sense of being can be understood in terms of idealism—an "erotic mind" that strives to incorporate all otherness into itself (*DDO* 142; *PU* 105).

The dialectical sense, like the univocal and the equivocal sense of being, is at once true and untrue to being. The dialectical sense of being, for Desmond, is truthful in that it points to the necessity of thinking through the ambiguity and instability of partial truths and of coming to have some intelligible understanding of being in its becoming and its otherness (*DDO* 124; *BB* 131, 141, 362). The dialectical points to the immanent development—the inherent exigence—of thought as it develops and comes to further articulation and determination (*EB* 123, 125).[43] However, the dialectical sense taken on its own tends to absolutize itself and its self-mediation such that thought thinking itself becomes a univocal totality that is deaf to any mediation but its own—a solipsistic circle that closes in on itself (*DDO* 124; *BB* xiv–xv, 163, 164; *PU* 14).[44] The problem with self-mediation's self-absolutizing is that it fails to take otherness or genuine plurality—as that which is other to thought thinking itself—seriously (*DDO* 118; *PO* 210; *BB* xiv–xv).[45] Reference to the other is always a subordinate moment to the self-mediating whole (*BHD* 2).[46]

The dialectical sense of being, again like the univocal and the equivocal, ultimately (in Desmond's view) subverts itself and intimates the metaxological sense beyond it—dialectical thinking is itself *aufgehoben,* so to speak. Desmond sees the dialectical sense as subverting itself in its failure to adequately pay attention to othernesses—transcendences and infinities within, without, and above—that resist the dialectical sense's total reduction to immanent unity and remain sources of persistent perplexity (*DDO* 4; *BB* xiv–xv). By failing to account for these othernesses, the dialectical sense fails in its own project of total self-mediation and calls for another—an otherwise—kind of mediation or dialectic that is not constrained by the dialectical sense's univocal ambition. The breakdown of the dialectical sense intimates the metaxological sense of being inasmuch as it presents another manner of dialectic, one displaying an awareness of other forms of mediation than self-mediation and "a more discriminating sense of otherness"—an openness to transcendences or certain irreducible excesses to self-mediation (*DDO* 4, 118–19; *BB* 137, 178).

## §4. The Metaxological

The fourth sense of the fourfold sense of being is the metaxological. This neologism of Desmond's refers to a *logos*—word, discourse, account—of the *metaxu*—the between, the middle, the intermediate. It is "a discourse concerning the middle, of the middle, and in the middle" (*DDO* 7; *BB* xii). The metaxological sense is a discourse *of* and *in* the middle—a thinking that is between the totalizing closure of rigid univocal "objective" thinking and the fragmented discontinuity of equivocal "subjective" thinking (*DDO* 28, 114, 207; *PO* 3–4; *PU* 108). The metaxological sense is also a discourse *concerning* the middle—striving to be mindful of what is at work in the happening of the ethos, the milieu, the between of being as our given place—to be attentive to the community of being's plurality of others in interrelation (*PU* 12; *GEW* 23, 25; *En* 130).[47] Thus, the metaxological focuses on thought in terms of interest or "*inter-esse*"—as being moved by wonder and perplexity at the fullness of our being in the between—our interest in *esse* arising from our *inter-esse* (*BHD* 137; *BB* 64, 452).[48]

The metaxological sense of being stresses plurality, "doubleness," difference, and otherness over oneness and sameness while seeking a form of unity that is a being-with that is not reductive to otherness—namely, a community. Desmond, in his concept of the metaxological, advocates an "affirmative doubleness"—a genuine plurality—that takes the *dia* of dialectic seriously and resists the reduction of the double—the plural—to a simulacrum of otherness in the self-division of the one in a single, dialectical process (*PO* 5; *BHD* 113, 114, 120, 274–75; *BB* 158, 163, 188, 196; *PU* 15).[49] Such a view of genuine doubleness or plurality places an accent on otherness (emphasizing Desmond's second requirement or exigency of thought) even in the context of togetherness (*BHD* 7, 81, 248, 272; *PU* 14–15).[50] Thus affirming otherness and togetherness leads the metaxological sense of being to present the relation between mind and being, between self and other, between the diversity of beings as a community—as a plurality of singulars in interplay in an "open whole" (*DDO* 127–28; *BHD* 129; *BB* 418, 451; *PU* 15).

The metaxological sense of being also focuses on mediated relations over the immediate relations of the univocal and equivocal senses. The metaxological is like the dialectical in its affirmation that the self and the other are neither absolutely same nor absolutely different (*DDO* 7; *BHD* 23; *BB* 129). However, unlike the dialectical, the metaxological sees the difference between the self and the other as being mediated from the side of the other as well as from the side of the self. This *double mediation* entailed in the metaxological sense of being consists of both *self-mediation* (thought thinking itself in thinking its other) and *inter-mediation* (thought thinking its other)[51] such that dialectical self-mediation is limited in its trajectory toward the self-enclosure of total self-mediation by the irreducible otherness of the other in its own relating to and mediating with consciousness (*BHD* 130, 176–77; *BB* 162; *PU* 15, 56).[52] Thus, the metaxological sense treats the middle in which the self and the other meet as a *plurally me-*

*diated* community in which the self is but one mediating center of power and thus should be hospitable to the mediation of the other out of its otherness (*BHD* 7; *BB* xii; *PU* 14–15; *EB* 481).[53]

From a hypothetical third-person perspective on the happening of being in the between, there is a situation of general *intermediation* in which there is an open community of singulars, "a plurality of centers of active being" mediating out of themselves with their others—multiple self-mediating wholes mediating with one another such that there is an excess to any single self-mediating whole (*DDO* 115; *BHD* 129; *BB* 188, 196; *PU* 15; *NDR* 48).[54] From the first-person perspective of the involved (interested, *inter-esse*, between-being) singular self there is, again, a situation of double mediation, of both self-mediation (of coming to intelligent self-articulation and self-understanding in relation to one's others) and intermediation (of seeking to come to terms with the other in its otherness as it manifests itself to us), so as to articulate our relations with our others intelligently while preventing closure—while obviating the temptation to reduce all mediation to self-mediation in the name of total(izing) intelligibility (*DDO* 116; *BHD* 8, 128; *BB* 163, 196, 418).[55] This intermediation of the metaxological sense stresses surplus otherness—it calls attention to and tries to find ways of intelligently talking about the overdeterminacy (neither reductive univocal determinacy, nor lacking equivocal indeterminacy, nor totalizing dialectical self-determinacy) that characterizes the community of being—the "between."[56]

The metaxological sense of being is a plurivocal way of speaking, in kind, of the plural community of being. This can be seen in two ways: first, in the way that the metaxological sense includes or takes up the truth of the prior senses of being; and second, in the way that the metaxological sense views genuine plurality, otherness, and transcendence in being. First, the metaxological sense of being is, for Desmond, the truth of the other senses—it takes up their plural perspectives on being, which "is said in many ways" (*PO* 60; *BB* 33; *BDD* 763).[57] The metaxological sense (or "metaxological realism") is superior in that it maintains the best of the thus-far partial truths of the preceding senses in a fuller and more inclusive and complex open whole that avoids the failings and blindspots of these more limited perspectives. The metaxological sense includes or reiterates or redeems the promise of the sense of unity and the lived immediacy of our community with being, the sense that we really do reach the other, intimated by the univocal; the awareness of a certain irreducibility to otherness, difference, indeterminacy, and rich ambiguity recognized by the equivocal; and the rejection of simplistic dualism (between self and other) and the sense of togetherness in the midst of difference understood by the dialectical. It does this without including the fixation on determinacy and blindness to complex otherness inherent in the univocal (or naïve realism); the discontinuous plurality of the equivocal (or skeptical empiricism); or the totalizing, self-mediating holism of the dialectical (or idealism) (*DDO* 142–44; *BB* 178).[58] It is thus, in its plurivocity, that the metaxological is the fullest sense of being—giving the fullest articulation of the overdetermined middle (*PO* 210; *BHD* 101; *PU* 12).[59]

The second way in which the metaxological sense is plurivocal is in how it lets there be genuine plurality, otherness, and transcendence in being. The plurivocity of the metaxological sense reflects the plurality of being in its character as an overdetermined excess made up of unrepeatable singulars (*BB* 34, 88, 465; *BDD* 761). Being is a manyness that necessitates a finessed many-sided thinking—able to regard simplicity and complexity, sameness and difference, clarity and ambiguity, stability and flux, immediacy and mediation, determinacy and indeterminacy, self-determination and overdetermination—in their relations and in their difference. In this facet (in its preference for the plural) the metaxological is a kind of reinstatement of equivocal difference (either/ or) after dialectical unity (both/and)—a both-either/or-and-both/and that sees genuine difference in the midst of community.[60] As such, the metaxological sense acknowledges the "being beyond totality" of certain irreducible transcendences or infinitudes that cannot be reduced to a single unity: the interior infinitude of the self, the exterior infinitude of becoming, the superior infinitude of the absolute (*BB* 201, 408). In its "letting be"—in its affirmation—of these irreducible plural otherness, transcendences, and othernesses in community, the metaxological sense of being intimates a kind of "agapeic mind"[61]—as is manifest at and as the culmination of Desmond's "phenomenology" of mind.

Before moving on, it should be noted that this fourfold sense of being and its unfolding logic pervades and gives structure to Desmond's work as a whole. It is seen in the development of consciousness in the next section. It undergirds the metaphysical vision that is the "open whole" of the metaxological community of being (in section IV of this chapter). The fourfold logic also manifests itself in the development (and hierarchical structuring) of the human self (in the "ethical selvings" of chapter 3, section III) and of human community (in the "ethical communities" of chapter 3, section IV). It also grounds Desmond's understanding of the different (more or less accurate) ways of thinking about God (see especially chapter 4, section III).

### Section III: A "Phenomenology" of Being-Between

In this section, I will lay out Desmond's—for lack of a better term— "phenomenology." Like the "logic" of the fourfold sense of being, this "phenomenology" speaks of the "how" of metaphysics. It concerns how being comes to manifestation in relation to thought and the progression or development of this relation between mind and being—between thought and its other. As such, this "phenomenology of mind" displays a complex correspondence with the fourfold sense of being inasmuch as it relates to the progression of individual consciousness. In relation to the thought of the relation between thought and being, Desmond's work in this area can be understood as a "philosophy of love" that traces the fecund tension between *eros* and *agape* as framed by his metaphysical (and ultimately religious) vision of being as a metaxological community (see section IV).[62] The progression here described follows a kind of chiastic structure (ABCBA) comprised of five moments: first astonishment, first perplexity, curiosity, second perplexity, and second astonishment. In this progression, the *agon* between *eros* and *agape* can be resolved, inasmuch as other views can be seen as possessing restricted scopes that focus on different parts of the (restless, if ultimately peaceful) whole.

### §1. First Astonishment

Astonishment arises in response to—is occasioned by—the enigmatic, overdetermined excess of given being—of the ethos (*BB* xiii; *EB* 21, 51). Thought is struck into astonishment by the "that it is at all": that there is something rather than nothing, the asymmetry between being and nothing, "the sheer being there of the world" (*PO* 33, 229, 236; *BB* 192; HT 25, 30; PR 112; BR 229; NDR 39; *HG* 3). The givenness of being in its otherness and fullness astonishes us (*DDO* 184–85; *BB* 8, 9; NDR 39; PR 112; *EB* 51). This initial astonishment at givenness is overdeterminate—an awareness of an original unarticulated plentitude prior to and exceeding all determinate facts and definitions (*DDO* 185; *BB* 8, 13, 179; BDD 736–38; *EB* 51; MC 11). Not merely indeterminate or lacking, this overdetermined givenness of being is recognized by astonishment as excessive—being is offered to mindfulness as an excess, a surplus, a "too much," an overfullness, a "pluperfection" (*BB* 221, 480; BDD 734, 737; NDR 39–40).[63]

This excess or fullness of being incites the astonishment or wonder that, for Desmond, is the origin of thought, the opening of mindfulness. Astonishment names this original wonder before being that is a joy or delight or trust in being—even a love of being (*BHD* 244–45; BDD 736; *PU* 137; *EB* 25–26). "We see this clearly," Desmond writes, "in the wonder of the child. Our mindful being is inherently a love of being and the light of truth" (*PU* 150). This astonishment or wonder is a reverence before being—an as-yet ambiguous recognition of its value (of being's goodness) apart from us (BR 225–26, 229; *EB* 40).[64] Such wonder, such astonishment is the originating pathos of thought, the opening of mindfulness, the advent of metaphysical thinking—the shock of otherness that impels the self-transcending of consciousness (*PO* 29; *BB* 8, 11, 13; *PU* 34; BDD 734, 763; NDR 39, 47; MC 10–11).[65] Astonishment has "the bite of an otherness, given before all our self-determining thinking: it opens a mindfulness that we do not self-produce."[66]

This first astonishment is encountered as an elemental immediacy—as an intimate strangeness. In astonishment, mindfulness is intimate with being. This intimacy is a spontaneously lived immediate bond—a "being-with" the other (*PO* 63, 64, 295; *PU* 67, 76). It is mind in communication or community with being (*BB* 201).[67] In astonishment, being appears to us as both intimate and strange—an otherness in which we are participating (NDR 47).[68] This dwelling in the intimate strangeness of being, that is astonishment, is at once *idiotic*—a private or singular existential happening (not a mere abstract category) with the individual I (*BB* 12)—and *elemental*—a spontaneous and irreducible, essential and perennial immediacy (*PO* 271–73, 287, 295; *BB* 8, 11; *EB* 26).[69] As such, astonishment manifests a kind of univocity—the lived, "rapturous" ("*prelapsarian*") univocity of the "immediacy to our initial immersion in being" (*BB* 47–48).

The excessive given being encountered as such an intimate strangeness is the giving, agapeic beginning that enables and empowers the self-transcendence of mindfulness in *desire*. Desire has its roots in and grows from a fullness—an affirmative attunement to or rapport with an anterior presence—that is more primal than lack (*DDO* 19, 28, 34, 127, 142; *BB* 115, 406; BR 216, 223; *EB* 87). In astonishment one finds an overdetermined resource that makes possible the promise of further determinate becoming (*PU* 70, 73). Prior to the active *conatus essendi*—the urge, the striving, the endeavor to be—there is a *passio essendi*—the patience or pathos or passion or undergoing or receptivity of thinking that is its agapeic astonishment before the fullness of being (*PO* 29; *BB* 8, 9; *EB* 372; *AOO* 291).[70] In astonishment, Desmond writes, "The givenness of being is offered for our beholding. We are patient to its giving in so far as we do not produce it, or bring it towards ourselves only for it just to be cognitively possessed by us" (BDD 736).

Such astonishment is called "agapeic" in that it is both the awareness of the givenness from the other and the spontaneous transcending of mind toward being—a joyful, celebrating, festive mindfulness (*PO* 229; *BB* 9).[71] "The first astonishment," Desmond writes, "is simply a mindful joy in this overflow. . . . a primordial *being pleased* with being, prior to all cognitive thematization and objective determination. . . . Our pleasure with simply being greets, and is greeted by, the elemental agape of being itself" (*BB* 11). There is here a dual opening of transcendence: first is the other's transcendence opening to us in the overdeterminate intimate strangeness of givenness (*passio essendi*); second is our opening to transcendence—the "vector of transcendence" that is our active transcending toward the other seeking determinacy (*conatus essendi*) (*BB* 5, 8, 11, 188; BDD 739; NDR 39).[72] With this second opening of transcendence—the self-transcending of thought—the eros over the agape of thought comes to the fore.

### §2. First Perplexity

The intimate strangeness of being gives rise not only to astonishment but also to perplexity. In perplexity, the focus of mindfulness is drawn to the strangeness of being, while the intimacy of being becomes recessed, ambiguous, ambivalent. Perplexity testifies to the infinite restlessness of desire within the intimacy of the self—that within desire there is not only the exigence to relate to the other as other but also the exigence toward self-development, self-determination, and wholeness (*DDO* 25, 26, 165, 167; *BB* 165, 190).[73] This tension between infinitude (regarding relating to the irreducible otherness of the transcendent others) and wholeness reflects that between the *passio essendi* and the *conatus essendi* in which the *conatus essendi* can proceed in such a way that it forgets or denies or puts-into-recess the dependence on the other implied in the *passio essendi* in order to give a greater emphasis to self-determination, self-will, and self-mastery—while in reality it is the givenness of being felt in the *passio* that makes the *conatus* possible (*BB* 324–26; En 133; *EB* 372; *HG* 135, 203–204).

There is a powerful equivocity to perplexity corresponding to the equivocal sense of being.[74] Desire is an equivocal thing insofar as it is driven by both fullness and lack—seeing its originating fullness as privation, as wanting—the "more" is seen as lack. Perplexed desire is driven by both the excess and the lack of the other (*DDO* 18, 23–24; *BB* 390, 401; *EB* 79, 87). Desire's "want" is the will to power that arises from (is dependent upon) the lack over which the will is powerless—the search for wholeness is made possible by the otherness of being that is beyond the bounds of the self-determining whole (*BB* 115; *EB* 87, 89, 119).[75] Not only is there an inner equivocity evident in desire, but there is an equivocity in given being—in the chiaroscuro of the ethos of being (*AT* 235, 250; *EB* 35, 41–42, 86–87, 123). Perplexity recognizes this equivocity in the "outer" overdetermination of being as it seeks determination—as well as the equivocity in the "inner" conflict of desire at the root of self-determination itself.

Desmond commonly describes perplexity as "erotic"—as a self-transcendence arising from an infinitely restless desire to overcome lack (*BB* 189, 248; *PU* 32; *BDD* 738, 740; CWSC 39; *EB* 324).[76] Erotic perplexity carries within it the dual exigency of desire—of self-fulfillment or completeness or wholeness on one hand, and openness to otherness or transcendence on the other (*PO* 55; *PU* 148; *EB* 324; 135).[77] This duality, as Desmond often notes, is reflected in Diotima's myth of the parentage of Eros in Plato's *Symposium*.[78] Eros is the child of *Penia,* or poverty, and drunken, sleeping *Poros,* or resource or plenitude (*BHD* 330; *BB* 276, 404; *PU* 11, 131; MC 12).[79] Thus, there is an inherent ambiguity in perplexity evident in a duality between fullness and lack, *poros* and *penia*—between the "agape" and the "eros" of perplexity, so to speak (*PU* 117; *BB* 6–7).[80] Despite this duality, perplexity tends to be erotic since it is driven toward the other in order to attain some completion, wholeness, or security of the self—the other is sought as something to be attained or acquired or possessed as an occasion for self-fulfillment (*PU* 117; En 136; *EB* 323–24).[81] However, perplexity, like desire, can be agapeic: driven by prior fullness to transcendence—driven to be genuinely self-transcending—to genuine relation to the other as other and as worthy in itself (*BB* 7, 86, 326). The driving lack/*penia* of eros, driven by the *conatus essendi,* can return/progress to the fullness/*poros* of eros that is at once the given (*passio*) prior excess (*poros*) and the fulfillment of eros's want.

Perplexity arises from (is roused by, is born of) astonishment before being's excessive otherness regarding the meaning of given being (*PO* 22; *BB* 14, 192; *BDD* 737). The excessive given encountered in astonishment is viewed in perplexity as indeed too full, such that the "too" of the "too full" of givenness is seen as a lacking—the overdetermined is seen as indeterminate, lacking determinacy. Thus perplexity, energized by a prior (over)fullness, is driven by the "lack" in the overdetermined-cum-indeterminate "fullness" toward greater determinacy (*BB* 6; NDR 40).[82] Indeterminate erotic perplexity—as an equivocal and troubled mindfulness seeking peace and resolution—is what makes us urgent to determine (*BB* 13, 165; *PU* ix, 106, 180; BDD 737–38).[83] The trajectory of this drive toward the determinacy of beings can be a drive away from the astonishing givenness of being such that perplexity can forget its source in such overdetermined otherness and take itself to be its own source—as mere indeterminate erotic lack seeking determinate fulfillment (*BB* 13–14).[84] In such as case, perplexity that ceases to be in communication with astonishment ceases to be perplexity—collapses into mere urge to determinate knowledge . . . but this brings us well into the domain of *curiosity* (NDR 47).

### §3. Curiosity

*Curiosity* is Desmond's name for the state of relations between mind and being in which the mystery of being is reduced to a series of determinate questions with determinate answers whereby being is domesticated—calculated and cut to fit our purposes. So it can be seen that with the advent of curiosity the intimate strangeness of being is in the process of being eclipsed. Being lacks intimacy in that it is seen as but a series of beings or objects. Being is a mere strangeness to be domesticated; beings are mere strangers over against us to be fixed and conquered—strangers to be made, by us, no longer strange (NDR 40, 43, 47).[85] At the heart of curiosity is desire that has forgotten any prior enabling givenness or fullness and has become a devouring willfulness seeking to incorporate and control and ultimately erase otherness (*DDO* 165–66; *EB* 211). This desire is wholly concerned with its own expanding wholeness without the second exigency of relation to the other as other—seeing all goodness, value, or worth in the other (indeed, in all of being) as nothing more than functions or projections of the self's desire (*BB* 402, 517–18; *EB* 24).

Curiosity is driven toward definiteness, determination, and univocity (BDD 737–38). Here, curiosity is seen, in Desmond's view, to provide a necessary function: to seek out further determinacy where it is available (MC 11). But this function can be potentially distorting inasmuch as curiosity fixates upon finding definite answers about the "what" of particular beings (over the more perplexing "that" of being, for instance) such that all being is considered to be determinately intelligible (BDD 737; BR 229).[86] Curiosity thus correlates to the univocal sense of being (*BB* 35; *PU* 205).[87] Curiosity's is an imperialistic, "postlapsarian" univocity (in contrast to the more passive spontaneous univocity of astonishment), seeking to dominate otherness in a self-projected unity—to impose a hegemony of the univocal in which being in all its resistant equivocity is reduced to a rational univocity cut to fit human interest (*BHD* 271; *BB* 48, 52, 64, 81; *PU* 205, 240).

Curiosity's imperialistic impulse comes to the fore in what Desmond calls *instrumental mind*. Instrumental mind is a calculative expression of erotic mind—of will to power over being's otherness that is a will to a manipulable univocity over the uncertainty of what is not determinately intelligible (*PO* 26, 121, 137, 158, 226, 306; *PU* 116; *EB* 46).[88] There is a dualism of fact and value that drives instrumental mind: on one side, the "degraded" or "deracinated" world as a valueless, inherently worthless thereness constituting a universal mechanism (the objectification of being);[89] on the other side, the projection of value onto the world so as to make what is "there" valued as useful—an instrument—to the self (the subjectification of value) (*PO* 333).[90] This instrumental mind inherent in curiosity is "an ungrateful child" in that it shuns or has forgotten its own birth in the overdetermined and inherently valuable givenness of being beheld in astonishment and contemplated upon in genuine speculative philosophy—the granted (the given) is taken for granted (neglected) in that it is not taken for granted (as given) (*PO* 242; *BHD* 20; *BB* 14, 202, 204–205; BDD 738; BR 224; MC 11–12).

Curiosity with its instrumental mind is, in Desmond's reckoning, the principal understanding of mindfulness as such in the modern ethos (*PO* 277, 306; *BHD* 49; BDD 738). This is so both in terms of the devaluation of being and in terms of the instrumental construal of value (*BB* 72, 517–18; *PU* 172; NDR 47). Such modern curiosity often issues in a scientism that denigrates any understanding falling short of the univocal standard of determinate intelligibility and its instrumental utilization of being (*BB* 82; BDD 748, 767). The result of this ascendant curiosity is the reconfigured modern ethos described above (I.§4.) with its elevation of autonomy as the sole value (and source of value), its devaluation and neutralization of being, and its suspicion, distrust and, ultimately, hostility toward the other.

Ultimately, for Desmond, curiosity can lead to its own self-destruction. First, the end (or purpose) of curiosity, the total determination of being, if achieved would spell the end of curiosity—after all is calculated and homogenized, there is no room left for curiosity (*EB* 40; MC 11–12).[91] Curiosity, if it is totally cut off from its sources in astonishment and perplexity, ceases to be curiosity—it is merely instrumental manipulation of mere thereness.[92] In addition to the former hypothetical failure (regarding the completion of the task of curiosity), Desmond calls attention to the latter reflexive and practical failure of curiosity. Second, the reflexive failure of curiosity is evident in how the urge to determinate intelligibility is itself not determinately intelligible—the desire for univocity, as with all desire, is itself equivocal (BDD 747; *EB* 119, 212).[93] Third, the practical failure of curiosity is evident in the continual failure of coming to complete determination—there is always a residuum, a fragment that mocks any present claims to completion (BDD 740). Finally, curiosity, whether it sees its failures or not, easily spawns *nihilism,* in that the instrumental revaluation of valueless being *itself* partakes in the same ontological, root valuelessness as its objects—the neutralization of being also neutralizes the being of the projectors of value, thus emptying out any so projected value (*BB* 71, 83, 508; *PU* 5, 39, 169, 171, 222, 227; *EB* 46; AT 236; BR 227; MC 14).[94] These breakdowns of curiosity can also be the occasion for the breakthrough of a second perplexity.[95]

## §4. Second Perplexity

*Second perplexity* is the return of perplexity—a disquieted mind before overdeterminate, unmastered otherness—after or beyond the determinate knowing of curiosity (*BB* 33, 35; *PU* ix–x). This second indeterminate perplexity arises from a failure, a "coming to nothing," a "being at a loss," a *breakdown* in thinking (*PO* 245–46, 248–49, 257–58; *BB* 204; *PU* 33; AT 248). This is the breakdown *of* the pretension of complete and absolute (erotic) self-mediation enclosing all otherness within univocal categories in order to be instrumentally utilized—the breakdown of totalizing curiosity and instrumental mind (*PO* 10, 46, 148, 210–11, 243; *BHD* 187, 263; *BB* 80, 192; *PU* 148, 243, 254; BDD 752). The curiosity's totalizing and univocalizing thought breaks *upon* (as it were) limiting, unmastered otherness that, while unrecognized, still intrudes upon thought and through its closure (*PO* 11, 243; *PU* 180, 255). The perplexity is induced by such enduring othernesses or transcendences: by the outer otherness and overdeterminacy of the givenness and goodness of being at all (*BB* 36; BDD 735; GEW 26); by the inner otherness and excess—the inner abyss—of thinking itself in its overdeterminate capacities for freedom and intelligibility (*BB* 35; BDD 735; *EB* 118); by ultimacy—otherness as transcendence itself, transcendence "as other"—as the ground and/or horizon of being and goodness, as the agapeic origin of being (*BB* 225, 268–69; *PU* 167–70, 209, 237; BDD 735; GEW 26, 29; *EB* 18, 495; *HG* 3, 5; *AOO* 3, 287–88).

After the breakdown of curiosity's univocal and instrumental mind, there are three options that present themselves—three directions in which perplexity can be developed, corresponding to the equivocal, dialectical, and metaxological senses of being (*BB* 204–205). *First,* perplexity can move in the direction of a nihilistic equivocity. Such a return to the equivocal can, Desmond writes, "turn into a skepticism, thence into a dissolution of all determinate intelligibility, thence into an exultation in the power to negate all mediations, finally hardening into a dogmatism of nihilism that insists there is no sense to be made and that no sense will be made" (*BB* 131). This is a despairing and truncated perplexity that dwells in and fixates upon the failure, the breakdown, the coming to nothing of the search for univocal meaning. It is a skepticism issuing from a self-lacerating dissolution of univocal curiosity that rejects the univocal and is left with only the equivocal (*PU* 197; BDD 762; *EB* 47). *Second,* perplexity can work in a dialectical direction. Here, the breakdown of univocal determinacy is seen to be merely a part of the process of self-determination that exceeds univocal determinacy. The dialectical trajectory of perplexity—here truly "erotic" perplexity—encounters resistant otherness as but something to be, but yet to be, incorporated within a larger dialectical whole. It seeks to attain a fuller and more determinate self-possession by making all that is other and so not possessed or controlled—outside of and thus threatening its wholeness—part of itself. Erotic perplexity, as envisioning itself as part of a process of dialectical self-completion and self-determination, circles or spirals toward a greater univocity and thus seeks to return to the full or total determinacy sought by curiosity ("this system will be complete . . . tomorrow") (*BHD* 117, 240; *BB* 8, 30, 155; BDD 747). *Third* and finally, perplexity can develop in the direction of the metaxological. Perplexity can mark a breaking of the circle of self-mediation that is also an opening toward otherness that exceeds self-mediation. This perplexity is a nihilism, a "coming to nothing" that is not despairing but is a readiness (a patience, a *passio*) for the coming of something, of a good or a fullness that is beyond the self's instrumental control. It is a breakdown that is the possibility of a breakthrough of a renewed astonishment, a remembering of a prior positive power (*BB* 41; *PU* 25, 249; BDD 752, 760; MC 15).

With this third trajectory, there is more of a true second perplexity—an equivocal place of tension between breakdown and breakthrough that is neither a nihilistic collapse into nor a dialectical eclipse of the breakdown of determinate curiosity. This tension is present in the intimate strangeness of being as the equivocal presence of the otherness of being still strange after curiosity—equivocally intimate, principally strange in its intimacy (NDR 40). The tension of second perplexity is manifest in eros and desire's not only seeking wholeness and completion so emphasized in the dialectical trajectory (*BB* 204–205; *EB* 217) or collapsing into themselves as despairing infinite lack as in the equivocal development (*BB* 518; *EB* 214), but also opening beyond self-mediation— beyond eros and desire—an "ex-centricity" of eros and desire toward relation and participation with otherness in its excess (*DDO* 24; *BHD* 333; *BB* 434; *EB* 88, 188, 355).[96] Second perplexity's openness to otherness is discernible in a readiness or a preparation or a patience for the coming breakthrough of second renewed astonishment and of agapeic mind (*BB* 38, 42, 204–205, 543; BDD 752, 760).[97] In this ground-clearing and preparatory function, second indeterminate perplexity beyond determinate curiosity is not something to be allayed and set aside—it is a metaphysical "insomnia" or "migraine" to be deepened and dwelt with as a radical struggle approaching truth beyond our measure (*BB* 492–93, 543; *PU* 25; MC 11–12).

To take a brief (perhaps critical) step back: On first glance, within this phenomenology, in particular in second perplexity and the transition to second astonishment, one can notice at this point a kind of break in the consistent unfolding of consciousness. Before second perplexity, thought (simply?) progresses/unfolds as a kind of Platonic *eros* (toward the other to thought) or Hegelian *Geist* (toward determinacy). At the breakdown of curiosity there appears, for the first time, *options* . . . implying that consciousness has a will, a choice in the manner of its progression. Was choice here before? If not, where did it come from? (One may as well ask where it goes, if it goes, in the transition to second astonishment.) By way of a possible answer, one should perhaps see the breakdown of curiosity's self-enclosed instrumental mind in the face of intransigent otherness(es) as a unique crisis in this particular (and particularly un-Hegelian) metaxological phenomenology of consciousness. For there is no clear way forward, no clear (dialectical?) progress. The unfolding desire of thought is brought—not to fulfillment, not yet—but to nothing. There are only so many things one can do with nothing—when one's supposedly sovereign self-mediations come to naught and one is left stunned, perplexed, at a loss. One can despair—see in the breakdown the "appearance" of the abysmal wind that makes all things flap emptily. One can try to paper over the hole (just short of the whole, almost there)—pretend that (this) nothing (n)ever happened—shake it off and press on dialectically toward consummate, consuming curiosity. Or one can recognize the breakdown and wait. The last sees this breach as the end of self-mediation—of one's erotic desire—alone. Desire reaches beyond its grasp—beyond itself—desire beyond desire—outside, beside itself. There are perplexities, tensions, paradoxes—living death, still motion—here in the waiting room, the antechamber of grace, of resurrection. (Does one attain it? Grasp it? Receive it? See it? Remember it? Awake one morning the same and yet unspeakably different?)

### §5. Second Astonishment

In Desmond's thought, there is the possibility of the return of astonishment in the midst of second indeterminate perplexity. Such a second astonishment is a re-turn to or re-petition of first agapeic astonishment—an astonishment reborn (BDD 768; *EB* 169), renewed (*BB* 159, 193; MC 13), reawakened (*BB* 192), recalled (*BB* 181, MC 12), refreshed (*BB* 41), resurrected (*BB* 193, 204; BDD 760; MC 13, 15), restored (*BB* 181) after the failure of the quest for fully univocal determinate knowledge. The wonder before given being that awoke thought in the first place can return at the limit of thought—where thought seems to have come to nothing.[98] This renewed astonishment before being is a kind of "posthumous mind"—a mindfulness after the breakdown of erotic mind (*BB* 192–93).[99]

This second astonishment is a reversal of mindfulness. It is a breakthrough of the otherness of the energy of being in its goodness (bespeaking something of an ultimate origin) (*PO* 92–93, 210–11, 253–54; *BHD* 187, 281; *BB* 543) calling forth our astonishment, our affirmation, our consent, our trust, our gratitude and our love of being—our agapeic festivity (*PO* 11, 254, 257–58, 296–97, 310, 365; *BHD* 250, 292; *BB* 192, 204; *PU* 164–65, 252, 255, 257; CWSC 51). This breakthrough is a gift for which one can be prepared, for which one can patiently and vigilantly wait in openness in the midst of perplexity, but it cannot be willed—one cannot choose to be gifted, to be astonished (*BB* 192; *PU* 122, 144–47; MC 12–13).[100] Such breakthrough in the midst of breakdown is a reversal of mindfulness from lack/absence to fullness/presence, from a self-mediating closure to an opening to otherness, from eros to agape (*DDO* 19; PO 211; *BHD* 331, 333; *BB* 500; *PU* 214–15).[101] Desire is reversed from an erotic self-transcending seeking to fill a lack with the acquisition of the other and to thus secure the wholeness of the self ("desire as lack") to an agapeic self-transcending that genuinely transcends the self inasmuch as it pours forth from a prior fullness and recognizes and affirms the other as good in itself ("desire as goodwill") (*DDO* 19, 164, 166–67).[102] In the former, the desiring (self) and the desired (other) are the same, forming a circle of self-wholeness in which the other is reduced to being a mere function of self-becoming; while in the latter, the desiring (self) and the desired (other) are genuinely different—providing for the possibility of genuine otherness, relation, and community.[103] This reversed desire-as-goodwill is the "second love" of agapeic relativity and openness to otherness that relativizes desire's "first love" of self-insistence (*PO* 188–89, 197, 254, 274, 310, 350; *PU* 155).

In such a reversal is revealed the central element of second astonishment described by Desmond in terms of *agapeic being* or *agapeic mind*. Agapeic mind/being is both constitutive of our being, our ontological reality, and a regulative ideal—our ontological participation in agapeic being (as freely given) bears the possibility and the promise (and possible betrayal) of our own active agapeic participation in being—our own being agapeic (*BB* 338, 415; *PU* 157, 215; *EB* 162).[104] Though the terms are largely interchangeable in Desmond's work, *agapeic mind* can be seen as this second, more self-conscious participation that entails a transformation of mindfulness that in turn entails a transfiguration of being for one—being able to see the ugly and hateful "in our more usual, domesticated senses" as lovely and lovable, valuable, worthy. We can see "the face of God" in the human form become ruined, decrepit, repulsive—as St. Francis kissing the face of the leper (*PU* 162–63, 221). This transformation of mindfulness arises from a rebirth of agapeic astonishment, a recalling and recognition of the excessive gift of being that is the opening for an ethics of gratitude and generosity—gratitude for the agape (the given gift) of being, calling one forth to become agapeic (giving) in generosity (*BB* 260–61; *EB* 169, 504; *HG* 140).[105]

The agapeic mind emergent in second astonishment is first, then, gratitude—a thanking, a seeing the given as given, as a gift—as an agapeic giving to us (*BB* 193–94, 506).[106] There is here, in the gratitude of agapeic mind, a recognition of and remaining true to one's *passio essendi*—the pathos, the "suffering," the coming-upon-one that shows our being, first, to be a gift—that we are not our own ground (*PU* 20, 254; *EB* 381).[107] Agapeic mind's gratitude is a reverence for the goodness, the worthiness of being—that being is not only given but is also good (*PO* 131; *PR* 120; *BR* 223–25, 227–29; *EB* 40, 45).[108] Such reverent gratitude is a basic love of being, in that agapeic mind appreciates and affirms the intrinsic goodness of being (*BB* 37, 509; *PU* 121, 149–50).[109]

Agapeic mind is also generosity—a generous excess giving out of the surplus of one's excess givenness (*BHD* 267, 292, 296–97; *BB* 407; *PU* 125–26; *CWSC* 51). This generous giving is a genuine/true self-transcendence toward the other as other, not a mere function of the self's self-mediation and self-determination (*BB* 498; *PU* 177, 250; *BR* 227).[110] Generosity gives to the other and not merely for a return to self. Agapeic mind, as such a generous vigilance regarding otherness (*BHD* 137), finds expression in the love of singular and particular others in their singularity and particularity (*BB* 193; *PU* 124, 177, 239). Singularity is the mark of otherness, of resistance to instrumental self-mediation that subsumes under a universal and makes useful. Agapeic mind's self-transcending, this movement of going out of the self to and for the singular other (*BB* 253; *PU* 211-12), is expressed in service—in making oneself available to serve, to give to the other (*BB* 490; *PU* 256; *EB* 161, 356). The generous giving in agapeic service is a freeing, a releasing (*BB* 514; *PU* 141),[111] an abandon (*BHD* 131-36), an "idiotic" letting the other be apart from one's projects of erotic self-recovery and self-constitution (*PO* 253, 266, 274; *En* 150). Agapeic mind gives to and affirms (and blesses and celebrates) the other in and as its own distinct and singular being.

The generous "let it be" of agapeic mind is ingredient in a broader, festive "amen" to being in second astonishment—an affirmation of being as good. The agapeic being in second astonishment gives rise to a kind of festivity—a festive being and mind that greets the fullness and goodness of given being with affirmation and celebration—with thought not only thinking but singing its other (*PO* 168, 259-61, 300, 303; *BHD* 302, 342; *BB* 193, 206; *PU* 252, 258).[112] This festive mind bespeaks what Desmond calls "golden being"—a transfigured vision that sees the intrinsic worth in and of being (*PO* 37, 40, 261-68, 281, 373). In this festive celebration of agapeic mind there is a kind of speculative laughter that is the coming together of the failure, the "coming to nothing," of one's best efforts to understand being (in second perplexity) and of the generous affirmation of the excess plenitude of being in its otherness—of an elemental "yes" to a plenitude that surpasses our grasp, not in its absence and emptiness, but in its overwhelming (astonishing) fullness and presence (*PO* 257-58, 372; *BHD* 17, 273, 292, 302; *MC* 12-13). Such a festive affirmation of the goodness of being in second astonishment entails what Desmond calls "posthumous mind"—a looking upon life and being as one dead, as one without ulterior instrumental motive, so that one sees the astonishing worth and goodness of being, beyond its value and good "for me" (*PO* 278-81, 300; *BHD* 115; *BB* 36-37, 192-93; *PU* 163-64; *EB* 379).[113]

Finally, as such an agapeic and festive mind, Desmond's second astonishment is a metaxological "idiot wisdom"—a singular mindfulness of the overdetermined intimate strangeness of being. Second astonishment is an idiot wisdom in that it, as agapeic mind, respects and affirms the enigmatic goodness of being ("idiotic" in the sense of affirming something strange, astonishing) in the singularity of being (*idios* as singular as opposed to public), in the excess or strangeness of being (*idios* as outside the sphere of the determinately accountable), and in the intimacy of being (*idios* as private) (*BHD* 292; *PU* 163-64, 197, 251, 257).[114] Thus, this idiot wisdom emergent in second astonishment and agapeic mind is a self-conscious return to the intimate strangeness of being—seeing the excessive "strangeness" of otherness not as a mere indeterminacy to be overcome and mediated but as an overdeterminacy that is always already with us, that is at the origin of mindfulness, and that is greeted in astonishment's renewal beyond the breakdown determinate thinking (*NDR* 47-49).[115] Second astonishment greets the overdeterminacy of being—the excess, the plenitude, the reserve of given being—as something to be affirmed, not as merely something to be dealt with, as a sign of the frustration of the attainment of the ideal of total determinacy (*DDO* 152–53; *PO* 260; BDD 759–63).[116] Perplexing breakdown and astonishing breakthrough *is* the proper functioning of thought—not an aberration—for *contra* univocal curiosity (which sees all being as intelligible and all intelligibility as determinate) metaxological second perplexity and astonishment recognizes that overdeterminate and other-wise being can exceed intelligibility as intelligibility can exceed determinacy. Second astonishment (before the overdeterminate, intimate strangeness of being) as idiot wisdom is thus metaxological in that it is a mindful return to the overdeterminacy of the givenness of being (*BB* 181; BDD 763; *EB* 51; HT 28; *HG* 70)[117] and an affirmative acceptance and maintenance of otherness (being is strange) (*PO* 253, 300; *BB* 35, 333) that is yet in community ("metaxological community") with otherness (the strange is intimate) (*PO* 211, 310)—a community that is plurally mediated and not reducible to a single overarching (erotic, dialectical) mediation (*BB* 8, 205).

### Section IV: Transcendences

With the conceptual groundwork of the fourfold sense of being and the "phenomenology" of mindfulness, Desmond moves from the "how" of metaphysics (from the manner in which it proceeds: through the fourfold sense of being, through a kind of unfolding drama) to the "what" of metaphysics (to that of which it speaks, its objects). As thought is opened to otherness, it seeks to understand this otherness—these others. This section will lay out the "what" of Desmond's metaxological metaphysics in broad outlines.

Metaphysics, in Desmond's understanding, tries to be faithful to the emergent happenings in the middle (*meta* as 'in the midst') that refer one to otherness and transcendence (*meta* as 'beyond, transcendent').[118] Such a meta-physics that is concerned with thinking otherness and transcendence from our situation in the midst of plural othernesses and transcendences is *metaxological*. A metaxological metaphysics is a speculative philosophy of non-identity—that holds a fundamental space for otherness and resists the urge to reduce being to the intelligible and intelligibility to the determinate. Metaphysics, if it is to have any hope of truly attending to that which is other to thought, must recognize the excess and overdetermination of the community of being. (This is so, for even the self of dialectical self-mediation and self-determination contains a transcendence that is beyond mediation and determination—a transcendence that also makes the self-transcending in mediation and determination possible.) Metaphysical meditation upon the excess overdeterminacy of being (that gives rise to the overdeterminate astonishment, indeterminate perplexity, and determinate curiosity described in the previous section) requires a likewise overdeterminate language that is metaphorical (*BB* 101–102, 208)[119] and hyperbolic (*BB* 218–19)[120]—carrying thought, indeed thought throwing itself, beyond itself in a vector of transcendence toward transcendence. The "objects" to be considered by such a metaphysics are then the plural "others" that constitute the metaxological community of being (*BB* 448). Desmond examines these "others" in terms of three transcendences: the exterior transcendence of beings in nature, the interior transcendence of the self, and the superior or ultimate transcendence of God.

### §1. Exterior Transcendence (T1)

The first transcendence, which Desmond refers to as "T1," is the transcendence of beings as other in exteriority (*DDO* 154; *BB* 206, 231; *HG* 2).[121] The beings in the exterior world or nature are transcendent in that they are not the product of our thinking (*HG* 3).[122] The otherness of the world precedes and exceeds our thinking of it. This "exceeding" is the overdetermination of outer being that resists any full reduction to univocal determination—there is always a reserve of otherness (*BB* 13). The transcendence of the world to our determinate thinking is due in part to its being self-transcending—its being as becoming, a universal impermanence (*BB* 88, 90, 143, 237, 256, 279–80). Exterior being as becoming does not easily conform to the univocal (*BB* 50, 238) but displays equivocity in its double coming to be and passing away (*BB* 88, 90, 291)—a process of differentiation in which things come to determinacy in a kind of dialectical process (*BB* 237, 284). The equivocal flux and becoming of the world for Desmond is not merely equivocal, not merely a formless and indeterminate dispersal inhospitable to any intelligibility—becoming is metaxological, a dynamic and intermediate happening where there is room for both the persisting equivocity of being and the possibility of intelligibility, determinate or indeterminate—being-between a totally determinate unity and an unintelligible mass.[123] Desmond describes this first transcendence of the external world of becoming as an *infinite succession*—an open, never completed plurality or series of particular beings in time and space (*DDO* 149–51; *BB* 207, 408, 448).[124] This first transcendence (T1) opens onto the other transcendences inasmuch as the overdeterminate happening of external being, first, gives rise to astonishment and a vector of self-transcendence (T2) toward this external other in human mindfulness (*BB* 179)[125] and, second, suggests a more radical sense of the infinite as a ground or an origin (T3) which makes possible the possibility and actuality of the world of beings (*DDO* 152; *PO* 138; *BB* 207, 231, 291; *HG* 3).[126]

### §2. Interior Transcendence (T2)

The second transcendence, which Desmond refers to as "T2," is the transcendence of the self (*HG* 2). There are two interrelated senses to this transcendence: the transcendence of the self's inward reserve of otherness;[127] and self-transcendence, or the self's active transcending as a vector of transcendence—as the restless power of human self-surpassing (*BB* 5, 7, 231, 407; *HG* 3, 203; *AOO* 268). The inward otherness of the self is the overdetermined source or fullness that enables self-transcendence—the agape at the root of the eros.

First, there is an intimacy (*BB* 383; *PU* 161, 202–203)[128] and an idiocy (*PO*

367; *BB* 187, 397; *PU* 55)[129] to the self—an inward otherness (*BB* 189, 384, 417; *PU* 202–203; *HG* 190)[130] that is marked by an irreducible, absolute and idiotic singularity (*BB* 532; *PU* 55, 57; *EB* 171, 186). The givenness of the singular "thisness" or "thatness" of the self is overdetermined—it is an excess, a "too muchness," a "more," a plenitude that cannot be exhausted or fully mediated in entirely determinate terms (*DDO* 151, 154; *BB* 13, 115, 183–84, 188; *PU* 59–61, 73, 144; *HG* 190).[131] This overdeterminacy of the inward otherness of the self is the transcendent reserve of the singular individual that is the funding source of the self's (self-)transcending.

The second facet of the self's transcendence is in its being self-transcending. Desmond links self-transcendence with the infinite restlessness of human desire. The self-transcendence of desire is an intentional infinitude that, in its dynamic restlessness, is not satisfied with any finite thing (*DDO* 12, 73, 85, 150–51; *EB* 212, 215).[132] This *intentional infinitude* of human desire in the midst of one's *actual finitude* (*DDO* 12, 75; *BB* 185; *HG* 203)[133] is a continual going-beyond (*BB* 156; *PU* 205) that is the expression of the excess of the self's inner infinitude (*BB* 206–207, 230, 448, 527; *EB* 215)[134]—the outpouring of the reserve of the self's overdetermined depths, the sprouting forth from an infinite root. This excessive self-transcendence is also a vector of transcendence toward an excessive and transcendent other—it is an urgency of ultimacy moving from transcendent fullness to transcendent fullness (*PO* 111; *BB* 155; *EB* 215).[135] Intentional infinitude, as intentional, enables articulate mediation with the multitude of beings in the world (T1) so as to form a wholeness—however provisional and "open" such a whole may be as existing in tension with the self's whole-exceeding infinity (or however prone to forming an instrumental totality) (*DDO* 26, 151; *BHD* 44; *BB* 446; *EB* 188).[136] This wholeness, the more determinate relating of the self to itself and to the world and God, Desmond describes in terms of different *ethical selvings*.[137] Finally, this self-transcending is an outreaching and an opening toward the metaxological community of excessive others (*BB* 230, 448; *PU* 205)[138]—toward other intentionally infinite but actually finite, inwardly transcendent and outwardly transcending selves (T2), toward the infinite succession of the exterior transcendence of the world (T1) (*PO* 23; *BB* 7) and toward the actual infinitude of superior transcendence (T3) (*DDO* 152; PO 111; *BB* 155, 207, 231, 378; *PU* 11, 250; *EB* 113–14, 214–18; *HG* 5, 7; *AOO* 268–69, 288, 291).[139] The more determinate shape of this kind of human dwelling-with is laid out in terms of Desmond's different *ethical communities*.[140] Indeed, this metaphysical understanding of human being is, for Desmond, the foundation of ethics—how we *are in relation* (ontologically) to the other of the self is the foundation of how we *are to relate* (regulatively) to the other.

§3. Superior Transcendence (T3)

The third transcendence (T3) is that of the divine or God (*BB* 231; *HG* 2–4; *AOO* 269). Desmond often refers to God as "transcendence itself"—not in the sense of an abstract category of "transcendence" but as the original transcendence that is the "possibilizing source" of the other transcendences (BB 231; *EB* 219; *HG* 3; *AOO* 269). Third transcendence is actual infinitude (in distinction from the infinite succession of becoming in T1 and the intentional infinitude and actual finitude of the self in T2) in the sense of a qualitative inexhaustibility in excess of all finitude (*DDO* 151; *BHD* 181; *BB* 408, 448).[141] This transcendence itself or actual infinitude is transcendence *as other*—it is not reducible to other transcendences (as a projection of our self-determination, for example) although it is spoken of in metaphors drawn from inner and outer transcendence (*BB* 231–32; *PU* 230; *HG* 3–4, 200). One such metaphor that Desmond sees to be particularly apt is that of height, such that third transcendence is a *vertical* transcendence: a higher transcendence, an ultimate (*BDD* 763–64; *EB* 219) other "beyond" all finite beings (*DDO* 198; *BB* 201, 208)—a transcendence *superior* to exterior (T1) and interior (T2) transcendence (BB 201, 231; *HG* 3; *AOO* 269). (Other metaphors of Desmond's that will be introduced presently and expanded upon in chapter 4 include ground, origin, and agapeic giver.) For Desmond, this "above" of third transcendence is the *huper* toward which human self-transcending thinking is thrown in contemplation of itself (T2) and the external world (T1)—thought about God is hyperbolic, thrown beyond itself toward a limit.[142] However, such a hyperbolic thought of divine transcendence is not of a mere indeterminate or empty beyond but of an overdeterminate fullness (*HG* 7).

One of the chief characteristics of third transcendence (like first and second) for Desmond is its overdetermination. As overdeterminate, God is neither an empty indeterminate idea nor simply a determinate being.[143] The overdetermination of divine transcendence is the excessive, surplus plenitude of the origin of being (*BB* 182; *HT* 34; *BR* 226; *HG* 7, 136).[144] This excess/surplus/fullness/too-muchness is a *reserve*—a persisting otherness, a holding back in a mystery beyond conceptual encapsulation and any holistic immanence (*DDO* 153; *BHD* 177; *BB* 495; *HG* 139, 187–88, 199ff.).[145] The infinite excess of the overdetermined reserve of third transcendence in its otherness is the ground of its transcending—it is out of the fullness of its reserve of otherness that the third transcendence creates, communicates, and is open to its others (HT 31; *HG* 200).[146] It is the overdeterminate and excessive *transcendence* of third transcendence that enables its *transcending* in the sense of its transcending itself in creation (originating being as other to it) and in relating to creation.

The preeminent metaphysical metaphor that Desmond uses for this third transcendence is that of the *origin*—more specifically, the *agapeic* origin (*BB* 208, 231, 330; *PU* 230; *HG* 3). God as the original transcendence is the origin of the "coming to be" of being—an answer to the question of being-at-all, why there is something instead of nothing.[147] As the origin, God is the possibilizing source and sustaining ground of being—not only bringing into being the other transcendences (T1, T2) but doing so in such a way as to enable their own possible self-transcendings (*BB* 263; *EB* 219; *AOO* 269).[148] The origin for Desmond is an *agapeic* origin in that it gives being its own being in otherness—whereas an erotic origin, such as Hegel's, is involved in (or just "is") a process of self-becoming, of self-othering and re-incorporation into self, in which the created other has only a provisional or illusory otherness (*BB* 495; *AOO* 287).[149] Such a metaphysical understanding of God[150] is the foundation for our proper relating to this God, in religion.[151] This God as agapeic origin is the ground of the metaxological community of being.

### §4. The Metaxological Community of Being

These three transcendences—of beings in the external world (T1), of selves (T2) and of God (T3)—constitute the metaxological community of being. This is a genuine community in that there are others in relation to one another—transcendences transcending themselves toward each other. Each is an overdeterminate fullness funding and impelling it to go out of itself toward its others. This metaxological community is neither a univocal monism (sheer unity) nor an equivocal dispersal of unrelated beings (sheer difference) nor a dialectically self-becoming and self-relating totality (unity including and absorbing difference within itself—difference as merely a vanishing moment toward unity). Community is *relation between others.* Both otherness *and* relation are equiprimordial and irreducible: for without otherness there can be no relation (there is only the same, the totality, the one), without relation there can be no otherness (the other disappears, "which other?").[152] Desmond's vision is of many different unities (transcendent others) in different relations (transcending mediations) with each other. Here genuine singularities are let be within an open whole—with (*cum*) one another. This plurally mediated metaxological community—this interweaving matrix of intermediation—is "the between."[153] All of the rest of Desmond's work—whether it be on the nature of human selves and communities (of the transcendence, transcending, and togetherness of T2) or of the nature of God (T3) and God's relation to the world (T1) and to humans (T2)—unfolds upon the stage of the open whole of the metaxological community of being. Metaphysics is the endeavor to behold and understand (and affirm and celebrate)—to mindfully dwell within—this community of others transcendent and transcending.

## Part Two: Metaxological Metaphysics and Radical Hermeneutics

Having summarized William Desmond's conception of metaphysics, I will now turn to examine how this conception provides a viable and preferable alternative to that represented in the work of John D. Caputo. Desmond's position can be seen as a viable alternative in two ways. First, Desmond's position is able to answer Caputo's critique of metaphysics by showing that the understanding of metaphysics represented in his work is not guilty of the errors that Caputo levels against metaphysics as such. Second, Desmond's position is able to genuinely address the motivating concerns that can seen to be inspiring Caputo's treatment of metaphysics. Beyond this, Desmond's position can be seen as preferable inasmuch as it presents a broader perspective from which the LeviNietzschean position can be seen to betray its motivating concerns and from which these concerns can be better addressed. Finally, this more capacious narration can be used to critique Caputo's own (de)constructive proposals regarding how to think about reality and how to think about thinking about reality.

*Section I: Desmond as Answering Caputo's Critique of Metaphysics*

§1. Abstraction

Caputo's first critique of metaphysics regards its *abstraction*. "The great mistake of metaphysics," Caputo writes, is "to think that we can come up with a pure, interest-free rationality" (*RH* 262). The grand "intellectual illusion" of the Western metaphysical tradition, from its opening gesture to its consummation, is its conception of thought as (at least ideally) disinterested or interest-free (*RH* 19). Metaphysics, for Caputo, is an essentially *abstract* enterprise seeking to achieve understanding through disinterested and disengaged speculation—above (*meta*) the flux that is our actual existence. Taking (Platonic) recollection and (Hegelian) mediation as its basic forms, Caputo sees metaphysical thinking as a turn toward abstraction—"to pure thought and disengaged speculation" (*RH* 32).

Desmond's conception of metaphysics can be seen to answer this critique in several ways. First, part of what Desmond considers to be good meta-physics (here, *meta* as "in the midst") is its awareness that it is *in medias res*—in the middle of things—in the midst of the excess givenness of the overdetermined community of being (BDD 761; *BB* 5; *PU* 25; *AOO* 3).[154] Second, Desmond's view of metaphysics as such a mindfulness of what is at work in the middle of our existence—of our inescapable being in relation to what is other (*PO* 11, 18; *PU* 22; HT 25; *AOO* 4)—presents a speculative mind that would be a watching of the play of life akin to ancient *theoria* that "contemplatively enjoys being as it is" and in which one is open and receptive to being in its otherness (*DDO* 216; *PO* 163; *BHD* 43).[155] Third, far from being disengaged and passionless, true speculative metaphysics for Desmond is born of our involvement with being—with what is happening—with being in its intimate strangeness. This excess or fullness of being incites the astonishment and the perplexity that, for Desmond, is the origin of metaphysical mindfulness. Astonishment is a wonder before being that is a joy or delight or trust in being—even a love of being (*BHD* 244–45; BDD 736; *PU* 137; *EB* 25–26)[156]—while perplexity develops out of a perplexity that testifies to an infinite restlessness of desire (*DDO* 25, 26, 165, 167; *BB* 165, 190). Fourth, metaphysics concerns a finessed and artful dwelling in the given ethos of being—a dwelling whose tasks include mindfulness of the intimately given community of being in which we are involved and that enables our thinking and being (*EB* 86–87, 123, 166, 169, 276; GEW 27). Finally, on Desmond's accounting, metaphysics as such a dwelling is not neutral, nor is the ethos in which it dwells. Metaphysics is trying to make intelligible our involvement in and being in the midst of (*inter-esse*) the given ethos of being that is encountered as charged with excessive value (in which the metaphysician is interested) (*EB* 17, 23, 177; *AOO* 292).

### §2. Universal System

Caputo's second critique of metaphysics concerns its being a *system*. For Caputo, a philosophical "system" entails a fixed set of universal rules—and indeed, a certain fixation on universality.[157] The universals involved in such a metaphysical system are to correspond to reality in a necessary way (*RH* 19, 32). Such a system of necessary and universal propositions presents, for Caputo, a violent hierarchy that "flattens out" and "levels off" the particularity, singularity, and individuality that pervade and complicate concrete existence (*DH* 203–204; *AE* 72–73; Meta 223).

Desmond sees such a critique as unfairly totalizing metaphysics in terms of a totalizing univocal system—a fascism of concepts (*BHD* 45; *BB* 344; *PU* 24, 217).[158] The kind of thinking that is fixated on systems of necessarily obtaining propositions applies not to metaphysics as such, but more to the univocal sense of being in which there is a heavy emphasis on determinacy such that all being is seen to be determinately intelligible—"that to be is to be intelligible, and that to be intelligible is to be determinate" (BDD 734, 762; *PU* 12). While Desmond sees the univocal sense as useful, even necessary—in that we need determination to identify and distinguish in the happening of the between (*BB* 48; *PU* 12)—it is when univocity is made the exclusive sense of being that one encounters the problems that concern Caputo, namely, its inability to account for the complexity either in the external object/other/being or in the internal subject/self/mind or in their relation to each other (*DDO* 6; *BHD* 6; *PU* 110).

Caputo's criticism can also be seen to apply to the dialectical sense of being inasmuch as it agrees with the univocal in taking all being to be determinately intelligible, though as the fruit of a more complex self-determining process culminating in a full systematic understanding of the whole of reality (in its more ambitious idealist versions) (*DDO* 142; *PU* 105; *EB* 117).[159] However, Caputo's critique does not apply to metaxological metaphysics in that such a way of thinking about reality strives to think in terms of an "open wholeness" rather than a closed, totalizing system. Such an "open whole" is a community of a plurality of singulars in interplay (*DDO* 127–28; *BHD* 129; *BB* 418, 451; *PU* 15)—a plural intermediation in excess to any single self-mediating whole (*DDO* 115; *BHD* 129; *BB* 188, 196, 451; *PU* 15; NDR 48).[160] The plurivocity of the metaxological sense reflects the plurality of being in its character as an overdetermined excess made up of unrepeatable singulars (*BB* 34, 88, 465; BDD 761). The metaxological emphasis on genuine plurality, rather than leveling or flattening, provides space for the singularity, for the "idiocy" of individual beings and selves—these including the singularity of the metaphysical thinker, for metaphysics is always undertaken in a particular between and bears the singular existential burden of its uncertain wager (*BB* 13, 45, 188).[161] Metaxological metaphysics, seeking to do justice to the overdeterminacy (neither reductive univocal determinacy nor lacking equivocal indeterminacy nor totalizing dialectical self-determinacy) of the surplus otherness of given being, requires a finesse that recognizes that the chiaroscuro of being, its ambiguous play of light and shadow—and our best intelligent understanding of being—extends beyond the horizons of univocal determinations and so disquiets our thinking and strains our language (*BB* 45; BDD 735, 764; AT 250; *EB* 79, 123, 166, 169, 276; BR 222).[162] Desmond himself presents a critique similar to that of Caputo's in his discussion of the instrumental mind (rampant in the modern ethos)[163] which seeks to impose a hegemony of the univocal in which being in all its resistant equivocity is reduced to a rational univocity cut to fit human interest[164]—in which being is a mere strangeness to be domesticated and made determinately intelligible (BDD 737; NDR 40, 43, 47; BR 229).

### §3. Static Unity

Caputo's third critique of metaphysics concerns its fixation on static unity. Caputo claims that metaphysics seeks intelligibility at the expense of movement and difference (BA 69). It does this by suppressing movement and subsuming difference into an absorbing unity (*RH* 20, 34; HKFM 207, 223).[165] With the suppression of movement and difference, metaphysics can impose an order that escapes and/or arrests the chaotic flux of existence (*RH* 1).[166] This privilege for static unity culminates in metaphysics' drive toward an abstract static system (previously noted) in which knowledge of reality is elevated to the totalizing unity of absolute knowledge.

Desmond's conception of metaphysics can be seen to answer this critique in several ways. First, Desmond, again, sees such a fixation on static unity as not being indicative of metaphysics as such but as describing the kind of stress on unity evident in the univocal and dialectical senses of being—in the univocal sense's stressing immediate unity and simple sameness over multiplicity and difference (*DDO* 6; *BHD* 6; *BB* xii; *PU* 12; BDD 762) and in the dialectical sense's stressing a mediated unity of the same and different produced from the side of the self to encompass the difference of otherness (*DDO* 6; *BB* 143, 175, 178). Second, regarding the subsuming of difference, Desmond's metaxological metaphysics advocates an "affirmative doubleness" that resists the reduction of the double—the plural—to a simulacrum of otherness in the self-division of the one in a single, dialectical process so as to envision being as a plurality of singulars in interplay in an "open whole"—a community of being whose "being-with" is not reductive of otherness (*DDO* 127–28; *BHD* 129; *BB* 418, 451; *PU* 15). Third, Desmond's own metaphysics sees external being (T1) in terms of a self-transcending becoming, a universal impermanence in which there is an equivocal coming to be and passing away in a process of differentiation that is nonetheless intelligible, if not in a fully determinate manner (*BB* 88, 90, 291). Finally, the plurality and becoming of being calls for a plurivocal and flexible (finessed) metaphysics in which "being is said in many ways" (*BB* xiii, 34). Desmond's fourfold sense of being is presented as such a plural and flexible framework that is able to deal with the complex interplay of many elements—unity and multiplicity, sameness and difference/otherness, immediacy and mediation, determination and indeterminacy, immanence and transcendence—that is entailed in our understanding of being (BDD 762).

### §4. Not Faithful to Life

Finally, Caputo sees all of these critiques as supporting his fundamental critique of metaphysics, namely, that it is not faithful to life. Metaphysics is dishonest to our severely finite human situation by making light of the difficulty of existence. It does this as an abstract system privileging static unity with which it gives an absolutely stable foundation for life—allaying our fears with the "assurances of the same" (*RH* 1; HKFM 213–14; *PT* 5). Metaphysics claims to provide a total knowledge of and privileged access to reality—it claims "to be *in on* The Secret and thereby to have surpassed the limits of offering a mere mortal interpretation" (*RH* 1, 288; *MRH* 3, 5). Such arrogant philosophical posturing is dishonest about the fix in which we find ourselves and thus supplants factual existence (*MD* 139).

Desmond sees such a critique as not justified if aimed at metaphysics as such and metaxological metaphysics, in particular. The *meta* of metaxological metaphysics is never just a "beyond"; it arises "in the midst" as an "interpretive fidelity" to the emergent happenings in the middle that refer one to otherness and transcendence (*BB* xiii, 44).[167] While seeking a mindfulness of what is at work in the middle of our existence—to be true to and to give the fullest articulation of the happenings in the middle—human metaphysical thinkers cannot escape the middle to gain a view from nowhere, a privileged viewpoint on reality (*PO* 11, 18; *PU* 22; HT 25; *AOO* 4). Far from providing the assurances of such a pure access to reality, metaphysics as Desmond conceives of it disquiets our thinking and strains our language—metaphysics is an insomniac, migraine-courting encounter and struggle with the excess of being that gives rise to the astonishment and perplexity that constitute the abiding engine of metaphysical thought (*BB* 45; BDD 735, 761, 764).[168] True speculative philosophy "introduces a rupture into habitual seeing" and engages with the irreducible perplexities that constitute a breakdown—a self-debunking—of thought's pretentious claims of self-sufficiency and absolute self-certain knowing such as one finds in totalizing curiosity and instrumental mind.[169] Within the overdetermined ethos of being, life is difficult due to the lack of simple univocal determinations (AT 250; *EB* 79, 123; BR 222)—due to the meagerness of our knowing and valuing and thus demanding a more finessed dwelling in the *chiaroscuro* of being (*EB* 123, 166, 169, 276).[170] This metaphysical finesse that the metaxological sense tries to articulate is a plurivocal saying arising from and dwelling with astonishment and perplexity before the perennially strange, enigmatic, overdetermined excess of given being (*PO* 22, 210; *BHD* 101; *BB* xiii, 14, 192; *PU* 12; BDD 737, 763; *EB* 21, 51).

### Section II: Desmond as Addressing Caputo's Motivating Concerns

Behind Caputo's critique of metaphysics and his more positive alternative to metaphysics, there can be seen to be certain motivating concerns. First, Caputo is concerned to avoid elevating the knowledge of reality to a falsely absolute status. This is a counsel for humility—for not putting too high a polish on our all-too-human determinations. Second, Caputo is concerned to avoid supplanting the living of life (difficulty, flux) with the knowledge of reality. This is a counsel for relevance—for not getting lost in the abstractions of thought and forgetting where one lives. By avoiding these two negatives, Caputo seeks, I think, to address a more basic positive concern. This is a concern to be honest and faithful to life—and to do so by having a way of thinking that is involved (interested, in the midst) in life in all its particularity and difference toward the end of directing one toward the difficulty of one's existence. Caputo's own alternative to metaphysics, his *radical hermeneutics,* is intended to be just such a way of thinking that is honest and faithful to life.

Desmond shares these concerns and is driven by the similar impulses of proper humility and honesty before what is. They are largely in a deep accord here regarding the most fundamental virtues of thinking about the world. Desmond, however, addresses these concerns from a metaphysical perspective. First, his vision of metaphysics avoids elevating knowledge of reality to a falsely absolute status. With regard to metaphysics' (univocal and dialectical) claims to absoluteness—its pretension of fixing truth determinately so as to attain self-certain and comprehensive consistency and coherence such as is found in totalizing curiosity and instrumental mind—metaxological metaphysics lives, not in its completion, but in its inevitable breakdown, in its self-debunking (*PO* 10, 46, 148, 210–11, 242–43; *BHD* 43, 187, 243, 263; *BB* xiv–xv, 73, 80–82, 192; *PU* 148, 243, 254; BDD 752; *AOO* 4). There is no completion or realization or consummation or end of metaphysics (*BB* xvi, 15; BDD 758). Metaphysics, for Desmond, is an uncertain venture entailing a certain inevitable failure, and thus calling for humility and finesse in the face of the meagerness of our knowing (*BB* xiii, 46, 192; *EB* 86–87, 123, 166, 169, 276). In fact, Caputo can be seen as being complicit with a high-handed dismissal of metaphysics—itself a totalizing gesture: metaphysics is reduced to the function it fulfills (the tyrannical order—against which we are the brave and virtuous transgressors) in the deconstructive system. One suspects there is lurking here an uncannily modern pretence to ("radical"?) newness and its concomitant prejudice against that which has gone before.

Second, metaphysics in Desmond's view avoids supplanting the difficulty of life with some kind of abstract knowledge. Metaphysics never truly leaves behind the singularity of the thinker for the anonymity of a system, for metaphysics is always undertaken in a particular between ("starts too late") and bears the singular existential burden of its uncertain wager (*BB* 13, 45, 188). Metaphysics is a mindfulness of what is at work in the "middle" of our existence, the happenings of our given place in being (*PO* 11, 18; *PU* 22; HT 25; *AOO* 4). This mindfulness is to enable a more artful dwelling in the given ethos of being—a dwelling whose tasks include mindfulness of the intimately given community of being in which we are involved and which enables our thinking and being (*EB* 86–87, 123, 166, 169, 276; GEW 27).

Finally, Desmond's metaxological metaphysics seeks to be faithful to the emergent happenings in the middle and thus to be honest and faithful to life. It is involved/interested (*inter-esse*) in the living of life (see §1 above). It is sensitive to and particularly mindful of particularity, singularity, and difference (see §3 above). It is honest with regard to life's difficulty (see §4 above). Metaphysics is to be an "interpretive fidelity" to the plural and overdeterminate happenings emergent in the middle, not an escape from them (*BB* xiii, 44).

In fact, one suspects a certain abstraction and forgetfulness in any perspective so reticent to attend to the most recurring human questions and perplexities: What is thinking? What is being? What is the relation between them? For Desmond, the speculative *arises from existential involvement.* To say it is always (or even primarily) an attempted escape from life is to be honest neither to life—to the existential fact of wonder and perplexity—nor to speculation.

## Section III: Desmond's Metaphysical Alternative to Caputo's "Metaphysics Without Metaphysics"

In addition to answering Caputo's critiques of metaphysics and addressing his motivating concerns, Desmond provides a metaphysical alternative to Caputo's alternative to metaphysics—one that is preferable to Caputo's radical hermeneutics, his "metaphysics without metaphysics." Beyond answering Caputo's central concerns arguably better than Caputo's own system, Desmond's thought can be used to critique/locate many of Caputo's main points and strong conclusions.

### §1. Radical Hermeneutics: Minimalism

Caputo's radical hermeneutics addresses what a way of thinking that is faithful to life should be. Radical hermeneutics stands as a bulwark against the assurances of metaphysics, seeing no grounding or foundation for interpretation to guide it and ensure its stability and fidelity (*RH* 6, 147). It affirms flux and becoming against metaphysics' stabilizing of the flux—"the uncircumventable futility involved in trying to nail things down" (*RH* 116–18, 211). Thus, the post-metaphysical rationality of a radical hermeneutics entails a minimalism that stays with the modest "finite facts" as they appear on the surface of experience and neither speculates about depths/beyonds nor overestimates the status and scope of its knowledge (GA 1–3; AE 38). Instead, it seeks a minimally restrictive or constraining idiom by favoring such constitutionally inadequate metaphors as flux, fluidity, movement, free play, instability, events, and happenings (RH 257, 262; AE 71; MD 140; MMD 28; MRH 180).

Desmond's work shows that one can have a grand, maximal vision that still has place for irreducible singularity—perhaps has a better place for it. The metaxological "grand narrative" is maximal without the pretence to legitimate or found itself by appeal to some neutral, universal reason—without being an incredible *meta-narrative*. For Desmond, metaphysics is not in the business of providing the assurances of a pure access to reality—it entails perplexity, disquiet, struggle, strain, and failure (BB xiii, 45; PU 25; BDD 735, 761, 764). Metaxological metaphysics is a discourse *of* and *in* the middle—it does not overestimate its grasp by envisioning an escape from the middle to gain a view from nowhere (DDO 28, 114, 208; PO 3–4, 11, 18; PU 22, 108; HT 25; AOO 4). Instead of nailing things down, metaphysics is an attending to astonishment and perplexities that rupture and constitute a breakdown—a self-debunking—of thought's claims of self-sufficiency and absolute self-certain knowing (PO 235–36, 242; BHD 43, 243; AOO 4).[171] Metaphysics is an "interpretive fidelity" to and a mindfulness of the emergent happenings in the middle, the between—to the "finite facts" on the surface of life—a being attentive to the community of being's plurality of others in interrelation (PO 18; BB xiii, 44; PU 12; GEW 23, 25; En 130).[172] Thus far, Desmond and Caputo agree on what thinking (called radical hermeneutics or metaxological metaphysics) should be up to and how it should carry itself, as it were.

Desmond's vision, however, does differ on some significant points. These "finite facts" in the middle are not merely lacking or indeterminate—and thus calling for a minimalist description—but overdeterminate. The metaphysician encounters and struggles with an excess of being as plural and "overdeterminate" that gives rise to the astonishment and perplexity that constitute the abiding engine of metaphysical thought (BB 46, 52, 204; PU 25; BDD 761). The modesty and humility of finite and all-too-human metaphysicians does not demand the abandonment of the deepest questions of philosophy—of being, of the self, of the world, of God. In fact, a fidelity to the surface happenings of the middle raises these perplexing questions about depths and beyonds in the first place. The "beyond" and the "in the midst" of metaphysics are intimately related—such that trying to be faithful to the emergent happenings in the middle (*meta* as 'in the midst') refers one to otherness and transcendence (*meta* as 'beyond, transcendent') (BB xiii).[173] Such a metaphysical meditation upon the excess overdeterminacy of being requires, not a metaphorics that is content to ask little of itself, but a likewise overdeterminate language that knowingly asks too much of language in the form of metaphor and analogy and symbol and hyperbole, for such is the best hope for naming (if always imperfectly) the fullness of the transcendences that surround us in the metaxological community of being—of the beyonds in our midst (BB 207–22).

## §2. Radical Hermeneutics: Repetition and *Inter-esse*

Over and against metaphysics' escaping the flux through abstraction and fixation on static unity, radical hermeneutics emphasizes being in and forging ahead in the midst of the flux in terms of repetition and *inter-esse*. Radical hermeneutics breaks with metaphysics' drive toward a static unity insulated from the vagaries of life. Caputo sees the exemplary movement of traditional metaphysics as a recollection seeking an original and pure presence uncontaminated by the arbitrariness and indeterminacy of our all-too-fluid human existence. Instead, radical hermeneutics emphasizes *repetition,* which represents how any unity, identity, or presence in life is one that is *produced* and not *found*—every "presence" as an effect of "repetition" (*RH* 4, 17). As such, repetition embraces a creative and productive movement into the difficulties of life where there is the possibility of novelty and genuine movement—against some eternal, preexisting, static unity (*RH* 3; HKFM 206, 210n, 212). This is the way of living *inter-esse*—in the midst of the rush of things. "The existing spirit," Caputo writes, "exists (*esse*) in the midst (*inter*) of time . . . in the midst of the flux. Its *esse* is *inter-esse;* its being is being-between, being-in-the-midst-of" (HKFM 220). The repetition at the heart of radical hermeneutics embraces this basic locatedness in the midst of temporal becoming (this passive *inter,* being-in-the-midst) and takes up the proper task of forging ahead in this situation (as an active *being, esse* in the context of the between) (*RH* 33). Radical hermeneutics thus presents this repetition as interestedness, as "the way of the existing individual" (HKFM 208).

Desmond, again, sees such a fixation on static unity not as being indicative of metaphysics as such but as describing the kind of stress on unity evident in the univocal and dialectical senses of being. Regarding metaphysics' (particularly in the form of recollection) fixation on pure presences, Desmond sees there to be (particularly in the phenomenon of astonishment) an overdeterminate presence that is not the foundation of a static system but the awareness of an original unarticulated plentitude prior to and exceeding all determinate facts and definitions that gets thought moving in the first place (*DDO* 185; *BB* 8, 13, 179; BDD 736–38; *EB* 51; MC 11). This first astonishment is encountered as an elemental immediacy—not as an immediate determinate knowledge but as an intimate strangeness (*PO* 63, 64, 295; *PU* 67, 76)—the lived, "rapturous" ("*prelapsarian*") univocity of the "immediacy to our initial immersion in being" (*BB* 47–48).

Regarding the unity or identity or presence that is produced by repetition, Desmond would see this as only half of the story. This kind of unity produced or constructed by the self in repetition maps onto what Desmond describes as self-mediation. There is for Desmond, however, from the perspective of the involved (interested, *inter-esse,* between-being) singular self, a situation of double mediation, of both self-mediation and intermediation, so as to articulate our relations with others intelligently while preventing closure—while obviating the temptation to reduce all mediation to self-mediation in the name of total(izing) intelligibility (*DDO* 115–16; *BHD* 8, 128; *BB* 163, 196, 418). Thus, second astonishment can be seen as a repetition, a re-turn to or re-petition of first agapeic astonishment, that is not produced by the self—a breakthrough, a gift for which one can be prepared, for which one can patiently and vigilantly wait in openness in the midst of perplexity, but it cannot be willed (*BB* 192; *PU* 122, 144–47; *MC* 12–13).[174] (This is actually close to the description that Caputo, following Kierkegaard, gives of religious repetition as a movement that is impossible to bring about on one's own and is ultimately a gift—as will be seen in chapter 4.)

Desmond's metaphysics also gives an alternative discussion of the possibility of genuine movement and novelty. As was recognized before, Desmond's own metaphysics sees external being (T1) in terms of being-as-becoming, as a universal impermanence that does not easily conform to the univocal (*BB* 50, 238) but displays equivocity in its double coming to be and passing away (*BB* 88, 90, 291)—a process of differentiation in which things come to determinacy in a kind of dialectical process (*BB* 237, 284). For Desmond, the equivocal flux and becoming of the world is not merely equivocal, not merely a formless and indeterminate dispersal inhospitable to any intelligibility—becoming is metaxological, a dynamic and intermediate happening where there is room for both the persisting equivocity of being and the possibility of intelligibility, determinate or indeterminate—a being-between a totally determinate unity and an unintelligible dispersal (such as one has a hard time not seeing to be suggested by Caputo's radical hermeneutics) (*BB* 88).[175] Regarding the notion of novelty that repetition is to defend, Desmond would hold that it is not a choice of either origin or novelty, but it is the nature of origin *as agapeic* that enables, makes novelty possible. It is precisely Desmond's metaphysics of agapeic origination that makes genuine novelty (and plurality and singularity and uniqueness) possible (*PU* 48).[176]

Finally, Desmond's metaxological metaphysics presents an alternative to radical hermeneutics' vision of human existence as *inter-esse*. Metaxological metaphysics is "a discourse concerning the middle, of the middle, and in the middle" (*DDO* 7; *BB* xii). The metaxological sense is a discourse *of* and *in* the middle—a thinking that is between the totalizing closure of rigid univocal "objective" thinking and the fragmented discontinuity of equivocal "subjective" thinking (*DDO* 28, 114, 207; *PO* 3–4; *PU* 108). The metaxological sense is also a discourse *concerning* the middle—striving to be mindful of what is at work in the happening of the ethos, the milieu, the between of being as our given place—to be attentive to the community of being's plurality of others in interrelation (*PU* 12; *GEW* 23, 25; *En* 130).[177] Metaphysics attempts to make intelligible our involvement in and being in the midst of (*inter-esse*) the given ethos of being that is encountered as charged with excessive value (in which the metaphysician is interested) (*EB* 17, 23, 177; *AOO* 292). Thus, the metaxological focuses on thought in terms of interest or "inter-esse"—as being moved by wonder and perplexity at the fullness of our being in the between—our interest in *esse* arising from our *inter-esse* (*BHD* 137; *BB* 64, 452).[178]

### §3. Radical Hermeneutics: Heterology

Radical hermeneutics counters metaphysics' urge to subsume everything within a singular, universal system with the awareness of abiding *difference*—it is "a philosophy of 'alterity,'" with "a relentless attentiveness and sensitivity to the 'other'" (*GNA* 453). Caputo describes radical hermeneutics as a philosophy of difference in terms of its being a "heterology"—both a heteronomism and a heteromorphism. *Heteronomism* views difference in terms of the particular and indigestible singular other as "marked by its idiosyncrasy, its idiomaticity, its uniqueness, its anomaly, its unclassifiability, its unrepeatability"—as standing against metaphysics' universal system of sameness (*AE* 42–43, 59; *MRH* 4, 179). The heteronomist sees reality in terms of the singular and idiosyncratic without there being any deeper structure (*AE* 94–95).[179] *Heteromorphism* views difference in terms of the plural, the multiple, the diverse, the changing and is concerned to keep the free-play of diverse and changing reality free of the closure of metaphysics' urge to static unity (*RH* 262; *AE* 42–43, 59). It keeps things open-ended, celebrates diversity and alteration, and happily greets unanticipated pluralities—seeking to "maximize the possibilities" and "to keep as many options open as possible" (*RH* 206, 258; *MRH* 6).

Desmond likewise considers his way of thinking to be a heterology, but in the sense of a different kind of practice of speculative philosophy—"a speculative philosophy of non-identity" in which thought is ultimately engaged in the task of thinking what is irreducibly other to thought (*BHD* 249). Metaxological metaphysics is a *heteronomism* considering being in its character as an overdetermined excess made up of unrepeatable singularities—as a general intermediation in which there is an open community of singulars (*DDO* 115; *BHD* 129; *BB* 34, 88, 188, 196, 465; *PU* 15; *BDD* 761; *NDR* 48). The ideal that Desmond puts forward in terms of agapeic mind in particular is a heteronomic vigilance regarding otherness, finding expression in the love of singular and particular others in their singularity and particularity—in giving to and affirming the other in its own distinct and singular being (*BHD* 137; *BB* 193, 253, 490; *PU* 124, 177, 211–12, 239, 256; *EB* 161, 356). Metaxological metaphysics (as an "idiot wisdom") respects and affirms the *idiocy* of being in the singularity of being (*idios* as singular as opposed to public), in the excess or strangeness of being (*idios* as outside the sphere of the determinately accountable), and in the intimacy of being (*idios* as private) (*BHD* 292; *BB* 186; *PU* 163–64, 197, 251, 257).

Desmond parts with Caputo's heteronomism inasmuch as the emphasis on singularity precludes any kind of deeper being-with or community in being. Here Caputo can be seen as representing Desmond's equivocal sense of being, which subverts itself insofar as remaining with sheer equivocity means not only the dispersal of being but the dissolution of mindfulness itself. The inherent drive of mindfulness cannot stop with equivocity's mere fragments; it calls for a deeper understanding of the differences, othernesses and ambiguities in the flux of being (*BB* xiv–xv, 132, 142).

Desmond's metaphysics is also heterological in the more *heteromorphic* sense. Metaxological metaphysics advocates an "affirmative doubleness" that resists the reduction of the double (the plural) to a simulacrum of otherness in a single, dialectical process (*PO* 5; *BHD* 113, 114, 120, 274–75; *BB* 158, 163, 188, 196; *PU* 15). This is a kind of reinstatement of equivocal difference (either/or) after dialectical unity (both/and)—a both-either/or-and-both/and that envisions being as a plurality of singulars in interplay in an "open whole"—a community of being whose "being-with" is not reductive of otherness (*DDO* 127–28; *BHD* 129; *BB* 178, 418, 451; *PU* 15). The metaxological also takes us to the truth of the equivocal sense of being in its recognition of the equivocity in being itself—in being's becoming as an ongoing process (a "universal impermanence") in which there is often an intermingling of opposites and in which univocal determinate labels thus have limited staying power (*BB* 88; *EB* 123). Again, the fixation on static unity that makes Caputo justifiably nervous is not, for Desmond, indicative of metaphysics as such, but descriptive of the kind of stress on unity evident in the univocal and dialectical senses of being (*DDO* 6; *BHD* 6; *BB* xii, 143, 175, 178; *PU* 12; BDD 762).

From Desmond's perspective, Caputo's notion of heteromorphic heterology takes the notions of plurality's free-play and freedom from closure to the extreme of a sheer equivocal diversity. The equivocal sense of being taken on its own presents a sheer plurality that is merely fragmenting. Here being and mind are set in opposition to one another such that there is no relation but only unmediated difference (*BHD* 6; *BB* xii; *PU* 12–13). Desmond, however, envisions a community of plural singulars rather than mere equivocal dispersal. The difference is the difference between equivocal difference and metaxological difference, where the latter includes the former's (heterological) emphasis on singularity and plurality while also seeing this plurality as an (at least potentially) intelligible community of complex relations. Metaxological metaphysics is a way of thinking about reality that strives to think in terms of an "open wholeness" rather than the kind of closed, totalizing system that rightfully concerns Caputo. Such an "open whole" is a community of a plurality of singulars in interplay (*DDO* 127–28; *BHD* 129; *BB* 418, 451; *PU* 15)—a plural intermediation in excess to any single self-mediating whole (*DDO* 8, 115; *BHD* 129; *BB* 188, 196, 451; *PU* 15; NDR 48).[180] The plurivocity of the metaxological sense reflects the plurality of being in its character as an overdetermined excess made up of unrepeatable singulars (*BB* 34, 88, 465; BDD 761). The metaxological emphasis on genuine (heteromorphic) plurality, rather than leveling or flattening, provides space for the singularity, for the (heteronomic) "idiocy" of individual beings and selves. Here Desmond provides a unified and complementary picture of the heteronomic singular and the heteromorphic plural, whereas in

Caputo's work these two (the Levinasian Rabbi and the Nietzschean Dionysius) are in deep, perhaps unmediatable tension with one another.

### §4. Critiquing Caputo's Conclusions

For Caputo, being faithful to life—being honest about the situation in which we find ourselves—brings one hard upon certain conclusions. First, there is the denial of any robust knowledge of reality (or metaphysics)—that the only acceptable "metaphysics" is one that recognizes that we do not (and cannot) know who we are or what is going on or what is true. Radical hermeneutics demands the humility to recognize the hard (difficult) truth that there are no hard (solid) truths . . . such as metaphysics claims (*RH* 146, 192, 258; *AE* 224–25; *MRH* 2, 12). Caputo's radical hermeneutics is then a basic "non-knowing"—not a metaphysical knowing but a passion driven by not knowing who we are or where we are going (*AE* 225, 230; *MRH* 2, 5).[181] Thus our understanding is always in a state of undecidability—of flux—in which we can never really say what is going on (*AE* 63, 99).

Second, there is the denial of the importance of metaphysics for life. Metaphysics, as Caputo understands it, stands in a position of fundamental opposition to our living of life as it truly is, in all of its ambiguity and difficulty, and we can and should (and ultimately cannot but) make our ways without it. Thus, radical hermeneutics as a thinking about reality after metaphysics, a metaphysics without metaphysics, moves in the opposite direction from metaphysics—from an abstract escape from the vagaries of existence to an interested involvement in the living of life. Factical life—anxious because of its lack of hard truths—is difficult in that we are not made safe by a metaphysical canopy and so have to make decisions against the backdrop of "undecidability" (*RH* 1, 189; *MRH* 4; *AE* 4). Finally, radical hermeneutics as an awareness of the difficulty of life leads one from metaphysics (as thinking about reality) to ethics (as regarding how one is to relate to others)—from "what" to "how" (*RH* 257).

Desmond's work stands to critique these strong conclusions of Caputo's "post-metaphysical" alternative to metaphysics. The general critique is that radical hermeneutics' denials are too radical and that they go to unnecessary extremes (specifically, the extreme of a false either/or) in order to address its motivating concerns. Desmond questions the rejection of metaphysics as expressed in the critique of "onto-theology"—of all metaphysics being considered to be one form or another of "onto-theology." Regarding Caputo's denial of any "hard truths" (in the first conclusion) Desmond grants the scarcity of true univocal determinations insofar as such cannot account for the complexity either in the external object/other/being or in the internal subject/self/being or in their relation to each other (*DDO* 6; *BHD* 6).[182] Moreover, Desmond would argue, this scarcity is not a problem for metaphysics as such, nor is it a reason to deny that metaphysics ever produces some knowledge of reality. Speculative philosophy not only entertains but mindfully safeguards irreducible perplexities that constitute a breakdown—a self-debunking—of thought's claims of self-sufficiency and absolute self-certain knowing in terms of univocal determinations (*PO* 242; *BHD* 43, 243; *AOO* 4).[183] It concerns itself with the limits, the extremities of thought (*BHD* 42–43). The lack of "hard truths" is more of the condition for the possibility of metaphysics—the perplexity that gets it off the ground—than its frustration. Or rather, the common frustrations of metaphysics are not its utter downfall but a possibly seminal, fecund, fruitful going to ground—an undoing, unraveling that allows an otherwise reweaving. In fact, it is the post-metaphysical perspective, such as is found in Caputo's radical hermeneutics, that is too totalizing—itself totalizing metaphysics in terms of a rigid totalizing univocity (*BHD* 45; *BB* 344; *PU* 24, 217).[184]

Regarding the "non-knowing" ingredient in the first conclusion of Caputo's radical hermeneutics, this can be seen, in Desmond's terms, as a despairing second perplexity. It is a perplexity become nihilistic equivocity—a despairing and truncated perplexity that dwells in and fixates upon the failure, the breakdown, the coming to nothing of the search for univocal meaning. It is a skepticism issuing from a self-lacerating dissolution of univocal curiosity that rejects the univocal and is left with only the equivocal (*PU* 197; BDD 762; *EB* 47).[185] In Desmond's metaphysics, however, there are other possible trajectories after the breakdown of the hope of total determinacy (III, §4). One can recognize the breakdown without giving up hope (despairing) of any other understanding of the overdeterminate givenness of being. Here radical hermeneutics unnecessarily closes down possibilities beyond the either/or of full univocal determinacy or total equivocal indeterminacy.

Likewise, radical hermeneutics' assertion of "undecidability," is an expression of what Desmond calls the equivocal sense of being. It calls attention to unmediated (even un-mediat-able) difference—seeing a sheer plurality and a fragmented dispersal that cannot be brought into any kind of a unity (*PU* 12–23). Desmond's critique here concerns the question of how to think otherwise than in terms of univocal determinacy (or of dialectical self-determination that has the former as its telos). Desmond suggests that a proper understanding of being should be metaxological, not equivocal—should think of being as overdeterminate, not merely indeterminate. The equivocal conclusion of radical hermeneutics points to a false either/or (univocal/equivocal)—for as the univocal tends to break down into the equivocal, so does the equivocal (as a strong conclusion about the unknowability of the world) tend, if it is honest, to break down and demand a more complex view of interrelationships in the community of being. The equivocal sense, again like the univocal, subverts itself in that remaining with sheer equivocity means not only the dispersal of being but the dissolution of mindfulness itself. There is no reason the absolute claim of equivocity should stand when all other absolute claims cannot.

Desmond's thought can also be used to critique Caputo's second conclusion about the insignificance of metaphysics for existing individuals. For Desmond, metaphysics is to take up residence "in the midst" of life, and questions about the "beyond" are not a function of wanting to escape the between but of being faithful to the transcendings and transcendences that intermediate there (*BB* xiii, 44). Desmond suggests philosophy as a mindfulness of what is at work in the middle of our existence—of our inescapable being in relation to what is other in terms of determinate or indeterminate intelligible mediation (or intermediation)—and thus intimately related to the living of life (*PO* 11, 18; *PU* 22; *AOO* 4).[186] Metaphysics is inescapable as our mindfulness of the happening of life; it proceeds from an inherent exigence—from our need to think it—for all reflection is dependent on and complicit in the question of the meaning of the "to be" that moves us to wonder and perplexity (*BHD* 341; BDD 758; NDR 48; *AOO* 2; MC 5).[187] Furthermore, metaphysics as Desmond understands it does not skirt the difficulty—the irreducible and intrusive perplexity—of life, but it deepens it.

From the perspective of Desmond's metaxological hermeneutics, the conclusions of Caputo's radical hermeneutics can be seen, not as a (postmodern) break with modernity, but as in basic continuity with modernity—particularly in terms of what Desmond calls the objectification of being and the subjectification of value. Desmond describes this as the "*double face* of modernity" (*EB* 41; *HG* 21–22; *AOO* 292; MC 3). Being is objectified in that it is neutralized or devalued or evacuated—emptied of any value or worth or goodness in itself—and made into a "merely empirical" mechanism (AT 235–37; NDR 46; *EB* 99; *HG* 21–22). The subjectification of value comes about as there is a "revaluation" of value in terms of human self-determination (AT 235–37).[188] This disjunction of being (knowledge of which is metaphysics) and value (the stuff of life and ethics) runs through radical hermeneutics like a great fissure: we poor, existing individuals on the side of (valueless) valuing—on the side of factical, equivocal existence—and metaphysics on the far unreachable side of being—on the side of abstract and universal totalizing systems.

Along these lines, Caputo can be seen as rightly identifying the problem with the totalization of instrumental mind but wrongly identifying instrumental mind with metaphysics as such—as the objectifying metaphysics on the far, inaccessible side of the fissure. This instrumental mind—as a will to a manipulable univocity over the uncertainty of what is not determinately intelligible (*PO* 26, 121, 137, 158, 226, 306; *PU* 116, 195; *EB* 46)—easily spawns nihilism, in that the instrumental revaluation of valueless being *itself* partakes in the same ontological, root valuelessness as its objects. The neutralization of being also neutralizes the being of the projectors of value, thus emptying out any so projected value (*BB* 71, 83, 508; *PU* 5, 39, 169, 171, 222–23, 227; AT 236; *EB* 46; BR 227; MC 14).[189]

Caputo's critique of the modern ethos ultimately does not escape modernity but retains its nihilistic conclusion regarding humanity's inherently worthless valuations as the sole source of value (the Nietzschean metaphysics without metaphysics of his LeviNietzscheanism). To escape the dark claim of the worthlessness and meaninglessness of all things and all human endeavor (perhaps Nietzsche too sought to outmaneuver this), there must be a value, a valuing that is more than our value, our valuing. Without this "more," our attributions of worth, our mere mores, ring hollow indeed. Radical hermeneutics perhaps does not go far enough—its postmodernism is perhaps all too modern. Desmond here sees the postmodern as partaking of the same modern ethos— postmodernism as more of a kind of "hypermodernism," a self-determination become self-laceration (NDR 41; *EB* 169–70; *AOO* 276).[190] Postmodernism, for Desmond, is modernism—a denizen of the same modern, reconfigured ethos— but taken to an extreme of deconstructing the sole constructions of value (human constructions) allowed by the modern ethos. Thus Caputo, in divorcing life and values from any thought of what is real, can be seen as perpetuating a hypermodern and ultimately nihilistic dualism between being and goodness, while Desmond wants to reexamine more deeply the relation between being and goodness—the charge of and hospitality to the good in given being. But this has already taken us well into the realm of ethics ...

# 3   Ethics

As in the previous chapter on metaphysics, this chapter (in part one) gives a systematic presentation of Desmond's understanding of ethics and (in part two) sets such an understanding up against that of Caputo for comparison. In particular, part one lays out Desmond's conception of the relation between being and goodness (in section I), his understanding of the nature of the human self as manifesting multiple "ethical potencies" (in section II), his depiction of the self's dynamic progression through seven "ethical selvings" that map onto his fourfold sense of being (in section III), and his understanding of the likewise progressive orders of community unfolding in the fourfold logic (section IV). In part two where this vision of ethics is compared to that of Caputo, Desmond's metaxological ethics is presented as a viable and indeed preferable alternative to LeviNietzschean ethics without/against ethics.

## Part One: A Presentation of William Desmond's Ethics

### Section I: Being and Goodness, Ethics and Metaphysics

The modern ethos provides the background for modern understandings of ethics in that it molds not only our values but our conception of value itself (AT 235; EB 19). Desmond sees a dualism or estrangement between being and goodness flowering into the fact/value distinction and into the absence of intrinsic worth that is one of the chief characteristics of the modern ethos (PO 160, 353; EB 194). This dualism in the reconfigured ethos produces a neutralization of the ethos and an evacuation of worth from being that leaves the human to dwell as in a valueless whole (AT 235–36, 250; NDR 46). The modern "good" or value is good or valuable because it is valued for a human project—the good is good because human desiring makes it so (MC 9; EB 31).[1] Thus being is instrumentalized—made the raw matter for human manipulation—totally (PU 227). Yet, Desmond argues, if being is valueless then humans are ontologically valueless as well, as are their valuations—there is no bank to cash the check of their bestowal of value upon being (EB 138; BR 228; PU 248).[2] This total collapse of value (when the check bounces, as it were) issues in nihilism, be it hidden or overt (PU 227; EB 31, 149, 154, 167).[3]

This modern ethos provides, for Desmond, the background for modern conceptions of ethics, particularly as it influences the meaning of the central concept of freedom. Freedom, in western modernity, is understood in terms of—if not simply as—autonomy or autonomous self-determination (PO 185; EB 160, 270; AT 233; BR 218). This understanding of freedom can be seen in thinkers from Descartes and Locke to Kant and Hegel. This freedom-as-autonomy is grounded in the "devalued soil" of the modern ethos (*EB* 133; *AT* 237), in that its relation to being in its otherness is ambivalent, equivocal—or rather it comes to see otherness itself as equivocal: valueless in itself but useful in our autonomous value-constructing projects (*PU* 121; *AT* 233; *EB* 169; *AOO* 271). Because of the lack of any inherent goodness or value in being or otherness, the autonomous subject is seen as the only possible source of value. And once autonomy is installed as the ideal, it works to maintain its autonomy as freedom from otherness (*PO* 173–74; *PU* 191). For the self-determining self to secure itself as truly autonomous, it alone must be the source of value—it is the source of what value there is in being in its otherness. Otherness is valuable because it is valued by an autonomous self. This reinforces the dualism between being and goodness (*EB* 137).[4] Desmond contends that there is, however, a way of thinking of the relation between being and goodness other than the modern dualism and a way of thinking of freedom (and thus ethics) other than modern, absolutized autonomy (*EB* 138, 158; *HG* 22).

Desmond's conception provides an alternative that affirms the inherent value of being in its otherness—a close interrelating of being and goodness. Desmond sees the "modern" view of the relation between being and value as being based on a contraction (or an "evacuation" or a "neutering") of the given ethos of being—on the modern ethos' overly determinate and univocal constriction of the overdetermined "between" (*NDR* 46; *EB* 99; *AT* 235).[5] Whereas the "modern" view sees the good as existing only as projected and defined by human desire, Desmond sides more with the "ancients," who saw desire as seeking the good because it *is* good—that there is good in being that is not fully reducible to our desiring (*AT* 235; *BB* 517–18).[6] Being and goodness, for Desmond, are related to each other—not in terms of any simple univocal identification or equivocal separation—but in terms of such metaxological relations or intermediations as the *promise* of goodness in being (especially regarding human being) (*PU* 192; *EB* 17, 162),[7] being's *intimacy* with the good (*NDR* 44; *EB* 21)[8] and being's *hospitality* to the good (*AT* 235).[9] Such an understanding of the interrelatedness of being and goodness issues in a different view of freedom: an ontological freedom that one has in being given to be—the prior "coming to be" that makes our free becoming possible, that possibilizes our possibility (*BHD* 80, 182)—a freedom not just "from" foreign or external domination but "to" become a more excellent self and then giving beyond the self "toward" the other (*EB* 317).

This bringing together of being and goodness in an understanding of the value or worth of being likewise brings metaphysics and ethics into a closer, more intimate, relation (*PO* 161).[10] Ethics and metaphysics, for Desmond, are inseparable and should not, and indeed cannot be, divorced from one another (*PU* 87, 223, 227; *AT* 235). Metaphysics cannot be divorced from the ethical in that metaphysics entails an ethical valuing of being and desire for, even love of, truth (*PU* 87, 108, 149, 177).[11] Neither can ethics be divorced from the metaphysical. Ethics, for Desmond, is metaphysical—is dependent on metaphysics— in that it entails an understanding of the relation between being and goodness, of what it means to *be* good (*PU* 39; *EB* 18).[12] Ethics entails articulating what is good or valuable or of worth in being (PO 160-61, 183, 189)[13]—particularly when it comes to that of human beings (*PU* 227).[14]

Finally, Desmond's conception of the deeper interrelation of being and goodness, of metaphysics and ethics, suggests meditation on the ground of the enigmatic value and goodness in being and thus the ground of ethics (*EB* 18-20). The error of more modern conceptions, for Desmond, is the endeavor to ground goodness and ethics solely in the autonomous self's groundless valuing.[15] In opposition to this, Desmond sees the more proximate ground of ethics to be metaphysics since it presents a conception of the ethos as a metaxological community of being—particularly when it comes to the understanding of the being of human selves in community (see the sections below).[16] The more ultimate ground, however, is the ground of this grounding community of being. The agapeic origin is the ground of being and goodness as the one that gives forth being to be as good in itself (*EB* 17, 20, 201).[17]

### Section II: The Plurivocal Promise of the Singular Self

Key to Desmond's understanding of ethics' relation to metaphysics is his philosophical anthropology—the way in which a metaphysical understanding of the self serves as a basis for a more concrete understanding of ethics in terms of different "ethical selvings" and ethical communities. Toward this end, I will summarize (in §1) Desmond's conceptions of the idiocy or singularity of selfhood, the infinitude and inward otherness of selfhood, the promise of original selfhood, and the freedom and development of the becoming self. I will then outline (in §2) what Desmond identifies as the ethical potencies of the human self.

### §1. The Metaxological Self

The human self, for Desmond, is characterized by an *idiotic singularity* (*PO* 361; *BB* 397; *EB* 170-71)[18]—by a felt irreplaceable uniqueness or originality—a singular integrity (*BB* 380, 397; *EB* 186).[19] This singularity is a "rich 'univocity'" (*BB* 383).[20] The idiot self is an "elemental self" (*BB* 381-84, 397). that has a non- or pre-objective[21] mindfulness of its being for-itself (*BB* 377, 379-80). The self senses, feels, is aware of this idiotic singularity intimately and elementally (*BB* 381-83).[22] Such mindfulness of the singular self entails a concrete awareness of the self's integrity (*EB* 186) and worth as a singular being (*EB* 188).[23] But this singular, idiotic self is also communal—always already in relation to otherness, whether in the self's own inward otherness (its transcendence) or its intimate relation with others (its transcending) (*EB* 170-71).[24]

The human self, in Desmond's understanding, is also characterized by its *infinitude*. Selfhood is the emergence in finite being of an infinitely restless desire (*DDO* 75; *BB* 401)[25]—of an intentional infinitude (*DDO* 75). The source of this infinite restlessness and intentional infinitude is the excess of the self—

the inward otherness of the self as an inner infinitude and as source of transcending (*EB* 215).[26] This transcendence of the human self (T2)—as both an inward otherness/excess/infinitude that is its transcendent source and a self-transcendence that is its transcending activity—has to do with the self's freedom and possibility (*BB* 231; *EB* 215).[27] The possibility of the self is the possibility of development both in its relation to itself—becoming a more articulated and determinate whole—and in its openness and relation to otherness (*DDO* 75; *BB* 384).[28]

Desmond brings these elements of the being of the self—of singularity and self-transcendence—together in his concept of the *original self*.[29] The self is original in two senses. First, the self is original in the sense of being unique, singular, original unto itself (*PO* 361; *BB* 380–81).[30] Second, the self is original in the sense of being a source of origination (*BB* 380).[31] In this second sense, there is an original power or energy of being in the self—an overdetermined ontological excess or plenitude or unmastered depth to the self's inward otherness (*PO* 51, 361; *BB* 401; *PU* 60).[32] As such, the original self (as constitutive of the being of the self) is the "indeterminate locus of selving" (of the self as becoming and developing) (*BB* 381). Thus Desmond writes of the *promise* of the singular self[33]—the way in which the self both is itself and becomes itself[34]—such that its being can be described as inexhaustible excess (its transcendence) and possibility (its transcending) (*BB* 384).[35] The promise of the self is the possibility of its self-transcending (*BB* 378),[36] be it in the direction of its self-becoming/realization (erotic) or of its relating to others (agapeic) (*PU* 78).[37]

The self's (self-)*transcendence* as *freedom* develops through a process of self-determination and self-mediation that is the becoming of the ethical self. The transcending power of human being comes to expression in its being as possibility—its perplexing and indeterminate freedom (*BB* 231; *PU* 191; *EB* 215; *AOO* 268).[38] This transcending of the self is a self-surpassing in which the self is self-determining and self-originating (*PO* 361; *HG* 3).[39] As such, the self's transcending/surpassing/originating/determining is a process through which the self becomes ethical in coming to relate to itself (understand itself) and shape itself (form itself in practice) in different ways—in different "selvings" (*BB* 378, 397, 525; *EB* 52).[40] In this process of selving (of the self's indeterminate ontological freedom/possibility forming itself in various ways), the self comes to understand itself in the light of different understandings of freedom.[41] But this selving is also (and, as Desmond argues, more basically) an intermediation with otherness beyond this self-mediation—seen in the way the higher forms of selving consist of coming to live in the midst of community with the other.[42]

The indeterminate original self then comes to and undergoes plural mediations and determinations. Within and outside of the singularity of the self there is a plurality. Desmond describes this plurivocal promise of the singular self in two ways in *Ethics and the Between*: in terms of the more abstract account of the *ethical potencies* and in terms of the more concrete account of the *ethical selvings*. He then goes on to describe the different kinds of *ethical communities* in which selves come to dwell. First, I will deal briefly with the ethical potencies before moving on to the ethical selvings and the ethical communities in following sections.

### §2. Ethical Potencies

Within the singular self there is a plurality of ethical potencies—a plurivocity of the good—for the good too is "said" in many ways. These potencies refer to the plurivocal ontological promise of being in the human self—the dynamic endowment out of which the self develops.[43] These potencies are the basic sources out of which the self comes to reflect more determinately on the indeterminate show of value—out of which ethics comes to dwell with the both the equivocities and the constancies in the ethos (*EB* 79, 191). The potencies are: the idiotic, the aesthetic, the dianoetic, the transcendental, the eudaimonistic, and the transcending.

The first two potencies are the idiotic and the aesthetic. The *idiotic* potency has to do with the self's elemental and yet indeterminate (or overdeterminate) intimacy with the good of being (*EB* 10–11).[44] This potency names the simple and (as mentioned above) singular pre-objective and pre-subjective awareness of the community of being as good on a primal and elemental level within oneself (*EB* 170–71).[45] The *aesthetic* potency, however, has to do with the showing of the worth of being in the body and to the senses—often expressed in terms of beauty (*EB* 11).[46] There is an indeterminate excess in the aesthetic display of value that issues in an equivocity that calls for constancies in our understanding of the good (*EB* 189–91).

The *dianoetic* potency seeks intelligible regularities or constancies in the midst of the ambiguities of polyvalent showings of the good (*EB* 11, 191). This potency names the drive to identify patterns of integrity and commonality—intrinsic values that command moral respect.[47] Such patterns or constancies would include perennial and elemental human concerns—that the gift of being or of life, in oneself and in the other, is something to be valued (for it is has inherent worth), honored, protected—not taken for granted but taken as granted, as a gift.[48] This potency retains a necessary place in being ethical even if there can be no complete univocal determination of the constancies (and such is to be guarded against) (*EB* 11, 196).

The next two potencies, the transcendental and the eudaimonistic, mirror on a more sophisticated and abstract level the dianoetic and aesthetic potencies. The *transcendental* potency is the power to name certain constancies that occupy a special position in that they are necessary for the possibility of ethical life (*EB* 11).[49] Desmond identifies two such conditions for the possibility of ethical being in the between: first, the metaxological relation or community between self and other (*EB* 11, 199–200)[50] and, second, the metaxological relation between the agapeic origin and the community of being. The *eudaimonistic*[51] potency, however, names value in terms of the fullness of human flourishing and resumes the idiotic and aesthetic potencies inasmuch it seeks to come to terms with the more indeterminate manifestations and embodiments of value in human being (*EB* 12). This potency has to do with an ethical dwelling that is less science than finesse—with more attentiveness to nuance and ambiguity—seeing excellence in terms of a feel for the whole of life.[52]

Finally, the *transcending* potency has to do with how the indeterminate or overdeterminate excess within the human exceeds and surpasses itself toward otherness. This restlessness points to an infinite dimension of the human being—a desire that is not satisfied by any finite good. It transcends us toward something transcendent of any finite good (*EB* 209).[53] This transcending takes various formations: be it equivocal transcending driven by unchecked desire as lack toward mania and boredom (*EB* 215), or erotic transcending seeking to affirm oneself and be one's own master (*EB* 216), or agapeic transcending consenting to the gift of being (gratitude) and letting go of what is one's own for the other (generosity)—a desire as openness to the other that is a true self-transcending (*EB* 217).

## Section III: Ethical Selvings and Agapeic Selving

The human being, in Desmond's understanding, becomes ethical through a *poiesis* of selfhood—through the process of the progressive unfolding of the self (*PO* 164; *BB* 415). This process of self-becoming broadly follows the lines of human development: from infancy and childhood through adolescence to adulthood and maturity (*EB* 223–24). The development of these different "ethical selvings" describes the development of will and desire from root indeterminate urge/willing through various self-mediations and transformations toward a (perhaps paradoxical) willing and desiring beyond willing and desiring (*PU* 70; *EB* 223–24). As such, the ethical selvings are the plural enactment of freedom—different kinds of freedom, different kinds of self-transcendence (*EB* 269).[54] These plural ethical selvings are the self-mediations of the good as the dialectical development of the self and its understanding of the good—as the coming to greater self-consciousness and a greater level of self-determination (regarding its will, desire, freedom, etc.) (*BB* 525–26; *EB* 223).[55] But this self-determination is also intimately connected to, dependent upon, and relating to the intermediation with the other in the broader community of being (as will be explored in the next section on ethical communities).[56] In this section, I will present Desmond's understanding of these plural ethical selvings, giving particular attention to the differences with regard to will and desire, freedom and relation to otherness (or love). For the sake of simplicity, I will organize the seven selvings (from *Ethics and the Between*) into the four more general categories of selving used in Desmond's other works and paralleling (more or less) the different forms of ethical community (as well as the fourfold sense of being).

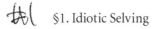

## §1. Idiotic Selving

### FIRST ETHICAL SELVING

The first of Desmond's ethical selvings is *idiot selving*. Idiot selving names the private and intimate elemental or original self (as discussed above) (*BB* 380–83). This selving is a richly "univocal" self—the self that is intimately aware of itself as itself, its mineness—the singular and unique becoming of the self (*BB* 379–83).[57] Idiot selving is a *prior* selving—prereflective, preobjective, pre-explicitly known—a "Self Before Self" that is the "root" self presupposed by all subsequent selvings (*BB* 381, 384; *PU* 63, 65). This prior, root idiot self is also the indeterminate and excessive source of origination of further selvings (*BB* 381–84; *PU* 65).[58]

This particular, idiotic selving can be understood as distinctive in terms of its relations to desire, will, freedom, and otherness. The idiotic self is the immediate and spontaneous eruption of *desire* as the self's elemental, urgent, and emergent power to be (*PO* 159; *EB* 223–24, 227).[59] Desmond describes the energy of this desire as a *root will* from which the self unfolds (*EB* 227–27; *BB* 415)—a double willingness that includes both self-insistence (the self's spontaneous affirmation of its own being) (*EB* 227)[60] and an intimate relation to otherness (*PU* 80; *EB* 227–28).[61] This first selving is characterized by an idiotic *freedom* as elementally given to itself (*PU* 78–80)[62]—a freedom to be itself—that is indeterminate in that it cannot be determined, for it is a source of determination but not totally autonomous in its determination because it does not give itself to be. It is indeterminate in its both being (relatively) and not (absolutely) being its own source/origin.[63] Finally, idiotic selving is characterized by a certain intimacy both with itself (*BB* 383; *EB* 228)[64] and with *otherness*—an elemental being-with the other, the always already being-present of the other to the self (*PU* 63–76).[65]

## §2. Aesthetic, Equivocal Selving

The next stage of development after the more immediate and univocal idiotic selving is aesthetic or equivocal selving. Aesthetic selving—as having to do with the body and the relation between inner and outer, subject and objects—is a more determinate, more manifest expression of the idiotic self as fleshed, located, and positioned in a world of others.[66] The aesthetic self is a between—the fleshed site of passage between the inner and the outer—an elemental community with otherness inasmuch as the self undergoes, suffers in its inwardness the "press" of being in its otherness (*BB* 385–87).[67] However, this community, as arising from a kind of vulnerability, is equivocal, for we need what is in the world and what we need can either be acquired or not, the latter condition constituting a threat to us.[68] It is in relation to this ambivalence about the "outer" that desire asserts itself—transcends itself—seeking to maintain itself by acquiring what it needs from what is other to itself. Thus desire as lack seeking to overcome itself becomes will as self-will—becomes a self-affirming and self-insistent willfulness (*DDO* 165; *BB* 385, 415). It is an equivocal, "devouring" love—loving the self and consuming the other—loving/hating the other as necessary/threatening (*BB* 389; En 136; *HG* 39).[69] Under this more general category of aesthetic or equivocal selving, Desmond describes two more specific ethical selvings (in *Ethics and the Between*): the second ethical selving of "the redoubling of will" and the third ethical selving of "the becoming of freedom" (*EB* 245, 269).

### A SECOND ETHICAL SELVING

Desmond's second ethical selving of the redoubling of the will has to do with the way that will comes to direct desire more determinately—a transformation of desire into a more decisive, directed self-mediation and self-becoming (*EB* 126, 245). Desire values what fills lack and thus fulfills it (*EB* 248). Desire becomes more determinate as it seeks and focuses on a particular outcome or object—but desire finds it cannot find univocal, definite satisfaction, for desire is excessive (*PO* 159; *BB* 392–93).[70] It is from this equivocal situation (the dis/satisfaction of desire) that desire is elevated and broadened, seeking not merely after this or that particular object, but after a certain state of being—a kind of wholeness to the self—willing to be a certain kind of person.[71] This happens with a redoubling of will—the will comes to stand above itself to judge itself, to be answerable for itself to itself.[72] With this redoubling of the will, there comes into being the consciousness of failure in terms of judgment—of one will (the judge, as it were) judging the other will (the judged) (*EB* 247). In this situation of failure and judgment, there can be a "refusal" in which the self refuses to identify with the judged and exclusively identifies with the judge, the higher—thus identifying with only one part of the redoubled will.[73] This ends up canceling the doubling, leaving only the will willing itself, affirming itself.[74]

### THIRD ETHICAL SELVING

Desmond's third ethical selving, described as "the becoming of freedom," takes up where the last one left off—with an "adolescent upsurge" (*EB* 223–24) This self-affirming of the will and desire comes to think of its relation to the other in terms of its freedom—in particular, in terms of its *freedom from* the objects of its desire. The desiring and willing self is free from what it desires in that it is beyond them—it always exceeds its objects.[75] It exceeds them while also needing them—the self is independent and free for itself and yet also dependent upon the others than one would be free from. Thus, this *freedom from* is an equivocal liberty.[76] Yet, in this third selving, *freedom from* the other is held to as an end—as establishing a kind of wholeness or integrity to the self—such that desire/will affirms itself over anything desired. The self-affirming will's dissatisfaction with the possessed other is seen as indicative of its superiority—I am more than this . . . and this . . . and this.[77] Desiring self becomes self-enjoying, self-seeking, self-circling, self-intoxicated—and

72   *Religion, Metaphysics, and the Postmodern*

would be self-generating (*EB* 289, 291).[78] Yet, in this self-circling, desire cannot "fill" itself, cannot "feed on" itself. Desire as "freedom from" becomes a *craving*, a would-be self-consummation (as self-completing) that is a self-consuming, a self-devouring that is ultimately despairing—an emptiness instead of sought fullness, an enslavement instead of sought freedom (from the other).[79] So faced with the self-willing will's desire becoming nihilistic craving, it can become apparent that some kind of *purpose* is needed to constrain or tame desire if the self is not to dissipate itself. This entails another kind of freedom and another kind of selving.[80]

### §3. Erotic, Dialectical Selving

Erotic selving (overlapping with what Desmond calls "erotic mind") has a less overtly antagonistic relation with the other as the prior "equivocal" selvings. Erotic selving is dialectical in the sense that it is focused on becoming something for itself *through the other*—it mediates with itself through the possession or appropriation of the other.[81] The dynamic of erotic mind moves toward mediated self-possession and self-completion (*BB* 402; *PU* 70, 113; En 136)—a self-relativity served by its other-relativity.[82] Here desire has become a directed self-becoming oriented toward the self's self-mediated wholeness or integrity (*PO* 159; *EB* 126). The erotic self intends to be a master, a sovereign—of both the other and the self—this is both its glory and its hubristic peril, for there is the temptation to close the circle of desire, making the self both desiring and desired without an openness to the other as anything other than an occasion for self-becoming (*BB* 402; *EB* 217). The erotic sense of freedom is thus closely related to the autonomy celebrated in modernity (AT 233; *EB* 160, 169, 326)—to a more mature, adult, self-actualized autonomy[83] that bears within it the seed or the promise or the possibility of a freedom beyond autonomy (*PU* 118, 191; CWSC 40; *EB* 160, 165).[84]

### Fourth Ethical Selving

Desmond's fourth ethical selving is a dialectical autonomy in which the self comes to further self-determination (*EB* 309, 320) seeking to appropriate the equivocities within itself and between itself and others.[85] Here the more adolescent "freedom from" is disciplined, tempered, and directed through the *work* of making something of oneself—which involves a calculating and self-disciplined negation or denial that is foreign to base self-assertion (*EB* 310, 316).[86] Dialectical autonomy's work is that of the adulthood of the will—of willing to be a certain self and thus transcending itself toward what is other (upon which one is dependent) in order to become such a self (*EB* 316, 320). Thus, this autonomy involves not only the negative freedom of "freedom from" the other but the more positive freedom of a "freedom to" become a certain kind of self (*EB* 309–10, 316–17, 320). There is, however, in dialectical autonomy the holdover from "freedom from" of the equivocal position of the other—that the other is needed, but needed as the object for the self's imposition.[87] With this equivocity at the heart of dialectical autonomy—the equivocity that autonomy (for the self) requires heteronomy (for the other)—there is the possibility within this selving of the tyrannous and the monstrous (*EB* 319–21).[88]

## 3 B    Fifth Ethical Selving

Erotic sovereignty, Desmond's fifth ethical selving, claims to deal with these equivocities in a higher form of "freedom to" (*EB* 321). The "sovereignty" of erotic sovereignty entails the higher autonomy gained in the confirmation and affirmation of one's powers of self-transcending (CWSC 38, 40; *EB* 323, 338) in relation to one's being with others (the "erotic" of erotic sovereignty) (*EB* 323).[89] The erotic sovereign transcends itself toward the other, impelled by lack, and finds in this experience that the transcending desire is a power (a transcending potency) that is more than mere lack—it returns to itself in affirmation of its free power as, at once, finite/dependent (in its lack and need of the other) and absolute/independent (in the excess of its self-transcending power to any lack) (*EB* 324, 328).[90] Erotic sovereignty is a "freedom to" become a certain kind of self, not in terms of a simple selfishness, but in terms of pursuing a great purpose—a purpose greater than itself (*EB* 323–34, 316, 338–39).[91] Thus sovereigns can be heroes, exemplars of human excellence and purpose.[92] Yet there is still in erotic sovereignty the peril, danger, and temptation of fixating upon oneself and one's glory—of thinking that one has achieved the highest freedom—such that one can become to the other a tyrant and a monster (*EB* 217, 330, 332, 339–40).[93] There can be in erotic sovereignty, as willing to be absolutely autonomous, an ingratitude toward the other that makes one's own being possible (*EB* 327, 330, 335).[94] Likewise, erotic sovereignty also contains within itself the possibility of remembering the other in thanksgiving (CWSC 40)[95]—the possibility of abdication of its sovereignty that can lead to a freedom beyond autonomy such as is found in agapeic selving.[96]

## 4    §4. Agapeic Selving

Erotic sovereignty has within it hints of a further selving that transcends it and yet realizes its promise—a self-transcendence beyond autonomous sovereignty (*BB* 411, 413–14; *PU* 191).[97] In agapeic selving, the closure tempting the erotic self is perforated and opened up (*BB* 407). The agapeic self is a self that has been decentered, has undergone an "unselving," and has been re-centered within community—it is a self that is "being-at-home in its not being-at-home with itself" (*BB* 409).[98] This decentering of the self is due to the double excess or otherness to which agapeic selving is opened and attends—to the inward excess/otherness of the original self in which the self is given to be by another as not self-generating (*BB* 406, 410) and to its willingness to be for the other, to be subject to the needs of the other, even to the point of sacrifice (*BB* 414; PU 70).[99] This agapeic willingness is a giving out of surplus to the other for the other—exceeding or transcending the self (from the excessive surplus of the self) toward the other (*PU* 70; En 144; *EB* 358).[100] Its desire for the other is an openness to the other in terms that are beyond self-desiring.[101] In the midst of this openness to double otherness, the agapeic self is a "between" as its love is an "interest"—an *inter-esse*—an affirmative being-between the excess of what is given to one and the other to whom one gives.[102] Thus, agapeic self is both an ontological reality—in the sense of being freely given to be for itself and for others—and a regulative ideal—in the sense of an ethical call to fulfill the promise of our being in giving to the other (*PU* 157-58, 195).[103] Agapeic selving also realizes the promise of other selvings: the recognition of the worth of the singular (self and other) intimated with the idiotic self, the affirmation of the goodness of being in its otherness intimated with the aesthetic self and the more complex interrelationship with the other in the midst of one's self-becoming intimated with the erotic self (*BB* 410-11).

This agapeic selving entails a conception and enactment of freedom that is different from that of prior selvings. Agapeic freedom is a freedom beyond or higher than autonomy—a freedom that both recognizes it is given from the other and uses its powers to give to others (*EB* 34, 161).[104] Agapeic freedom is not a freedom *from* or *to* but *toward,* toward the other in a true self-transcendence. This "freedom toward" is an *agapeic* release (*BB* 410; *PU* 191, 196; *CWSC* 40) in which the self is released toward the other—being able to affirm and consent to the other as having value and worth in excess of the other's usefulness for the self (*PO* 202; *PU* 193; *EB* 137, 201)—and the other is released from the self.[105] Here, the will becomes *goodwill,* a willingness beyond willfulness to be put in the relative position and to be vulnerable in service to the other.[106]

## 4A    Sixth Ethical Selving

Desmond's sixth ethical selving is that of agapeic service and friendship. This service entails a difficult laying of the self open to the other and to the reality of the metaxological between—as saturated with giving without (immediate) return (*EB* 217-18).[107] This opening to the other includes both gratitude and generosity. The agapeic self has gratitude ultimately to God for its being as a good and original power in itself (*EB* 220).[108] This gratitude, for the agapeic self, in turn generates within one, charges one with, a generosity toward the other (*EB* 177, 220)[109]—recognizing our giftedness, our givenness from the generous other, we in turn give to the other as we have been given to—with a self-transcending creativity giving to the other and not asking for a return (*BB* 407; *EB* 355-56).[110] With this generosity, the will in the selving of agapeic service becomes a willingness—a willingness to help, to be available to the other (*EB* 347-48, 358, 506).[111]

Desmond sees friendship as involving this kind of willingness (*EB* 364). In friendship, there occurs a mutual giving, a reciprocity or symmetry in which the self gives to or serves the other, and the other gives to or serves the self (*EB* 356, 358; *HG* 40). One could say that one's service (one's giving to the other) is necessary but not sufficient for friendship—there needs to be a mutual "serving" as it were. (A service without symmetry, reciprocity, or mutuality would be suffering, as will be seen below.)

Finally, agapeic service entails a transformation of freedom. While service is often thought of as below autonomy in terms of subordination or servility, agapeic service sees that it is in fact autonomy that entails an enslavement of other and self to self (*EB* 347; *HG* 181).[112] Agapeic service, however, is a freedom—a "freedom towards" the other as good in itself and for itself—it is a creative freedom that gives freedom (*EB* 347, 510).[113] In this freedom toward the other in generous agapeic service there is a true self-transcendence that is not exhausted by autonomous self-determination (*EB* 353–54).

4β  SEVENTH ETHICAL SELVING

Desmond's seventh and highest ethical selving is that of suffering. This suffering is the pathos of accepting and affirming the other, of letting the other be, that expresses the *passio essendi* of human being in its primal receptivity—its suffering the given (*PO* 286; *BB* 6; *PU* 20, 255; En 131; *EB* 219, 367–68). This suffering is a return to the first idiotic, elemental self (*EB* 367–68)[114]—a return to an intimacy with the other as good (*EB* 367–68, 370).[115] Here, suffering is a kind of *askesis*—a breakdown that strips the masks of false selvings, that would be self-originating in their self-determination, to the first original self that is a self given from an origin beyond the self (*EB* 110).[116] With the awareness of this origin comes a communion with the ultimate in the suffering, in the *passio essendi*, of the self that opens beyond the merely ethical and into the religious (*PO* 370; *EB* 367–68).[117]

As with agapeic service, this *suffering of the given* (in gratitude) is the seed of giving (generosity) to the other—our suffering the other helps us give to the other and understand those who suffer (*PU* 255; *EB* 111–12, 365). One's new awareness of one's "freedom from" (here given from another, from the origin) spurs one in the direction of a more radical "freedom towards."[118] This "freedom towards" the other to the point of the *suffering of giving* (suffering the giving) is a new willingness[119] that is intimate with the other (*EB* 365, 498, 500) and is willing to suffer with and for the other even in the absence of reciprocity. The suffering of the highest selving is compassion—a suffering with and for the other (*BB* 450, 454).[120] Here, the highest selving is shown to be opened beyond itself—a post-self, a "self-less" selving—toward the other and the communal (*EB* 365–67).[121] At the same time (as mentioned above), this highest selving comes to the limit of ethics as regarding selving and moves toward the religious—the self is opened horizontally toward others in community as it is opened vertically toward the agapeic origin (*DDO* 174; *EB* 367, 377–78).[122]

*Section IV: Ethical Communities and
the Community of Agapeic Service*

Ethics, for Desmond, is a process of selving in the broader context of and toward the forming of different kinds of communities (*BB* 409; *EB* 120). Community has to do with different modes of togetherness, of being-with, and different social embodiments of value (*PO* 162; *BB* 417; *PU* 81). The different kinds of ethical communities constitute different determinate formations, diverse articulations of ethical community (*EB* 196–97, 199–200). These different determinate kinds of community derive, for Desmond, from the given metaxological community or ethos that is prior in the sense of a transcendental, metaphysical ground that makes possible these different formations of ethical community (*DDO* 127).[123] As the highest selvings are those that best understand and live out the reality of the self (as given and self-transcending), so do the higher ethical communities dwell in a closer relation to the primal ethos, the metaxological community of being.

### §1. The Community of Intimacy, Idiocy, Family

The first of Desmond's ethical communities is that of the intimate and idiotic community of the family. The community of the family is an idiotic, elemental, prior being-with that forms and nurtures (or fails to nurture) the young self's potencies. The family mediates the intimate sense of the good of the idiot self and shapes its impression of aesthetic good—of beauty and pleasure. The family provides a context in which one comes to understand and accept certain dianoetic norms—be they tacit or explicit—along with a transcendental sense of the unconditional in one parents' love. In this first, intimate community, there is instilled respect for the self's seeking after excellence, one's eudaimonia, in the special attention and reverence for the singularity of the child. Finally, it is within the family that one is oriented toward the infinitudes of human transcending—in the encouragement to press on and seek the highest—and divine transcendence—imaging one's relations of reverence toward, dependence upon. and intimacy with the divine (*EB* 385–86. See *EB*, chap. 13).

### §2. The Community of Distracted Desire and Serviceable Disposability ( EQUIVOCAL & AESTHETIC)

The second of Desmond's ethical communities is the community of distracted desire and serviceable disposability. This community is driven, at least initially, by a desire for self-preservation and self-perpetuation (*BB* 435). The world is seen as a web of utility, of serviceable disposability, in which one works to acquire and exploit other beings as "goods." It is a thorough-going pragmatism in which all otherness is evaluated in terms of use and expedience. This results in the dominion of instrumental use-values, in that the community of the between has value or worth only in relation to its use for human desire—in itself, it is useless and thus worthless (*BB* 437; *EB* 443).[124] The desire that drives this community of serviceable disposability is deeply equivocal—it gives communal expression to the equivocity of human desire. The other is the valued object, but it is not valuable for itself. The other is desired for the satisfaction of desire, which is never satisfied and continually desiring (*BB* 435; *EB* 416–17, 444).[125] The other is only thought of as for the self, for the self's consumption and exploitation (*EB* 416–17).[126] There is, in this kind of ethical community, no point or purpose save the multiplication of satisfactions of desire—while there is no satisfaction (*BB* 437; *EB* 443). In the end, the empty and craving self in the context of such a community—seeking but not finding satisfaction in the otherwise worthless and purposeless others in the community—can only seek diversion or distraction from itself. "The selves of distracted desire," Desmond writes, "are the most bored beings, for our diversions reach an empty satiation where we know ourselves simply as disgust with self" (*BB* 436; *EB* 443). Thus, the community of serviceable disposability is, in the end, a community of distracted desire.

### §3. The Community of Erotic Sovereignty

With the community of erotic sovereignty comes a community that values excellence beyond utility—there are self-justifying excellences to be sought that are at once supreme and useless.[127] This seeking after higher ("sovereignty") excellence is also a seeking for self-fulfillment ("erotic") (*BB* 439). In the community of erotic sovereignty, such a seeking results in a community of selves seeking to achieve wholeness through an ascent to self-mastery (*BB* 440, 544)[128]—a community that gives selves back to themselves as autonomous (*BB* 439, 448–49). In this kind of community, there is a respect for the other—a companionship with other sovereigns (or would be sovereigns)[129]—such that one comes to oneself through the other's recognition.[130] Thus, the community of erotic sovereignty is, at its best, a community of justice that celebrates immanent excellences—often in the person of the hero (*BB* 453).[131]

The gains of the community of erotic sovereignty over the community of serviceable disposability and distracted desire include the recognition, first, of the infinite reserve of worth in the human self and, second, of the co-implication of the self with the other—of self-relation as being dependent on other-relation (*BB* 443–45). However, there is danger implicit in the community of erotic sovereignty—namely the danger of a dialectical totalism, a larger wholeness as absorbing, subsuming, and thus forgetting otherness, singularity, infinitude, excess (*BB* 445–49, 479, 481).[132] Ultimately, erotic sovereignty in itself cannot fully incorporate the religious extremes of the idiot self (in its intimacy with the divine other) and the religious community of agapeic service.[133] The community of erotic sovereignty does, however, have the potential (in recognizing singularity, otherness, infinitude, and religious ultimacy) to open onto a different, agapeic kind of community—as the dialectical to the metaxological (*BB* 443, 448–49; *EB* 161, 506).[134]

### §4. The Community of Agapeic Service

For Desmond, the ethos as the intermediating community of self-mediating wholes is full of, "criss-crossed by," agapeic relation—given to be and giving to others (*BB* 451; *EB* 476).[135] The ethos as the community of being (metaphysically considered) holds within it the promise of the human community of agapeic service (ethically considered) (*EB* 161).[136] In this highest of ethical communities, there is a generous serving—a giving of oneself beyond self-interest, even to the point of sacrifice (here service includes the possibility of suffering) to the other as worthy or good in itself (*BB* 450–53; *HG* 39)—in which the self is centered beyond itself, decentered or ex-centered, so as to result in a fundamentally other- or community-oriented self.[137]

In his understanding of *agapeic community,* Desmond presents an understanding of community *as metaxological* (as at once exceeding and preserving—teleologically suspending, transfiguring—the erotics of a closed dialectic) that includes both disinterest and interest, agape and eros, sacrifice and reciprocity. The community is thus more fundamental than the individual (though in a way that specifically preserves the singularity, otherness, idiocy of the individual) both ontologically and ethically. The genuine agapeic selving is a selving beyond selving, a potentially sacrificial giving from and unto community. Thus the unilateral moment of the gift is to be but a moment.[138]

This community of agapeic service is a community of freedom, of agapeic release—a community in which freedom is beyond being merely hoarded as autonomous freedom for-self but is given to the other as others (divine and human) have given one freedom (*BB* 199, 448–90; *PU* 191).[139] This kind of community also entails in its agapeic service and release of the other a twofold idiocy—first, an intimate and elemental community with otherness even in idiotic inwardness (*BB* 385, 456, 535; *EB* 171) and, second, a love of the other as irreplaceable in its idiotic singularity (*BB* 542).[140]

The community of agapeic service, for Desmond, has significant religious resonances—such that such a community is seen largely in terms of religious community. As agape, as the divine gift of creation, enables ontological community, so does agape enable our agapeic service, our participation in the broader agapeic community. The agapeic generosity of the community of agapeic service is born of gratitude to the origin for its generosity (*EB* 171, 220, 365, 507),[141] such that there is in agape a double service, both ethical and religious.[142] Religious community consists in how the togetherness of the divine and human transforms human community (*EB* 171)[143]—instilling it with a generous trust and patience (as one gratefully recognizes the origin's trust and patience in its creative release) that is not giving up on the promise of the good in the other (*BB* 455; *EB* 510). The love of the other in the community of agapeic service—the giving (and trusting and waiting on) even to the point of suffering—is, in Desmond's reckoning, so difficult as not to be sustainable on our own, such, first, that it feels called forth by superior transcendence (*EB* 197, 218),[144] and, second, that we need help from beyond ourselves to be equal to its call (*EB* 217–19).[145] The end result of this kind of community is its being as a witness to and as a finite image of its agapeic origin, of God's agapeic generosity (*EB* 452, 491, 495)[146]—this divine service as lived out in ethical service toward the other and as enacted in divine festivity, in religious celebration, in the agape(ic) feast.[147]

Desmond's understanding of the metaxological nature of agapeic *community* as embracing eros as well as agape sheds light on recent discussions of the nature of the gift, of love and of reciprocity. Marion, following a broadly Levinasian trajectory (in a manner similar to Derrida and Caputo), rejects reciprocity inasmuch as its "economy" cancels out the agapeic gift as an expenditure without return.[148] Milbank (and Pickstock) advocate a kind of erotic reciprocity—a gift-exchange that is more true to the nature of the gift and of love. Agape is ultimately fulfilled in a community, a *polis*.[149]

The highest ethical selving for Desmond is that of agapeic service and suffering—here Marion (and Levinas and Derrida and Caputo) would agree. However, this is not the end of the story for Desmond—nor is it the beginning of the story. For, first, the enabling "beginning" or condition for the possibility of such agapeic selving is the given matrix of the metaxological community of being in general and the original self in particular; and, second, the end of agapeic giving, service, suffering is beyond itself—it is the agapeic community of (mutual) service. Love or charity is ultimately gratuitously received exchange. The enabling reciprocity of the intersubjective (ontological) community (the metaxological community of being) is a precondition for the gift as the gift (from the individual perspective) is for reciprocity. Desmond's work echoes Milbank's observation that one must think in terms of ontology, of metaphysics, to see this—thus Marion's more restricted, though correct as far as it goes (which is not far enough), vision of individual gift-giving as enabled by a prior agape.[150] The unity of agape and eros that appears in Marion's work involves not as much the broader ("erotic") reciprocities of the community but the fulfillment and pleasure that is part of the "one love"—the latter, however, if one thinks metaphysically, opens onto the former as its whence.[151]

In seeing the unilateral moment of the agapeic gift as not the *telos* of ethical being (or being as such) but a moment within the broader and more fundamental reality of the agapeic community, Desmond recognizes, as does Milbank, that the internal, individual *psyche* must be properly oriented within the external *polis*—agape must be oriented beyond egotism and self-sacrifice toward the communal (agapeic) "feast." Thus, genuine agape (viewed from the broader perspective of the metaxological community) is not a pure gift but a purified gift-exchange. Here, human community is realizing the promise of the primal community of being.[152]

Milbank describes this broader, genuine agapeic community in terms of an asymmetrical reciprocity or an "aneconomic economy" in which gifts are given and returned non-identically (asymmetrically). Marion gives a qualified affirmation of *this kind of* non-identical reciprocity, "a reciprocity that is out of phase."[153]

Speaking theologically, between Fall and Consummation—in our fallen state—the present human embodiment of true community will, as not yet perfected, be saturated with giving without returning, with service that is a suffering (in the present); yet it is precisely this willingness to give, to serve, to suffer that is necessary for (is a condition for the possibility of) true community. In this between-time, alas, the *ecclesia* is born (cannot be born but) through a cross.

## Part Two: Ethics with/out Metaphysics

Having summarized William Desmond's conception of ethics, I will now turn to examine how this conception provides a viable alternative to that represented in the work of John D. Caputo based on three points. First, Desmond's position is able to *answer* Caputo's *critique* of ethics by showing that the understanding of ethics represented in Desmond's work is not guilty of the errors that Caputo levels against ethics as such. Second, Desmond's position is able to genuinely *address* the motivating *concerns* that can seen to be animating Caputo's treatment of ethics. Third, Desmond's position is able to be used to *critique* the *conclusions* of Caputo's own (de)constructive proposals regarding how to think about ethics.

### Section I: Desmond as Answering Caputo's Critique of Ethics

### §1. Dependence on Metaphysics

Caputo's first critique of ethics regards its dependence upon metaphysics (see chapter 1, part two). The basic problem with ethics for Caputo is that it is based upon metaphysics and functions toward the same end—to give (false) stability to life. Ethics seeks to elevate its knowledge of its subject matter through metaphysics—it is "a (certain) metaphysics (of morals), a metaphysics charged with making obligation safe" (*RH* 5, 73). Caputo thus sees ethics, as dependant on failed (in his view) metaphysics for its ground, to end up being groundless (*AE* 24–25, 237).

Desmond's conception of ethics can be seen to answer this critique. Whereas Caputo sees (true) ethics and metaphysics as ultimately distinct and thus sees their intermingling in terms of ethics being infected by a necessarily suspicion-arousing foreign (onto-theological) agent, Desmond sees that ethics and metaphysics are inseparable and should not, and indeed cannot, be divorced from one another (*PU* 87, 223, 227; *AT* 235). As metaphysics cannot be divorced from the ethical—as metaphysics entails an ethical valuing of being and desire for, even love of, truth (*PO* 163; *PU* 87, 108–109, 149, 177)—so ethics cannot be divorced from the metaphysical as ethics is dependent on metaphysics, in that it entails an understanding of the relation between being and goodness, of what it means to *be* good (*PO* 344; *BB* 509; *PU* 39, 223; *EB* 18) and of what is good or valuable or of worth in being (*PO* 160–61, 183, 189)[154]—particularly when it comes to that of human beings (*PO* 160, 187; *PU* 227). Being and goodness, for Desmond, are related to each other—not in terms of any simple univocal identification (the elevation of ethical knowledge that Caputo wants to avoid) or equivocal separation (that Caputo advocates)—but in terms of such metaxological relations or intermediations as the *promise* of goodness in being (especially regarding human being) (*PO* 160; *PU* 192; AT 235; *EB* 17, 51, 162), being's *intimacy* with the good (*BB* 535; NDR 44; *EB* 21) and being's *hospitality* to the good (AT 235).[155]

### §2. A System of Universal Rules

Caputo's second critique of ethics concerns its seeking to be a system of universal rules. Ethical systems, like and as metaphysics, privilege a kind of static unity—finding a fixed point of reference to absolve ethical reflection from the arbitrariness of existence so as to provide a stable foundation for ethical relations. Such ethical system-making thinks that ethical existence permits formulations in hard irrevocable rules—in "universal, rational, or natural laws" (BA 66–67; *RH* 212). The problem with such ethical laws and principles is that they, in Caputo's estimation, cannot speak to individuals making particular choices in particular situations (*RH* 38–39, 104–105; *AE* 73), for ethical existence is entangled in such a situation of groundlessness, singularity, particularity, novelty, transcendence, and incomprehensibility that it resists any kind of universal ethical rule (*AE* 14; *MRH* 173).

Desmond's conception of ethics can be seen to answer this critique in several ways. *First,* it does not advocate a simple, static unity but a dynamic plurality—a plurivocal ethics. There is a plurality of ethical potencies referring to the plurivocal ontological promise of being in the human self—the dynamic endowment out of which the self develops (*EB* 10). Desmond's conceptions of ethical selvings and ethical communities are plural enactments of freedom—different kinds of freedom, different kinds of self-transcendence.[156] *Second,* ethics for Desmond is not about formulating hard irrevocable rules as much as it is about naming the constancies *and* the fluidities that are operative in ethical existence. Certain ethical potencies focus on the intelligible regularities or constancies (such as the dianoetic and the transcendental), while others focus on the more equivocal fluidities (such as the aesthetic and the eudaemonistic) of life such that there is a plurivocity describing the complexities of our ethical situation (*EB* 79, 191). Even within this plurivocity, there can be no complete univocal determination of the constancies (and such is to be guarded against) (*EB* 11, 196). *Third,* Desmond's ethics gives special attention to the singularity—to the idiocy—inherent in ethics. The human self, for Desmond, is characterized by an idiotic singularity, a singular integrity, an original unto itself (*PO* 361; *BB* 380–83, 397; *EB* 170–71, 186). It is out of this singularity that the plural promise of the self—in terms of potencies, selvings, and communities (*BB* 377, 384)—unfolds toward the highest (agapeic) selvings and communities in which the singular *other* is valued and loved in its unique and irreplaceable singularity (*BB* 410–11, 542).[157]

### §3. Faithful Neither to Life Nor to the Other

Caputo's third critique of metaphysics concerns its failure to be faithful to life or to the other. First, (metaphysical) ethics is not faithful to life in that it gives a false stability or safety to life and thus ends up making light of life's difficulty (*AE* 4, 97). Second, ethics, as building upon and complicit in faithless metaphysics, is not faithful to the other. Within metaphysical ethics, ethical existence with and toward the other—in all of its risk and difficulty—is supplanted with a kind of abstract knowledge. Life (and obligation) is more difficult and risky than ethics would allow (*AE* 4).

Desmond's conception of ethics can be seen to answer this critique in several ways. *First,* regarding the charge of not being faithful to life, Desmond presents the descriptive goal of his ethics not as making for stability and "safety" in our ethical decisions as much as intelligently dwelling in the ethos as it is—with all of its ambiguities and equivocities—with the aid of metaxological metaphysics. *Second,* regarding the same charge, the more prescriptive side of Desmond's ethics (in his understanding of the "higher" selvings and communities) sees the better ethical dwelling as precisely that which is the most difficult and least safe—agapeic service to the other, even to the point of suffering that is so difficult as to be unsustainable on one's own (*EB* 197, 217–20).[158] *Third,* regarding the charge of infidelity to the other, Desmond's ethics is shot through with precisely the ideal of relating to the other as a good in itself. The process of selving is ultimately oriented toward an intermediation with otherness beyond self-mediation—seen in the way the higher forms of selving consist of being opened beyond oneself toward the other and the communal in a compassionate willingness to suffering with and for the other (*BB* 450, 454; *PU* 151; *EB* 223, 365–67). In the highest of ethical communities, there is a generous serving—a giving of oneself beyond self-interest to the other as worthy or good in itself (250. *BB* 450–53; *HG* 39)—in which the self is centered beyond itself so as to result in a fundamentally other- or community-oriented self.[159] *Fourth,* Desmond recognizes the abiding difficulty of relating to the other in the way in which the other keeps getting co-opted in human selving and community. Desmond's metaphysical ethics gives some explanation of how and why this is difficult in terms of kinds of willing, freedom, and desire dominant in different selvings and their concomitant communities.

### Section II: Desmond as Addressing Caputo's Motivating Concerns

Behind Caputo's critique of ethics and his more positive alternative to (metaphysical) ethics can be seen to be certain motivating concerns. First, Caputo is concerned to avoid elevating the knowledge of ethical guides, norms, or laws to a falsely absolute status. Second, Caputo is concerned to avoid supplanting genuine, difficult ethical existence with such ethical guides, norms, or laws (falsely elevated). By avoiding these two negatives, Caputo seeks, I think, to address a more basic positive concern. This is a concern to be honest and faithful to life and to the other—and to do so by having a way of thinking that is involved in the relation to the other in its particularity and difference toward the end of directing one toward the difficulty of such a relation. Caputo's own alternative to ethics, his *post-metaphysical ethics "against ethics,"* is intended to be just such a way of thinking that is faithful to the other.

Desmond, however, addresses these concerns from a metaphysical perspective. First, Desmond's view of ethics avoids elevating knowledge of ethical guides to a falsely absolute status. He is largely concerned with seeking to be true to the given situation in its complexity and plurality. There are, again, both constancies *and* equivocities/fluidity in our ethical existence (*EB* 79, 191). Beyond any simple gesture of flux *über alles*, Desmond suggests more of a true plurivocity in which different potencies focus on the constancies, and others on the fluidities. Even when it comes to his more prescriptive agapeic ideal, Desmond is not focused on ethical rules as much as on a more holistic vision of better/higher selvings and communities. One wonders how to envision a LeviNietzschean community of impossible responsibility—of groundless, pure giving. Can one even think of it as a community? It seems so focused on the moment of the serving and suffering agapeic individual (which Desmond would affirm but go beyond) that it is difficult to see what a community of such individuals could be if any kind of return or reciprocity—or, more importantly, a giving to one *prior* to one's agapeic giving to the other—is denied. For Desmond the community is the final reality, the broader excessive mutuality that enables agapeic selving (along with all the lesser selvings) and is the end of such agapeic individual sacrifice.

Second, Desmond's view of ethics avoids supplanting genuine, difficult ethical existence with such ethical guides/laws/rules. Desmond likewise wants a vision of ethics that tries to deal with life in its ethical fullness. He wants, and presents, not a set of laws but a more holistic vision of multiple potencies, selvings, and communities that describes our ethical reality and gives us some direction toward a better way of being and relating to those around us. Desmond's ethics has a similar view of the degree of difficulty involved in genuine ethical existence as that of Caputo inasmuch as it has the same high ideal of agapeic service and even suffering for the other. One wonders if, within Caputo's framework, ethical existence so bereft of any funding source or community is so difficult as to be impossible. How can one think of one's ethical existence as impossible without (perhaps through a strange, subtle deconstructive yet abstractly speculative *Aufhebung*) abandoning it, or at least abandoning any thought of it?

Third, Desmond's view of ethics is a way of thinking about ethical existence that is faithful to the other. In Desmond's vision, agapeic love of and giving to the other as good and valuable in itself is the highest, is the ideal. Agapeic selving realizes the promise of the other selvings (*BB* 410–11). However, this agapeic service and freedom toward the other in its singularity as worthy and good is, for Desmond, based on a certain metaphysical understanding of the human self and of the metaxological community of being. Our agapeic being is both an ontological reality—in the sense that one is freely given to be for oneself and for others—and a regulative ideal—in the sense that there is an ethical call to fulfill the promise of our being in giving to the other (*PU* 119, 157–58, 195; *EB* 197). Agapeic being toward the other is an ethical dwelling that is in harmony with the metaphysical understanding of the community of being as metaxological. There is a "why" for Desmond's ethics rooted in the nature of the "others" around (within, above) us. In comparison, it seems that Caputo's "why" is emptied, is as empty as the "other" about whom/which we can say (metaphysics) only enough to demand our utter obligation. One can reasonably wonder if this saying is truly enough to make (reasonably) such demands.

### Section III: Desmond's Metaphysically Informed Alternative to Caputo's "Ethics Without (Metaphysical) Ethics"

In addition to answering Caputo's critiques of ethics and addressing Caputo's motivating concerns, Desmond provides a metaphysical alternative to Caputo's alternative to metaphysical ethics. In other words, Desmond's ethics can be presented as a viable and indeed preferable alternative to Caputo's post-metaphysical "ethics without ethics." Beyond answering Caputo's motivating concerns arguably better than Caputo's own system, Desmond's thought can be used to critique/locate many of Caputo's main points and strong conclusions.

### §1. Heterology

Post-metaphysical ethics—as an ethics (a way of thinking about relating to the other) without ethics (ethical systems)—seeks to be *faithful to the other*. Caputo describes such a faithful ethics in terms of a heterology. Caputo summarizes such a heterological ethics using Augustine's: "*Dilige, et quod vis fac*"—"Love, and do what you will."[160] This follows the dual trajectory of the heterology of the project of radical hermeneutics, that of heteronomism (*dilige*) and heteromorphism (*et quod vis fac*) (*AE* 41, 121). *Heteronomism* is the sober, self-effacing posture of being responsive to the call of the other and the call to love (*dilige*) the other—of placing one in the position of a "*non-coercive heteronomy*" (*AE* 42–43, 55, 61; *MRH* 186). Ethical heteronomism takes the form of *obligation*, such that a post-metaphysical ethics is an ethics of obligation. "Obligation," Caputo argues, "is what is important about ethics, what ethics contains without being able to contain" (*AE* 18). Such heteronomic obligation finds expression in an "hyperbolic" sensitivity to the other (GNA 266)—a radical partiality to the singular, individual other that is before one (*AE* 191, 225). This privileging of radical, ineffable, unanticipated singularity in obligation entails a deeper awareness of difference—of the other as other (*MRH* 175, 179; *AE* 74–75, 246; *DH* 196–206). *Heteromorphism* is the more Dionysiac posture of celebrating difference (*et quod vis fac*) as multiplicity and diversity (*AE* 42–43, 61, 121–22)—a nonexclusionary egalitarianism that seeks "to let many flowers bloom" (*OR* 62; *RH* 254–55, 260, 288; *AE* 39). Caputo describes ethical heteromorphism as a letting be, a "generalized *Gelassenheit*" that lets "all things be what and how they are" (*RH* 288) and seeks to be maximally nonconstraining—proceeding "in such a way as to keep as many options open as possible" (*RH* 258–59, 264; *AE* 41, 121). Ultimately, a properly heterological, post-metaphysical ethics must come around to include both the heteronomic Rabbi and the heteromorphic Dionysiac (*AE* 64–65).

Desmond's ethics is likewise a kind of heterology, including both heteronomic and heteromorphic elements. His ethics displays a (metaphysical) ethical *heteronomism* in several ways. *First,* Desmond likewise sees love in terms of an agapeic service that is something beyond autonomy—a freedom that both recognizes it is given from (dependent upon) the other and uses its powers to give to others (*BB* 199; *CWSC* 40; *EB* 34, 161). *Second,* Desmond likewise sees an agapeic, heteronomic passion for the other as the core of ethics, but this is based on his metaphysics. The agapeic decentering of the self is due to the double excess or otherness to which agapeic selving is opened and attends—to the inward excess/otherness of the original self in which the self is given to be by another (not self-generating) (*BB* 406, 410) and to its willingness to be for the other (*BB* 408, 414; *PU* 70, 144), its willingness to be put in the relative position and to be vulnerable in service to the other (*DDO* 164, 167, 190; *CWSC* 41, 51; *EB* 169, 192, 217–18). *Third,* Desmond's conception of agapeic selving and community entails a love and a recognition of the worth of the other as irreplaceable in its idiotic singularity (*BB* 410–11; 542).[161] This valuing of the singular is based on Desmond's metaphysical conception of the genuine plurality and the unique singularity and inherent worth of selves as beings within the community of being (*BB* 188; *EB* 186–88).

Desmond's ethics displays an ethical *heteromorphism* in several ways as well. *First,* agapeic selving and agapeic community entail a certain freedom and release. Agapeic "freedom toward" is a creative freedom that gives freedom—a true self-transcendence that is not exhausted by autonomous self-determination (*EB* 347, 353–54, 362, 510). It is an agapeic release (*BB* 410; *PU* 191, 196; *CWSC* 40) in which the self is released toward the other—being able to affirm and consent to the other as having value and worth in excess of the other's usefulness for the self (*PO* 202; *PU* 193; *EB* 137, 201)—and the other is released from the self (*BB* 261; *PU* 147). *Second,* this agapeic release is a "letting be"—a kind of "*Gelassenheit*" (*BB* 410; *PU* 191, 196; *CWSC* 40). This letting the other be expresses the *passio essendi* of human being in its primal receptivity—its suffering the given (*PO* 286; *BB* 6; *PU* 20, 255; En 131; *EB* 219, 367–68). *Third,* there is, again, a plurality entailed in Desmond's conception of the ethical potencies, selvings, and communities. This is not, however, sheer plurality—at least with the selvings and communities there is a kind of hierarchy such that the heteronomic (the agapeic) guides and structures the heteromorphic (the plural selvings and communities). The higher, heteronomic agapeic selvings realize the promise of the plural other selvings (*BB* 410–11). Such a hierarchy is necessary if one wants to have any (agapeic or heteronomic) ideal. This sort of hierarchy (of the heteronomic over and maintaining the heteromorphic) is supported by Desmond's metaphysics in that the highest selvings and communities are those that best understand, live out, and dwell in the reality of the self (as given and self-transcending) and the metaxological community of being.

### §2. Post-Metaphysical Ethics: Minimalism

Caputo's post-metaphysical ethics is also a minimalist ethics. A post-metaphysical ethics proceeds from the foundationless foundation of radical hermeneutics—it takes place in the withdrawal of any deeper grounding or metaphysical certification (*AE* 37; *RH* 236, 239). Such an ethics is, as following the project of radical hermeneutics, a minimalism—seeking a maximally "open and undetermined" and "weak and nonconstraining" notion of the Good (*RH* 257; *AE* 33, 41). The one regulative principle, that of obligation, is simply an "event" or "happening" of obligation. "Obligation," Caputo writes, "happens"— and this happening is groundless, in a void, without any evident further "why" (*AE* 6, 14, 25, 192, 225, 237).

Desmond parts with this kind of minimalism insofar he sees metaphysics as being valuable, if not necessary, for ethics. Instead of seeing ethics and/or obligation to the other as being foundationless, Desmond suggests the foundation of a metaphysical conception of the self and of community as providing a guide for seeing which selvings and communities dwell in a closer relation to the primal ethos, the metaxological community of being. The agapeic self is an ontological reality, in the sense of being freely given to be for itself and for others, and *because of this reality* it is also a regulative ideal, in the sense of ethical call to fulfill the promise of our being in serving or giving to the other (*PU* 119, 157–58, 195; *EB* 197). This service entails a difficult laying of the self open to the other and to the reality of the metaxological between—as itself saturated with giving without return (*EB* 217–18).[162] One's generous agapeic regard for and obligation to the other does not happen without a why, but because of gratitude. Gratitude generates within one, charges one with, a generosity toward the other (*EB* 177, 220)[163]—recognizing our giftedness, our givenness from the generous other (and metaphysics for Desmond endeavors to map this communal and ontological reality), we in turn give to the other as we have been given to—with a self-transcending creativity giving to the other and not asking for return (*BB* 407; *EB* 354–56).

### §3. Post-Metaphysical Ethics: Ethical Repetition

Central to Caputo's post-metaphysical ethics is the idea of ethical repetition. This ethical repetition is the task of becoming oneself as an ethical self in the midst of the flux of existence without the knowledge of any prior guide or foundation (*RH* 17, 21, 28–30, 58; HKFM 207, 209–10). In ethical repetition the individual seeks to constitute, to produce the self in relation to the other (*RH* 30, 58; HKFM 207). Ethical repetition also presses toward a privilege for the other that is at once a de-centering the self. Ethical repetition is in need of the other (*RH* 30). Thus, ethical repetition deconstructs its own project in that, in order to achieve itself, it has to become something else. This "something else" is a "hyperbolic" ethics—a religious ethics—that is even further purified of metaphysics. It is thus that an awareness of the difficulty of ethical life leads one to the use of religious language.

Desmond likewise sees ethics as entailing a similar becoming of a self as Caputo describes in his ethical repetition, but within the context of a metaphysical understanding of the self. *First,* Desmond describes the self in terms of selving—of processes and projects of becoming. The self metaphysically understood in Desmond's terms of "original selfhood" is an originating or becoming self. The original self (as constitutive of the being of the self) is the "indeterminate locus of selving" (the self as becoming and developing) (*BB* 381). Thus, for Desmond, the metaphysical conception of the self is not in opposition to the thought of a self that is in a process of becoming. *Second,* the agapeic self is a self that has been de-centered, has undergone an "unselving," and re-centered within community (*BB* 409, 453; *CWSC* 41). This de-centering or "unselving" that is at the summit of ethical selving comes about through an *agapeic release* (*BB* 410; *PU* 191, 196; *CWSC* 40) in which the self is released toward the other—being able to affirm and consent to the other as having value and worth in excess of the other's usefulness for the self (*PO* 202; *PU* 193; *EB* 137, 201).— and the other is released from the self.[164] *Third,* this de-centering involved in the process of ethical becoming suggests the advent of a religious ethics in Desmond's work as well. The love of the other in the community of agapeic service is, in Desmond's reckoning, so difficult, first, that it is manifest as needing to be called forth by superior transcendence (*EB* 197, 218, 220), and, second, that we need help from beyond ourselves to be equal to its call (*EB* 217–19). Here, agapeic suffering can be a kind of *askesis*—a breakdown that strips the masks of false selvings, that would be self-originating in their self-determination, to the first original self that is a self given from an origin beyond the self (*EB* 110, 367). This highest selving comes to the limit of ethics as regarding selving and moves toward the religious—the self is opened horizontally toward others in community as it is opened vertically toward the agapeic origin (*DDO* 174; *EB* 367, 377–78).[165]

## §4. Strong Conclusions

For Caputo, being faithful to the other—being honest about the situation in which we find ourselves when it comes to our ethical relations—brings one hard upon certain conclusions. The *first* conclusion is the denial of (the possibility of) metaphysical knowledge of ethical guides. This is the denial of ethics inasmuch as it entails a metaphysical knowledge of ethical guides—the only acceptable ethics is one that operates without metaphysics—that is, without the aforementioned "ethics." Post-metaphysical ethics sees that we act lacking unshakable metaphysical foundations and thus with a heightened awareness of our insecurity—of our "fear and trembling" (*RH* 239; *AE* 191). We are, again, in a situation of undecidability, in which we have to make ethical decisions and judgments without any sure guidelines that would answer our questions ahead of time (*AE* 3, 63). The *second* conclusion is the denial of the possible significance of metaphysics for ethical knowledge. Even if one could have metaphysical knowledge, it would be of no value for truly ethical living. Obligation (true ethics) and metaphysical (not true) ethics are incompatible. Obligation is the core of ethics that metaphysical ethics is based upon and betrays, that scandalizes metaphysical ethics, and to which post-metaphysical ethics seeks to be faithful (*AE* 5, 18).

Desmond's work, in effect, critiques these strong conclusions of Caputo's "post-metaphysical" alternative to ethics. The general critique is that the denials of Caputo's post-metaphysical ethics of obligation are too radical and that they go to unnecessary extremes (specifically, the extreme of a false either/or) in order to address its motivating concerns. *First,* regarding the denial of the possibility of metaphysical knowledge of ethical guides—regarding the impossibility of ethics, for Caputo, as following from the failure or impossibility of metaphysics—Desmond provides a powerful challenge.[166] Regarding the descriptive side of ethics denied in this first conclusion: when it comes to the difficulty and complexity of thinking of the metaphysical foundations of ethics, Desmond sees pluralities of elements to be dealt with, but this is complexity, not impossibility. Desmond's "metaphysical guides" are not determinate, univocal, metaphysical principles but are metaxological—a description of ethical life in terms of the plural potencies (some necessarily indeterminate and some more determinate) and the plural concrete descriptions of projects of selving and being in community in their interrelation. Metaphysics is involved, for instance, in seeing how there is within the singular self a plurality of ethical potencies that refer to the plurivocal ontological promise of being in the human self (*EB* 10). These potencies are the basic sources out of which the self comes to reflect more determinately on the indeterminate show of value—out of which ethics comes to dwell with the both the equivocities and the constancies in the ethos (*EB* 79, 191).

Regarding the prescriptive (the more properly ethical?) side of ethics in this first conclusion, it can be seen that, for Caputo, metaphysical guides are supposed to make the ethical life easier to navigate. But for Desmond, his explicitly metaphysical ethics entails as high a demand and difficulty as the ideals in Caputo's own vision inasmuch as it has the same high ideal of agapeic service and even suffering for the other. Desmond's ethical ideal of agapeic being is a high and difficult one, and his metaphysical ethics gives some explanation of how and why this is difficult (regarding the various tensions and imbalanced tendencies in the doubleness of human desire and will coming to expression in different conceptions of freedom in relation to the other). The love of the other in the community of agapeic service—the difficult laying of the self open to the other (*EB* 217–18) and the giving (and trusting and waiting on) even to the point of suffering—is, in Desmond's reckoning, so difficult as to not be sustainable on our own resources, such that it feels called forth by superior transcendence (*EB* 197, 218, 220), and that we need help from beyond ourselves to be equal to its call (*EB* 217–19, 494).

Desmond likewise challenges Caputo's denial of the significance of metaphysical knowledge for ethical life. Again, this judgment about the uselessness of metaphysics for genuine ethical existence is based on how Caputo sees the two as being fundamentally at odds. Caputo denies the significance of metaphysics because he has defined metaphysics in such a way that obligation, or any serious engagement with lived existence, would be allergic to it.[167] For Desmond, however, ethics and metaphysics are inseparable (*PU* 87, 223, 227; *AT* 235). A metaphysical understanding of the self serves as a basis for Desmond's more concrete understanding of ethics in terms of different "ethical selvings" and ethical communities. These different determinate kinds of selving and community derive, for Desmond, from the given metaxological community or ethos that is prior in the sense of a transcendental, metaphysical ground that makes possible these different formations of ethical community (*DDO* 127; *EB* 197).[168] These metaphysical foundations are significant for the ethical life in that Desmond's metaphysical understanding of community and of the self coheres with and supports precisely the kind of high regard for the other that Caputo wants from ethics. For Desmond, a metaphysical understanding of reality and the high and difficult demand of the agapeic ideal are of a piece—they cohere harmoniously; whereas for Caputo these two stand in stark contrast to each other, such that his view of ethical obligation is "against ethics" inasmuch as ethics partakes of the poisoned well of metaphysics. But, in the end, if Caputo's critique of metaphysics as such, and any ethics tainted thereby, does not stand—as it does not in relation to Desmond's metaxological metaphysics and ethics—then there is no good reason to accept Caputo's extreme either/or severance of thinking (about being, about reality) and doing (good unto the other, as one ought).

# 4   God and Religion

In this chapter, we will examine (in part one) Desmond's understanding of God (and of the nature of our understanding of God) and religion as it is manifest in his discussion of the status of God-talk in the modern ethos (in section I), of how we can and should talk about God and the "ways" one can come to have some manner of knowledge of God (in section II), of the particular characteristics that such a God might have (in section III), and of the kind of religious relations humans might have with such a God (in section IV). In part two, this vision of God and religion is compared to that of Caputo; in so doing, Desmond's conception is presented as a viable and indeed preferable alternative to LeviNietzschean religion without religion.

## Part One: A Presentation of William Desmond's Philosophy of God and Religion

### Section I: God and the Modern Ethos

#### §1. The Modern Ethos

Modernity has made religion and thought about God problematic. Clues to this difficulty can be gleaned from an understanding of the modern ethos. The modern ethos, for Desmond, is a reconfiguration of the primal ethos (AT 250; GB 2–3). This reconfiguration has resulted in a "contraction"/ "evacuation"/"neutering"/"degrading" of the given ethos of being—an overly determinate and univocal constriction of the overdetermined "between" that has lost a feel for the fullness of the ethos (BB 71; NDR 46; EB 99, 167; AT 235)[1]—that has come to cut off mindfulness from the deeper, overdeterminate resources of the primal ethos, or the between (EB 44–45; GEW 23; MC 9).[2] This modern deracination of the ethos finds expression in a dualistic opposition between fact and value—a divorcing of being and goodness (PO 158; BB 72, 103; AT 236, 248; BR 227; EB 24). The modern instrumental mind—a will to a manipulable univocity over the uncertainty of what is not determinately intelligible, seeking to have determinate knowledge and control over beings—is driven by this dualism (PO 26, 121, 137, 158, 226, 306; PU 116, 195; EB 46).[3] The dualism of fact and value that drives instrumental mind comes to manifestation in the twofold process of the *objectification of being* and the *subjectification of value* that Desmond describes as the "*double face* of modernity" (HG 21–22; AOO 292; MC 3; GB 2).[4] On one face, being is objectified—the "degraded" or "deracinated" world is a valueless, inherently worthless, "merely empirical" thereness constituting a universal mechanism (PO 158, 366; BB 71; AT

235–37; NDR 46; BR 227; *EB* 46, 99; *HG* 21–22); on the other face is the subjectification of value that comes about as there is a "revaluation" of value in terms of human self-determination and a projection of value onto the world so as to make what is "there" valued as useful—an instrument—to the self (AT 235–37; *PO* 333, 353; BR 224). Thus, the instrumental mind of the modern ethos is, for Desmond, "an ungrateful child" that shuns or has forgotten its own birth in the overdetermined and inherently valuable givenness of being beheld in astonishment and contemplated upon in genuine speculative philosophy—and has also, as a not at all unrelated parallel, shunned and forgotten God (*PO* 242; *BHD* 20; *BB* 14, 202, 204–205; BDD 738; BR 224; MC 11–12).[5]

## §2. God and Modernity

Modernity's instrumental mind, with its dualistic objectification of being and subjectification of value, leads to the problematic status of God in modernity. Divine transcendence has become problematic and devalued in modernity—such that there is a modern "allergy to transcendence" (*HG* 4; *AOO* 271–72). In the wake of modern fact/value dualism—of its lost attunement to the richness of the between—the world is stripped of signs and traces of the divine (PR 108; GEW 16; *GB* 19–20).[6] Desmond writes of the problem of God in modernity in terms of an *antinomy of autonomy and transcendence*. The relation between the two is an antinomy such that in absolutizing one, one would relativize the other (*EB* 32–33, 353; *HG* 22; *AOO* 275).[7] Modernity has largely opted for absolutizing human autonomy, leaving the strange animal of a relativized transcendence (*EB* 353; *HG* 4; *AOO* 269, 283; *GB* 23–24). Thus taking upon itself the mantle of absoluteness, the modern self is made to be a double—as Desmond would say, a false double—of God (AT 250; *GB* 19, 21–22). What God remains is a relativized transcendence that survives as but a projection of our own power—yet another inherently worthless instrument to be wielded by us strangely diminishing sovereigns (are we losing our clothes? our mantle borrowed from our fiction?) in our little war with being.[8] How then to speak of God again upon this disenchanted earth of modernity?

In *God and the Between*, Desmond recalls that of old the philosopher's vocation entailed a concern about the question of God—but recently, in modernity, there is has grown a silence about God—not of reverence but of indifference . . . irritation, hostility (*GB* 1). He sees the advent rather, in the last couple centuries, of a dark origin—projecting the worthless self (its valueless creations of value) onto the origin (*GB* 24–26)—tracing a genealogy from Kant to Hegel to Schopenhauer—from the autonomous self as epistemic arbiter of the knowable world to *Geist* as rational origin of the unfolding world to the blind tyrannical Will at the root of all things—following the "downward arc" of our self-determining being toward an ultimate darkness, a nihilism. But this nihilism is also a coming to nothing that is unbearable, that can be a "reopening in us of the porosity of being" (*GB* 29) beyond godlessness into a newly reawakened in a second perplexity and a second astonishment (*GB* 32). The modern ethos has effected a kind of bewitchment—that Desmond discusses in terms of a "postulatory finitism"—that has "cast a spell in which atheism seems self-evident" (*GB* 2).

Desmond sees the need to address this bewitchment by seeing the background presuppositions that characterize our modern (now postmodern) ethos (*GB* 2). He proposes a process of "unclogging"—of becoming open again to what is communicated in the "too muchness" of the primal ethos (*GB* 3, 5). This unclogging/reopening to the primal ethos progresses in a fourfold manner: existentially—an elemental "yes"—an "idiotic rebirth" of intimacy with being (*GB* 12, 36);[9] aesthetically—an aesthetic recharging (*GB* 37–40) in renewed awareness of manifest "sensuous givenness" of the beauty and goodness of other-being (*GB* 12) quickening of our senses to the beauty and ugliness that come to us unbidden (*GB* 39); ethically—an erotic outreaching that is our self-surpassing (*GB* 40–43) and our integrity, our being true to what we truly are . . . are to be (*GB* 12); and religiously—seeking to pass beyond the false doubles of God to begin to seek the truth about the divine mystery (*GB* 13)—an agapeic resurrection to our community beyond self-determination with otherness within (in the abyss of the self [T2]), without (in other humans [T2] and in the otherness of the world around us [T1]), and above—our being with ultimate transcendence (T3) (*GB* 43–44).

*Section II: Ways to God*

§1. Religion and Philosophy (and Religion)

The task of thinking about God in the wake of modernity is, for Desmond, one to be shared by religion and philosophy. Desmond sees philosophy and religion as independent (at least to a certain extent) and interrelated integrities such that philosophy can be regarded as a separate discipline that can think about religion and that to which religion refers.[10] Philosophy and religion are interrelated in that each can change as a result of dialogue with the other—philosophy (as metaphysics) and religion display a certain porosity between each other and thus should not be divorced from one another (*HG* 8).[11]

However, within this relationship, religion is for Desmond closer to "the ontological roots of things" (BR 213–14, 226)—it is the deeper and more intimate matrix (the mother tongue) of our thinking, especially our thinking of God (*HG* 17).[12] Desmond's primary configuration of the relation between philosophy and religion is not as much (indeterminate, religious) faith seeking (determinate, philosophical) understanding as it is philosophy's coming to show an opening to divine transcendence (BDD 766–67) and religion after itself coming to a standstill, to nothing, to a breakdown (all of sorts) in perplexity before the astonishing excesses in being (*HG* 191).[13] (One can see even at the outset how this follows Desmond's "phenomenology" from a primal, enabling religious astonishment (as intimate matrix) to philosophical perplexity and curiosity to philosophy's second perplexity opening toward a second, reborn, religious astonishment.) This going-beyond-itself of philosophy, Desmond describes as a different poverty of philosophy—its fulfillment in being called, from within itself, beyond itself (*HG* 191).[14]

Desmond's work on religion and God is then an endeavor to think philosophically in a religious register. It involves contemplation and meditation upon worthy otherness, upon the ultimate and transcendent (GEW 21; BR 223).[15] The philosophical perplexity induced by enduring otherness breaks the circle of self-mediation and leads to the thought of ultimacy. Speculative philosophy, in this mode, not only entertains but mindfully safeguards irreducible perplexities and concerns itself with the limits and extremities of thought (*PO* 242; *BHD* 42–43, 243; *AOO* 4).[16] This kind of philosophizing is a speculative watch—a wakeful watching for signs of absolute otherness in finitude and a guarding watch against ascribing the absolute to the finite (*BHD* 81–82).[17] It is in this watchful tension that one must find ways to speak of God (whose ways are not our own).

By way of brief excursus, one would be remiss to pass by at this point without mentioning a certain tension or ambiguity between reason and faith or philosophy and theology in Desmond's thought. To be more specific, it could be observed that Christian theology informs his philosophy at points where there are thinly veiled Christian concepts, such as creation, agapeic suffering service (*imitatio Christi*), needing divine aid (grace) for higher selvings and community, and the consummate agapeic community of religious service (church). To do this without an explicit theology could leave one with an overly effective "apologetics" that may threaten to make theology redundant—if philosophy alone can yield these theological concepts. There is a possible logic of dualism here, where philosophy on its own can perform such that theology is redundant, unnecessary, rejected. Perhaps Desmond would benefit from a more positive account of revealed, confessional theology. Indeed, Desmond might need to "come out of the closet" as a theologian as well—to be able to give a more robust accounting (and so remedy a kind of incompleteness in his present accounting) of the indeed necessary relation between, not only philosophy and religion, but philosophy and theology. Such would only benefit philosophy and theology and the metaxological community between them. However, it must be said that Desmond's reticence about confessional theology is understandable—especially insofar as he has made his career speaking to a philosophical field that tends to be (especially earlier in Desmond's career) suspicious of, if not hostile to, confessional theology.

### §2. How to Speak of God

How then speak of God? Desmond's answer is that we should speak of God metaxologically. This needs to be unpacked before going on to look at the various signs of and "ways" to God in the between. Laying out how to speak of God (in Desmond's thought) we will follow a course that gets progressively more concrete: from speaking in terms of the middle generally to those of indirection to metaphor to hyperbole.

## FROM THE MIDDLE

In speaking metaxologically, we should speak of God from the middle—speaking as from the middle. Speculative philosophy is, for Desmond, a mindfulness of—an attending to—what is at work in the middle, the midst of our existence (*PO* 11, 18; *PU* 22; *AOO* 4).[18] We cannot name God (or anything for that matter) but from the middle (*DDO* 181). Thus, there can be—for our eyes that cannot clearly or fully see the beginning or ending or depths or heights of being from our often ambiguous location—no immediate, direct access to God, who is to us more an enigma (*DDO* 206). From our intermediate position God cannot be determined directly or (in Desmond's terms) univocally, because humans cannot be on a par with God (as the transcendent other) conceptually (*PO* 136; *EB* 79; *HG* 8). Because of the middle position of humanity with its attendant ambiguity, there is need for us to speak of God, if we so speak, by means of indirection.

## INDIRECTLY

Speaking of God metaxologically entails speaking with images and representations that involve a certain doubleness. For Desmond, to speak indirectly is to speak imaginatively—in terms of representations that are intended to do the work of imag(in)ing an original (*HG* 9–10). In the case of God, no finite determinate (univocal, intending to be direct) category will do, for the original that is to be imaged is at the boundary of human understanding.[19] Thus, if one is to talk of transcendence, one must live with the risk of equivocity (*GEW* 22);[20] for such talk is necessarily representational and indirect—able to conceal in its revealing (*PO* 111, 136).

This indirect speech entails a certain doubleness. God is the ultimate transcendence that is beyond all images/names, which no image can exhaust, and because of this the naming of God risks a fundamental violence of objectifying God—of turning the infinite into a finite object (*PO* 157)[21]—and of producing an idolatrous counterfeit double of God (*BHD* 103, 174; *HG* 8–9).[22] However, this risk is inevitable, for we need—"cannot but need"—images and names to speak of God at all (*PO* 113; *HG* 8). We are thus in the tension of a double situation where naming and imag(in)ing God is both *necessary* (otherwise God is to us a nameless nothing) and *impossible* (in the sense that all names/images fall short of univocally determining the transcendent other to which they refer) (*PO* 133–35).[23] The best names, then, for Desmond, are those that name their failure to be The Name (*PO* 135–36)[24]—that exhibit iconic speech in naming metaxologically (*PO* 135).[25] In this manner of speaking about God—in its caution, reticence, diffidence about making claims about God (*PU* 189; *HG* 8)—God can remain other in our thinking about (naming/imaging) God. There is in indirect speaking a space of difference—a degree of equivocity—that can be maintained between the name/image and God and can function to guard the threshold of the enigma of transcendence.[26]

METAPHORICALLY

For Desmond, such indirect speech about God is, more specifically, metaphorical.[27] Metaphysical metaphors are speculative categories (or "image-less images") (*DDO* 26; *BB* 504; *PU* 208)—such as original selfhood (*DDO* 39, 186), agapeic and erotic being (*PU* 211), creation (*BB* 269; *HG* 131), the absolute original (*DDO* 13, 179, 182), and the agapeic origin (*BB* 166, 211, 251, 261; *PU* 230), to name a few. Such metaphysical metaphors are intermediating names that entail a "carrying between" (*metapherein*)—a carrying across a gap—a speaking of the "beyond" or transcendences "in the midst" (*meta*) of our actual finitude (*DDO* 182; *BB* 45; *PU* 208).[28] A metaphor is a way to articulate what is beyond univocal determination (*DDO* 27; *PU* 99, 207–208, 250)[29]—an "as" (or metaphorical "is") that identifies an excessive (ontological) "is" (*BB* 310)[30] but resists (the seduction of) reducing (or elevating) the likeness (the "as") to a univocal identity (an "is") such that the result is a complex identity, "a certain identification."[31] A metaphysical metaphor, when used of God, is a concrete saying of perplexity that preserves reference to a beyond, to an otherness, and respects the enigma of the ultimate (*BB* 209; *PU* 209).

HYPERBOLICALLY *Throws us to transcendble*

Desmond further focuses the indirect saying involved in metaphor in his concept of the *hyperbole*. A hyperbole is a thought (image, name, etc.) that, in its attending to certain phenomena, has an immanent exigency—an urgency, a restless dynamism within the immanent, the present—that propels one to the thought of the transcendent. With the hyperbolic, one is "thrown," propelled "by our being" beyond (*huperballein*) ourselves and beyond the hyperbole toward the ultimate and transcendent—from our being between toward the "being above" of transcendence (*BB* 218, 222).[32] This patient being thrown, being "in the throes," is "an undergoing which is an overgoing"—"a releasing transcendence drawing us upwards" (*GB* 127). Hyperbolic thought has to do with how something *in* experience (immanence) suggests something *beyond* experience (transcendence)—with something disproportionate or asymmetrical to finitude in the midst of finitude (HT 30; BR 227).[33] The hyperbolic is, for Desmond, a *via eminentiae*—a way of excess (*BB* 219, 221) that brings one to the thought of that which exceeds determinate categorization (HT 23; NDR 48). In hyperbolic indirection, we are made aware of a "divine disproportion"—the reserve of the "radical excess" ultimate of transcendence such that "we feel the need to pile excess upon excess" (*GB* 127). The metaxological hyperbole resumes the deeper promises of the prior indirections—the (more univocal) metaphoric "is," the (more equivocal) analogical "like (as)," the (more dialectical) symbolic "with," are included in the (more metaxological) hyperbolic "above" (*GB* 128).

This overdetermined talking about overdetermined reality involves an *affirmative equivocity*—a constitutive ambiguity, a persistence of paradox (signifying such a saying's ultimate failure to univocally identify, "pin down," ultimate transcendence) that obtains when one comes to think transcendence, to think that which is beyond thought (*BB* 217–19; *HG* 69).[34] As such, as a way of excess, the hyperbolic is connected with a reborn, second astonishment and agapeic mind (a breakthrough after breakdown)—a thinking akin to praise (if not simply that) that names the worthy other in a manner that affirms its otherness and worthiness (*BB* 219).[35] Here there is for Desmond a *reversal* involved in the hyperbolic, in that there is a coming to see the finite measures (metrics) that we employ to refer to the ultimate as lesser reflections of the more fundamental and prior reality of the ultimate as an infinite measure that is beyond our measure, asymmetrical to us and ours.[36] Whereas a common conception (perhaps not foreign to Caputo's) sees talk of the ultimate as but "hyperbolic" (as exaggerated, figurative, "unreal") talk about the finite (reality), Desmond's idea of the hyperbolic is a reversal of this—it is how our understanding of finite realities impels or propels ("gives rise to") our thinking toward something more than the finite which is not sufficient unto itself. Such suggestive, impelling finite happenings (to which we will turn below) are what Desmond calls the "hyperboles of being"—these excessive happenings are signs pointing beyond themselves (in various ways) toward ultimacy (PR 113–15; BR 227; *HG* 7).[37]

We now turn to the various hyperboles of being. For Desmond, these are sundry ways to God—signs of God in the othernesses of the between (*PO* 343; GEW 24).[38] We will consider these ways under the broad categories of the overdeterminate transcendences in the between—the exterior transcendence of being in nature (T1) and the interior transcendence of the self (T2)—that point to a superior transcendence beyond the between (T3). These signs in these othernesses bring one to a perplexity—that God does not quell as a univocal answer to a determinate question—but that points to God as an intimate stranger, who utterly transcends us and whose indeterminate signs and traces utterly surround and indwell us.[39]

### §3. Ways to God from Exterior Transcendence

The hyperboles of being are happenings experienced in finite being that point beyond themselves.[40] In this section, we will look at the hyperboles of being that are encountered in Desmond's first transcendence (T1), in the infinite succession of beings in the external world of becoming (*DDO* 149–51, 154; *BB* 206–207, 231, 256, 408, 448; *HG* 2).[41] Generally, these hyperboles consist of the encounter with external transcendence as suggesting or intimating a transcendent ground or origin—the world's ultimate ground in an origin (*DDO* 152; *PU* 205; *HG* 7).[42] This is the hyperbolic thought of creation (*BB* 267; *AOO* 5–6; *HG* 131).[43] It is in the following ways that finite being images, in its intermediate being, an ultimate ground or origin.[44]

### The Givenness of Being

The first hyperbole of external being is the hyperbole of the givenness of being. The phenomenon from which this hyperbole arises is the finitude of creation in its being given to be at all (*DDO* 184–85; *BB* 8, 9; *NDR* 39; *PR* 112; *EB* 51; *HT* 30, 34; *HG* 203).[45] Thought is struck into astonishment by the "that it is at all": that there is something rather than nothing, "the sheer being there of the world" (*PO* 33, 229, 236; *BB* 192; *HT* 25, 30; *PR* 112; *BR* 229; *NDR* 39; *HG* 3, 203).[46] The perplexity that arises from the givenness of being has to do with the more basic "coming to be" of being—the question of why there is being rather than nothing (*HT* 28, 34; *EB* 192–93; *HG* 131).[47] There seems to be an ontological dependency of finite being as a whole[48]—a sense of the whole as a universal impermanence, an open whole, that points beyond itself (*BB* 293; *PU* 225; *HT* 39; *GEW* 28)[49]—and thus "presents itself as something originated."[50] This hyperbole of the givenness of being suggests or intimates an origin that makes possible (possibilizes) the possibility and actuality of being at all (*DDO* 152; *PO* 138; *BB* 207, 231, 291; *HT* 36; *HG* 3; *AOO* 268).[51] The coming to be of being—that it is at all—suggests the metaphysical hyperboles of creation (*HT* 23–25)[52] and of an absolute original that gives the given (*DDO* 181, 184, 188; *HT* 39–40).[53]

### The Plural Community of Being

The community of being, not only in its sheer givenness but in its plurality, is another hyperbole of being that intimates a particular kind of ground and origin. The community of being is experienced as a plenitude (*BB* 264, 514), as a genuine plurality (*BB* 338; *PU* 238)[54] in which there is true, irreducible otherness and singularity in interrelation and intermediation (*BB* 330, 338; *HT* 39–40).[55] Such a community as plural plenitude of finite being suggests a particular kind of "giving" that originates such a "given" (*PO* 8, 39, 113; *BB* 511; *EB* 195). In Desmond's terms, such an origin would be an *agapeic origin*—an origin that gives finite otherness to be, lets otherness be other and sustains it in its otherness (*BB* 263; *PU* 137, 220, 238).

### The Intelligibility of the World

Another external hyperbole of being is that of the intelligibility of the world. The external world is experienced as orderly, as ordered, as exhibiting an integrity and a harmony that makes it intelligible (*BB* 339, 510; *PU* 227). This intelligibility of the world, as structured and orderly, exhibits design as a sign that suggests an origin that is the ground of our epistemological trust (*PO* 228–29; *BB* 345, 359, 514; *PU* 225).[56] This epistemological grounding is in astonishment and perplexity before the manifest order of the world, not a univocal determinate grounding that (onto-theologically) functions to stabilize the world for our instrumental manipulation—for we are not equal to the enigmatic ground (intelligibility exceeding our determinate understanding bespeaking an origin also thus excessive, if not beyond our intelligible grasping).[57] Intelligibility itself begs an explanation—whence intelligibility? The question hyperbolically suggests the idea of a trustworthy and ordering origin of the world.[58]

## THE GOODNESS OF BEING

The final hyperbole of external being is that of the goodness of being. We experience the ethos of being as charged (if indeterminately) with value—as bearing an inherent or intrinsic worth (*BB* 510, 513; *PU* 5, 225, 228; *EB* 23, 75–76, 177, 219–20; *AOO* 292).[59] It is because of this more excessive pre-existing goodness or worth in being that we can think goodness or value or worth at all (*PU* 228; GEW 23, 25; En 130; *EB* 17). We encounter this over-determinate and indeterminately given goodness of being with astonishment and perplexity (*BB* 36; BDD 735; GEW 26). Such astonishment is a general *reverence* before being—a recognition of being as being worthy in itself, beyond any instrumental valuation (BR 215, 225–26, 229; *EB* 40).[60] This general reverence for being is a sign of a source—of a more primal giving and affirmation as good from an origin toward which a deeper (or higher) reverence is due (BR 222–29).[61] Desmond understands this source that is intimated in our encounter of the goodness of being in terms of an agapeic origin that, in creating the world as good in itself, is the ground of the unity of being and goodness (*BB* 208, 551; *PU* 226–27, 230; *EB* 200).[62] The agapeic origin is the ground of being and goodness as the one that gives forth being to be as good in itself (*EB* 17, 20, 201). With this final hyperbole of external being—regarding goodness and the ground of the good—we are already crossing a threshold into the hyperboles of internal being that are the ways to God from human being.

## §4. Ways to God from Interior Transcendence

In this section, we will examine the hyperboles of inner being. The phenomena here under consideration are those that cluster around Desmond's second transcendence as the transcendence of the self's inward reserve of otherness (*BB* 201) and as self-transcendence or the self's active transcending as a vector of transcendence—as the restless power of human self-surpassing (*BB* 5, 7, 231, 407; *HG* 3, 203; *AOO* 268). Generally, these hyperboles consist of the encounter with internal transcendence as suggesting or intimating a transcendent ground—a transcendent other that is at the origin and *telos* of the self's idiotic transcendence and of human self-transcending. The inward, intentional infinitude and actual finitude of the self suggests a more radical sense of the infinite (*BB* 207; *HG* 190).

## THE INFINITE WORTH OF THE IDIOTIC SELF

The first hyperbole of interior transcendence is that of the idiocy of the self. With the idiot self there is an infinite value revealed in the ontological roots of the human being (*PO* 143).[63] We experience as a givenness the phenomenon of the intrinsic, infinite value of the person—both within ourselves and in relation to other singular individuals (*BB* 527; *EB* 138). With this singular infinite worth there is no finite measure—there must be another infinitude, an infinite measure *other than* the human, to be on a par with it and to make sense of the infinite worth *of* the human.[64] This suggests that there is a relativity to the ultimate that grounds the worth of the singular self—as singular and free, as an original self (*PO* 186; *PU* 241; *EB* 496).[65] There is, then, in the intimacy of the idiotic self—in its singular "thisness"—a being in relation to the ultimate—a sense of God as the (exceeding and transcendent) origin of the excessive worth of the singular self (*PU* 100–101; *HG* 5, 93, 188–89).[66]

The following hyperboles of internal being concern desire. Desire's self-transcending is an outreaching and an opening toward the metaxological community of excessive others (*BB* 230, 448; *PU* 205)[67] and toward the actual infinitude of superior transcendence (T3) (*DDO* 152; *PO* 111, 204; *BB* 155, 182, 207, 231, 378; *PU* 11, 250; *EB* 113–14, 214–18; *HG* 5, 7; *AOO* 268–69, 288, 291). There are here two sides to desire: in its urgent outreaching toward and transcending and in its porous opening to the ultimate other.

### SELF-TRANSCENDING DESIRE: THE URGENCY OF ULTIMACY, THE *CONATUS ESSENDI*

The anomalous being of the human is that of infinite desire in finite being.[68] This desire is a self-surpassing toward transcendence in general and more radical "transcendence as other" in particular (*BB* 155; *AOO* 268).[69] Such a self-transcending has a hyperbolic vector of transcendence (*PU* 182)[70]—an excessive drive toward an excessive, "Unequal," other (*EB* 213; *HG* 93).[71] Desmond describes this desire or eros as the "urgency of ultimacy"—as an absolute, infinite restlessness for the absolute or the ultimate (*BHD* 44; *BB* 155, 182; *EB* 74, 324)[72] that is not satisfied by any finite good.[73] Such a restlessness is an infinite neediness, an infinite lack, not needing or lacking itself but another good beyond itself (*EB* 367; *AOO* 287).[74] Desire's urgent, self-transcending restlessness for an ultimate good/end (*DDO* 197; *BB* 229) suggests a more radical, disproportionate sense of the infinite, an "actual infinitude" in excess of its own infinity—an infinity that coexists with the desiring human's actual finitude and is thus not what it seeks (*BB* 207; *PU* 204; *HG* 3).[75] Desire's intentional infinitude, as something that is absolute about the self, images and refers beyond itself to a more original source (as the absolute original of our original selfhood) (*HG* 3, 7; *AOO* 6, 269, 288).[76] It is thus that thought thinking itself becomes thought thinking its other, thinking the unthinkable, that which is transcendent to thought.[77] This self-transcendence in the urgency of desire is also an opening to ultimacy, and this opening shows a being-with transcendence (a *passio essendi*) that is prior to and enabling the self-transcending urgency of ultimacy (*PU* 11; *EB* 74).

### SELF-TRANSCENDING DESIRE: POROSITY, THE *PASSIO ESSENDI*

Another hyperbole of internal being, another happening that brings one to the thought of God, is a primal porosity—an intimate commun(icat)ion with God in the interior depths of the self (*AOO* 292).[78] In human self-transcendence, there is a *passio essendi*—a passive suffering and givenness, a gift from the other—that is prior to the *conatus essendi*—to our striving endeavor to be (*HG* 97, 203–204; *AOO* 288).[79] There is a prior *agape*, a prior fullness, a prior being-in-relation to transcendence that is the ground of self-transcendence (*BB* 208, 221; *PU* 250)[80]—a divine festivity (*poros*) that is in the idiotic roots of self-transcending *eros* (*PU* 135; *EB* 157). Here, more basic to desire is an openness, an opening or patience to the other—here, to the ultimate other (*BB* 5; *PU* 204; *EB* 217).[81] In this *passio*/opening/patience, self-transcendence is ruptured by, called forth by, and released toward transcendence as other (*EB* 113–14).[82] A sense of divine transcendence is communicated in intimacy of the self.[83] Desmond describes this intimate commun(icat)ion between God and the self in the self as a porosity—an experience of being-with or dwelling with that suggests a transcendence beyond or superior to self-transcendence (*EB* 362–63; PR 108; *AOO* 290, 292).[84]

### The Call of the Good: Agapeic Selving and Community

The final hyperbole of internal being is, broadly, that of the call of the good. The call of the good that is experienced in being ethical refers one to a ground of the good—a good beyond finite goods—a *huperagathos* that must be so disproportionate in order to be proportionate to the exorbitant good we experience in the between—in the experience of the goodness of being and in being called to agapeic being (*EB* 20, 93, 200, 493).[85] The human good refers to more ultimate good as a condition for the possibility of ethical being (*EB* 170). This experience of the call of the good is a being commissioned, being constrained by ultimacy in relation to the other (*BB* 414).[86] As such, the call of the good beyond the self is the ground of agapeic selving and community—a good beyond the self to which one is called even to the point of suffering, of service without reciprocity.[87] Thus, when this call is answered and embodied in a community of agapeic service, such a community can be a witness to the agapeic source—likening itself to the generosity of the agapeic origin (*EB* 165, 502).[88]

### §5. The Hyperboles of Being in *God and the Between*

In *God and the Between*, Desmond provides a more elegant presentation of these hyperboles of being that maps onto his fourfold sense of being. *The idiocy of being* is the "that it is" of given being (*GB* 11). This "idiocy" is that which is so singular and intimate that it is resistant to determination (*GB* 128–29)—that is also the immediate "taste" of the goodness of given being (however ambiguous) in the face of its possible nothingness (*GB* 131)—the shock, the "bite" of the actual, of the striking reality of being in its otherness to us (*GB* 133). This givenness of being is a disquieting phenomenon that lends itself to a metaxological "reformulation" of more traditional "proofs" (*GB* 130)—of the cosmological proof into a meditation of what it might mean for all that is to have come to be and the hyperbolic "cause"—a cause unlike any finite cause—that this brings to mind (*GB* 131–32). Desmond sees in Aquinas's third way a meditation upon the radical contingency of all finite being conjoined with the fact of its existence (*GB* 132–33)—what it might mean that anything is actual at all.

*The aesthetics of happening* attends to the glory and beauty of otherness in the external, given world "incarnated in the beauty and sublimity of finitude" (*GB* 12)—to the "marvelous intricacy" of order manifest in the world's sensuous showing (*GB* 134, 138–40). Included in this phenomenon is the conjoining of inner and outer intricacies in the marvel of intelligibility.[89] In the aesthetics of happening we see the singularity of things—not just that it is, but that it is *this*—and these singulars in a network of intermediation (*GB* 135). We see the beauty and sublimity of creation and of our human creations—in the breaking forth from an inward otherness something that is more than us, something surprising and strange (*GB* 136). We see the "fugitive" nature of beauty that "invites us to the *boundary* of the sublime" (*GB* 135). This is Desmond's reconfiguring of Aquinas's fifth way or of the argument from design to the hyperbolic thought of a maker beyond determinate making, a *poiesis* that truly originates beyond any forming we can imagine.

*The erotics of selving* attends to our being "infinitely self-surpassing"—our being "as beyond measure in terms of ourselves as measure, we point and are pointed to a measure exceeding finite measure" (*GB* 12)—our porosity in ourselves beyond ourselves to the ultimate other. This includes the two sides of desire (the *conatus* and *passio essendi*) (*GB* 142–43) as well as the call of the good on the singular self's ethical being (*GB* 145–48) described above. Here we behold the transcending power of reason itself—"the erotics of reason"—as pointing toward a more "Anselmian" approach to the ontological proof—a prayerful following of the movement of thought to the ultimate (*GB* 143–44).

Finally, *the agapeics of community or communication* is the hyperbole of being that is our being in receiving and giving (*GB* 12)—that community is *a priori*, elemental, that an open wholeness of plural singularities in relation is the basic reality of the world around us, within us (*GB* 151). Here we see that even in the intimacy of our secret selves we are with another, never alone, always already in communion with another before and with and after us (*GB* 153). Here we see the reaching of the highest human communities in agapeic service beyond, into a religious register—participating in a community beyond us enabling a loving giving, a solidarity, that seems or is beyond us, beyond our finite capacities—such that the (more than) human community of agapeic service is itself "a hyperbolic sign of transcendent good" (*GB* 156).

*Section III: The Metaxological God*

§1. Counterfeit (Univocal/Equivocal and Dialectical)
Doubles of God

Thinking about God, for Desmond, entails a vigilance in discriminating false doubles of God (*HG* 10)[90]—a guarding against counterfeit doubles presenting a God that is not God (*HG* 2).[91] Such counterfeit doubles mimic the original they purport to image—reflecting only a part of the original but so focusing on that part as to distort its imaging of the original.[92] Avoiding such counterfeits also involves guarding against the idolatry that "stalks thought" (*PU* 229). Such idolatry often involves an instrumentalizing of God—a reducing of the overdeterminate, transcendent metaxological God to a manipulable univocity.[93] These counterfeit doubles, these idolatrous gods are dead gods, amounting to little other than the human will to power that projects them[94]—a God that is not God. In Desmond's work, the counterfeit doubles of the metaxological reality of God are presentations of God as contracted into the univocal, equivocal, dialectical senses of being.

### The Univocal God

The univocalization of God entails an objectifying of God that is also an absolutization of univocity (*BB* 96; *PU* 110).[95] The univocal God is the static, univocal eternity—absolute in its immutability and stasis beyond time and becoming—that has been, as Desmond recognizes, pervasive in the western philosophical tradition (*DDO* 89–90; *PU* 171).[96] This univocal God is exemplified in the *Ens Realissimum*—a static eternity that is a self-thinking thought fixed outside of time (*PU* 202).[97] The univocal God can be seen as an expression of onto-theology—as an idealized projection of objective mind (*PU* 111)[98] that can become an instrumentalization of God, a mere univocal explanation.[99] Such a use of God as a foundation—as a means of securing ourselves in the world, as a self-projection of our power (PR 109)[100]—is, in the end, a use of God that makes God useless. It makes God redundant, dispensable when the order of the world and the self (to which God is utterly transcendent) is taken as self-sufficient.[101] Thus, the univocal conception of God can be seen as generating an oppositional dualism—equivocal difference between God and the world, the between (*BB* 58).[102]

### The Equivocal God

The univocal understanding of God begets a dualistic understanding of God and the world.[103] This dualism—this fixation of God as eternal outside of the world of becoming—leaves the world devalued and degraded, for if there is a dualistic opposition between God and the world, God cannot be the ground of goodness or value in the world—there can be no relation between the two (*EB* 20; *GEW* 16).[104] The God intended as a ground, in the end, cannot function as a ground—God's relation to the world becomes equivocal. What this theological dualism does ground is the fact/value dualism so pervasive in the modern ethos—such that what the dualistic conception of God has torn asunder (being and goodness), no human will be able to put together.

This equivocal dualism between God and the world of beings in the between is problematic in several ways (*DDO* 108). The conception of God as a static eternity is equivocal inasmuch as it is self-frustrating: one cannot seek to have any relation to it; it cannot act in relation in relation to the world; it cannot have originated the world; and it cannot be the ground of that to which it is antithetical (*DDO* 96–99; *EB* 25). On one hand, God as a static eternity is a nugatory transcendence—unavailable for any relationship with the world or humans—for God is defined only negatively, in opposition to the world (*DDO* 99).[105] On the other hand, the only kind of relationship that is often left in a dualistic conception of God—that of the eternal origin and ground of the world of becoming—ultimately serves to make God redundant (*DDO* 99; *PU* 170; *EB* 24). God as static eternity does not serve the intended use of securing the world, for such an entity, by definition, cannot originate or ground the entities in the world becoming to which it stands in opposition.

### THE DIALECTICAL GOD

Finally, this equivocal dualism can lead to a dialectical conception of God.[106] In the long run, the oppositional relation of dualistic opposition and equivocal difference in dualism tends to undercut itself and issue in a kind of dialectical monism (*DDO* 204).[107] Desmond describes this dialectical god as an *absorbing god*—a closed whole that subsumes all parts, all otherness within itself, within its oneness (*DDO* 202–4; *BHD* 128).[108] Desmond (with Hegel in particular in mind) also describes such a dialectical god as an *erotic origin,* a god that originates the world with the goal of reconstituted self-relativity—in order to achieve absolute self-mediation (*BB* 242, 245).[109] This idea of an erotic origin can come to expression in the conceiving of God in terms of human divine sovereignty—of a social will willing itself (*EB* 25, 474).

Desmond sees several problems in this dialectical conception of God. The dialectical (absorbing, erotic) God subsumes and so dissolves the difference between God and humans (*PO* 135, 310). This again makes divine transcendence redundant, for there is ultimately no divine (ultimate) other to the world (*HG* 6). In fact, with the dialectical God, all otherness is ultimately temporary, provisional—there is no true plurality or irreducible otherness.[110] The originating and the originated entailed in the erotic origin is ultimately illusory—there is only self-origination (*DDO* 202–204). Finally, the dialectical God as an erotic origin is an empty, indeterminate origin. Its originating is driven by a lack—needing to become determinate—and not proceeding out of a fullness (*BB* 247–48).

In *God and the Between,* Desmond gives an extended systematic presentation of many different ways of thinking about God. In Part II he uses his fourfold sense of being as a way of locating and progressing through some of these understandings of God, exploring how God is thought in an univocal register in such perspectives as Pantheistic and Parminedian Monism, Platonic and Plotinian understandings of the One, the "geometrical" understanding of God as might be seen in Leibniz, and certain Dualisms (*GB* 49–72). Under the "Equivocal Way" he treats the equivocities involved in our understanding of God arising from nature's aesthetic happening, the doubleness evident in the joy and suffering in life, the mixture of the good and evil in our experience, and the inwardness of the self (*GB* 73–90). In the chapter on the "Dialectical Way,"

Desmond treats of the mediation between the univocal an equivocal understandings of God, the religious and philosophical approaches to God. Through examining Kant and Hegel as exemplary, Desmond moves toward a mode of mediation that points beyond a dialectic that would ultimately reduce one side (the equivocal, the religious) to the other (the univocal, the philosophical) (*GB* 91–115). In all of these ways, Desmond brings out moments in our thinking through our understanding of God where the different senses of being illuminate aspects that contribute positively to a properly metaxological understanding of God. In Part III of *God and the Between,* Desmond explores the plurality of conceptions of God or divinity as traditionally understood in terms of monotheism, polytheism, gnosticism, pan(en)theism, and mysticism.

## §2. The Metaxological God

The metaxological sense of being is a vision of being that entails genuine otherness, transcendence, and difference in the midst of community. Central to this vision is the way in which divine otherness or God relates to this metaxological community. If being is an overdetermined excess made up of unrepeatable singulars that constitute genuine difference in the midst of community, does this have a bearing on how we are to talk about God? Toward this end—that is, thinking God metaxologically—Desmond uses two principle terms to encapsulate his conception of God: superior transcendence and the agapeic origin.

### SUPERIOR TRANSCENDENCE

One of the key elements in understanding God metaxologically for Desmond is that of seeing God in terms of a superior transcendence. In Desmond's metaphysics there is, in addition to the transcendence of the being of nature (T1) and the self-transcending transcendence of human being (T2), a *third* transcendence (T3) which is identified with the divine or God (*BB* 231; *HG* 2–4, 7; *AOO* 269). Desmond, following in the tradition of the great monotheistic religions, is concerned with defending God's genuine transcendence—over against the potent(ial) counterfeits—as a nonnegotiable (*PU* 189; *HG* 9). Desmond often refers to God as "transcendence itself," as the ultimate and foundational transcendence (*BB* 231; *PU* 230; *EB* 219; *HG* 3; *AOO* 269).[111] This divine transcendence is spoken of in terms of metaphorics of height and depth, of "the extremes of space" (*DDO* 198–99). God is the depth of the world as its immanent (though different), intimate (though reserved), originating, and supporting ground (*DDO* 199). Of more significance in the present context, the metaxological God is described in terms of height as a "vertical transcendence"—an infinitude that is *huper,* "beyond" or "above" all finite being (*DDO* 198; *BB* 201, 208; *HG* 7).[112] This "vertical" divine transcendence is a superior transcendence (beyond interior and exterior transcendence)—an absolutely superior otherness (*BB* 201, 256–57; *HG* 3, 59) that has an essentially asymmetrical relationship with humans and the world (*HG* 49).[113] There is a "divine *disproportion*"

(*BHD* 182). Desmond describes this superiority of God in terms of the ultimate (BDD 763-64)—God is "the Unequal Itself" (*BHD* 182; *PU* 235).

Desmond characterizes this superior and ultimate transcendence, not as an empty "beyond," but as an otherness characterized as plenitude—as actual infinitude and as overdetermined, excessive reserve. Third transcendence is *other* to the other others, the other transcendences—not reducible to a mere projection of the transcendence of the becoming of the world or of human self-determination (*BB* 231–32; *PU* 230; *HG* 3–4, 200; *AOO* 6). God, in the metaxological conception, is not a product of projection but of hyperbole (*BB* 256–57; *HG* 4). That is to say that the metaxological God is not mere "hyperbole"—an exalted way of speaking about something else (say, ethics)— but an hyperbole in the sense of a thinking that finds itself beyond itself, on a trajectory toward an infinite other, an actual infinitude that cannot be fully subsumed under or comprehended in terms of finitude or of lesser infinitudes like the infinite succession of external becoming (T1) or the intentional infinitude of original selfhood(T2) (*DDO* 151; *BB* 408, 448). Desmond describes the otherness of God as a "reserve"—as in something that is held back, that retreats, that withdraws (*BB* 495; HT 31). Superior transcendence, in itself and for itself, remains for us an enigma, a mystery that retreats beyond the veil that is the limits of human comprehension and mediation (*BB* 258).[114] The reserve of divine transcendence is a persisting otherness that remains beyond, exceeds the bounds of any holistic immanence (*BB* 495, 502; *HG* 187–88, 199ff.). Concomitant with this reserve is the necessity that our speech about God be indirect, metaphorical.[115] Desmond describes this "reserve" not as an indefinite or indeterminate or empty otherness (*HG* 7), but as an overdetermined plenitude (*BHD* 181; *BB* 19, 182; *PU* 230; HT 34).[116] Divine transcendence is a qualitatively inexhaustible excess (*BB* 19, 182, 255)[117]—it is the "reserve of the full" (*HG* 198).

Desmond's metaxological presentation of divine transcendence is not merely utter transcendence, transcendence without relation to the world and to humans—thus collapsing into an equivocal dualism between God and the world that ultimately erases first the "between" and then God altogether. Metaxological divine transcendence is an *original* transcendence—not merely "beyond" but also "before." It is "original" as first and as originating. Its overdetermined excess/fullness/plenitude is the reserve that grounds its power of origination (*DDO* 188; *HG* 3, 136) out of which transcendence originates genuine others.[118] As such, it is the "possibilizing source" of the other transcendences— a transcendence (T3) that begets, that is the original source of transcendence (T1, T3) (*BB* 231; *EB* 219; *HG* 3; *AOO* 269). The overdeterminate and excessive *transcendence* of third transcendence enables its *transcending* in the sense of its transcending itself in creation (originating being as other to it) and in relating to creation.

One metaphysical metaphor that Desmond has used in his presentation of this "original" aspect of divine transcendence (and here we are already moving into the next section) is that of the *absolute original*. Desmond describes the absolute original in terms of wholeness and infinitude (*DDO* 188–96; *HG* 8). The absolute original is *absolute* in that it is *whole*—an ultimate unity in itself, neither lacking for fulfillment and needing nor dependent upon the world for self-completion (as with the erotic origin, the dialectical God). It is its own (self-originating) whole (*DDO* 189, 192).[119] The absolute original is *original* in that it is *infinite,* for it is its infinity (its transcendent reserved otherness to the finite) that grounds its power of origination (*DDO* 192; *BB* 502).[120] Inasmuch as wholeness alone yields an univocal God[121] and infinitude alone yields an equivocal God,[122] both of these incomplete options leave one with a God that can have no possible relation to the world as other. Within the absolute original, however, wholeness and infinitude open onto each other so as to yield an "open wholeness" (*BB* 502).[123] Its "absoluteness" is not its absence of relation but its giving in relation (or, rather, the *manner* of its giving, as we will see below).[124] Its infinitude is not an escape from finitude but is the ground of its openness to finitude as a power to originate (*DDO* 189; *BB* 502).

### The Agapeic Origin

#### "Origin"

The central metaphor for God in Desmond's work to date is that of *agapeic origin.*[125] Before examining the agapeic dimension, I will first explicate the original/originating dimension. God, for Desmond, is centrally the original transcendence (*HG* 3)—the origin and creator of the world that is other, transcendent to the creation, to the becoming of the world (*BB* 447; *PU* 187).[126] There is, in the metaxological conception of God, a clear (and distinctly monotheistic) alternative to the "holistic self-creation" of the dialectical God (*HG* 8).[127] The transcendence of the origin—of God as the unique, singular, "first" and "primal" giver (*BB* 506; *EB* 202, 505; *HG* 136; *AOO* 6)—entails a radical sense of origination, a "genuine" origination that is absolute and unconditional (*DDO* 197; *AOO* 6, 288).[128] Such creation is a hyperbolic thought, a metaphysical metaphor for something that exceeds determinate intelligibility (*BB* 269; *HT* 23; *HG* 131).[129] God's origination is creation *ex nihilo* (*DDO* 242; *BB* 262)—bringing being into being from nothing. The nothing so names the "qualitative difference" between the radical origin and the radically originated and the "hyperbolic asymmetry" between the creator and the creation such that the latter's being is utterly dependant on the former.[130] Thus, as created from nothing, as coming to be in an unconditional origination that is bound by nothing, the created universe is "shadowed" by the nothingness (*nihilo*) from which (*ex*) it was made (*creatio*)—nothingness is ontologically constitutive of finite creation (*BB* 269; *HG* 129–30).[131]

The agapeic origin is the possibilizing source of being-at-all. The origin's originating of finite being (creation of creation), as a radical creation out of nothing, has to do with the primal "*coming to be*" of finite being (*HG* 128–31).[132] God here is an answer to the question of why there is something rather than nothing, the question of being-at-all, and as such is presented as the ground of "the fact itself"—the fact of given finite being at all (*DDO* 180–81, 188).[133] The agapeic origin is the "possibilizing source," "the primal and ultimate power of creative possibilizing," the ground of possibility that makes being able to be at all (*BB* 231, 335, 338).[134] It is the original power of being (*BB* 330, 335) that is the sustaining (and thus relatively or rather relationally immanent) ground of being and thus human origination and creativity (*AOO* 288).[135]

The origin of the world is not an empty transcendent beyond or an erotic lack or defect seeking fulfillment (*DDO* 193; HG 139), but an always-already-full-ness. The agapeic origin's origination issues from a "superplus" (*HG* 139) surplus—a plenitude that is "an excess of completion and wholeness" (*DDO* 193; *BB* 166, 255, 330). Creation does not come from a compulsion, from a desire to remedy a defect, but from an already present completion, a perfection or "pluperfection" (*DDO* 193; *BB* 215).[136] The origin's wholeness beyond lack, far from being the basis of God's merely (univocal/equivocal) insular, static self-enjoyment, is a surplus out of which it transcends itself in asymmetrical creation—creation of the other that is not merely a function of self-relation (as with the dialectical, erotic origin) (*BB* 215, 255).[137]

Finally, the agapeic origin is the source of the community of created being as plural, singular, and good. The agapeic origin is the originating and sustaining ground of the metaxological community of being (*PO* 113; *BB* 263). As such, it is the ground (the source and sustainer) of the genuine, nonreductive plurality of creation (*DDO* 180; *BB* 264, 338; *AOO* 293)[138]—a true community of plurality made up of unique (idiotic) singularities in communicative relation to one another (*BB* 330; *PU* 48; HT 40). This created plural yet singular community of being bears a certain doubleness—at once independent of and dependent upon God as agapeic origin. It is independent of the agapeic origin in that the origin originates the other *as truly other* and thus as given to itself, freely released into being for itself (*PU* 187, 218; *EB* 202; *AOO* 6).[139] In giving being to the other, God gives the gift of free otherness to the other. Finite being is ontologically dependent upon the origin in that there is yet an asymmetrical relationship between them as finite being has been radically originated from nothing by the origin—its being as finite, as having come-to-be, points back to its origination and to its origin (*HG* 164).[140] Finally, finite beings are given to be themselves as good in themselves—as bearing inherent value from but not for the sake of the origin (so as to make the value of finite being extrinsic, instrumental for divine self-fulfillment) (*BB* 186, 511–12; *PU* 196; *EB* 44; BR 229; *HG* 140).[141] Here we are already moving into the "agape" of Desmond's agapeic origin.

### "Agapeic" Origin

The agapeic origin, as Desmond's preeminent metaphysical metaphor (*BB* 208, 231, 330; *PU* 137, 207, 230; *HG* 3) or "hyperbole" (HT 39–40) for God, designates the particular character of God's/the origin's creation/origination as *agapeic*. As intimated above, agapeic origination is creation not from lack but from surplus or plenitude.[142] Here, the agapeic origin is to be understood in contradistinction to the erotic origin, which, because of some lacking in itself (some indeterminacy or lack of wholeness or completion), seeks to produce/ fulfill/complete *itself* in the production of creation—a creation always provisionally other. The agapeic origin does not need to produce itself in its origination—it is "always already itself."[143] The agapeic origin is instead a *plenitude* that freely originates out of a fullness and not a lack or internal necessity (*BHD* 79–80; *BB* 166; *PU* 188, 207, 231; *HG* 135)—a "creative excess" out of which genuine creation happens (*BB* 256, 261).[144]

Agapeic origination generously gives forth genuine otherness (*PU* 196).[145] It lets the other of creation be as other (as other to the agapeic origin) (*BHD* 80; *PU* 216–18, 231; *HG* 70; *AOO* 288)[146]—as an irreducible otherness (*BHD* 90; *BB* 261–62) "in itself" (*BHD* 80, 116) and for itself (*BB* 262, 448; *EB* 164).[147] The being of the world is "released"—given as free from the origin—into being for itself (*BB* 257, 263–64; *EB* 164, 200; *HG* 136; *AOO* 6). Thus, agapeic creation cannot be reduced to self-mediation (*BHD* 80; *PU* 218–19; *AOO* 287).

In giving otherness, the "agapeic One" gives rise to more than one, to a genuine plurality (*HG* 138). Desmond describes this in terms of an affirmative doubling or redoubling that is not the self-division of the One but a "real Secondness" (*BHD* 120; *BHD* 80–81, 116; *PU* 220).[148] Thus, agapeic creation is the source of difference and plurality (*DDO* 242; *PU* 238; *EB* 502; *HG* 70)[149]— the excessive generosity that gives rise to plurality (*BHD* 81).[150] The plurality of the created world is composed of singulars—finite beings that are not only other to God but other to each other (*BB* 184–87, 193, 263, 330, 496; PU 48, 100, 239–41; *EB* 164, 502; *HG* 136).[151] The agapeic origin is thus the ground of singularity and genuine ("idiotic") selfhood as well. As creator of this plurality of singulars, the agapeic origin is the giver of "the between," "the middle" as the "space of open being" (*BB* 262).[152] God is the original (originating) ground of metaxological community of being (*DDO* 242; *PO* 8, 113; *BB* 263; *PU* 137, 234, 238).[153]

In all of this, the "agapeic" character of the agapeic origin's creation/ origination is best described in terms of the "gift." God's creation, the giving of being to be as other and for itself, is a gift (*PU* 133, 144, 196, 216–17; *EB* 505)[154]—a true gift of love.[155] It is a giving that gives the given as a gift. Agapeic creation is a gratuitous origination, a "*non-possessive dispensation*" (*DDO* 191),[156] an act of pure generosity exceeding itself for the sake of the other— not merely giving *something* to the other but giving the other to be as such, giving the other itself (*BB* 418, 501; HT 41; BR 224; *EB* 207).[157] There is a disproportion and asymmetry in the directionality of giving—God's creative gift is something that could not ever be returned; it would ever exceed any attempt.[158] It is difficult for us to think this excessive gift, to think agape—it is foreign, other, transcendent to our (all too erotic) conceptual economies (*BB* 410, 542; *PU* 195).[159]

Creation as agapeic gift implies a certain freedom in created being. Beings and human beings in particular are given, are "released" into (*BB* 257, 264; AT

250),[160] an ontological freedom, a freedom to be for themselves as other (*BHD* 182; *BB* 79; *EB* 138)[161]—a freedom "given from," a being given free(ly) from, the agapeic origin.[162] In creating, the agapeic absolute "absolves" itself from its creation—makes it other and free.[163] In so doing, the agapeic origin allows creation the freedom to absolve itself from the origin such that there is a permitting, a "letting be" of evil—a patience to evil (*BB* 263; AT 250; En 150)[164]—that can be horrifying to us (*PU* 249).[165] Yet there is a conceptual consistency between the existence of the agapeic origin and the existence of evil, for a creation without the possibility of evil is not the result of agapeic creation, not truly other to the creator, not released, free.[166]

As agapeic, for Desmond, the origin is good or rather, the Good (*BB* 71; *EB* 281).[167] The agapeic good is not extrinsic to God; God is "agapeic transcendence," the "free identity of being and the good" (*PU* 195). And, as the agapeic origin gives forth being, so does it give goodness to being (*BB* 71; *PU* 195, 216–17; *EB* 495, 503).[168] God creates being as good for itself, as valuable in itself. God creates the world and says "It is good" (BR 224).[169] As such, the agapeic origin is the original ground of goodness in being (*EB* 200, 496).[170] And, as such, it can provide both a way out of the nihilism of instrumental mind and a ground for our trust in being and knowledge (*BB* 71, 359).

### Agapeic Sustaining

For Desmond, God as the agapeic origin is not merely the source of being, but has a continuing relationship with created being. This relationship, with regard to humans at least, is an intermediation, a double mediation between creation and Creator (*PU* 204). Here we will briefly set out God's side of this continuing relationship; we will look at the human side in the next section: on "religion."

God's continuing relationship with being, with the creation, arises out of God's continuing agapeic regard for being. God loves being, loves it for itself, continues to see it as good in itself (*EB* 491).[171] God "lets the sun shine equally" on all—loving even the evil, the hateful, as yet possessing inherent goodness—with what is to us a "reckless," "terrifying," "monstrous" generosity (*BB* 544).[172] This loving God is "absolutely interested" in being—loving being all the way "down to" the unique and irreducible singularity of created being.[173] God's agape, as the creative source of difference, otherness, and singularity in being, persists—God unconditionally loves the singular as something of infinite worth (*BB* 193, 200, 259, 277, 542; *PU* 239; *EB* 188).[174] Out of this abiding love, God calls and re-creates and sustains the metaxological community of being to be an agapeic community. Creation is given as good, yet is given with the promise (not the necessity) of freely entering into agapeic community with God and others. We humans are called forth into this community, called to realized the promise of agapeic community (*BB* 414; *EB* 218).[175] We freely fail, however, to answer this call, to realize this promise.

God's love, however, persists. God, in Desmond's understanding, is less an erotic sovereign compelling obeisance than an agapeic servant[176] who is compassionate, involved *with* our *sufferings* (*PU* 235–36; *EB* 371)[177]—who suggests a *com-passio essendi,* vulnerable, open, patient, in communication with our weakness (*HG* 137; En 150). This agapeic God acts with a "condescending" love, entering into the midst of the community of the beloved (*BB* 544; *EB* 207). Seeking to save us—to redeem defection from the good, to renew, to re-create "in place of de-creation" (*BB* 531; En 150)[178]—God, for only God can do it, acts to bear the burden of evil.[179] In the bearing of this burden, God offers yet another agapeic asymmetrical relation to human beings, that of forgiveness (*HG* 64–65). Thus a continuity is joined between agapeic creation and agapeic re-creation (En 150).[180] We cannot but be brought to think here of the incarnation, the suffering servant, the cross, resurrection, reconciliation.

God also works to sustain agapeic community. The agapeic service and community to which God calls us is not sustainable by our will alone but requires God's gracious, forgiving, re-creating, sustaining power.[181] Our agapeic service needs a willingness, a goodwill, a new will beyond self-will—it needs gracious help—a release to reverse the gravity its fall (*EB* 218).[182] Giving this help, God is our secret partner[183] who provides needed help in sustaining agapeic community (*EB* 217–19, 486). Religious community exists partially as recognizing its dependence upon God for the fulfillment of agapeic community and appealing to God for help.[184] Thus, with the sustaining power (grace) of the agapeic God, human community can become an agapeic community that is the finite image of, that hyperbolically points toward, God as agapeic origin and sustainer, creator and re-creator.[185]

### God in *God and the Between*

Desmond expands on the his portrayal of God as Agapeic Origin in *God and the Between* in terms of the "God Beyond the Between" (chapter 7) and the "God Beyond the Whole: The Theistic God of Creation" (chapter 12). Seeing the Agapeic Origin as the Creator of the world who transcends the world but is yet revealed in the immanence of the world in the hyperboles of being,[186] Desmond writes of the prior "reversed" movements corresponding to the hyperboles of being—the divine descent (originating being in its singularity, creation in its aesthetic glory, selves in their erotic and loving dynamism reaching out beyond ourselves, community in agapeic and metaxological intermediation) the prior to our responding ascent, assent (*GB* 164–65).

In chapter 12 of *God and the Between,* Desmond provides an extended meditation on the "hyperbolic" concept of creation and what it entails regarding God's character, the nature of the world as a "whole," the singularity of God in relation to singularities in creation, the affirmation of actuality, the nature of the intelligibility of the world, the contingent becoming of beings within the world, and the nature and existence of evil—all of this making manifest the profoundly intimate community (not dualism, not redundancy) between the between (the creation) and the Agapeic Origin of the between. The final chapter of *God and the Between* (chapter 14) is a *tour de force*: a hyperbolic re-imaging of the traditional "attributes" of God—through the lens of God as the excessive and Agapeic Origin of the metaxological community of being in "Ten Metaphysical Cantos." God is represented as being beyond being, as the one that exceeds oneness, as the eternal fullness that possibilizes time, as the incorruptible constancy of the divine agape, as the asymmetrical absolute that yet intermediates with creation, as the singular absolving absolute that communicates and lets beings be as singularities, as actual infinitude, as the power that gives power for the empowering and possibilizing beings in their freedom, as the being-true that knows more than the sum of all things, as the good beyond and before and after all known and imaginable determinable goods.

### Section IV: Metaxological Religion

### §1. Religion

In the context of Desmond's metaxological metaphysics that sees the world as a community of being given by the agapeic origin, "to be," he says, "is to be religious."[187] For Desmond, "religion" (against the common modern usage) is not a dimension, a discrete part, of life, but has to do with our dwelling in being as such—our being (T2) in relation to the origin and sustainer (T3) of the community of created being (T1, T2). The between, ethos of being, is a "secret commons" between creation and God (*EB* 506). The self that has (re)awakened to second astonishment is a "metaxologically open self" that has become initiated into "being religious"—to a celebration, a reverence, a sense of the sacred, the inherently good, in the between that hyperbolically refers beyond the between to its agapeic origin (*BB* 41–42).[188] There is, in the singular intimacy of the religiously awakened self,[189] a "porosity" (*HG* 10, 97)[190] to, an intimate communion with, the divine. This intimacy, this porosity is connected with our *passio essendi*—our "being given to be" that "signifies our disproportion to ourselves" by pointing us beyond ourselves to that which gave us to be (*BB* 415; *HG* 204).[191] In the depths of the singular idiotic self, there is a radical intimacy (*HG* 188–89), an "absolute" or religious community or "being-with" the ultimate (*EB* 500; *HG* 188).[192] Being religious has to do with this intermediation, this ultimate relationship between ourselves and God (*EB* 486; *HG* 9, 188).

In Desmond's work, being religious comes to expression in two principal ways: gratitude and generosity. Recognition of the gifts of the agapeic origin "solicits" in us the "hyperbolic life" of agapeic being (*PU* 232).[193] This agapeic religious being is "sabbatical"—seeing and celebrating the goodness of creation as the gift of the Creator.[194] This gratitude for the gratuitous and generous creation of the agapeic origin also inspires "a different 'return'" of the gift of creation in the co-creation of agapeic community with God and with others.[195] Being religious is being in community with God—responding to God's agapeic gift with gratitude (recognizing, celebrating and thanking for the gift) and generosity (becoming agapeic ourselves in giving to others in community).

## §2. Gratitude

Religion as our being in relation to God, as our response to the gift of God, entails our recognition and appreciation of God's gift and our becoming gift-giving ourselves. Religion involves the agapeic mind emergent in second astonishment—agapeic mind as gratitude—a thanking, a seeing the given as given, as a gift—as an agapeic giving to us (*BB* 193–94, 202, 506). It is closely connected with becoming an agapeic self—a self attending to otherness in two areas. First, the agapeic self attends in gratitude to the excess/otherness in which the self (and the world around it) is given to be by another, by a superior divine otherness (*BB* 406, 410). Second, the agapeic self attends in generosity to the human other in its willingness to be for the other, to give to the other (*BB* 414; *PU* 70).[196] In this section, we will focus on the first attending. Furthermore, in Desmond's understanding of religion—under what I am here describing with the more general category of "gratitude"—there seems to be a progressive (from indirect to direct) unfolding: from a breakdown of erotic mindfulness and a breakthrough to an awareness of genuine otherness, to a recognition of the goodness of being, to an affirming celebration of the goodness of being, to thanksgiving to God for the good gift of being, to worshipping and praising God as the Good, the origin, the superior.

Religion, for Desmond, as operating within second astonishment, involves a breakdown and a breakthrough—one might call it a conversion—within the self. This breakthrough is described as a gift, as a visitation for which we can prepare, as something that cannot be willed (BDD 760; CWSC 51). This religious breakthrough comes beyond the breakdown or failure of self-will (*PO* 254, 257–58, 296; *EB* 181)—its precondition is a reversal of self (such as in Desmond's second perplexity) (*PO* 211; *BB* 500–503). It comes to us as an expression of our *passio essendi*—our primal receptivity and intimacy with other. It is an exalting blessedness (in that one has been blessed, given a good gift, raised up) (*EB* 126)[197] that sustains and is sustained by a radical humility before the gift-giving Other (for the good I have, I am, I have received) (*BB* 221–22; CWSC 51).[198] The religious opening in the self is a breakthrough to appreciating (and so affirming, celebrating and trusting in) the gift of the origin—in short, to gratitude (*BB* 543; *PU* 252; CWSC 51). Opening beyond oneself, one may see the goodness of being in itself.

Being religious progresses in recognizing the goodness of creation beyond one's merely instrumental good. We meet being not as something neutral, neutered, but with reawakened (second) astonishment (*PO* 158; BR 225–26)—with a sense of reverence before the inherent or ontological worthiness or goodness of being "beyond instrumentalizing" (BR 215).[199] This reverence is connected with a reborn agapeic mind—a transformation of mindfulness, of vision (*PU* 162, 221; *EB* 492)[200] in which being is transfigured as saturated with goodness—the world comes to be seen as the "sacramental earth."[201] In this one comes to see creation more as God sees it, through sabbatical lenses as it were—one says, *imitatio dei*, "It is good" (*BB* 545; *HG* 140).

Beyond simply recognizing the goodness of being, the reverence of being opens onto a religious festivity—a "festive being" that celebrates of goodness of being (*PO* 260, 300). This celebration of being is agapeic, the agapeic festivity of agapeic mind (*BHD* 302; *PO* 300; *PU* 252, 258)—whose idiot wisdom affirms, consents to the goodness of being (*PO* 297, 303; *BB* 193; *EB* 479). This affirmation/consent entails a kind of trust in being (*PO* 127–28; *BB* 473, 455), a metaphysical faith "in a goodness not of one's making" (*EB* 377–78; *BB* 545). Being religious in celebration laughs (*BHD* 302, 342; *PO* 257–58)[202] before, and speaks to being as good and as gift, and says "Let it be,"—yielding to the goodness in unmastered otherness (*PO* 253)—"yes,"—affirming and welcoming and consenting to being in its plenitude as good (*BHD* 17, 302, 342; *PO* 253, 303; *BB* 194; *PU* 258)—"amen" (*BB* 42, 206).

The celebration of the gift naturally opens toward gratitude to the Giver. Being religious is, more deeply, gratitude to God as the generous origin of being, as the ground of good, for the goodness of being (*BHD* 95; *PU* 258; *CWSC* 51; *EB* 479). It seeks to "return goodness in the 'yes' to its origin" (*EB* 195)—to be a largess, a generous giving in the face of the gift (*BB* 193), a "being agapeic" toward the agapeic origin.[203] Seeing the goodness of being as a gift, we seek to thank the giver. Gratitude for the goodness of being ultimately makes no sense without God (*CWSC* 51). At the least, our ontological gratitude is a thanks that doesn't know who to thank.[204] Gratitude shows that true festivity, true celebration of the goodness of being, is impossible without the sacred (*EB* 479), for to thank is to grant an excessive asymmetry to the giver, to divine generosity.[205]

The festive gratitude for the goodness of being in being religious finds its fullest expression in worship.[206] Reverence, seeing the good in being as good, is first due to the origin of the good and being (*EB* 195). Worship is this reverence as a hyperbolic and liberating release (BR 216, 221)[207]—freeing us from ourselves and being propelled beyond ourselves—toward the superior other (*HG* 59). In worship, one transcends oneself and places oneself before the transcendent, the ultimate—such that one's pretense fades to praise of the other without demand, to communication without temptation to dominion.[208] In worship, one confesses that God alone is good, is supremely good, is the Good that is the source of the good (*EB* 197, 217). This doxological height of being religious joins together the absolute otherness of God with the absolute intimacy of the singular self.[209] This joining, this porosity, this community is nothing less than the intimate and hyperbolic communication of prayer—as the idiotic and elemental being-with God, an agapeic proximity with the transcendent yet condescending agapeic origin of the world and of the self so intimately bared (*BB* 460; EB 177; BR 213–14).[210]

Grateful worship joins together reverent appreciation, festivity, and thanksgiving in a celebration of "the ground of the world" in gratitude for the gift of being.[211] This holistic doxological being religious enacts and instantiates a solidarity, a participation between the human and the divine, between the profane and the sacred (*BHD* 101).[212] Worship is an agapeic feast—a festive celebration of and in the midst of community of being, of and in intimate communion with God—that looks around to the gift of being and looks up to the Giver, celebrating the former, thanking the latter for the former, praising the latter as the latter (*BHD* 98, 101; *EB* 512).[213] In genuine gratitude, one freely gives praise in "return" to God. Here we see the complex interweaving of gifts and gift-giving in religion: gratitude (as recognizing and celebrating God's gift) is itself a gift—God's gift begets a non-identical reciprocity of gratitude to God and generosity to others, building an agapeic gift-giving community in the midst of the agapeically given metaxological community of being, as we are sustained by the same community, by God's gift of and through the community. In being thus gratuitously giving, the worshiping community becomes a witness to and a finite image of its agapeic origin, of God's agapeic generosity (*EB* 452, 481, 491, 495).[214]

### §3. From Gratitude to Generosity

In Desmond's understanding of religiousness, gratitude to the divine Other gives rise to generosity toward the human other—to an agapeic community. Gratitude for the (agapeic) gift of being calls forth, commissions, (agapeic) generosity—"the gift of agapeic being solicits in us the gift of agapeic being" (*PU* 232; *BB* 414).[215] Gratitude—recognizing and celebrating that one has received the gifts of being and goodness within and without, thanking and praising the Giver, the agapeic origin—as if it cannot do justice to, cannot contain, the excessive gifts it receives, itself generates, gives forth, charges one with (*EB* 177, 220)[216] an ethics of generosity born of, springing from, incarnating gratitude.[217] The gift calls for repetition—for a different return.[218] It is as if the first commandment, to love (thank, praise) God (as the agapeic origin)—to enter into agapeic community with God—gives forth from its (gratuitous) excess and sustains the second commandment, to love the neighbor, to become an agapeic (serving even unto suffering) self opening toward (participating in, contributing to the creation of) agapeic community.[219] We love God by being agapeic to the other and so liken ourselves to the origin (*EB* 498).[220] Here the agape (the excessive gift) of the origin, recognized and celebrated in gratitude, breaks through the closure of the erotic self (*DDO* 19; *PO* 211; *BHD* 331, 333; *BB* 500; *PU* 214–15) and effects a reversal from lack to agape—issuing from a prior fullness and seeing the other as good (*DDO* 19, 164, 166–67).[221] This is the union of divine and ethical service (both agapeic communication)[222] where the latter arises from the former.[223]

Here, as gratitude become generosity (thanksgiving become giving), being religious involves agapeic being as ontological and regulative. In gratitude, we recognizing our ontologically agapeic being (as a gift, as generously given). Generosity is our active participation in being agapeic, our seeking to be true to the (regulative) agapeic promise of our given being (*BB* 338, 415; *PU* 157, 215; *EB* 162).[224] Seeing our being as a gift "given over" by (freely given from) the agapeic origin spurs us to "give ourselves up" (to freely give) towards the other.[225] This agapeic giving to the other can give rise to the community of agapeic service as arising, ultimately, then, from gratitude (as religious community) (*EB* 171, 220, 365, 507).[226] The human agapeic metaxological community is then grounded in the ultimate—as ontologically, so ethically (*BB* 263).

§4. Generosity

In religious gratitude, one becomes aware of and celebrates and thanks and praises the agapeic origin for its generosity—one affirms what God is like, one beholds God's agape. In religious generosity, one becomes what God is like—one becomes agapeic. From this perspective, religious gratitude involves a certain metaphysical speculation—a wonder before the excessive goodness of being becomes religious regard for God. Generosity is then the living—living ethically—in light of this regard. In religious gratitude one has a transfigured metaphysics; in religious generosity, a transfigured ethics. (However, it must be noted that this distinction/pairing should not be taken too strictly, for gratitude is already ethical, a right way of being before God, and generosity is always metaphysical, regarding the excessive metaxological community of being and its origin with agapeic mind.) In beholding the excess of the metaxological community of being, of agapeic creation, we revere, thank, praise the agapeic origin. This transfigured mindfulness, agapeic mind, calls us to agapeic being, to become agapeic selves, to make agapeic communities—to be agapeic after and with God.

Religious generosity, the being agapeic of being religious, begins with the agapeic mind in which beheld being is transfigured (*PU* 162, 221).[227] Agapeic mind, in consenting to seeing being and one's being as a gift of generosity, solicits generosity; it is the turning from grateful beholding to generous becoming.[228] Our all-too-common lack of agapeic mind, of agapeic generosity, our erotic selfishness, requires gratitude's awakening.[229] In agapeic mind, we are called beyond our self-enclosure to agapeic being,[230] called by an "immanent exigence"—something immanent within being and within us, its being an agapeic gift, that calls us from beyond, from on high. We are constrained by ultimacy as the agapeic origin of being and our being (*PO* 159).[231] This call of the good ultimately only makes sense in a religious register, by thinking the source of being, of the primal ethos,[232] for we ethically consider humans to have inherent value because they are part of, the crown of, an inherently valuable creation. God is the origin (original ground) of both this general and this more particular human being and value.[233]

Agapeic mind opens onto agapeic being—a transfigured being in the face of transfigured being. Agapeic being, as a more general orientation in one's being, is a generous giving out of one's excess givenness (*BHD* 267, 292, 296–97; *BB* 407; *PU* 125–26; CWSC 51). Agapeic mind become agapeic being is a genuine self-transcending toward the other, a being with the other that lets the other be as other (*PO* 253, 266, 274; En 150)—a giving beyond self, not seeking a return (*BB* 498; *PU* 177, 250; BR 227).[234] This agapeic being finds expression in service—in making oneself available to serve, to give to the other (*BB* 490; *PU* 256; *EB* 161, 356).

For one to actively incarnate this agapeic being is to participate in agapeic selving, to become an agapeic self. Agapeic selving as the highest selving is a selving beyond selving. It is beyond itself "vertically" as a religious selving, a becoming of a subject (subject to and) in community with God (*DDO* 174; *EB* 367, 377–78).[235] It is also beyond itself, is a being beyond oneself,[236] "horizontally"—decentered in willingness to be for other (*BB* 414; *PU* 70).[237] The agapeic self is commissioned, called beyond itself to service, to "giving itself" to the neighbor (*BB* 414; *EB* 498), and so likens itself to (imitates) the agapeic origin in its agapeic generosity.[238]

Being religious reaches its fullest expression in agapeic community—in what Desmond calls the religious community of agapeic service (*EB* 481, 483ff). This is a community of agapeic selves before God existing in mutual service, in true community. It is a community serving God and the neighbor (*EB* 509).[239] The religious community of agapeic service is the consummate community in that it presents the apotheosis of the bond of trust that exists in all true human community (the binding together, *re-ligare*) (*EB* 485, 510).[240] One could say that as human community as such is based on reaching beyond the self in trust and self-giving, so the religious community of agapeic service entails a comprehensive "reaching beyond": "down" to the roots of being as good (as trustworthy) and as gift, "up" to God as the agapeic origin and sustainer of being and human community, "in" to the self as an inherently (and excessively) valuable and freely given donation, "out" to the neighbor as likewise valued and worthy to be served. With God's sustaining aid,[241] the community of agapeic service participates in the work of God in community with God:[242] in likening itself to the agapeic origin in agapeic service (in giving sustaining aid)[243] and in becoming a finite witness to, image, or revelation of the agapeic origin in its loving generosity (*BB* 286).[244]

## Part Two: Metaxological Philosophy of God and Religion vs. Religion without Religion

Having summarized William Desmond's conception of God and religion, I now turn to examine how this conception provides a viable and preferable alternative to that represented in the work of John D. Caputo. Desmond's position can be seen as such an alternative based on three points. First, Desmond's position is a viable alternative in that it is able to *answer* Caputo's *critique* of metaphysics by showing that the understanding of God and religion represented in Desmond's work is not guilty of the errors that Caputo levels against metaphysical understandings of God and religion as such. Second, Desmond's position is a viable alternative in that it is able to genuinely *address* the motivating *concerns* that can seen to be inspiring Caputo's treatment of God and religion. Third, Desmond's position is an arguably preferable alternative inasmuch as it narrates/locates, "out-narrates," Caputo's position—showing Desmond's as possessing a broader and greater explanatory reach. Along these lines, Desmond's position can be shown to possess the possibility of fulfilling Caputo's own motivating concerns better than Caputo's own vision.

### Section I: Desmond as Answering Caputo's Critique of Religion

Desmond's vision is a *viable* alternative to Caputo's in that it answers Caputo's critiques of religion and God-talk, showing that his critiques need not be the case. Here Desmond shows how a conception of God and religion informed by metaphysics *escapes* Caputo's narration/location of "metaphysical" conceptions of God and religion, as such. Desmond's position answers Caputo's critiques and thus is a possible, viable position on Caputo's terms.

### §1. Elevating the Knowledge of God to an Absolute Level

Caputo critiques traditional metaphysical understandings of God and religion as promoting an absolutely stable onto-theo-logical framework in which God is a highest being and first cause that functions to guarantee or stabilize such a stabilizing framework. These onto-theo-logical frameworks, however, are never more absolute than their finite makers—are always thus "deconstructible" (*Rel* 2; *OR* 113). Metaphysical religion makes absolute pronouncements about God, but these are never more than contingent human artifacts; it confuses the infinite transcendence of God with human religion, elevating the latter to the status of the former (*MRH* 255; *OR* 93–94). Such religious systems present themselves as attaining a rigorous and certain status that is, in fact, beyond human capacities—they are falsely absolute.[245]

Desmond's metaxological metaphysical conception of God and religion can be seen to answer this critique in several ways. His metaphysical meditations on God and religion have to do with what are, for him, irreducible perplexities— that which lies at the limits and extremities of thought (*PO* 242; *BHD* 42–43, 81–82, 243; *AOO* 4). It explicitly guards against ascribing the absolute to the finite (*BHD* 81–82, 136). When it comes to God, we have no direct access. From our intermediate position, God cannot be determined directly, for we cannot be on a par conceptually with a God that no name or image can fully capture (*PO* 134–36, 157; *EB* 79; *HG* 8). We always speak of God "from the middle" (*DDO* 181); thus, speech about God must be an indirect attempt to name an overdetermined plenitude (*BB* 502). The best names for God are not absolute (utterly univocal determinations) but are metaphysical metaphors, indirections that name their failure to be The Name (*PO* 135–36; *PU* 210), that carry with them an affirmative equivocity—the ambiguity and paradox (signifying such a saying's ultimate failure to univocally identify, "pin down," ultimate transcendence) that obtains when one comes to think transcendence, to think that which is beyond thought (*BB* 217–19; *HG* 69, 127). Such sayings of perplexity do not elevate themselves to a falsely absolute level, preserving reference to God as that which is beyond our ken, so respecting the enigma of the ultimate (*BB* 209; *PU* 209).

## §2. God of the Same

Caputo critiques metaphysical understandings of God and religion as fixated on universality and static unity. This happens at the expense of canceling out a proper regard for the singular, the fluid, the different. This kind of theological system presents God as an ultimate static unity—as a "God of the same"—that is subordinated to Greek ontology (HKFM 223; *PT* 113, 336).

Such a critique misses with regard to Desmond's metaxological metaphysical conception of God and religion. Central to Desmond's conception of God as agapeic origin is the manner in which such a God gives rise to a genuine plurality (*HG* 138). God as agapeic origin is the source of the metaxological community of being (*DDO* 242; *PO* 8, 113; *BB* 263; *PU* 137, 212, 234, 238) as a community of difference, plurality, and singularity (*DDO* 242; *PU* 238; *EB* 502; *HG* 70; *AOO* 293).[246] The plurality of the created world is composed of singulars—finite beings are not only other to God but other to each other (*BB* 184–87, 193, 263, 330, 496; *PU* 48, 100, 239–41; *EB* 164, 502; *HG* 136).[247] God, for Desmond, functions as first the ground of plurality and singularity—of the different—before the Same.

In Desmond's metaphysical understanding, God is no static unity. This is what he explicitly rejects in his own critique of the univocal God. The univocal God—which has been, as Desmond recognizes, pervasive in the western philosophical tradition (*DDO* 89–90; *PU* 171)—is a static, univocal eternity that entails an objectifying of God that is also an absolutization of univocity (*BB* 96; *PU* 110), an instrumentalization of God, a mere univocal explanation.[248] This univocal God ends up being self-frustrating, is equivocal inasmuch as it is a transcendence without relation; it cannot act in relation to the world; it cannot have originated the world; and it cannot be the ground of that to which it is antithetical (*DDO* 96–99; *EB* 25). Desmond's metaxological metaphysical conception of God as an intimate stranger, who utterly transcends us and whose indeterminate signs and traces utterly surround and indwell us, is explicitly other to such a God of the Same.

## §3. A Falsely Stable Foundation

For Caputo, metaphysical religion functions to give life a false stability. It makes light of and thus undercuts the difficulty of a properly religious faith. It seeks a "heavenly hook" to "bail us out and lift us above the flux of undecidability" (*MRH* 193; *PT* 334). Metaphysical religion and the metaphysical God make light of the radically finite situation of human life in the midst of the flux.

Desmond's metaxological metaphysical conception of God and religion escapes this characterization and critique. For Desmond, God cannot be determined directly and is to us an enigma to which we have no direct access and is only thought indirectly, with a degree of irreducible ambiguity (*DDO* 206; *PO* 136; *EB* 79; *HG* 8). Our perplexity is deepened, not quelled, by the hyperbolic thought of God. Thus, if one is to talk of transcendence, one must live with the risk of equivocity (GEW 22),[249] for such talk is necessarily representational and indirect (*PO* 111, 136). The thought of the infinite God is not an escape from finitude but a transformed mindfulness of finitude, an affirmation of the finite as good in all its heteromorphic plurality and singularity. Our religious dwelling with this God, far from making things easy, begins with a breakdown, a failure, a reversal of our attempts to control life, to subject it to our rational power for our manipulation and ease (*PO* 211, 254, 257–58, 296; *BB* 500–503; *EB* 181).

### Section II: Desmond as Addressing Caputo's Motivating Concerns

Behind Caputo's critique of religion and his more positive alternative to (metaphysical) religion and God-talk can be seen certain motivating concerns. First, Caputo wants to avoid elevating the knowledge of God to a falsely absolute status—he wants thought about God (and in general) to be properly humble. Second, Caputo wants to avoid supplanting a properly religious faith. Behind both of these concerns is a desire to avoid being dependent upon a faithless metaphysics—a metaphysics that is an abstract speculation that oversteps the boundaries of human thinking and distracts one from genuine religious existence.

Desmond's work can be seen to address Caputo's concern to avoid elevating the knowledge of God to a falsely absolute status. As stated above, Desmond's version of metaphysical speculation about God entails meditating on irreducible perplexities and enigmas—a speaking from the middle of that to which we have no direct access. This chastened metaphysical thought, all too aware of its lack of absoluteness in its thought of the absolute, embodies a necessity that our speech about God who is qualitatively inexhaustible excess (*BB* 19, 182, 208, 255) be indirect, metaphorical (*BB* 502). Such a metaxological understanding of God is a saying of perplexity that refers to divine otherness while respecting the enigma of the ultimate (*BB* 209; *PU* 209). It guards the threshold of transcendence, consciously and cautiously maintaining a space between the image and God who remains other to our thinking about God (*BB* 219; *PU* 189; *HG* 8).[250] If anything, a robust denial of the possibility of knowledge of God would be a (falsely absolute) grasp beyond one's reach.

Desmond's work can also be seen to address Caputo's concern to avoid supplanting a properly religious faith. For Caputo, metaphysical religion exchanges religious life in all of its difficulty (embodied in a passionate love of God embodied in the love of the other) for a fixation on abstract and certain propositions so as to give life a stable foundation. Generally, Desmond's metaxological speculative philosophy is a mindfulness of what is at work in the middle, the midst of our existence (*PO* 11, 18; *PU* 22; *AOO* 4)[251]—in particular, of the hyperboles of being as happenings in finite being that point beyond themselves (*HG* 138). It is from this perspective that Desmond sees a metaxological metaphysics as contributing positively to genuine religious faith and thought about God. Desmond's metaphysics arises from a seeking to be faithful to life—a seeking to get beyond the modern deracinated ethos that has come to cut off mindfulness from the deeper, overdeterminate resources of the primal ethos, or the between (*PO* 228; *EB* 44–45; GEW 23; MC 9). The relation between philosophy, or metaphysics in particular, and religion need not be one of the former's domination and contamination of the latter. Indeed, if one understands religious belief—inasmuch as religious belief always has some kind of content—in anything short of an anti-intellectual frame, some kind of (even minimal) thoughtful reflection seems to be necessary and beneficial. In this kind of posture, philosophy, for Desmond, can refer beyond itself, give way, yield to religion—such that his primary configuration of the relation between philosophy and religion is that of philosophy's coming to show an opening, a porosity to divine transcendence (*BDD* 766–67). Metaphysical philosophy finds its fulfillment in being called, from within itself, beyond itself (*HG* 76, 191). For Desmond, metaphysics actually contributes to a properly religious life—a life of gratitude and generosity toward God and one's neighbor. The difference between Caputo's and Desmond's conceptions of God and religion can largely be traced back to their respective understandings of metaphysics.

### Section III: Desmond as Providing an Alternative to Caputo's "Religion Without Religion"

In addition to answering Caputo's critiques of religion and addressing his motivating concerns, Desmond provides a metaphysical alternative to Caputo's alternative to metaphysical religion. Desmond's metaphysical understanding of religion and God is not only a viable alternative to Caputo's "religion without religion" but is preferable inasmuch it can locate and critique, can "out-narrate," Caputo's position in a broader vision.

#### §1. Denial of Knowledge of God

Caputo's post-metaphysical "religion without religion" begins with the death of the God of metaphysics—of onto-theo-logy—the God that is tailored to fit knowledge (*RH* 271; *Rel* 2; *MRH* 174). Such religion is a "religion without religion" that can live with or without any particular or determinate claims to religious knowledge (*OR* 3). Caputo ultimately denies the possibility of metaphysical knowledge of the absolute or God and rejects it as a mask for absolute knowledge.

Desmond is likewise critical of such an onto-theological instrumental understanding of God, while maintaining some kind of knowledge or understanding of God that is not reducible to onto-theology. His understanding is concerned with guarding against counterfeit doubles, dead gods amounting to little other than the human will to power that projects them (*BHD* 104; *HG* 2, 9). The univocal understanding of God as static, univocal eternity—absolute in its immutability and stasis beyond time and becoming—has been, as Desmond recognizes, pervasive in the western philosophical tradition (*DDO* 89–90; *PU* 171). This conception of God as a static eternity—as a means of securing ourselves in the world, as a self-projection of our power (*PU* 171; PR 109; *EB* 44)—self-destructs in that it ultimately serves to make God redundant (*DDO* 99; *PU* 170; *EB* 24). Such a God is unavailable for any relationship with the world or humans—for God is defined only negatively, in opposition to the world (*DDO* 99; *BB* 240). God as static eternity does not serve the intended use of securing the world, for such an entity, by definition, cannot originate or ground the entities in the world of becoming to which it stands in opposition. However, this univocal-become-equivocal metaphysical understanding is not the only game in town for Desmond. His metaxological understanding of God makes robust claims to knowledge about God—as agapeic origin, as the origin and creator of the world that is transcendent to the becoming of the world (*BB* 447; *PU* 187; *AOO* 6), as a singular, "first" and "primal" giver (*BB* 506; *EB* 202, 505; *HG* 136; *AOO* 6)—without aspiring to absolute knowledge.

For Desmond, God (as mentioned above) cannot be determined directly, univocally. When it comes to God, we must speak indirectly. No finite determinate (univocal, intending to be direct) category will do, for the original that is to be imaged is at the boundary of human understanding (*PU* 207). We must speak indirectly, but speak we must. There is an inevitable risk in naming God, for we need images and names to speak of God at all, while understanding that all names/images fall short of univocally determining the transcendent other to which they refer (*PO* 113, 133–35; *HG* 8). Metaphors are such intermediating names beyond univocal determination—concrete sayings of perplexity that preserve reference to a beyond, to an otherness, and that respect the enigma of the ultimate (*BB* 209; *PU* 209). More specifically, Desmond sees his naming of God in terms of hyperbole. Such is a thought that, in its attending to certain phenomena, has an immanent exigency that propels one to the thought of the transcendent—it is something in experience, something disproportionate or asymmetrical to finitude in the midst of finitude, that suggests something beyond experience, a transcendence (*HT* 30; BR 227).

Desmond's claims to knowledge about God arise from these happenings in our experience—from the hyperboles of being. These are, for Desmond, indirect signs of God in our midst, in the between. His hyperboles of external being (encounters with external transcendence as suggesting or intimating a transcendent ground or origin—the world's ultimate ground in an origin) (*DDO* 152; *BB* 207, 506; *PU* 205; *HG* 7) are *the givenness of being*, of the world's being given to be at all, that there is something rather than nothing (*DDO* 184–85; *BB* 8, 9, 473; NDR 39; PR 112; *EB* 51; HT 35; *HG* 203);[252] *the plural community of being* as a plenitude (*BB* 264, 514), as a genuine plurality (*PU* 238)[253] that intimates a particular kind of ground and origin; *the intelligibility of the world* as orderly, ordered, as exhibiting design as a sign that suggests an origin that is the ground of our epistemological trust (*PO* 228–29; *BB* 359, 514; *PU* 225, 246);[254] and *the goodness of being,* the ethos of being as charged (if indeterminately) with value—as bearing an inherent or intrinsic worth (*BB* 227, 510; *PU* 5, 225, 228; *EB* 23, 75–76, 177, 219–20; *AOO* 292).[255] Beyond the external signs of God in our midst, Desmond identifies certain hyperboles of internal being such as *the infinite value of the idiotic self* (*PO* 143);[256] desire's *urgency of ultimacy,* an absolute, infinite restlessness and desire in our finite being for the absolute or the ultimate that is not satisfied by any finite good (*BHD* 44; *BB* 155, 182; *PU* 11; *EB* 74, 209, 215, 324);[257] desire's *porosity or the passio essendi,* as a deep openness, an intimate communion with God in the interior depths of the self (*AOO* 292);[258] and *the call of the good,* the call into agapeic being, selving and community refers one to a ground of the good—a good beyond finite goods (*EB* 20, 93, 200, 493, 502–503).

### §2. Religion as the Passion for the Impossible as a Structure of Experience

Caputo sees religion as a passion for the impossible that constitutes a (if not the) structure of experience. As a passion for the impossible, this religious passion looks for the new, the unexpected (*PT* xxiv, 202; *MRH* 258; *OR* 9, 11). This structure of experience is the "religious side" of everyone (*OR* 11). Caputo sees this passion for the impossible as the love of God—"God" that is the impossible we passionately desire—which is religion (*OR* 1, 113; *PT* 332; *MRH* 258, 263). The passion of life is interchangeable with love of God.

For Desmond, passion as a structure of experience and religion are closely connected as well. Human being, for Desmond, possesses an infinite desire in the midst of finite being. It is a self-surpassing toward transcendence (*BB* 155, 208, 231; *EB* 215; *AOO* 268.)—a hyperbolic vector of transcendence (*BB* 378; *PU* 182)—an "urgency of ultimacy"—an infinite restlessness for the absolute or the ultimate (*BHD* 44; *BB* 155, 182; *EB* 74, 324).[259] This impossible passion (actually finite but intentionally infinite) (*DDO* 152; *HG* 3, 7; *AOO* 6, 269, 288) suggests a more radical, disproportionate sense of the infinite, an "actual infinitude" in excess of its own infinity (*DDO* 152; *HG* 3, 7; *AOO* 6, 269, 288). For Desmond, there is also a *passio essendi* in human self-transcendence prior to the *conatus essendi* (the urgency of ultimacy) (*HG* 97, 130, 203–204; *AOO* 288, 291). This *passio essendi* is a porosity more basic to desire—an openness, a given opening to the other (*BB* 5; *PU* 11; *EB* 217).[260] This intimacy, this porosity—our "being given to be"—"signifies our disproportion to ourselves" by pointing us beyond ourselves to that which gave us to be (*BB* 415, *HG* 204).[261] It is an intimate always-already-being-in-communion with God in the depths of the self—a more passive passion, something given, opened prior to our striving (*AOO* 292).[262]

There is, however, a critical difference between Caputo and Desmond (we will return to this again below). There is a difference between saying that x *is* y—that "God" is the impossible part of our impossible passion, the infinity of our desire—and that x leads to, or entails y (goes beyond itself toward something other). "God" is not merely the impossible that we desire, keeping the focus on the present passion of our experience. "God," for Desmond, is the other to which the impossible (in/finite) passion of human being points, refers, is thrown. "God," for Desmond, is not a hyperbolic way of speaking of our excessive desire (the new, the impossible of experience)—fully reducible to a generic placeholder for the otherwise indifferent object for our uncannily infinite desire. For Desmond, such experience and desire is itself what is hyperbolic. Such a hyperbole throws beyond itself; it moves from experience to something beyond experience, from our being between toward the "being above" of transcendence (*BB* 218, 222, 256).[263] It is an exigency that cannot remain fixated on the experience, the happening itself. Such happenings, "hyperboles of being," refer beyond themselves toward ultimacy (*PR* 113-15; *HG* 7, 138, 187-88). The impossible infinity of human desire and passion is a sign, not of itself, but of another.[264]

### §3. Heterology

#### HETERONOMISM: *TOUT AUTRE*

The God of Caputo's religion without religion is the "God of the other" (*AE* 59; *PT* 5, 113). This God is the "the impossible," "the coming (*l'invention*) of the other" (*PT* 71-76). Thus, true religion for Caputo is closely related to relation to the other in general. In fact, religion is structurally identical to obligation—obligation to a singularity that is higher than the universal (*AE* 19). Religion is the absolute bond (*ligare*) with the Absolute (*AE* 18).[265] In obligation and religion, one is subject to a call, an unconditional solicitation. The relation that is obligation—that we have with every singular, human "other"—is identical with the relation that is religion—that we have with a singular, "absolute," wholly "Other."[266] Every other is wholly other, such that the name of God is a "place holder" for the other.[267] Religion and God are thus hyperboles of obligation, of ethics—religion is a *hyperbolic* way of speaking of obligation, of one's "hypersensitivity" to the demands of the other (GNA 466).

For Desmond too, there is a close connection between religion and ethics—between one's relation to God and one's relation to others. Desmond likewise meditates upon the experience of the call of the good into agapeic community, of a being commissioned, a being constrained by ultimacy in relation to the other (*PO* 159; *BB* 414). Desmond thinks of the ethical call of the good as referring one to a ground of the good—a *huperagathos* that must be disproportionate in order to be proportionate to the exorbitant good we experience in the between (*EB* 20, 93, 200, 493, 502-503). Desmond also defends God's otherness, God's genuine transcendence—"vertical," superior transcendence—an absolutely superior otherness (*BB* 201, 256-57; *HG* 3, 59) that has an essentially asymmetrical and disproportionate relationship with humans and the world

(*BHD* 182; *HG* 49, 59). This divine transcendence is to be guarded over against potential counterfeits (*PU* 189; *HG* 9).

However, again, the religious for Desmond is not simply reduced to another phenomenon (desire above, here obligation). Religion is not mere hyperbole—an exalted way of speaking about something else (*DDO* 151; *BB* 408, 448). Obligation or ethics in Desmond's vision, instead finds itself beyond itself, on a trajectory toward an infinite other—obligation points to something more than obligation. The call of the good, as Desmond's version of obligation, calls us beyond ourselves. In Desmond's hyperbole, again, one is propelled from experience to something beyond experience (*BB* 218, 222, 256).[268] Desmond's idea of the hyperbolic is a kind of reversal of Caputo's talk of the ultimate as but "hyperbolic" (as exaggerated, figurative, "unreal") talk about a concrete finite experience or reality, here human obligation—rather, our understanding of the concrete finite realities impels or propels ("gives rise to") our thinking toward something more than the finite that is not sufficient unto itself.

In Desmond's conception of religion in which the religious and the ethical are connected but not identified, related but not the same, the love of God gives forth from its (gratuitous) excess and sustains the love of the neighbor.[269] We love God by being agapeic to the other and so liken ourselves to the origin (*EB* 498).[270] The general shape of the relation between religious regard for God and ethical regard for the human other is that of the latter arising from the former, be it explicitly or implicitly.[271] For Desmond, love or generosity arises out of, is solicited, called forth by, gratitude for the agapeic gift of being (*PU* 232; *BB* 414; *EB* 220). Our being called to love the other—to obligation—only makes sense, for Desmond, in a religious register, for it calls us to regard humans with an inherent value (*PO* 159; *GEW* 27). Whence this value? Ethical obligation, treating one's neighbor as a being of inherent value, only makes sense by thinking the source of such value in an agapeic origin.[272]

### Heteromorphism: Undecidability and Affirmation

The heteromorphism involved in Caputo's post-metaphysical understanding of religion has to do with the fundamental, constitutive undecidability attendant to religious belief (*RH* 281; *MRH* 200, 210; *PT* 57–61). Religious faith is undecidable inasmuch as it is co-constituted with, must include, the anti-religious tragic sense that sees a persistent abyss, an anonymous nothing behind life—that sees life and its suffering as an innocent and meaningless becoming (*OR* 120, 124; *AE* 245; *RH* 282, 288; *GA* 16). The tragic view, in which flux rules all, cannot be excluded or silenced—there is undecidability between it and the religious view (*RH* 269, MMD 28–29). Caputo's religious obligation to the other is thus but a construal on the face of the abyss (*OR* 118; *AE* 244–45). The meaningless nothing of the tragic sense cannot be excluded; it is always a valid reading of the phenomena. Inhabited by this fundamental undecidability, religion without religion will always be other to knowledge.

For Desmond, a valueless, anonymous nothing is not taken for granted as a given. Such a nihilistic vision, which must always remain an interpretive option for Caputo, is rather, for Desmond, the product of the modern milieu of instrumental mind come to self-consciousness in Nietzsche. Modern instrumental mind is manifest in the twofold process of the *objectification of being*—yielding the "degraded" or "deracinated" world as a valueless, inherently worthless, thereness (*PO* 158, 366; *BB* 71; AT 235–37; NDR 46; BR 227; *EB* 46, 99; *HG* 21–22)—and the *subjectification of value*—the "revaluation" of value in terms of human self-determination and a projection of value onto the world so as to make what is "there" valued as useful—an instrument—to the self.[273] Desmond recognizes with Caputo that this modern nihilistic vision is severely problematic to religion such that he writes of a modern "allergy to transcendence" (*HG* 4; *AOO* 271–72) in which the world is stripped of signs and traces of the divine (PR 108; GEW 16).[274] But this, however, is not the end of the story. The goodness of being is, for Desmond, fundamentally evident in our experience of the world—it is the very opening of thought in astonishment. Likewise, in Desmond's understanding of God and religion, the thought of God arises from one's experience of the "hyperboles" of external and internal being—it is not reducible to a mere projection (whether of the becoming of the world or of the human self) (*BB* 231–32, 256–57; *PU* 230; *HG* 3–4, 200; *AOO* 6).

Desmond, in fact, proposes or affirms another nothing—another cosmic nothingness. As created from nothing, the created universe is "shadowed" by the nothingness (*nihilo*) from which (*ex*) it was made (*creatio*)—nothingness is ontologically constitutive of finite creation (*BB* 269; *HG* 129–30).[275] However, this nothing does not stand in a tension of undecidability with the religious view. It makes sense in the religious narrative. The between of the religious view (for Desmond) is not the undecidable and disjunctive between of faith/nihilism but the affirmative, metaphysical between of the community of being suspended between God as agapeic origin (as the origin and sustainer of being) and nothingness.

Likewise, Desmond offers another religious heteromorphism—one not so much an undecidability as a fundamental affirmation of the community of created being as plural, singular, and good. The agapeic origin is the source of genuine difference and plurality (*DDO* 242; *PU* 238; *EB* 502; *HG* 70)[276]—of a true community of plurality made up of unique (idiotic) singularities in communicative relation to one another (*BB* 330; *PU* 48; HT 40). This affirmation of the plural community of being as good is other to any thought of being as a meaningless or anonymous abyss. Thinking the ground of the good in the agapeic origin can provide a way out of the nihilism of instrumental mind (*BB* 71, 359). Against any basic undecidability, Desmond's religion beholds the goodness of being and affirms it. (This affirmation, indeed *any* affirmation, trumps undecidability. An affirmation in the face of risk, uncertainty, even a fundamental undecidability is no longer undecidable. The affirmation is a decision—"being is good," "God is real," "God loves us": these may be false, but they are not undecidable for one who has affirmed them. Confession and undecidability are mutually exclusive.) Being religious recognizes the goodness of creation beyond one's merely instrumental good. Religion is a "festive being" that celebrates of goodness of being (*PO* 260, 300). In religion, God is affirmed and thanked and praised as the ground of value—the origin of goodness in being (*PU* 227). It is a gratitude for the gift of being that makes no sense without God (CWSC 51). Religious worship, as with all being religious for Desmond, is not undecided; one confesses that God is the Good that is the source of the good (*EB* 197, 217).

It must be said that, beyond these differences, there are some *striking* similarities between Desmond's religious gratitude and Caputo's Nietzschean heteromorphic affirmation of play of the world. In his more recent work, Caputo affirms "the sovereign beauty of the world and the sovereign joy of life" (*WoG* 92), echoing his earlier exuberant "Dionysiac" celebrating alteration and the many (*AE* 42–43, 59). Religion is where our "yes," our affirmation of the goodness of being, meets and echoes God's "yes," God's original benediction (*WoG* 67, 89). This faith "in existence itself" affirms the goodness of being—that "life glows with the 'good' " (*PhTh* 72; *ADG* 49). Such is a Dionysian *Gelassenheit*—a "letting be" of the play of things (*RH* 258–59, 264; *AE* 41, 121)—that lets "many flowers bloom" (*OR* 62; *RH* 254–55, 260, 288; *AE* 39).

One might even say that Desmond's vision of religious gratitude incorporates and affirms Nietzschean yea-saying and affirmation of the world— perhaps Desmond sees the religious piety within the Dionysian festivity. The Nietzschean "yes" to the world is not, for Desmond, opposed to a religious vision; in fact, Desmond would see the religious understanding of the world as the proper home of the Nietzschean "yes"—a "yes" to the world that unfolds as gratitude to the origin. The good origin does not evacuate the world of its goodness; such would be a dualistic (equivocal) eternity or an erotic (dialectical) origin. The goodness and beauty of the world is so great, greater than its finite being can contain on its own, that we are made to think hyperbolically, thrown beyond ourselves and the wonderful world, of a deeper and higher good beyond the world, perhaps beyond being. We are brought to the thought (celebrating, thanking, praising) of the agapeic origin.

### §4. "God"/"Love"

For Caputo, there is also an undecidability between God and love. They are subject to an endless substitutability/translatability (*PT* 52; *OR* 126)[277] such that one cannot know whether "love" is a way of telling us something about God or if "God" is a way of telling us something about love (*OR* 6, 25, 134). Caputo concludes that "God" is less a name of a who or a what than a "how"— whose force is more pragmatic than semantic (*OR* 115, 135, 141; PMDG 304). Ultimately, it does not matter what, God or love, exemplifies what—only loving action matters (*PT* 338). It does not matter if a properly religious faith is "religious" (talking about God) or not, as long as it is loving (*OR* 114; GA 17–18).

One can "be deeply and abidingly 'religious' with or without theology, with or without the religions" (*OR* 3). Any kind of knowledge of God is thus insignificant for religion—it (religion) can do without it (knowledge). The undecidability between God/love is thus meant (by what? whom?) to elicit deeds. As religion is reducible to obligation without remainder, so "God" is reducible to love without remainder.

For Desmond, the "religious" and the ethical are connected but not identified. There is a kind of union of divine and ethical service where the latter arises from the former (*EB* 505). God, for Desmond, is fundamentally loving, is the agapeic origin. God loves being all the way down to the unique and irreducible singularity of created being.[278] God's love is persistent and compassionate—condescending and in communication with our sufferings, our weakness (*BB* 544; *PU* 235–36; *EB* 207, 371; *HG* 137; *En* 150). We love God by being agapeic to the other and so liken ourselves to the origin (*EB* 165, 286, 498, 507).[279] This likening is not a simple identification but a complex relation. Our loving, our being agapeic is a finite witness to, an imitation, image, or revelation of the agapeic origin in its loving generosity. Love, agapeic selving—a giving beyond self, not seeking a return (*BB* 498; *PU* 177, 250; *BR* 227) that finds its expression in service (*BB* 490; *PU* 256; *EB* 161, 356)—is for Desmond the highest selving, a selving beyond selving. For Desmond, *re-ligare* and *obligare* are not interchangeable (the former disappearing into the latter), but both are present together (the latter issuing from the former) in the religious community of agapeic service—the consummate community that presents the apotheosis of the bond of trust that exists in all true human community (*EB* 485, 510).[280]

Here as elsewhere, the central difference between Desmond and Caputo has to do with the place or status of metaphysics. Caputo's religion without religion is a religion without metaphysics that need amount to anything other than ethics, thus it naturally follows that any talk about a supreme being or object of religious devotion, God, would shift into the supreme ethical value, love. Religion "without religion," without metaphysics, is a religion of love with (inasmuch as largely identified with love itself) or without (as metaphysical) God. In Desmond's work, however, a metaphysical discourse about God (as superior transcendence and agapeic origin) is maintained. When Desmond speaks of God, he is speaking of something other than something we "do." What's more, and quite contrary to Caputo, Desmond sees the metaphysical dimension of religion as positively contributing to its ethical dimension. Agapeic generosity is our active participation in our gratefully acknowledged ontologically agapeic being and our seeking to be true to the (regulative) agapeic promise of our given being (*BB* 338, 415; *PU* 157, 215; *EB* 162).[281] Generosity is the ethical living in light of what one beholds and affirms in gratitude. In religious gratitude one has a transfigured metaphysics; in religious generosity arising from gratitude, a transfigured ethics arising from transfigured metaphysics. Love does not arise out of nothing. Even as lovers, we do not create *ex nihilo*. To be honest to love, we must think its whence—out of the excess goodness of being given agapeically (thus our ontologically agapeic being) by the agapeic origin (*BHD* 267, 292, 296–97; *BB* 407; *PU* 125–26; CWSC 51).

The place of gratitude is telling. An explicit understanding of gratitude is largely lacking in Caputo's work, for God as giver is deemed unnecessary—for what would one be thankful? One is to give to the other in obligation, but has one received a gift? No gift, no Giver. For Desmond, however, religion as our being in relation to God is our response to the gift of God, and entails our recognition and appreciation of God's gift and our becoming gift-giving ourselves. This seeing being as gift, and thanksgiving for it as such, makes no sense without God (CWSC 51).[282] Gratitude shows that true (Dionysian?) festivity, true celebration of the goodness of being, is impossible without the sacred (*EB* 479), for to thank is to grant an excessive asymmetry to the Giver, to divine generosity.[283]

For Caputo's religion without religion, all that matters is that one loves the other. Yet, in Caputo's schema, how can the other (every other) come to us as if from on high demanding *ob-ligare, re-ligare*? Is not, must not, this recognition of inherent worth and goodness happen within a broader ethos of a broader story about the goodness of being as such? Does the restricted ethos that will say nothing of being cut one off from the deeper resources that fund and enliven and nurture our obligation to the other? (Can the LeviNietzschean be surprised when one sees the other as inherently worthless, as worthless as anything and everything? Does one's surprise and shock and disgust at cruelty, far from confirming one's nihilistic vision, demand something more than such a vision has to offer?) Beyond this, Desmond recognizes that an infinite worth other than human is needed to make sense of, to give one reason to believe in, the singular infinite worth of the human individual (*EB* 188–90).[284] Beyond bare obligation, Desmond sees creation itself, the giving of being to be as other and for itself, as a gift (*PU* 133, 144, 196, 216–17; *EB* 505)—a true gift of love, demanding nothing in return (*PU* 221, 231–32). We are empowered, inspired to give by the great gifts of God. Metaphysics is central to this empowering. Only with metaphysics can one say: "This is good," "This is a gift," "God is the Giver." Gratitude says what and whence. There is no non-metaphysical gratitude. And if we are not grateful, how can we love? How can we give without first receiving a gift? How would we know what love is?

We need help to love. We are helped to love. There is no place for this for the LeviNietzschean—the brave lover making otherwise valueless evaluations of the other on the face of the abyss. But is s/he loving? If so, how? Caputo's vision, in the end, is neither dark enough (why do we so lack love?) nor light enough (does love not surround us?). For Desmond, God's giving not only shows us what love is but funds and encourages our own generosity. It is difficult for us to think love, the gift, agape—it is foreign to our erotic, selfish thoughts (*BB* 410, 542; *PU* 195).[285] We need God's help to be agapeic. In Desmond's vision, God works to sustain agapeic community with God's gracious, forgiving, re-creating, sustaining power.[286] God is our secret partner in loving the other, in creating agapeic community.[287] Gratitude recognizes our dependence and God's excessive gift. Beyond the impossible agonistics of Caputo's religious vision—of ethics versus metaphysics, of love versus God, of generosity without gratitude—is the metaxological community of Desmond's vision—a religion that is gratitude and generosity, God and love, metaphysical and ethical and more.

# Conclusion: Divine Hyperbolics, Two Visions, Four Errors

I see in the representative positions of Desmond and Caputo two "postmodern" ways of thinking about religion. These two ways diverge fundamentally and severely on the question of the proper relation between religion and metaphysics. They also represent, in the end, two different understandings of the "hyperbolics" involved in religion. My contention throughout has been that Desmond's positively metaphysical vision of religious belief is a viable—and, indeed, preferable—alternative to Caputo's deconstructed, "post-metaphysical" vision of religion.

## Summary

On the way to seeing Desmond's alternative to Caputo's vision of religion, I have presented his distinctive understanding of metaphysics. Desmond's metaxological metaphysics is an account of (or an accounting by way of) the *metaxu*—the between, the middle, the intermediate—an "interpretive fidelity" to the emergent happenings in finitude that is open to signs of the beyond in its midst. Situated between the totalizing closure of rigid univocal thinking and the fragmented discontinuity of equivocal thinking, metaxological metaphysics works from the basis of a vision of being as a community, as a genuine plurality of irreducible singularities in interplay.

For Desmond, the best attempts to speak of God metaphysically are likewise metaxological. Speaking from the middle, from our intermediate position, we find that we must speak of God indirectly. More specifically, Desmond sees this naming of God in terms of hyperbole. Desmond's hyperbole is a thought that, as attending to certain phenomena, has an immanent exigency that propels one toward the thought of the transcendent—something disproportionate or asymmetrical to finitude in the midst of finitude—something in experience that suggests something beyond experience, a transcendence. Desmond's claims to knowledge about God arise from these happenings in our experience—from the hyperboles of being—from these indirect signs of God in our midst, in the between.

Reflecting on these hyperboles of being, Desmond describes a metaxological God that is a superior transcendence—an otherness that has an essentially asymmetrical relationship with humans and with the world. The central metaphor for God in Desmond's work, however, is that of agapeic origin—the source, through a radical and gratuitous origination, of the world as a true community of plurality made up of unique singularities in communicative relation to one another.

For Desmond, then, being properly religious is being in community with this God—with this agapeic origin—by responding to God's agapeic gift with gratitude (recognizing, celebrating, thanking for the gift) and generosity (becoming agapeic ourselves in giving to others in community). Gratitude for the generous creation of the agapeic origin inspires "a different 'return'" of the gift of creation in the generous co-creation of agapeic community with God and with others. Desmond's understanding of God and religion, and the understandings of metaphysics (of our metaxological relation to being and of the metaxological community of being) and of ethics (of agapeic selving and agapeic community) that it entails, is a viable and preferable alternative to that of Caputo.

## Hyperbole

These two visions—these two ways of thinking about religion in relation to metaphysics and ethics—can be seen acutely in their understandings of the "hyperbole" involved in religion. In Caputo's LeviNietzschean understanding of religious hyperbole, Levinasian ethical religiosity has undergone the Nietzschean hammer such that no positive (metaphysical) religious belief can remain—"religion" remains as but an exalted way of speaking about ethics. "God" is here a "placeholder" for the human other. Religion and God are *hyperbolic* ways of speaking of one's "hypersensitivity" to the demands of the other. This non-metaphysical hyperbole keeps to the surface of experience alone. Yet allowing the surface alone, the surface ultimately disappears. The deconstructability and yet persistence of the surface, of the phenomena, points to that beyond the surface—to a needed height or depth. The surface/phenomena then becomes a sign of something other, propelling one to think beyond it.

For Desmond, hyperbolic thought has to do with how something *in* experience (in immanence) suggests something *beyond* experience (transcendence). With the hyperbolic, we are "thrown," propelled beyond ourselves and our present experience toward the ultimate—thrown from our being between toward the "being above" of transcendence. Whereas Caputo sees talk of the ultimate as merely "hyperbolic" (as exaggerated, figurative) talk about the finite (about "reality"), Desmond's idea of the hyperbolic is a reversal of this—it is how our understanding of finite realities cannot remain fixated on the experience, the happening itself, but entails an immanent exigency that drives or impels our thinking toward something more than the finite—the finite is not sufficient unto itself. "God," for Desmond, is not a hyperbolic way of speaking of obligation or of our excessive desire—not fully reducible to a generic placeholder for the strange call to love or the otherwise indifferent object for our uncannily infinite desire. For Desmond, such experience, such obligation, such desire *is itself* what is hyperbolic.

## Postmodern Theology?

In looking at Desmond and Caputo with an eye toward the project of a "postmodern" theology, we come upon a kind of irony. One might say that Caputo's postmodern theology is, in the end, quite modern. In its broad reductionist project, it is nothing terribly new—yet another apology to religion's cultured despisers. One hears in the LeviNietzschean dithyrambs the cool echoes of the Enlightenment Religion Project to "help" religion—to rehabilitate an old chum that has fallen on hard times. Here one identifies a given domain of human experience as "religious." One then *renders* religion in the terms of that human domain. The signs in human being and experience of a divine other undergo transmutation—a reductive reversal—such that the divine is now merely a hyperbolic sign of the human. Religious language is retained as a cipher. This rendering that is the essence of modern religion is a kind of procrustean bed. God stretched and cut to fit—a holy sheet (shroud?) for the now hollow (now hallowed) naught-but-human bed. So Caputo's "postmodern theology" is neither all that postmodern (its project is modern), nor is it all that concerned about God (its object, in the end, need not be anything but finite humanity).

Desmond, however, takes these signs in human immanence as . . . *signs*—as pointing to something that exceeds them, to an agapeic origin, to God. Desmond, though, would disclaim the label "postmodern theology." He is simply a philosopher, a religious philosopher at best, not a theologian. And the "postmodern," for Desmond, is equivocal. The more common kind of postmodernism—"the muffled tramplings of the *Zeitgeist*" (*PU* 23)—is for Desmond a "hypermodernism" still subject to the ethos of modernity and its evermore-suspicious will to power now turning in, knives unsheathed, on itself—modernity's nihilistic chickens coming home to roost (*AOO* 276; *EB* 37). Yet Desmond also recognizes a dissident postmodernism (an agapeic postmodernism?) open again to God and to the neighbor.[1] It is in this perhaps dissident mode that Desmond's metaxological understanding of metaphysics and religious belief may provide us with a more robust way forward—a return beyond spent, cynical modernity to a constructive and affirmative conception of religion and metaphysics that could be construed as truly, if quite differently, "postmodern."

## Four Errors

In closing, I would like to suggest that Desmond's work can be seen as presenting the relation between metaphysics and religion in terms of an affirmative "both/and"—by way of a "neither/nor/nor/nor." More specifically, by looking at Desmond's thought through the concerns of postmodern theologians like Caputo, one sees four errors to avoid when it comes to thinking of and relating to God. *First,* one must guard against the dubious and unwarranted transition from knowledge of the absolute to absolute knowledge—the triumphalist dogmatism that mistakes truth about the divine as a truth that *is* divine and so unassailable.[2] *Second,* one must guard against the dubious and unwarranted transition from knowledge of divine truth as necessary for religious existence to seeing such knowledge as sufficient to constitute religious existence—one mistakenly moves from the necessary to the sufficient, as if assenting to certain propositions were all there is to being religious. *Third,* recognizing the first error, one must avoid performing a reverse conceptual slippage from the impossibility of absolute knowledge to the impossibility of knowledge of the divine—that if we cannot think *as* God (as God thinks), that we may not think *of* God. *Fourth,* recognizing the second error, one must avoid a reverse conceptual slippage from seeing knowledge of the divine as insufficient to constitute religious existence to seeing knowledge of divine as unnecessary for religious existence.

Caputo and those like him rightfully exhort us to turn from the two former errors only to fall squarely into the two latter errors. In Desmond's understanding of God and religion, we have a way to affirm some kind of knowledge of the absolute/divine (against the third error) while denying absolute knowledge (against the first error)—a way to affirm the necessity of such knowledge for religious existence (against the fourth error) while denying its sufficiency (against the second error). Thus, Desmond's metaxology proposes a metaphysical way of talking about God that is possible (through the hyperboles of being) but not absolute (because of our middle position)—in which metaphysics is valuable (informing the content of our ethical and religious being) but not sufficient (looking toward a more holistic life of community between metaphysics, ethics, and religion).

Desmond's thought—of religion, being-between, metaphysics, and the postmodern—denies and avoids all four of these errors and so opens a way forward toward an affirmative conception of God and religion.

# Notes

## Introduction

1. See Thomas A. F. Kelly, ed., *Between System and Poetics: William Desmond and Philosophy after Dialectic* (Ashgate, 2006), 4–5.

2. I do not discuss secondary material on Desmond's work inasmuch as it is either interacting with his interpretation of Hegel (as is seen in the volume of *Owl of Minerva* [36:2] dedicated to his work) or using Desmond's ideas to help understand another area or to serve a role in a constructive project (as in Kelly's volume).

## 1. Caputo

1. "Philosophy is only possible *as* meta-physics" (HKFM 207).

2. "We do not 'Know' ourselves or one another, that we do not 'Know' the world or God, in some Deep and Capitalized way" (*MRH* 5).

"We do not know who we are, not if we are honest" (*RH* 288).

"We are not (as far as we know) born into this world hard-wired to Being Itself, or Truth Itself, or the Good Itself, that we are not vessels of a Divine or World-Historical super-force that has chosen us as its earthly instruments" (*MRH* 1).

3. "I use the word 'metaphysics' rhetorically to nail just what it is about philosophy that makes me nervous. Just when philosophy gets to be transcendental, just when it gets to be pretentious, just when it thinks that it has things nailed down, that's just what I'm after" (*MD* 139).

4. "We have not been given privileged access to The Secret." (*MRH* 1).

5. "The desire of philosophy is to bring the flow to a halt in the system, to confine the rushing river within the fixed borders of its categories, to lay a systematic grid over it to contain its movements and allay our fears" (HKFM 207).

"The real obstacle to understanding human affairs lies in the tendency to believe that what we do . . . admits of formulation in hard and irrevocable rules" (*RH* 212).

6. "Thought can flourish only in the element of necessity and essence, and it can appropriate becoming only at the expense of what is definitive for it, viz., its very contingency" (*RH* 19).

7. It is thus that "classical metaphysics foundered on the problem of individuals" (*AE* 72).

"The universal never quite fits, can never quite be fitted into the concrete. The individual situation is always more complicated and it is never possible to anticipate, to have in advance, the idiosyncrasies of the particular, never possible to prepare the universal for the disruptiveness of the singular" (*DH* 203–204).

8. "Metaphysics suffers from the systematic misfortune of containing what it cannot contain, of harboring what it cannot protect . . . like a man who has swallowed something he cannot digest" (*AE* 73).

Metaphysics is "tossed back and forth between two impossibilities: the failed universal and the impossible singular" (*DH* 204).

9. "Parmenides set the stage for onto-theo-logic by so privileging unity, that multiplicity and diversity have been suspect ever since" (BA 69).

"Philosophy means meta-physics, the attempt to suppress movement, arrest the flux, stabilize the rush of experience" (HKFM 207).

10. "Philosophy is scandalized by movement and has always argued in one way or another against it" (HKFM 207).

"Metaphysics is comfortable only with a world of presence and absence, with Being and its negation. And it has always had the greatest difficulty in focusing on what is between them, on that movement which neither is nor is not but somehow fluctuates between the two" (HKFM 223).

11. "The essential tendency of metaphysics to arrest the flux" (RH 34).

12. "Metaphysics, from beginning to end, from Plato to Hegel, systematically searches for a way to arrest the play and allay our fears" (HKFM 213–14).

13. Radical hermeneutics "has no standing and no position, and it makes no attempt to get behind *physis*, beyond the flow" (RH 147).

14. Radical hermeneutics is "not an exercise in nihilism . . . but an attempt to face up to the bad news metaphysics has been keeping under cover" (RH 6).

15. AE 228. See RH, chapter 3.

16. "The best sort of concepts are those which are internally structured to point to their own inadequacy" (MRH 180).

17. The logic of the *sans* is that "according to which 'X *sans* X,' is not a simple negation, nullification, or destruction, but a certain reinscription of X, a certain reversal of movement of X that still communicates with X" (PT 100).

18. Derrida "shows that presence is the 'effect' of a process of repetition, that representation precedes and makes possible the very presence it is supposed to reproduce, that repetition is 'older' than what it repeats" (RH 4).

19. "*That*, if anything, is *who we are*, the ones who do not know who they are, and whose lives are impassioned by the passion of that non-knowing" (MRH 5).

"We are left with nothing, but with the passion and the not-knowing" (OR 127).

20. "There is/*es gibt* only . . . the plurality of particulars" (AE 71).

"The fact in all its 'facticity,' that is, in all its particularity as a fact, can be relieved of its irrationality only by being stripped of what is proper to it and lifted into the heavens of eidos" (MRH 4).

21. "To speak of what happens is to give up thinking that events make sense all the way down" (AE 234).

"The sum and substance of events is nothing other than the events themselves" (AE 235).

22. "Once we stop trying to prop up our beliefs, practices, and institutions on the metaphysics of presence, once we give up the idea that they are endowed with some sort of facile transparency, we find that they are not washed away but liberated" (RH 7).

23. The term "jewgreek" is Caputo's appropriation of Derrida's appropriation from Joyce in *Writing and Difference*, 153. It is "a clustering of quasi-philosophical discourses would have allowed what is Greek to be inwardly disturbed by its other and what is other than Greek to find something of a philosophical idiom" (AE 36).

"Jewgreek thinking," in contrast to metaphysics' (Greek) fixation on pure origin, greatness, presence, "embraces contamination, impurity, miscegenation, and dissemination. . . . the derivative, the non-originary, the secondary, and the repetitive. . . . the small, the insignificant, the marginal, the low-down and no-account . . . the time immemorial of justice and the placelessness and homelessness of the outcast . . . the invisibility of what cannot manage to emerge into presence" (*DH* 7).

24. Undecidability functions "to raise the intensity of the decision, the 'responsibility' for the decision. The more decidable things are, the more rule-governed they are and the more easily we can excuse ourselves for what we have done by saying, 'this is really not my doing, it's the rule'" (PMDG 304).

"Undecidability adds spice to life because it makes decisions possible, and indeed constitutes the very condition of possibility of decisiveness. The opposite of undecidability, it must be insisted, is not 'decisiveness,' as the Defenders of the Good and the True contend, but *programmability,* deducibility. A real decision requires undecidability, requires being in a situation where the deck is not stacked in favor of one option, where the only way a solution can be resolved is through *judgment* and *decision.* Undecidability is an account of judgment, not an attack upon it" (GA 7).

25. Caputo describes "the end of ethics" thus: "The business as usual of ethics has given out and the ethical verities that we all like to think are true . . . are now seen to be in a more difficult spot than we liked to think" (*MRH* 172).

26. These three points are Caputo's use of Derrida's "aporias of judgment" (*AE* 104–105).

"If someone really demands a principle or a foundation, if they want a cognitive basis, a theory, or a principle, before proceeding, they will, I fear, never get underway" (*AE* 38–39).

27. "Ethics makes safe. It throws a net of safety under the judgments we are forced to make, the daily, hourly decisions that make up the texture of our lives. Ethics lays the foundations for principles that force people to be good; it clarifies concepts, secures judgments, provides firm guardrails along the slippery slopes of factical life" (*AE* 4).

28. Caputo cites Augustine's Commentary on the First Epistle of John, in Migne, *Patrologia Latina,* vol. 35, p. 2033.

29. "Structurally, one is always on the receiving end of an obligation" (*AE* 11).

30. "In the economy of obligation, the I is always structurally an agent body while the other—which enjoys a place of primacy—is structurally flesh" (*AE* 213).

31. "Justice in itself," Caputo writes, is "the unique and particular justice that is cut to fit the particular needs of the individual, that is subtly suited to each individual in all individual's most secret singularity" (Meta 203).

32. "Obligations are our hyperbolic act of affirming infinite worth, of attaching hyperbolic significance to the least among us" (*AE* 246).

33. Ultimately, a properly heterological, post-metaphysical ethics must come around to include both the heteronomic Rabbi and the heteromorphic Dionysiac. "For heteromorphism is too pluralistic to exclude grave and solemn keepers of the law from its premises, and heteronomism is too obliging to the other to exclude these multicolor polymorphs from attending synagogue if they wish" (*AE* 64).

"If heteronomic piety without laughter makes me uneasy, heteromorphic gaiety without obligation is no less disturbing" (*AE* 65).

34. "But eventually the bravado of ethical repetition must come to grief. In the ethical, one needs only oneself, and that is its illusion" (*RH* 30).

35. "Religion, which is a human practice, is always deconstructible" (*OR* 113).

36. "If faith and theology understand themselves well, if they learn to speak of themselves and of God well . . . then they understand that they cannot, that they are structur-

ally unable . . . to close the circle, finally and effectively to assure their own destination, truth, and validity" (*PT* 59).

"The faithful need to concede that they do not cognitively know what they believe in any epistemologically rigorous way" (*OR* 111).

37. "That very finite Hellenistic creature called 'God' is being cut to fit the narrow needs of Greek ontology, of Parmenides and Plato, who were scandalized by time and motion and change" (*PT* 336).

38. "Genuine repetition . . . occurs only when the individual does not see how he can go on, when every human resource is exhausted" (*RH* 31).

39. *MRH* 263, quoting ("sans . . .") Jacques Derrida, *Parages* (Paris: Galilée, 1986), 25.

"The name of God has a special way of functioning as the name of what we love and desire" (*MRH* 258).

40. The God of the other is "the name of *the* impossible, of novelty, of the coming of the Other, of the *tout autre,* of what is coming with the shock of absolute surprise, with the trauma of absolute heterogeneity" (*PT* 113).

The religious dimension is inherent in heteronomism itself insofar as it is an "openness and responsiveness to what comes to us from without (*ab extra*), from on high, in short from the other" (*AE* 59).

41. "The Other is not infinity but a partiality to which we are unapologetically partial" (*AE* 19).

42. "The *re-ligare* in Derrida, . . . Kierkegaard and Levinas . . . is the *ob-ligare,* the bond of responsibility to the singularity of the 'wholly Other,' the bond of the one-on-one of the self to the Other" (*DH* 210).

43. The face of the other is "an intervention from without, a command issued from the hidden depths of the other. . . . The respect the other commands plays on the mystery of depths we cannot fathom" (*RH* 276).

44. Derrida, *Donner la Mort*, 68.

45. "The other is *any* other, God or someone or something else. So love means love the other as other, any other, any wholly other" (*PT* 49).

46. "The name of God is very powerful, full of force, of pragmatic effect, ordering us to the neighbor, directing our desire, *le désir de Dieu,* to the neighbor" (PMDG 304).

47. Caputo sees the "impossible relation" of the "absolute relation to an absolute" as rather a way of talking of the Other's unconditional claim on us—the Other's relation to us "in a very powerful, unconditionally commanding way" that calls on us to respond "decisively and unequivocally" (*AE* 80).

"The absolute Other is not, *stricto sensu,* an ineffable alterity but a fabulous tale . . . one of the best ways we have of saying that something is not only such-and-such, but very much so, indeed quite excessively, hyperbolically so" (*AE* 82).

48. "To love God is to love something deeply and unconditionally. But it is also true . . . that to love deeply and unconditionally is to be born of God, to love God" (*OR* 6).

"Is love a way of exemplifying *God*? Or is God a name we have for exemplifying *love*?" (*OR* 25).

"God is the name of love. God is the name of what we love" (*OR* 134).

49. "The 'other' is an example of what is named with the name of God; the name of God is an example of what is named by the 'other.' God is the exemplar of every 'other,' the other is the exemplar of God" (*PT* 52).

50. "How easily saying 'God is love' slides over into saying 'love is God.' This slippage is provocative and it provides us with an exceedingly important and provocative ambi-

guity, opening up a kind of endless substitutability and translatability between 'love' and 'God'" (*OR* 5).

51. "In the translatability of the love of God it is we who are to be translated, transformed, and carried over into action" (*OR* 140–41).

"So if we say 'God is love,' that means that we are expected to get off our haunches and *do* something" (*OR* 115).

52. "True religion, genuine religiousness, means loving God, which means a restlessness with the real that involves risking your neck; it means serving the widow, the orphan, and the stranger . . . *without* getting trapped by the claim to a privileged divine revelation made by the particular religions" (*OR* 114).

"What if the most religious thing you can do, service to the neighbor and the stranger, requires that we not think or believe *at that moment* anything religious at all, so that the religious doctrine, the thematic religious content, would actually get in the way of the religion? . . . What if religion can be itself only if it is a 'religion without religion'?" (GA 17–18).

## 2. Metaphysics

1. *BB* 44: "'*Meta*' is being in the midst; '*meta*' is also reference to what is beyond, what is transcendent. Metaxological metaphysics must think the doubleness of this tension between being in the midst *and* being referred by self-transcendence to the transcendence of what is other, what is over and above."

*BB* 44: "If metaphysical thinking, as I claim, takes shape in the milieu of being, the question of transcendence has nothing to do with a leap out of being into the void, but with the deepest mindfulness of what is emergent in the middle itself."

2. *BB* 5: "Metaphysical thinking is precipitated in the between. We find ourselves in the midst of being. . . . we have already begun."

3. *PU* 25: "Repeatedly Kant laments the 'mere random groping' of metaphysics prior to his own putting of metaphysics on 'the secure path to science.' I think that beyond all determinate science there is a groping that indicates a more radical metaphysical struggle. This groping suffers from an essential perplexity about the meaning of being that give the thinker a kind of metaphysical migraine, or insomnia."

4. *BB* 46: "Perplexity gives us a kind of metaphysical migraine."

5. BDD 735: "There may be indeterminacies or overdeterminacies about the ontological situation that demand metaphysical finesse which does not conquer astonishment or perplexity but deepens and disquiets thinking even more radically."

6. *BB* 12: "The call of metaphysical thinking is singular in its idiotic origins."

7. *BB* 17: "I suggest that such deconstructions of metaphysics as totalizing univocity themselves totalize the nature of metaphysics. In claiming to be free of totalizing thinking, they exhibit totalizing thinking relative to traditional metaphysics. As they seem to take the speck out of metaphysician's eye, they overlook any beam in their own. They do not do justice to the *plurivocal nature* of metaphysical thinking."

Indeed, the critique of metaphysics itself becomes a new metaphysics—the preference for the finite as but another metaphysical preference. See John Milbank, *Theology and Social Theory,* 106.

8. *BB* 15: "There is no such thing as the completion of metaphysics. To claim such a completion indicates a complete lack of understanding of what is at play in agapeic astonishment. . . . The true consummating of metaphysics is not the overcoming of aston-

ishment, but the infinite renewal of the opening to transcendence that comes first to us in it. And there is no completion of this renewal."

BDD 758: "There is no end of metaphysics, precisely because the sources of metaphysical thinking are in a beginning that always exceeds complete objectification."

9. AOO 2: "In our progress beyond 'metaphysics,' do we not drag metaphysics with us? This is what one would expect if there is no escaping the fact that to be human is to be shaped by fundamental orientations to being, and by implicit understandings of what it means to be."

MC 1: "I am not entirely sure what is meant by post-metaphysical thinking, but if we think of metaphysics as asking for fundamental reflection, more or less systematic, on the basic senses of the 'to be,' or of what it means to be, metaphysics will never be a practice we can put behind us."

10. AOO 271: "Despite the bad name metaphysics has had of late, the need for metaphysics has not ceased. Sometimes it takes forms that do not officially present themselves with the calling card marked 'metaphysics.' "

Milbank likewise recognizes this inescapability—that "we *have* to say 'how things are in general,' to be able to say anything at all." See *Theology and Social Theory*, 300.

11. *BHD* 249: "Is there possible a speculative philosophy of non-identity, a philosophical thinking that lives in an uncompromising acknowledgement of the irreducible others of self-thinking thought? I answer yes. I answer also that a thinking through of self-thinking thought leads us in this speculative direction."

12. HT 25: "Philosophy is just the thoughtful engagement of the sources of intelligibility immediately at work in the between. . . . Philosophical thought is struck into astonishment by the advent of what is other to thought at home with itself. Moreover, the idea of philosophy as autonomous self-mediating reason is of limited truth."

13. *DDO* 216: Speculation as "a rebirth of ancient theoria . . . need not imply the construction of idle theories . . . but rather, a rational openness to *die Sache selbst*."

*BHD* 8: "The deepest openness of speculative mind is the impossibility of the ultimate closure of thought by itself and in itself."

14. *BHD* 9: "Self-mediating thought must be genuinely open to the otherness of being, even in all its forms dissident to complete conceptualization. . . . This second exigence is so important that honest speculative reflection may find its self-mediations broken or ruptured on forms of otherness that its categories cannot entirely master."

15. *BHD* 243: "One of the supreme nobilities of speculative metaphysics is its willingness to mindfully return again and again to such ineradicable yet essential perplexities."

16. *BHD* 17: "There is a speculative laughter that issues from the festive celebration of being by agapeic mindfulness. This speculative yes to the community of being in no way subordinates the otherness of being to any conceptual whole constructed by the philosopher's mind. The yes of this laughter is a festive gesture towards the metaxological openness of agapeic being."

17. En 130: "This I call the between: the ontological ethos of plurivocal community of being in which the self-mediations and intermediations of beings come to be more determinately."

18. Such is "an ontological state which is fitting for something which is receptive of being." See Kelly, *Between System and Poetics*, 6.

19. In the work of Alain Badiou, true value always begins with an event, not with being, with being-as-being. With Desmond, however, being itself is charged with value. This is due, as will be shown in chapter 4, to the singular *event* of the origin of being.

Desmond's theistic vision undercuts and bridges Badiou's estrangement between being and event. See Alain Badiou, *Being and Event;* Peter Hallward, *Badiou: A Subject to Truth,* 78.

20. AT 235: "The ethos is the basic milieu in which determinate values come to form, but in itself it is in excess of determination. Ethos is indeterminate in an overdetermined sense: not merely neutral, but an equivocal medium of possibility or an in-between of promise. Here ethics and metaphysics cannot be entirely divorced; changes in one are reflected in, or influence changes in the other."

21. *EB* 86–87: "The ethos wherein we find ourselves is equivocal, and we must learn the art of dwelling with this. There are many ways of dwelling, but the art of every dwelling demands a truthfulness to what is given and shown in the ethos. The equivocal is not simply our defect, nor are we to wallow in confusion. There is a truth of the equivocal but it is more than the univocal, not less, and other approaches are necessary to reach it."

22. GEW 27: "Metaphysics, at its most deep, requires philosophical mindfulness of the primal ethos of being."

23. *PO* 228: "The order we make is grafted onto another order that we ourselves do not produce."

See Radical Orthodoxy's narrative regarding the post-1300 refiguration and evacuation of being effected by Scotus and other late medieval and early modern thinkers.

24. BDD 760: "The general spiritual ethos is pervasively pragmatic and oriented to instrumental problem-solving. We give our concern to things about which we can do something, where we seem able to will it and bring them under some control."

25. AT 248: "The absence of inherent good in the ethos is covered up by excessive noise about our purported creation of value. We distract ourselves from the death of the ethos with encomiums to our self-proclaimed creativity."

26. See AT. Badiou's work betrays just this objectification of being as the purely empty and mathematically formal domain of being qua being and this subjectification of value as the instrumental and historical (though intending a kind of universality) domain of the event, of truth, of the subject. Badiou's ontology presents the evacuated ethos of modernity as described by Desmond—a sterile, neutral, empty thereness that is no richer for its anonymous infinite unfolding. This stripped, evacuated being—as the matrix of a pure instrumentality, being is only good for this or that human project or truth-process—extends to humans themselves. As goodness or value or worth is extrinsic to being, so is it extrinsic to inherently worthless humans, who only become subjects of worth relative to a particular truth-process unfolding a particular event. See Alain Badiou, *Ethics: An Essay on the Understanding of Evil,* 59; Badiou, *Being and Event,* passim.

27. *EB* 37: "In the main the ethos of modernity (and postmodernity) has continued its wonted line, interpreting it in terms of distrust vis-à-vis the equivocity of the given ethos, and in terms of a will to power that begins to pass out of the power of the will of autonomous selfhood."

28. NDR 45: "To what extent is deconstruction a victim of the devaluation of being in modernity? Are deconstructive thinkers still in the same ethos which breeds the quasi-deconstruction of modern self-determination?"

29. Radical Orthodoxy makes this point, that the "modern" and the "postmodern" share the same nihilistic ontology repeatedly. See Catherine Pickstock on the nihilist aspect of the "immanentist cities" in her *After Writing: On the Liturgical Consummation of Philosophy* (Oxford: Blackwell, 1998), 3.

30. *BB* 15: "Relative to the view that I am developing, what has supposedly been completed in the so-called realization of metaphysics is not metaphysical thinking at all."

*PU* 23: "I do not think of myself as a post-modern. If what I say has any relevance to what is going on—and I would be disingenuous to deny that I think it does—this is not primarily because I keep my ear to the ground to hear the muffled tramplings of the *Zeitgeist*. It is because I think there is a matter to be thought which all the philosophers have tried to think."

31. *BB* xii: the "fourfold understanding of being"; *DDO* 237: "the quadruplicity."

32. Badiou makes the basic, axiomatic decision to see being as number and thus ontology as mathematics, mathematics as "being thought," as the thought of being as such. In this vision, nature and number are substitutable; number is the ontological substructure of nature. Here, in Badiou's mathematical ontology, thought is directly engaged with being as such; there is no distance between thought and being. Desmond makes another basic decision: to see being as an excessive, substantial fullness other to thought not fully reducible to the determinately intelligible. See Badiou, *Being and Event*, 140–41. Hallward, *Badiou*, 51–55.

33. *PU* 110: "To objectify being is to univocalize it. But this is to entrench dualism by rigid separation of the subjective and objective. This entrenched dualism is incompatible with the community between mind and being which is presupposed by the truth of objective mind."

34. The manner in which Deleuze's univocity of being generates a plane of pure, unmediatable difference between beings (a sameness without sameness passing into equivocity) and his insistence on this thoroughgoing difference disables any *understanding* of difference (a difference without difference reverting to univocal sameness) reflects how the univocal sense passes into the equivocal sense and shows the kind of mad dialectical interplay that arises without an understanding of mediation and relation that enables any understanding of real difference. (It must be said, though, that there are different ways to read Deleuze's "univocity of being.") Milbank recognizes just this generation of pure, unmediatable heterogeneity from the univocity of being in Duns Scotus. See Gilles Deleuze, *The Logic of Sense*, 179–80; Deleuze, *Difference and Repetition*, passim. Milbank, *Theology and Social Theory*, 304–305.

35. *BB* 82: "The will to absolute univocity is self-subverting, and cannot evade its own opposite, equivocity. This very insistence on univocity itself proves to be equivocal, for no univocal meaning can be given to the univocal insistence."

36. BDD 762: "The *equivocal* sense accentuates diversity, the unmediated difference of being and mind, sometimes to the point of setting them into oppositional otherness."

37. *BB* 88: "Equivocity is not always just our failure of univocal logic, but is rooted in the character of being itself. . . . Thus the ideal of the cut and dried is an abstraction from this becoming, with a provisional truth. Being as becoming, as flux, as temporal, as process, as ongoing—in a word, creation in the universal impermanence—undermines every effort completely to stabilize being as an aggregate of univocal substances, or units."

38. *BB* xiv–xv: "The thinking of this other causes us to think in terms of the equivocity of being. In turn, the coherent thinking of this equivocity drives us beyond equivocity to dialectic. Equivocity absolutized subverts itself, and calls for a more positive mediating mindfulness, in order to be true, not only to the transcending of thinking, but also to the truth of being as other to thinking."

39. *BB* 445: "The dialectical sense of being tends to resolve oppositions by subsuming them into a larger subsuming whole, all the way to the whole of all wholes, which is the absolute absorbing totality."

40. *PU* 13: The dialectical "recognizes the self-transcending dynamism of thought in its restless surpassing of limits, whether they be the fixations of being by univocal thought, or the dissolute, unmediated differences of equivocal thought."

41. *BDD* 762: "The *dialectical* sense emphasizes the mediation of the different, the re-integration of the diverse, the mediated conjunction of mind and being. Its mediation is primarily self-mediation, hence the side of the same is privileged in this conjunction."

*BHD* 2: "The logic of dialectical self-mediation includes a reference to what is other, but also always ends by including that other as a subordinate moment within a more encompassing self-mediating whole."

42. *BB* 161: "The dialectical sense, like the univocal, thinks that to be is to be intelligible, and that to be intelligible is to be determinable. But unlike the univocal interpretation, this determinate intelligibility is not a static state of affairs but a coming to determinacy in the very happening of becoming itself."

43. *BB* 134: "Dialectic has to do with the nature of the *immanent* development of mind and thought; with the meaning and intelligibility of being as *inherent* in being itself; with the conviction that the immanence of the former development is intimately related to the inherence of the latter intelligibility."

44. *BB* 164: "The insight of dialectic into the pervasive work of self-mediation can cause it to *absolutize* this mediation as marking the community of being, the happening of the between now called *the whole*."

45. *PU* 14: Dialectical self-mediation reduces "*all otherness* to a form subordinated to the putative primacy of such absolute self-mediation. . . . Such a dialectic converts the mediation of self and other into two sides of a more embracing and singular process of total self-mediation. The thought of everything other to thought risks getting finally reduced to a moment of thought thinking itself. Thus, Hegel's speculative unity is marked by, as we might call it, a kind of 'dialectical univocity.' "

*BB* 289: "If dialectic is exhausted in terms of a self-completing mediation, the eventuation of genuine pluralism becomes a mere vanishing medium, devoured by the all-absorbing totality."

46. *BHD* 11: "Hegel counts to three, but in dialectically counting to three, he is finally counting to one. . . . Hegel does not finally count beyond one at all."

47. *PO* 18: "Philosophy is an attempt at mindfulness of what is at work in the middle, considered as the metaxological community of being."

*MC* 16: "The metaxu first is to be seen as a happening: the milieu or ethos of being within which we find ourselves."

48. *BB* 452: "In a literal sense, being between is an *inter-esse,* where the interest is in the being of the *inter*."

49. *BHD* 117: "Dialectical doubleness is a misinterpretation of metaxological doubleness. If not freed from this misinterpretation, dialectic produces a simulacrum of real otherness . . . and circles around its own fetish of absolute self-mediation."

*BB* 142: "Is it just the self-doubling of one voice, or is it the doubling and redoubling of a plurality of voices, not reducible to one single overriding voice? . . . Traditionally dialectic has tended to the first answer, while the metaxological offers the second."

*BB* 163: "The doubleness of mediation is so affirmed as to obviate any temptation to the reduction of pluralized interplay to a singular play of one power with itself."

50. *BHD* 272: "The question of otherness should be posed genuinely from dialectic, not from below it."

51. *DDO* 7; *BHD* 8, 128, 278, 309. Marion's encounter with the flesh of another in which I become flesh, become myself, is an example of this kind of interdependence.

Marion's understanding of this relationship as being without confusion or mixing (not reducible to Desmond's dialectical absorption) and without separation or division (not reducible to Desmond's equivocal dispersion) resonates, though his thought is in tension with this elsewhere, with the kind of reciprocity seen in Desmond's intermediated metaxological community of being. See Jean-Luc Marion, *The Erotic Phenomenon,* 127.

52. *DDO* 108: "Both on the side of the self and the other, we must grant a positive sense of identity and difference. . . . For this ineradicable pluralization cannot be understood in terms of dialectical self-mediation alone. The form of mediation between two terms, each of which is dialectically self-mediating, cannot be itself dialectical self-mediation, but requires the fuller form of metaxological intermediation."

53. *BDD* 762–63: The metaxological sense "puts stress on the mediated community of mind and being, but not in terms of the self-mediation of the same. It calls attention to a pluralized mediation, beyond closed self-mediation from the side of the same, and hospitable to the mediation of the other, or transcendent, out of its own otherness."

54. *DDO* 8: "The intermediation of the metaxological relation grounds an open community of self and other. Beyond mere unity, beyond sheer manyness, beyond manyness within a single unity, it entails a community full of unities, each of which is inexhaustibly manifold within itself."

*BHD* 81: "Metaxological intermediation is simply respect for the richness, complexity and community of Ownness and otherness that is going on, always and already. Ownness and otherness and metaxological community escape beyond final encapsulation."

*BB* 451: "This intermediation shapes the *inter* such that it can never be closed by either side alone, or even by both sides together, for the very *inter* is kept open just by the openness of the participants in this community. The participants are in excess of self-mediation, the interplay of the participants is in excess of self-mediation, and yet there is mediation. This is metaxological intermediation."

55. *DDO* 115: "Though there is a deep mutuality in intermediation between self and other, there is also a recognition of what might be termed a reciprocal asymmetry between them. By this I mean that, mediation notwithstanding, there remains an essential recalcitrance, not only to the self, but also to the other, which intermediation acknowledges and lets be. The asymmetry is reciprocal because each side recognizes the irreducibility of the other to itself."

*PU* 203: "Our mediating is itself double: it is a self-mediating in which we ponder our own being; it is also an intermediating with what is other, whereby we seek to come to terms with, metaphysically and existentially, the meaning of being in its otherness."

In *DDO*, Desmond writes of intermediation as itself including *both* of these mediations—thought thinking itself and thought thinking its other—not just as the latter. See *DDO* 114–15, 117.

56. *HT* 28: "We need a metaxological approach to acknowledge the affirmative surplus of the overdeterminate, beyond determinacy and self-determination."

57. *BB* 34: "The plurivocity of metaxological metaphysics takes up Aristotle's *to on legetai pollachōs.*"

58. *MC* 16: "Then a metaxological metaphysics bears on our efforts to offer a logos of the metaxu: this is a mode of articulation of the happening of the metaxu. In this latter task, the univocal, equivocal, and dialectical ways of being and mind are each taken to be ways of trying to articulate the metaxu. Each exhibits characteristic emphases, characteristic underemphases: something is expressed, something recessed. A metaxological metaphysics tries to take the next step with a more faithful articulation of the metaxu, in

terms of the deepest definitions of sameness and otherness, identity and difference, and the forms of relation and interplay between self and other, and so on."

*BB* 177: "The metaxological reiterates, first a sense of otherness not to be included in dialectical self-mediation, second a sense of togetherness not reached by the equivocal, third a sense of rich ontological integrity not answered for by the univocal, and fourth a rich sense of ontological ambiguity not answered for either by the univocal, the equivocal, the dialectical."

59. *BDD* 763: "The metaxological is the truth of the univocal, the equivocal, and the dialectical. When we try to articulate it, we are trying to find the right words for what is given in the overdeterminacy of the original astonishment. The other three senses help to articulate the truth of the metaxological, but we risk error when they are absolutized and claimed to cover the entire milieu of being."

60. *BB* 178: "I suggest that as dialectic tries to redeem the promise of univocity beyond equivocity, so the metaxological tries to redeem the promise of equivocity beyond univocity and dialectic."

61. *BHD* 266, 302; *PU* 105. For a somewhat similar (though independent) presentation, see Milbank on charity as entailing a positive, gratuitous, freedom-giving relation to difference in *Theology and Social Theory*, 422.

62. Kelly, *Between System and Poetics*, 5–6.

63. *BDD* 736: "There is always an excess in astonishment. Something is both given to mindfulness, and yet is in excess of what mindfulness can grasp clearly and distinctly in that given."

*NDR* 45: "Return once more to thought as seeded in astonishment; astonishment is original: being given as too much, as overfull."

64. See note 32 on Badiou above. Value (here the value of being as such) is no mere relativistic projection, it is (in Badiou's terms) rooted in the event of the origin of being (so fundamentally displacing Badiou's terms). See chapter 4.

65. *BHD* 244: "Wonder (*thaumazein*) is the pathos of the philosopher, Socrates and Plato say, and also its archē, as Aristotle reiterates."

*NDR* 39: "An original astonishment stuns us, rocks us back, impels an exodus of transcending towards beings."

One could see this astonishment as an at once universal and singular *event* (in one's own consciousness) in a sense akin to Badiou's that is the foundation of an understanding of being otherwise than Badiou's—as full and not empty, as good and not neutral. In relation to Marion's work on love, Desmond can agree that love in the sense of that being given is primordial with regard to consciousness, while seeing one's relation to the other as more porous than does Marion, who opposes "the lover" and "the thinker." As we are seeing, love—that given—continually founds, funds, enables thinking. Love, the agapeic, is thought's origin and *telos*. Marion, *The Erotic Phenomenon; PO* 29; *BB* 8, 11, 13; *PU* 34; BDD 734, 763; NDR 39, 47; MC 10–11, 28.

66. MC 11: "Astonishment is a precipitation of mindfulness before something admirable, or loveable or marvelous, communicated from an otherness that has the priority in speaking to the porosity of our being. It comes to us, comes over us, and we open up in response. We do not first go towards something, but find ourselves going out of ourselves because something has made its way, often in startling communication, into the very depths or roots of our being, beyond our self-determination. We are struck into astonishment."

67. *PU* 63: "The intimacy of being, while not completely articulable in determinate univocal fashion, is communicable; it is communication itself."

*PU* 66: "Elemental self-transcendence and community are inseparable, so much so that an elemental 'being-with' is constitutive of the idiotic I itself. The nature of the intimate self is 'being with': being with self, and being with what is other to self."

68. NDR 37: "Intimate strangeness refers to the middle condition of our thought of being: being is strange because it has an otherness, indeed marvel, of which we are not the conceptual masters; it is also intimate, in that this very strangeness allows no stance of thinking 'outside' being—we are participants in what we think about."

69. *PO* 272: "The elemental is such that its expression is just its simple being. There is no disjunction between expression and being."

70. En 131: "There is a being given to be, before the being given affirms its own 'to be.' . . . Put differently . . . there is a *passio essendi* more primal than any *conatus essendi*: a suffering, or *passio*n of being more elemental than any endeavor to be, or striving to be."

This prior *passio essendi* resonates at once with Milbank's (theological) understanding of our primordial ontological receptivity (that even the "I" is given) and with Marion's understanding of the priority of the love of the other—of the question, "Does anyone love me?" See Milbank, *Theology and Social Theory*, xviii; Marion, *The Erotic Phenomenon*, 20–26, passim.

71. *BB* 179: "This overdetermination is the manifest transcendence of being as original plentitude, as itself the festive agape of being."

72. *BB* 188: "Agapeic astonishment is from the outset an inarticulate coming towards us of the intimacy of being, and a going towards it, on our part, in an opening of mind towards its otherness. This intimacy of being rouses to itself in the mindful singularity of the thinker struck into astonishment."

73. *PU* 9: "Desire [is] a metaphysical opening to being, being in its otherness, as well as the self-development of the human being in its own ineluctable search for its own wholeness."

74. BDD 762: "The *equivocal* sense accentuates diversity, the unmediated difference of being and mind, sometimes to the point of setting them into oppositional otherness. Perplexity in its restless encounter with troubling ambiguities can be correlated with this sense of the equivocal."

75. *BB* 110: "The equivocal is nowhere more evident than in human *desire*."

76. BDD 739: "I call perplexity erotic because it arises out of a troubled sense of lack and desire: as ignorant, one lacks definite knowledge of the other that is given to mindfulness in astonishment; and yet one desires to overcome that lack of ignorance."

77. *DDO* 126: Desmond describes Platonic *eros* "as both a drive to self-fulfillment and an arrow to the beyond."

78. *Symposium,* 203a ff. cited on *PU* 131.

79. *BHD* 329: "Eros, as a between, is a mingling of his father, contrivance, resource, *Poros* . . . and his mother, poverty, *Penia*. I take this to imply that for us mortals in the middle, eros as lack always contains the promise of something more than lack."

*PU* 135: "The trace of divine festivity is in the very conception of eros, when Penia sleeps with drunken Poros who has stumbled intoxicated from the feast of the gods. The trace of the agape of the gods is an origin *before* the awakening of eros to its own beginning in lack."

80. *BB* 7: "The eros of perplexity is driven to transcendence, troubled initially by a sense of lack. . . . The agape of perplexity is prior to the eros of perplexity, because the lack of eros could not drive beyond itself at all in the first place, were it not energized by an anterior power of being that cannot be described in purely indigent terms."

81. *BB* 249: "The other serves the reconstitution of fulfilled self-relativity on the part of erotic being."

*EB* 354: "Eros is a mode of transcending in which we are impelled beyond self in order to attain some wholeness of being beyond the initial lack. It carries self beyond itself from lack to wholeness, and does so in relation to an other who serves to overcome that immanent lack. I go towards the other out of lack, but in coming to the other I come to some wholeness of self, and being whole can claim some freedom of self-determining being. The surpassing of self towards the other comes back to the self, in the fulfillment it seeks in possessing the other."

*BDD* 739: "I call perplexity erotic because it arises out of a troubled sense of lack and desire: as ignorant, one lacks definite knowledge of the other that is given to mindfulness in astonishment; and yet one desires to overcome that lack of ignorance. The beginning of perplexity is this indigence of knowing, out of which indigence there is a movement of self-transcendence towards the other. I also call this movement erotic because the other sought is sought for the sake of alleviating perplexity's own troubled mindfulness."

82. MC 11: "*Perplexity* follows astonishment, in that the 'too muchness,' being given, calls forth our thinking about what it might mean at all. The thinking in perplexity is sometimes troubled by its own inability to be the measure of what gives itself as worthy for thought. In perplexity we move away from the primal astonishment and the beginning of our own determining thinking emerges. For we try to put the question now, more and more; and the more we seem to find an answer to our perplexity, then the less the 'too muchness' seems to exceed the measure of our thinking. We allay the trouble of thinking by both determining our thinking, and by seeking determinate answers, and thinking we have the determinate measure of all being as other."

BDD 759: "Erotic perplexity is lacking just in its lack. The very restlessness it expresses is itself grounded in a prior, more affirmative, energy of being that cannot be expressed in merely lacking terms. . . . Lack becomes restless just because in lack there is an affirmative original energy driving lack out beyond itself. This more original source is, from the start, beyond lack."

83. BDD 737: "Perplexity is not patience to the otherness of being in quite the same way as is the original astonishment. In its troubled mindfulness there works a vector of self-transcendence that would go towards this otherness of being, and if possible overcome its own perplexity. Perplexity is felt as a lack of definite cognition, driving our beyond itself to overcome that lack."

*EB* 53: "We cannot live indefinitely with perplexity. We want to know *definitely* what is good in the between. We want to secure ourselves against vulnerability."

84. *BB* 16: "Let us not forget the crucial ambiguity in the transition from agapeic astonishment to erotic perplexity—namely, the birth of the latter out of the former, but the possible forgetting of the former in the latter's sense of lack or ignorance."

85. NDR 40: "As our perplexity becomes more focused into definite curiosity, thinking and the sense of being turn more towards the determinate: being as determinate beings, thinking as determinate thought. Here begins the temptation to turn from the intimate strangeness. Being becomes just strange—now just beings: beings also seem as strangers over against us, without any intimacy, or intimation of something beyond the determinate. Here surfaces knowing as a more aggressive curiosity: the otherness is a strange thereness to be conquered; fixed, placed, made subject to my cognitive project. Thus we find the process of domestication, of sedimentation."

86. BDD 734: "We have this inveterate tendency to think that to be is to be intelligible, and that to be intelligible is to be determinate."

87. BDD 762: "Correlative to the univocal sense of being is the search for determinate solutions to determinate problems, impelled by specific curiosity."

88. *PU* 195: "In our time the hegemony of instrumental mind seems to be completing itself inexorably. All being is more and more instrumentalized. Our erotic self-transcending has reached out to being-other and progressively appropriated its difference as other; we have made it to be for the self, for ourselves alone."

89. *PO* 158, 366; *BB* 71; BR 227; *EB* 46. See I, §4 above.

90. *PO* 353: "What is there, what 'is,' has no intrinsic worth; worth is merely an instrument of the projecting self, already set in opposition to being. The fact/value distinction is an expression of this ethical/ontological estrangement."

BR 224: "If the world is worthless, we cannot stand a worthless world, we must make it worthy, worthy of us, and that means we must make it our instrument."

91. *PU* 226: "Being has been so thoroughly instrumentalized in modernity that the mind-set we inhabit is sometimes a prison-house of assumption. Neutralized of any intrinsic value, being is made a means to an end, namely, to serve our desire, flattened into something that only is for us. The ontological yes of the 'It is good' is silenced."

92. On the manner in which positivistic science's instrumental mind cuts itself off from its own indeterminate sources, see Milbank, *Theology and Social Theory,* chap. 9.

93. *BB* 64: "The originating 'dream' of univocity remains a surd that univocity cannot explain. . . . The scientific love of truth as univocal is a love that is not itself univocal."

BR 222: "The desire thus to make everything determinately known is itself more than determinate."

94. *BB* 509: "If the creation is valueless in itself, then the human being as a participant in creation is also ontologically valueless, so likewise his human construction is ultimately valueless. Every effort to construct values out of himself will be subject to the same deeper, primitive, ultimate valuelessness. Human values collapse ultimately into nothing, if there is not a ground of value in the integrity of being itself. . . . Only subtle self-deception can avoid the collapse of our constructions into the ontological nihilism that is said to affect the whole of being in itself."

*PU* 223: "In sum: if being itself has no value, we can give it no value, for our own being itself, and everything we do, including our giving of value to being, ultimately has no value. The human giving of value to being is finally without value."

MC 14: "We can claim to create value in the valueless whole, and so seem to save it from the indifferent insipidity of mere thereness, but what happens when we remember that we are also parts of or participant in this valueless whole? We also exhibit the same valuelessness of the valueless whole—from the standpoint of the whole—hence our claim to be the source of value looks like self-serving or special pleading."

95. *BB* 81: "Out of mathematicized univocity, scientific theory might turn around again into metaphysical perplexity about the enigma of being . . . In a word, this acme of determinate knowing can open up the possibility of the second indeterminate perplexity."

96. *DDO* 85: There is "a certain decentering of desire toward otherness, even in moments of wholeness; we find the breaking open of any close circle of merely monadic self-relation."

*BHD* 331: "How does the erotic drive of the philosopher finally relate to the other? I suggest that the telos of this drive indicates a reversal of directionality right at the end. . . . in finding its own self-mediation more energetically and mindfully activated, the philosopher discovers the opening of this self-mediation beyond self-mediation: openness to the other becomes more accentuated the more deep or high erotic self-mediation becomes."

97. *BB* 156: "Agapeic astonishment is renewed on the limit, in the reborn metaphysical mindfulness of the *second* perplexity beyond all determinate knowing."

98. *PU* 34: "It is as if the wonder that is said to be the originating pathos of the philosopher *reappears* after he has done his best job in giving a determinate logos. The indeterminate perplexity reappears, wonder resurrects itself, in a different sense of being at a loss, now at the limit of logos i[t]self."

99. Milbank observes something like posthumous mind from a theological perspective, of a transfigured vision of the world in terms of gift informed by the belief in the resurrection of the dead. John Milbank, *Being Reconciled: Ontology and Pardon* (London: Routledge, 2003), 151.

100. BDD 760: "We cannot will astonishment. It is given. It is a gift. There is required preparation, waiting, purified willingness, opening, tireless thinking. There is a willingness beyond will to power. . . . Something from beyond self must be allowed to give itself, if it will give itself at all."

101. *BB* 261: "Agapeic being is a movement of creative origination that goes forth from itself, from its own surplus, but it does not go forth for the sake of itself; it offers the other being, for the sake of the other. Its self-transcendence is truly self-transcending, since there is a kind of *releasing reversal* between self and other: the self is othered such that the other is given a freedom of being from the giving self. . . . The self-transcendence that is a reversal of self is a giving of genuine separateness to the other. Freedom is this separation."

102. *DDO* 167: Desire as goodwill "reveals that desire may be more than an erotic rush from lack to wholeness, that it may be an agapeic pouring forth from a wholeness already real."

103. *EB* 217: "If erotic sovereignty is tempted to close the circle of desire, and make self both desiring and desired, by contrast, agapeic service cannot close any circle, for the desired is not the same as the desiring—when I desire I desire the good as other to my desire: the communal reference to the good as other is in the dynamism of our self-transcending."

104. *PU* 119: "Agapeic mind expresses something that is both a regulative ideal and an ontological reality, somehow constitutive of our most intimate being."

105. *PU* 232: "The gift of agapeic being solicits in us the gift of agapeic being. We, too, must be the release of the divine freedom of generosity."

*EB* 220: "The agape of being is first given to us, but we are called to an agapeic being which is the doing of living, in an ethics of gratitude to the origin, and of generosity to self and other. The agape of being intimates a fullness, but it is not being full of oneself. One does nothing to merit it, and no payment is exacted, for it offers itself simply as the life of the good, a life we are to live. It has no reason, beyond itself, which is to be beyond itself, in being itself."

106. *BB* 202: "What is taken for granted can be what is acknowledged as granted; and hence there is the grateful mindfulness that sees what is given just as given, as a gift; to take for granted is to appreciate the gift granted."

107. *BB* 414: "There is a kind of return to the first, because agapeic acting, willing, creating, doing are germinated in passion, suffering, imitation, patience. The passion of being that is always already spread out in the elemental I, returns in the end."

108. BR 215: "What is reverence? . . . a worthiness beyond instrumentalizing."

BR 226: "Reverence is a happening in which the worth and the being-there of the other are conjoined."

*EB* 195: "It is with reference to love of this surplus of the gift that all reverence, gratitude, respect, dignity, obligation and consideration are alive. Reverence: it is worthy in itself."

109. BR 227: "Agapeic mind also beyond the ontological nihilism which reduces being's otherness to a worthless thereness. . . . Agapeic mind is a love of being: a love that knows that being is worthy of affirmation as good in itself."

110. *BB* 33: "We reach out to what is other in self-transcendence, but there is in agapeic mind a transcendence different to that of erotic perplexity that wills finally and always to return to self."

*BB* 206: Agapeic mind is "the self-transcendence of mindfulness as it goes towards the other as other, and not just simply as a mirror of itself, or a means to mediate with its own self. It is genuinely self-transcending, for it is the thinking of the other in its otherness. . . . It thinks beyond itself, thinks in excess of its own self-mediation. And so such a communicative mindfulness is the living exemplification of a coming into the community of being."

111. *BB* 261: "Agapeic being is a movement of creative origination that goes forth from itself, from its own surplus, but it does not go forth for the sake of itself; it offers the other being, for the sake of the other. Its self-transcending is truly self-transcending, since there is a kind of *releasing reversal* between self and other: the self is othered such that the other is given a freedom of being from the giving self."

112. *BHD* 17: "There is a speculative laughter that issues from the festive celebration of being by agapeic mindfulness. This speculative yes to the community of being in no way subordinates the otherness of being to any conceptual whole constructed by the philosopher's mind. The yes of this laughter is a festive gesture towards the metaxological openness of agapeic being."

*BB* 42: "Festive being is an amen to the being in its gift and largess."

113. *PO* 278: Posthumous mindfulness is "a thinking from the future when we are dead, about the ontological worth of the present, imagined from beyond death as our past."

*BB* 37: "I suppose that I am dead, and can look at being from beyond the fret and fever. I would have nothing to gain, nothing to lose. I would look at being without ulterior motivation. I would not look upon it for myself. I would want to see its otherness as other. . . . Such would be entailed by posthumous honesty: a willingness to let the truth of other-being emerge for itself. . . . Since I look on being from beyond death, and look on it for the truth of its otherness, might not my mind be agapeic? For I am imagining that I behold being from its otherness; I go towards its otherness as other, and I have no reason to interfere with it. . . . As thus posthumous, agapeic mind would be love of being in its intrinsic good. . . . If being would so appear from beyond, is it not *now* so from within, as we live it, though now we cannot see it so?"

*BB* 192: "Suppose one were dead and came back to one's time, looking for the things of time, the beings and companions and happenings of the middle that shaped one's being here with a sense of intrinsic worth of value. Posthumous mind is this speculation of agapeic mind looking on the happening of the between, beyond the lies of life and beyond the negativity of death."

114. *BB* 186: Idiot wisdom is "a mindfulness that respects the intimacy of being, its

idiotic being, in all the gift of its thereness, and indeed its transcendence to every determinate science we construct to remake it in the services of our categorical structures."

115. NDR 48: "We need to think of being in terms of surplus overdeterminacy rather than as empty indeterminacy—the evacuated sense of being. . . . The intimate strangeness means rethinking being as full. This might be called to a kind of hyperbolic thought, in the sense of what exceeds all complete fixation in determinate categories."

116. BDD 766: "The excess of overdetermined manifestation proves to be ever drawing thought, ever daring to extend to the extremes, ever renewing it when it wearies, redoubling it beyond self-determination and all its putative completions. It strikes us into astonishment again, disturbing the complacency of our conceptualizations with a perplexity that may be deepened but never will be totally dissolved."

117. BDD 763: "The metaxological is the truth of the univocal, the equivocal, and the dialectical. When we try to articulate it, we are trying to find the right words for what is given in the overdeterminacy of the original astonishment. The other three senses help to articulate the truth of the metaxological, but we risk error when they are absolutized and claimed to cover the entire milieu of being."

118. BB 44: "'Meta' is being in the midst; 'meta' is also reference to what is beyond, what is transcendent. Metaxological metaphysics must think the doubleness of this tension between being in the midst *and* being referred by self-transcendence to the transcendence of what is other, what is over and above."

119. BB 45: "Metaphor is a carrier in the between; it ferries (*pherein:* to carry) us across a gap; or it is the carrier of transcendence; it is in the midst as *meta,* and yet an image of the *meta* as beyond, as transcendent."

120. BB 218: "We are thrown towards transcendence by our being" as "a metaphysical *exigency.*"

121. This understanding, of a distance between thought and being entailed in an other-than-univocal understanding of this relation, distances Desmond from Badiou, who sees thought as directly engaged with being. See Hallward, *Badiou,* 55.

122. AOO 268: "The transcendence of such beings consists in their not being the product of our process of thinking; their otherness to us resists complete reduction to our categories, especially in so far as they simply are, or have being at all."

123. BB 57: Desmond observes that even with Heraclitus "the flux of happening is shot through with *logos.* . . . Becoming . . . is intermediate, as the happening of the between: it is between form and formlessness, indefiniteness and determination."

BB 88: "Equivocity is not always just our failure of univocal logic, but is rooted in the character of being itself. Being is metaxological, hence plurivocal. The process of becoming provides the dynamic ground of univocity. Thus the ideal of the cut and dried is an abstraction from this becoming, with a provisional truth. Being as becoming, as flux, as temporal, as process, as ongoing—in a word, creation in the universal impermanence—undermines every effort completely to stabilize being as an aggregate of univocal substances, or units."

124. BB 256: "Finite beings are differentiated in a process of becoming that, as open-ended, does have its indefiniteness. Finite beings partake of the originated infinitude of endless succession and the universal impermanence. But that derivative infinity is not the underived infinite."

In Badiou's understanding, being as being is infinite—nature is an infinite multiplicity. Desmond parts company with Badiou's assertion that one is forced to choose between an infinite God and a finite nature, on the one hand, and atheism and an infinite nature, on the other. In Desmond's understanding, an infinite nature is not inconsistent with the existence of an infinite God. God need not be the erotic One that Badiou assumes. One suspects the difference here is, in part, one of *theologies*—of understandings of God—as much as of philosophies of nature or the infinite. Again, Badiou's understanding is based on an axiomatic (militant) decision against God (as what Desmond would call the erotic origin, the absorbing God) and for the infinity of being. Desmond makes another axiomatic decision that includes an infinite God and an infinite world. See Badiou, *Being and Event*, 142–45, 148; Hallward, *Badiou*, 81.

125. *BB* 11: Astonishment "comes from *transcendence as other*. . . . Yet in opening the self, it initiates the vector of *transcendence in the self* and its going towards being-other with express mindfulness."

126. *BB* 293: "Creation as universal impermanence, as it were, reaches beyond its open wholeness to its own transcendent ground."

*AOO* 268: "What makes possible both their possibility, as well as their actuality? . . . Why beings and not nothing? . . . The possibility of transcendence as *other* to their transcendence is opened by such questions."

127. *BB* 201: "This *being beyond totality* refers to the beyond of innerness to totalization, the abyss of idiocy in the immanence of self-transcendence."

128. *BB* 374: "There is a certain intimacy of self-relation that is not included in a determinate system, not even a self-determining system, since it is the source of such . . . [a] system."

129. *BB* 384: "The idiocy of the self in this inwardness is an opening to otherness within itself. Indeed its excess suggests the promise of an inexhaustibility."

*PU* 61: "By the idiocy of singularity I intend no privatistic atomism, though I do mean a privacy of the intimate. I intend it also in this sense: there is a certain excess of being characteristic of what it means to be a self, which can never be completely objectified in an entirely determinate way. This is an affirmative overdetermination."

130. *BB* 187: "The metaxological sense differs from the dialectical in denying that the innerness of the singular is entirely determinable in terms of self-mediation. This innerness is what I called the intimacy of being of the singular. And while it is self-mediating, it is not a closed self-sufficiency, but opens inwardly into its own idiocy."

*HG* 190: "If we are talking about the *infinite inwardness* of self, there is this immanent otherness which is most intimate to the self and yet is not owned by self, and can never be. Its most intimate being is other to its own self-possession; something exceeds self-mediation, this inward infinity, even in the most intensive of self-mediations."

131. *PO* 361: "Original selfness cannot be exhausted by any determinate what; as a this, it is a singularization of the power of being whose unity is not univocal; it shows a certain indeterminacy, in the sense of being overdetermined and hence not exhaustible in terms of univocal predication."

*BB* 187: "The metaxological sense differs from the dialectical in denying that the innerness of the singular is entirely determinable in terms of self-mediation. This innerness is what I called the intimacy of being of the singular. And while it is self-mediating, it is not a closed self-sufficiency, but opens inwardly into its own idiocy."

132. *BB* 189: Regarding the infinitude in the intimacy of the singular self, it is "only because of this, does our characteristic desire exhibit an infinite restlessness. We transcend ourselves again and again in desire; we are satisfied with this determinate thing, only to find dissatisfaction resurrected on satisfaction, and another search initiated; and there seems to be no determinate limit to this restless self-transcendence."

133. *BB* 230: "We are self-transcendence that will not rest, intentionally infinite even

in being actually finite, an opening, not just to this being or that, but to being *simpliciter,* and the community of being."

*EB* 215: "Infinite desire emerges in finite being."

134. *BB* 401: "The excess of the self . . . is the source of its infinite restlessness."

*EB* 190: "The infinitely restless desire attests to the 'too muchness' at the idiotic source."

For Badiou, we are infinite inasmuch as we think infinitely, as we can think mathematically about being qua being that is infinite. This is an "ordinary" infinity that has to do with being as such. One becomes extraordinary, Immortal, when one becomes (a) subject to a truth—when one becomes a militant for a particular if universalizable truth. For Desmond, the infinity of the human is not of two distinct orders—one necessary, formal, and abstract, one particular, accidental. The distinctive coexistence of the infinite and the finite in the human for Desmond is intrinsic, metaphysical, constituting a genuine philosophical anthropology. Hallward, *Badiou,* 67; Badiou, *Ethics,* chap. 4.

135. *DDO* 24: The infinitude of desire testifies to the fact that "we are always oriented to something more" in "an incessant process of going beyond limited satisfactions."

*EB* 215: "The anomalous being of the human is revealed in this freedom of infinite desire. Infinite desire emerges in finite being—excess of being rises up in the human being as selving: transcending as more, and towards the more. This 'more' means enigmatic otherness in inwardness itself: the very interiority of being is the coming to show of infinity, the transcending power of the being, the transcendence towards infinity of the human being."

136. *DDO* 150: Intentional infinitude "helps to rescue the infinite succession of becoming from being solely a scattering or equivocal process. Intentional infinitude specifically refers to the power of and open dialectical self-mediation displayed in the articulation of human desire."

*BB* 157: Intentional infinitude "is intentional to the extent that the restlessness of self-transcendence can be directed through the self-mediating powers of thinking itself."

Milbank likewise understands (again from a theological perspective) the desire at the core of human nature as wanting to be both at home (toward wholeness) and abroad (toward infinite). Milbank, *Being Reconciled,* 210.

137. See below: chapter 3, part one, section III.

138. *BB* 408: "The metaxological space between self and other is a middle between infinitudes. As well as the self's inward infinitude, there is recognized the infinitude of the other. This other infinitude can be the infinite succession of external becoming, the universal impermanence; it can be the self-mediating infinitude of an other self; it can be the actual infinitude of the absolute origin."

139. *BB* 182: "The vector of self-transcending is an infinitely restless seeking of unconditional transcendence."

*PU* 204: "Our transcending being is unfolded as the quest of ultimacy. The field of being and our being in that field, both point beyond themselves. . . . [W]ithin the self-transcending urgency of desire, we find an opening to the ultimate other. We are the interior urgency of ultimacy, this other is ultimacy as the superior. . . . The point is not to appropriate the ultimate in its transcendence to human self-transcendence, nor yet to depreciate the energy of human self-transcending."

140. See below: chapter 3, part one, section IV.

141. *BB* 255: "We must think of infinity here as other than an infinite succession or series. We must think of *qualitative inexhaustibility* rather than quantitative accumula-

tion and summation. In a sense, such qualitative inexhaustibility is more than humans can think."

142. *BB* 256–57: "The way of transcendence is hyperbolic. Transcending thinking finds itself thrown upwards at an ultimate limit. Any metaphysical arrogance is entirely out of place, for this hyperbolic thinking is marked by a paradoxical humility. It is thrown into the face of the absolutely superior, a face of excessive dark, as much as a face of excessive light."

143. *BB* 19: "We have to recall the overdetermined excess of original being. This agape of being is manifested in the determinations of beings, but it is not a determinate being simply, not even the highest being in the sense with which God is often identified—namely, the *ens realissimum.*"

*HG* 7: "Third transcendence is not an empty indefinite but overdetermined in a surplus sense: God as hyperbolic. . . . If this is so, God could not be comprehended under any finite category of the possible or real. It would be above, *huper, über* them, and yet be the original power to be at its most ultimate."

144. *BB* 330: "God thought metaxologically would be . . . the overdetermined excessive plenitude of the free original power of being."

*AOO* 269: "Transcendence itself would be in excess of determinate beings, as their original ground; it would be beyond self-transcendence as its most ultimate *possibilizing source.* . . . In excess of determinacy and our self-determining, it would be overdetermined transcendence which, as other, would not be a merely indefinite beyond to finite being."

145. *HG* 197–98: "The hyperbolic full is always excess, whether in its communication of itself and to what is other, or in terms of what remains reserved as absolute surplus even in its self-communication."

146. *BB* 502: "There are two sides to this ontological truth of the origin as other. The first is its open wholeness, the side of its communicative being that is turned towards finite being. The second is the excess of its infinitude, which is really the ground of its unmastered openness, and which remains other and in enigma, 'dwelling in inaccessible light which no one has seen or can see' (1 Tim. 6:16). This side is the *reserve of its otherness,* preserved as other, remaining beyond and transcendent. The side turned towards us is in community with finitude, though, as shown, it gives an inkling of what remains in reserve. This hiddenness of the ultimate truth again invokes our need of images and metaphors, themselves both true and untrue, double. . . . This reserve is significant because it unequivocally reverses our anticipation that we can reduce the truth of the origin to our truth, be on a par with it in our conceptual mediations."

147. *HT* 34: "Coming to be is hyperbolic happening. What is suggested is an overdetermined source of origination out of which coming to be unfolds. To speak of 'creator,' I suggest, is a way of putting us in mind of this other source."

148. *BB* 231: "T3: The transcendence of the *origin*—this would be *transcendence itself,* not as the exterior, not as the interior, but as the superior. This would be the *huper,* the above. The way of transcendence as hyperbolic throws us towards it. Since it is in excess of determinate being, as its original ground, it would be beyond the doublet of possibility and reality. It would be what we might call the *possibilizing source* of both possibility and realization; but it could not be just a possibility, nor indeed a determinate realization of possibility. It would have to be real possibilizing power, in a manner more original and other than possibility and realization. It would have to be 'possibilizing' beyond determinate possibility, and 'realizing' beyond all determinate realization."

*HG* 3: "T3: Here I refer to original transcendence as still *other* to the above two senses. What might this be? Can we speak of *transcendence itself*? Rather than the exterior transcendence or the interior, can we speak of the *superior*? How superior? Transcendence itself would be in excess of determinate beings, as their original ground; it would be in excess of our self-transcendence, as its most ultimate possibilizing source. It would be beyond the ordinary doublet of possibility/reality, as their possibility source; it could not be just a possibility, nor indeed a determinate realization of possibility."

149. *HG* 136: "The agapeic origin does not produce itself in giving creation. It is always already itself—superplus power of origination, overdeterminate, not in 'need' of finite determination. Finitude is not its own determination, but is a released happening that is given its own promise of being creative. This God gives the being of creation."

150. See below: chapter 4, part one, section III, §2.

151. See below: chapter 4, part one, section IV.

152. One suspects that the fundamental preference for univocity (in Deleuze and Badiou) will ultimately undercut, on one side or the other, any possibility of understanding the nature of community and, therefore, of understanding the nature of otherness (difference, plurality) or of relation. The univocity of being flowers into a nihilistic equivocity, in which identity and relation disappear. In Desmond's terms, this debilitation of our thinking of the community of the between (indeed of community and between-ness as such) is due to the entrenched thinking of the modern ethos that has constricted and deracinated the primal and enabling (whence this strange urge to univocity? To understanding?) ethos of the metaxological community of being. On the roots of this univocal modern (post-modern? . . . post-post-modern?) ethos, see Pickstock, *After Writing*, passim.

Desmond's work, however, resonates with some of Deleuze's concerns. Both Deleuze and Desmond argue for the priority of relation, of an open intermediation that avoids any closed static whole or equivocal dualism. Both also present a fundamental regard for difference, singularity, and plurality. One might argue, however, that Desmond's metaxological community of being better provides for relation and singularity (otherness) than Deleuze's ontological univocity/monism. Deleuze maintains the univocity/monism of being in order to provide for difference and becoming such that difference operates within a more basic static unity. Desmond presents a community of othernesses/transcendences in dynamic non-reductive inter-relation. Here unity/identity is not needed to found difference. (Also, while Deleuze sees such relation and singularity as being devalued by the idea of a transcendent God, Desmond sees all of this as fully compatible with his understanding of God as agapeic origin, see chap. 4.)

153. Milbank presents such a community of difference in harmony and ultimate ontological peace again from a theological perspective. Distinctly opposed to this ultimately harmonious vision of community is Badiou's militant subjects in eternal struggle against, forcing into (themselves ever creating anew?) the totalitarian state(s) of the situation. See Milbank, *Theology and Social Theory*, 434, 440. Badiou, *Being and Event*, 93ff.

154. *BB* 5: "Metaphysical thinking is precipitated in the between. We find ourselves in the midst of being. . . . we have already begun."

155. *BHD* 8: "The deepest openness of speculative mind is the impossibility of the ultimate closure of thought by itself and in itself."

156. *PU* 150: "Knowing is a delight in being. We see this clearly in the wonder of the child. Our mindful being is inherently a love of being and the light of truth."

157. HKFM 207: "The desire of philosophy is to bring the flow to a halt in the system, to confine the rushing river within the fixed borders of its categories, to lay a systematic grid over it to contain its movements and allay our fears."

*RH* 212: "The real obstacle to understanding human affairs lies in the tendency to believe that what we do . . . admits of formulation in hard and irrevocable rules."

158. *BB* 17: "I suggest that such deconstructions of metaphysics as totalizing univocity themselves totalize the nature of metaphysics. In claiming to be free of totalizing thinking, they exhibit totalizing thinking relative to traditional metaphysics."

159. *BB* 161: "The dialectical sense, like the univocal, thinks that to be is to be intelligible, and that to be intelligible is to be determinable. But unlike the univocal interpretation, this determinate intelligibility is not a static state of affairs but a coming to determinacy in the very happening of becoming itself."

160. *DDO* 8: "The intermediation of the metaxological relation grounds an open community of self and other. Beyond mere unity, beyond sheer manyness, beyond manyness within a single unity, it entails a community full of unities, each of which is inexhaustibly manifold within itself."

*BHD* 81: "Metaxological intermediation is simply respect for the richness, complexity and community of Ownness and otherness that is going on, always and already. Ownness and otherness and metaxological community escape beyond final encapsulation."

161. *BB* 12: "The call of metaphysical thinking is singular in its idiotic origins."

162. HT 28: "We need a metaxological approach to acknowledge the affirmative surplus of the overdeterminate, beyond determinacy and self-determination."

163. *PO* 277, 306; *BHD* 49; BDD 738.

164. *PO* 26, 121, 137, 158, 226, 306; *BHD* 271; *BB* 48, 52, 64, 81; *PU* 116, 205, 240; *EB* 46.

165. HKFM 207: "Philosophy means meta-physics, the attempt to suppress movement, arrest the flux, stabilize the rush of experience."

166. *RH* 34: "The essential tendency of metaphysics to arrest the flux."

167. *BB* 44: "If metaphysical thinking, as I claim, takes shape in the milieu of being, the question of transcendence has nothing to do with a leap out of being into the void, but with the deepest mindfulness of what is emergent in the middle itself."

168. *PU* 25: "This groping suffers from an essential perplexity about the meaning of being that give the thinker a kind of metaphysical migraine, or insomnia."

169. *PO* 10, 46, 148, 210–11, 235–36, 242–43; *BHD* 43, 187, 243, 263; *BB* 80, 192; *PU* 148, 243, 254; BDD 752; *AOO* 4. *BHD* 243: "One of the supreme nobilities of speculative metaphysics is its willingness to mindfully return again and again to such ineradicable yet essential perplexities."

170. *EB* 86–87: "The ethos wherein we find ourselves is equivocal, and we must learn the art of dwelling with this."

BDD 735: "There may be indeterminacies or overdeterminacies about the ontological situation that demand metaphysical finesse which does not conquer astonishment or perplexity but deepens and disquiets thinking even more radically."

171. *BHD* 243: "One of the supreme nobilities of speculative metaphysics is its willingness to mindfully return again and again to such ineradicable yet essential perplexities."

172. MC 16: "The metaxu first is to be seen as a happening: the milieu or ethos of being within which we find ourselves."

173. *BB* 44: "If metaphysical thinking, as I claim, takes shape in the milieu of being,

the question of transcendence has nothing to do with a leap out of being into the void, but with the deepest mindfulness of what is emergent in the middle itself."

*BB* 44: "'*Meta*' is being in the midst; '*meta*' is also reference to what is beyond, what is transcendent. Metaxological metaphysics must think the doubleness of this tension between being in the midst *and* being referred by self-transcendence to the transcendence of what is other, what is over and above."

174. *BDD* 760: "We cannot will astonishment. It is given. It is a gift. There is required preparation, waiting, purified willingness, opening, tireless thinking. There is a willingness beyond will to power. . . . Something from beyond self must be allowed to give itself, if it will give itself at all."

175. *BB* 57: Desmond observes that even with Heraclitus "the flux of happening is shot through with *logos*. . . . Becoming . . . is intermediate, as the happening of the between: it is between form and formlessness, indefiniteness and determination."

176. *BB* 294–95: "The fecundity of creation gives rises [*sic*] to the newness of the 'once' that is infinitely pluralized in the marvel of singularity. Such a pluralization is a repetition that never repeats itself, that never reiterates the univocal same. Creation is an ever-fresh, never-diminished origination of singularity."

177. *PO* 18: "Philosophy is an attempt at mindfulness of what is at work in the middle, considered as the metaxological community of being."

*MC* 16: "The metaxu first is to be seen as a happening: the milieu or ethos of being within which we find ourselves."

178. *BB* 452: "In a literal sense, being between is an *inter-esse,* where the interest is in the being of the *inter.*"

179. *AE* 71: "There is/es gibt only . . . the plurality of particulars."

*AE* 234: "To speak of what happens is to give up thinking that events make sense all the way down."

*AE* 235: "The sum and substance of events is nothing other than the events themselves."

180. *BHD* 81: "Metaxological intermediation is simply respect for the richness, complexity and community of Ownness and otherness that is going on, always and already. Ownness and otherness and metaxological community escape beyond final encapsulation."

181. *OR* 127: "We are left with nothing, but with the passion and the not-knowing."

182. *PU* 110: "To objectify being is to univocalize it. But this is to entrench dualism by rigid separation of the subjective and objective. This entrenched dualism is incompatible with the community between mind and being which is presupposed by the truth of objective mind."

183. *BHD* 243: "One of the supreme nobilities of speculative metaphysics is its willingness to mindfully return again and again to such ineradicable yet essential perplexities."

184. *BB* 17: "I suggest that such deconstructions of metaphysics as totalizing univocity themselves totalize the nature of metaphysics. In claiming to be free of totalizing thinking, they exhibit totalizing thinking relative to traditional metaphysics. As they seem to take the speck out of metaphysician's eye, they overlook any beam in their own. They do not do justice to the *plurivocal nature* of metaphysical thinking."

185. *BB* 131: "Equivocal thinking can turn into a skepticism, thence into a dissolution of all determinate intelligibility, thence into an exultation in the power to negate all mediations, finally hardening into a dogmatism of nihilism that insists there is no sense to be made and that no sense will be made."

186. HT 25: "Philosophy is just the thoughtful engagement of the sources of intelligibility immediately at work in the between."

187. AOO 271: "Despite the bad name metaphysics has had of late, the need for metaphysics has not ceased. Sometimes it takes forms that do not officially present themselves with the calling card marked 'metaphysics.'"

MC 1: "I am not entirely sure what is meant by post-metaphysical thinking, but if we think of metaphysics as asking for fundamental reflection, more or less systematic, on the basic senses of the "to be," or of what it means to be, metaphysics will never be a practice we can put behind us."

188. AT 248: "The absence of inherent good in the ethos is covered up by excessive noise about our purported creation of value. We distract ourselves from the death of the ethos with encomiums to our self-proclaimed creativity."

189. BB 509: "If the creation is valueless in itself, then the human being as a participant in creation is also ontologically valueless, so likewise his human construction is ultimately valueless. . . . Only subtle self-deception can avoid the collapse of our constructions into the ontological nihilism that is said to affect the whole of being in itself."

190. NDR 45: "To what extent is deconstruction a victim of the devaluation of being in modernity? Are deconstructive thinkers still in the same ethos which breeds the quasi-deconstruction of modern self-determination?"

## 3. Ethics

1. BB 517–18: "When the ancients said that desire seeks the good because it is the good, they were superior to the moderns who said that the good is good because desire seeks it."

EB 168: "Is not late modernity anomalous in this regard? We have set ourselves up over against the surplus of otherness; stripping it of the charge of the good, we have also stripped it of the signs that point towards the ground of the good. As we saw, being there becomes worthless. In tandem, we set ourselves up as ground of value who impose on this valueless thereness values of our construction."

This estrangement between being and the good—of the objectification of being and the subjectification of value—is very much present in Badiou's understanding of humans as inherently worthless and of ethics (his "ethics of truths") as not arising from what is, for what is is nothing more than neutral pure multiplicity (Badiou, *Ethics*, 28, 59). On the problem of the estrangement of being and goodness, see Milbank, *Being Reconciled*, 17.

2. BB 509: "If the creation is valueless in itself, then the human being as a participant in creation is also ontologically valueless, so likewise his human construction is ultimately valueless. Every effort to construct values out of himself will be subject to the same deeper, primitive, ultimate valuelessness. Human values collapse ultimately into nothing, if there is not a ground of value in the integrity of being itself."

3. BB 509: "The human being is a living nihilism masquerading as ethical, if there is no ontology of the good, if the good is not grounded in being itself, or if being is not primally good."

4. NDR 43–44: This is related to what Desmond calls "the antinomy of autonomy and transcendence": "Absolutize autonomy and you must relativize transcendence; but if transcendence cannot be so relativized, autonomy must itself be relativized."

5. AT 236: "Suppose such an ethos of 'neutralization' is itself an ontological contraction of the given milieu of being as saturated with value."

(N.b.) The "phenomenological" experience of this ethos was addressed more specifically in the first and third sections of the first part of the previous chapter.

6. *EB* 248: "Some say: the good is the desirable; it is what is desired; desire defines the good, not the good desire. This is a widespread modern view, from Hobbes onward. The ancients took the other side of the ambiguity: the good is the desirable, it is desired as desirable, but it is desirable because it is good; the good is desired because it is good, not good because it is desired. I take the second view to be the truer, but the first has its partial truth."

It should be noted that Desmond is here speaking quite (if not too) generally when he speaks of the "modern" (he might be here thinking of a certain prevalent scientific reductionism) and the "ancients" (he is likely thinking of Plato). There were, of course, ancient nihilists as well as modern mystics.

7. *PO* 160: "The ethical is an articulation of being as good, the charge of being in us that we become, actualize, the given promise of the good."

*AT* 235: "Ethos is indeterminate in an overdetermined sense: not merely neutral, but an equivocal medium of possibility or an in-between of promise."

*EB* 51: "The ethos is one of promise, and so open to different shapings in terms of the plurality of the potencies of the ethical." See section II below.

8. *BB* 535: "The immanence of the good concerns its working in the intimacy of being itself. This intimacy refers both to the idiocy of the self, and to the community between ethical selves that sustain each other with respect for their inherent worth."

9. *NDR* 44: "One of the richest ways of speaking of [being] would be to say: it is hospitable to the gift of the good. It is enveloped by a light of worth. The metaphysical milieu, the ontological ethos of our philosophizing, requires reflection in terms of this, reflection on this hospitality of being to the good."

10. *PU* 39: "The question of the worth of what is, the very worthiness of being . . . [t]his question points to a convergence of metaphysics (as asking about the meaning and truth of being) and ethics (as asking about the goodness of being)."

11. *PO* 163: "All being mindful is ethical."

*PU* 109: "There is an existential ethical side to objective knowing as participatory in a community of mind and being. Objective knowing counsels detachment, disinterest. But these are ambiguous counsel, since they seem to deny the *value* of objective inquiry itself."

12. *PO* 344: "Being ethical is a way of being of desire: desire is an articulation of being that is always already charged with value. . . . Ethics is the hermeneutics of this charge."

*BB* 509: "The human being is a living nihilism masquerading as ethical, if there is no ontology of the good, if the good is not grounded in being itself, or if being is not primally good."

*PU* 223: "Again metaphysics and ethics are inseparable. Without proper metaphysical ground, ethics is groundless."

13. *PO* 160: "The ethical is an articulation of being as good, the charge of being in us that we become, actualize, the given promise of the good."

*PO* 161: "We value according to an ontological sense of being, the self-knowledge of which we often lack."

14. *PO* 160: "The ethical, as care for the good, is a way of being, articulating what we are in a manner that from the outset shows a configuration of being always already charged with the good. The ethical is an articulation of being as good, the charge of being in us that we become, actualize, the given promise of the good."

*PO* 187: Respect for the other "follows from what we might term the metaphysical worth of personhood."

15. *EB* 45: "This is nonsense, of course, since the ground, even while giving growth, must always remain other; the flower is only relatively self-growing and never self-grounding. The self-grounding flower is folly. But we will ourselves to be thus blooming."

16. *EB* 199–200: "There is a transcendental/ontological meaning of metaxological community which is the ground that makes possible determinate formations of ethical community such as we find in definite forms of ethical selving and communal intermediation."

17. *PU* 225: "How can we speak of such value as intrinsic to being? The language of 'creation' points in a direction which cannot stop short of metaphysics, indeed a certain theology. Creation is good because to be is to be a value; to be a value is to be so because one is valued; but who is the one that values the creation? The most radical answer is that the origin does."

18. *BB* 383: "This elemental self is idiotic, again in the Greek sense of the *idiōtēs:* the private, the intimate—what is on the edge of, or outside, or other than—more publicly available generalities or neutral universals."

19. *BB* 380: "This elemental self is itself and nothing but itself. Perhaps we may speak of its simplicity and indivisibility, though this will have to be further qualified. We might say that to be a self is to be an original unto oneself."

*BB* 381: "The human self—and this is felt singularly by each singular self—has an ineluctable sense of itself as itself and itself alone."

20. *BB* 380: "The univocal sense offers us a first approach to this singularity of self. A self is itself and nothing but itself."

21. *BB* 381: "This nonobjective selfhood is a singular mindfulness of the original power of being that senses and feels itself as a unique becoming that is for itself in the vast enigma of the universal impermanence."

*EB* 171: " 'Idiocy' " also names an indeterminate pre-objective and pre-subjective 'awareness' that is not any definite awareness, and that floats with a pre-determinate sense of 'self' that is no definite self, and that yet precedes any definite formation of self, and out of which crystallize different formations of selving."

22. *BB* 381: "The human self—and this is felt singularly by each singular self—has an ineluctable sense of itself as itself and itself alone."

*BB* 397: "It is this sense of idiotic integrity, incomparable singularity, that is felt by the primal, elemental I."

23. *EB* 200: "The idiot self concretizes the infinite value in the ontological roots of human being as given to itself by the origin."

24. *BB* 384: The elemental self is "as idiotically my own, and as never possessed even while my own, it is never owned by me. It is an inward otherness, more intimate to inwardness [than] all its own self-possessions. The idiocy of the self in this inwardness is an opening to otherness within itself."

*EB* 170: "The intimacy of the idiocy is both a self-intimacy and also an unthematic mindfulness that self is with others always and from the start. The ontological definition of the intimate "*solo*" is always to be with the other, even when not knowing this, and indeed when not knowing itself."

25. *EB* 215: "The anomalous being of the human is revealed in this freedom of infinite desire. Infinite desire emerges in finite being—excess of being rises up in the human being as selving: transcending as more, and towards the more. This 'more' means enig-

matic otherness in inwardness itself: the very interiority of being is the coming to show of infinity, the transcending power of the being, the transcendence towards infinity of the human being."

26. *BB* 384: "The idiocy of the self in this inwardness is an opening to otherness within itself. Indeed its excess suggests the promise of an inexhaustibility."

*BB* 401: "The excess of the self . . . is the source of its infinite restlessness. A pure whole is never restless with itself; it is perfect and needs nothing; or it is perfectly at home with itself. Not so the human self as original."

27. *HG* 3: "T2: Here I refer to the transcendence of *self-being* such as we meet especially in the self-surpassing power of the human being. The meaning of possibility can here be defined immanently rather than just determined externally. There is possibility as freedom, perhaps even as the promise of free finite creativity."

28. *DDO* 189: "As an intermediate original, the self revealed itself as double—that is, both as a desire for immanent self-relation and as infinitely open in terms of its exodus into what is beyond. It desires to be whole; yet, as infinitely open, it may become actively originative in relation to otherness. Wholeness and infinitude in this sense can be seen as two ultimates defining man's deepest relation to himself and otherness."

29. See regarding original selfhood: *DDO* 35–67.

30. *BB* 380: "This elemental self is itself and nothing but itself. Perhaps we may speak of its simplicity and indivisibility, though this will have to be further qualified. We might say that to be a self is to be an original unto oneself."

31. *PU* 78: "If there is an indeterminacy to the idiot I that is original, 'original' does not imply atomic substance but source of origination. The original indeterminate I is free as an originative source of being."

32. *BB* 380: "To be a self is to be a distinctive center of original power of being."

*PU* 60: ". . . an indeterminate power that is prior to any determination and that exceeds every determination, whether effected by the self itself, or by the social networks of relations which consolidates its communal identity. This is the ontological power of original selfness."

33. *BB* 377: "In sum: the promise of singularity, concretized in the being for-itself of creation, selves through things and intelligibilities, and begins to be mindfully realized in the human self."

34. *PU* 57: "We become ourselves, but we are already ourselves; and we become the selves we already are, because we are not the self we might be, given the promise of being that is given to us as being this person."

35. *PU* 192: "Possibility as creative is ontological. It refers to the promise of being as concretely offered in the between, a promise that is given, but that is not completely actualized in its givenness. Promise may be a gift that has to be actualized, or actualize itself in freedom. Ontological promise is especially evident with the human being as free. Creative possibility reveals the transcending energy of being itself; in the promise of human freedom, the original power of being becomes freely self-transcending."

36. *BB* 397: "The *dynamism of self-transcendence* specifies the promise of this original self."

37. *BB* 390: "[T]his self is . . . an affirmative openness to what is other to itself, and to the to-be-realized realization of its own promise of being."

*PU* 70: "There is both erotic and agapeic promise in the intimacy of being, in the idiocy of selfhood."

38. *HG* 3: "T2: Here I refer to the transcendence of *self-being* such as we meet espe-

cially in the self-surpassing power of the human being. The meaning of possibility can here be defined immanently rather than just determined externally. There is possibility as freedom, perhaps even as the promise of free finite creativity."

39. *BB* 380: "The indeterminacy of the original self is to be understood affirmatively as a source of origination. As a power of determining, we can also call it a source of spontaneity and freedom."

*BB* 392: The self is "original of itself to the extent that its doing of itself also makes it to be the kind of being that it is."

40. *PO* 164: "Ethical mind in its fullness . . . [is] an achievement, the product of a process of development . . . we must *become* ethical. Here we have the risk of soul-making: being ethical involves a *poiēsis* of selfhood, the self-becoming of the human being in praxis with respect to its ideal perfection."

*BB* 379: "Selving, like being, is plurivocal."

*EB* 223: Ethical selvings (which are dealt with in Part III of *Ethics and the Between*) have to do with "the self-mediation of the good from rudimentary desire to agapeic freedom beyond autonomy."

41. The different selvings and concomitant freedoms will be expanded upon in section III below.

*EB* 269: "If the freedom that ferments in ethical selving is not univocal but plurivocal, it follows that there are different freedoms, corresponding to different formations of self-transcending."

42. *EB* 223: "Of course, we cannot separate the self-mediation of being good from intermediation with the other. But for purposes of clarification, self-mediation can be correlated with a more dialectical slant, intermediation with a more metaxological. In truth, ethical selving is intermediated through and through, and hence metaxological. The intermediate sustains the self-mediation."

43. *EB* 10: "The ontological promise of the power of the 'to be' receives such plurivocal articulation in terms of what I will call the *potencies of the ethical*."

*EB* 10: "We are plurally endowed with the ethical promise of diverse potencies of the original power to be."

44. *EB* 170: "'Idiocy' names the initially unarticulated intimacy with the good."

45. *EB* 171: "The community of being as good comes to indeterminate mindfulness in the *innerness of selving* that is the mysterious coming to self in primal self-awakening to the 'to be.'"

*EB* 171: "I connect this with the elemental, non-determinate mindfulness of *simply being*. This indeterminate awareness/non-awareness of simply being is saturated with the value of being, but we cannot uninterruptedly endure this value."

46. *EB* 177: "The worth of being is shown aesthetically in the ethos—given to our senses and our bodies."

*EB* 179: "The more standard contrast of aesthetics and ethics cannot be finally upheld. We think of beauty as an aesthetic category, but it is also ethical. Beauty is the singular formation of harmonious integrity of being within the ambience of value pervading the ethos."

47. *EB* 192: "Ethical mindfulness is intensive attunement to the play of sameness and difference in the ethos, where insistent and subtle constancies emerge in the flux of impermanence."

*EB* 192: "The constancies reflect dynamic patterns of integrity and commonality in the changing flux of the ethos. They are forms of 'being together' that, already at work, make a call on humans to realize more fully their given promise."

48. *EB* 196: "What do we find is the constant? We approach very close to the elementals: worship and thanks, reverence and honor, love, birth, marriage, death, covetousness and liberality, possession and hospitality."

*EB* 196: "I think the *ten commandments* offer a succinct codification of the constancies as passing from God's absolute constancy, and the gift of the "to be," through the other more qualified constancies related to self and other: mortal life, family, marriage, birth, death, one's place in the sun, what one may possess and what one should not usurp; the elementals above named. The point is not mindless submission to dead law. The constancies formulate deep and elemental exigencies of human being, formulate them often as tasks, but tasks based on what we are, for what we are is an openness to become what we are and answer the exigencies immanent in our being."

49. *EB* 199: "What I mean by transcendental here is not any logical or epistemological possibility; it is ontological as pertaining to the constitution of what it means to be, and what it means to be good."

50. *EB* 199: "But do we find constancies so insistent as to be called transcendental in the general sense that without them determinate ethical living would not be possible? I think the agapeic relation between origin and the ethos is transcendental in that sense, as well as the metaxological relation between self and other within the ethos. Both relations condition the possibility of more determinate possibilities of selving and being together."

51. Sometimes Desmond has the eudaimonistic follow the dianoetic in sequence to accentuate the dialectical to and fro between the more stable/constant/univocal and the more fluid/variable/equivocal.

52. *EB* 203: "The needful discernment is neither a fixation on rigid principles nor a lax yielding to every passing impulse. It is principled and yet ever vigilant to the nuance of situation. It is a *living constancy* in the midst of the passing."

53. *EB* 212: "A restlessness emerges that testifies to an infinite dimension to human desire. We cannot force all desire into the mould of finite appetite. To live in terms of that forcing is to deform ourselves. The infinite restlessness must be given allowance to be itself. Allowing it so, however, risks futility on one side, our coming into something more transcendent, on the other."

54. *EB* 269: "If the freedom that ferments in ethical selving is not univocal but plurivocal, it follows that there are different freedoms, corresponding to different formations of self-transcending."

55. *EB* 223: "In Part III, I consider the self-mediation of the good from rudimentary desire to agapeic freedom beyond autonomy."

56. *EB* 120: "Ethics entails a process of selving in community, and a process of communication between selves. Ethical self-mediation occurs within the intermediation of the ethos."

*EB* 223: "Of course, we cannot separate the self-mediation of being good from intermediation with the other. But for purposes of clarification, self-mediation can be correlated with a more dialectical slant, intermediation with a more metaxological. In truth, ethical selving is intermediated through and through, and hence metaxological. The intermediate sustains the self-mediation."

57. *BB* 382: "This nonobjective sense of self suggests the nonreducibility of the inner feeling of mineness."

*BB* 383: "This elemental self is idiotic, again in the Greek sense of the *idiōtēs:* the private, the intimate—what is on the edge of, or outside, or other than—more publicly available generalities or neutral universals. This idiotic singularity points to a rich 'univocity' that is not subsumable in any system of categories."

58. *BB* 380: "The indeterminacy of the original self is to be understood affirmatively as a source of origination. As a power of determining, we can also call it a source of spontaneity and freedom."

*BB* 397: "The *dynamism of self-transcendence* specifies the promise of this original self. The risk run here is always that of self-distraction, or self-loss, or self-betrayal, or self-deformation; though again the self that loses itself is still the primal integrity for itself; it has, however, betrayed the promise of its own originality."

*PU* 60: "This inexhaustibility of selfhood, exceeding determination, conceptual or social, is the idiocy of its being."

59. *PU* 70: "Desire erupts in the idiotic self, it surges up in the flesh, elementally and unbidden. It comes to be shaped in a process of selving. Instead of the dissolution of determinacy, there is the fuller unfolding of this power to be into a distinctive self with a plurality of determinate self-manifestations."

*EB* 223: "*First selving:* the idiocy of root will surges up as spontaneous desire/need—elemental self-insistence."

60. *EB* 228: "The root will is always at work, even when self-determination mediates it. There is goodness to this root will: the self-insistence is the very energy in which the unique self-being of this being gives expression to itself. Every being is thus, simply as a being of dynamic energy; this is the spontaneous affirmation of its own being, of this being as good, and of the good of this being."

61. *EB* 228: "The root will is in the idiot self: sheer idiosyncrasy in one sense, but in another sense it is the intimacy of being, and hence the happening of deep presence both to self and to others. The truth of community, of communicative being with a uniquely personal intonation, is already there in the root will."

62. *EB* 270: "First freedom is given to us as the release into being for ourselves."

63. *PU* 78: "Freedom cannot be reduced to a determinate power. . . . To be free in itself, the source of freedom must be beyond univocal determination; for it cannot be fixed. And it cannot be fixed because it is a fixing or source of fixing, a shaping and not at first a shaped product."

*PU* 78: "Freedom is not ultimately erotic, nor simply for the self. Put otherwise, the indeterminate freedom of the idiot I is not autonomy. For the intimacy of being is double, hence its being for itself is also heteronomous."

64. *PU* 161: "There is a truth to the *cogito* argument—the self in being denied or deceived cannot be denied to be. I see this as the ineradicable intimacy of being, the idiocy of self-being."

65. *PU* 66: "Elemental self-transcendence and community are inseparable, so much so that an elemental 'being-with' is constitutive of the idiotic I itself. The nature of the intimate self is 'being with': being with self, and being with what is other to self."

*PU* 76: "Is the idiotic I just thought thinking itself? No, for its intimacy with the other is always already there from the outset."

*EB* 171: "This idiocy is an awakening. The community of being as good comes to indeterminate mindfulness in the *innerness of selving* that is the mysterious coming to self in primal self-awakening to the "to be"—a coming that is of the essence to singular self-hood and yet irreducibly communal, at once a relation to itself and a relation to what is other."

66. *BB* 384: "In certain respects, the idiot self is prior to aesthetic selving, because the latter is already 'objectified' in the body, positioned, 'posited,' there, hence more determinate than the idiotic I."

*PU* 66: "This idiotic self comes to more manifest expression with the *aesthetic I*—

aesthetic in its ancient and widest connotation concerning sensible and sensitive being. Being-there as other is given as aesthetic presencing; so also the sense of self is emergent as aesthetically intimated. By the aesthetic self I mean the self in the prereflective and preobjective feeling of itself as fleshed."

67. *BB* 386: "The aesthetic self is a site of flow and passage, in and out. In the element of the flesh it is already a between."

68. *BB* 388, 390. The other as t(h)reat?

69. *DDO* 166: Self-will's "devouring willfulness . . . cannot endure the pathos, the suffering, of difference. Indeed, in that it hates what it cannot control, there is really a despair, both of itself and of otherness, in its defiance of finitude."

70. *EB* 249: "Desire is indeterminate as simply desire, but determinate as oriented to this particular outcome. It is always both: indeterminate/determinate, and yet again more than any determinate desire. There is a univocity to the process: I desire this, this, this—and the "this" can often be determined with strong univocity: food, drink, shelter. . . . Yet this univocity leads to this good, this good and so on, *ad infinitum*. It is this *multiplication* that introduces the *more* in *equivocal form*. The excess of desire meets the excess of things, always more than desire, and at the same time desire is more than they. They are more than it can possess; it wills to possess more than they can give. There is a double "more," on both sides. The *ad infinitum* of desire suggests *futility: ad nauseam*. It is the same damn thing again and again, in every different object. And as the same, it is now not anymore the more that desire seeks. An orgy of satisfaction comes to sing the dirges of dissatisfaction."

71. *EB* 245: "Hence desire is not just for this and that but also for *its own* fulfillment. This appears with will: not just the will to this or that; but the will to be such and such a person. Not only do I will to have, or do, or be, such and such. *I will myself* to be such and such, in having or doing or being such and such. This is a more decisive self-mediation than any immediate happening of desire."

72. *EB* 245: "Will thus is always implicitly an answerability for self. To will is to be answerable: to be open to acknowledge that what has been willed has been willed by *this* self, as the original of *this* willing. This answerability means the root will that merely insists on itself here decisively steps in the direction of ethical responsibility. The will that is answerable for itself is more than the will that insists on itself. Answerability lays itself open to judgment, while self-insistence calls for attention to itself, announcing its being there as a claim on the other."

73. *EB* 248: "So the intrepid self-doubling, redoubling of the will, risks being the refusal whereby the self falls into evil, even as it elevates itself in the reiteration of its own self-infinitizing. Will willing to be itself absolute, to be itself the absolute: this is, in one sense, a natural development of the root will; in other sense, it is the result of a perversion of the doubleness that necessarily emerges in the self-unfolding of the root will."

74. *EB* 249: "What of the *will willing to be itself absolute*? This is a self-doubling that expresses the root energy of our being as self-transcending. But this is a self-transcending that does *not* transcend self. The self-doubling is no doubling at all; it is the insistent reiteration of the I as alone to be affirmed, and as I alone. This is a will to self-reiteration: self-insistent solitude in the absolute of will willing itself."

75. *EB* 280 "In its upsurge, desire discovers freedom both in its power to possess this thing and that, and in its dissatisfaction in excess of all these possessions. Its knowing of this 'more' about itself means it is 'free from' these things: it is beyond them, even though it needs them. Its dissatisfaction paradoxically is inseparable from its *superiority*: it tastes the unlimited range of its self-transcending, and sees this lack of limit as

revealing its power. Its unhappiness shows its power, even though as it ages more it will know more from this the meaning of its impotence. Now here the virgin freshness of desire, new to its own restlessness, is intoxicating. Desire is desire affirming itself as desire. Its drunkenness consists in its own self-intoxication, even as 'freedom from' takes form out of the will willing itself, or self-affirming affirming itself."

76. *EB* 271: "This first freedom opens equivocity: equivocity between our dependence on the other origin, our relativity to other things and persons in creation, and our own integrity of being for self. I said that my being is an affirmation of the 'to be' in the self-affirming of my being for self. This affirmation is a freeing of the original power of the 'to be.' It is a primordial *ontological* freedom."

77. *EB* 280: "Its knowing of this 'more' about itself means it is 'free from' these things: it is beyond them, even though it needs them. Its dissatisfaction paradoxically is inseparable from its *superiority*: it tastes the unlimited range of its self-transcending, and sees this lack of limit as revealing its power. Its unhappiness shows its power, even though as it ages more it will know more from this the meaning of its impotence. Now here the virgin freshness of desire, new to its own restlessness, is intoxicating."

78. *EB* 280: "Desire is desire affirming itself as desire. Its drunkenness consists in its own self-intoxication, even as 'freedom from' takes form out of the will willing itself, or self-affirming affirming itself."

*EB* 297: "Desire would be self-generating; self would generate self. Any releasing of desire into freedom as itself given to it, will be redefined in terms of the circle of the self-generating, self-seeking self-enjoying self. There is no gift."

79. *EB* 289: "Despite appearances, this self-circling excitation of desire desiring itself is not fulfilled desire. Desire fills itself with itself. One is 'full of oneself,' we say. Is this fulfillment: 'being full of oneself'? Is it the plenitude of agapeic generosity that would give beyond itself? Is it the power to bestow itself on the other? No. It is the self-consummation that consumes itself and only itself, and in its own self-consumption finds the bitter taste of its own nothingness. . . . Despair here is an empty self full of itself, circling on empty in its own lacking fullness with self."

*EB* 299: "What is craving? A hunger that gnaws at itself as an emptiness that is never replete, that must be infinitely fed, even as it ceaselessly devours everything. Craving: desire that is mine and that is not mine anymore, for I am not free in my craving. Craving: my desire is freed but so freed that it is the prisoner of necessitation, hence not free at all."

80. *EB* 289: "Without some purpose desire dissipates itself. But to have some purpose is to be more than 'free from'; it is to be 'free towards . . .' If we have made our settled abode in 'freedom from,' we are in trouble. Why? Because purpose *constrains* desire. If I have a purpose I am not 'free from' anymore, and have to direct, discipline desire towards that objective. This means placing restraint on desire."

*EB* 290: "Purposes may serve to arouse desire initially; but since freedom is 'freedom from,' purposes must now serve to deflect the energy of desire back to desire itself. The particular purpose arouses desire, desire energizes itself towards it, but the 'freedom towards' is again overtaken by 'freedom from.'"

81. *BB* 402: "The self-transcending restlessness of desire here seeks wholeness but it subordinates the other to the goal of its immanent self-satisfaction. The erotic self finally tries to appropriate the other to itself and make it serve the riches of its own immanent self-satisfaction"

*EB* 358: "Eros returns the self to itself through the other."

*HG* 40: Erotic love is "a kind of self-mediation in and through the other. I come to myself more fully in and through the other, the other gives me to myself in the fuller form beyond initial lack."

82. *PU* 105: "By erotic mind I will mean a relativity of mind to what is other to self, but a relativity that subsumes what is other into the self-relativity of the mind seeking its own self-satisfaction and self-certainty. Erotic mind goes to the other beyond itself, but its self-transcendence is impelled by its own lack which it would fill by appropriating the other. Its relativity to the other serves this fulfillment of its own initial lack. The truth of the other affords the truth of self-fulfillment."

83. *PU* 191: "Erotic freedom is 'for-self'; it is autonomy, *auto-nomos*, law of the same."

*EB* 224: "*Fourth selving*: beyond an equivocal liberty ethical selving works for an adult autonomy, not least by dialectically seeking to appropriate its own powers of negation. *Fifth selving*: adult eros seeks its sovereignty (there is 'autonomy' and mature autonomy)."

84. *EB* 161: "Dialectical freedom as erotic sovereignty is already in seed beyond autonomy, because its community with the allowing other is already immanent in its self-determining."

85. *EB* 309: "The root self-insistence is to be further transformed in a willing of self that *seeks to appropriate the multiple ambiguities of its own internal equivocity, and the recalcitrances of resisting others.*"

86. *EB* 309: "Autonomous self-determination is indeed self-insistent, but now the naiveté of my own self-affirmation has been tempered: I have tasted the despair in an undirected intoxication of desire; I have known the dubious fidelity of others who stand more against me than with me; coming to myself, I must calculate for myself and not be prodigal; I must work and not spend, and work for myself; and work for myself as *one works to make oneself be something*. I must climb out of the sty of the hired hand and be my own master, owning not only my own property, but my own life. I see my further freedom is closely connected with negation and work, beckoning me to autonomy as a dialectical freedom, and perhaps the further selving of erotic sovereignty."

87. *EB* 318: "If its own self-determination is the meaning of freedom, the other cannot be completely fitted into the seamless circle of its own self-mediation. Something is here inherited from the ambiguity of 'freedom from.' For the latter, to be free for self is to be free from the other as a restraining curb; hence the latency of hostile relations: the 'from' is shaped by the negation that springs up with the 'no' to the other standing in the way of my freedom. But since there is no escaping the other, the other must be 'put in its place.' Autonomy continues 'freedom from' into 'freedom to,' and in terms of the will willing itself. And it is this continuity of the will willing itself that inevitably places the other in an equivocal position."

*EB* 320: "Dialectical self-mediation, as autonomy, subjects the other to its own becoming subject."

88. *EB* 317: "Autonomy risks always the return of its own 'freedom from' in the shape of the self as a unit of power, indeed as negative power turned to predatory power, that is, as implicitly tyrannical in the idiocy of the heart, there where the monstrous slumbers."

*EB* 319: "*Within* the freedom of autonomy, the absolute willing of itself by the tyrannical will comes to arise. This tyranny is not the opposite of autonomy; it is the monster that has always slept in the cellar of will willing itself and that now crawls out triumphant under the mask of self-legislation to proclaim itself finally as the absolute work."

*EB* 321: "What is tyranny but the most powerful will willing itself in relation to the other? This means that autonomy, as this tyranny, is exactly *heteronomy.* The logic of the one willing itself is that there but be *one absolute* autonomous self-determination. Short of that there will always be others to relativize the absolute autonomy. This logic of autonomy must become totalitarian, and hence produce the most tyrannical heteronomy, relative to all others except the all-devouring one. Some of this we have seen in modernity."

89. *BB* 439: "The coming of the self to itself, in its outgoing towards the other, is erotic sovereignty. It is erotic, because the self proceeds through its transcending from its own lack to self-fulfillment; it is a sovereign because its togetherness with others gives the self back to itself, with a confirmation of itself and its powers. The community of erotic sovereignty gives selves to themselves as autonomous."

One can see a similarity between Badiou's subject's participation in a truth procedure that incorporate and expands the domain of a "truth" and Desmond's erotic sovereign.

90. *EB* 323: "Finite beings mix the exigence to be and lack. The elemental self-insistence of a being is inseparable from its lack of its full self. It insists on itself in face of its own lack, and to overcome its threat. The becoming of desire shows the urge to be free, and to be free as self-affirming, in such a wise that the lack internal to finitude is met and mastered."

*EB* 329: "Erotic self-transcendence goes out of itself towards the other. It goes out needing the other to fulfill its lack, and finds its own desire to be more than lack, for how else could it surpass itself, were it not already an affirmative center of transcending being."

91. *EB* 324: "What does it mean to 'come to itself' (again that phrase)? It is not any simple selfishness. Sovereignty is pursued in view of a *purpose greater than the particular self.* Recall the fanaticism of purpose mentioned before: it takes over the whole self, seems to be greater than one. So with sovereignty: the search is to overcome the shabby condition of one's present limits."

92. *EB* 339: "It seems to be your passion to demonize erotic sovereignty. But No. Erotic sovereignty, qualified by openness to transcendence as higher than itself, can show us the glory of the world. In the upbuilding of communities of justice, sovereigns who have come into a maturity of self-possessed freedom, are essential. They are essential to show us something of the realized promise of immanent excellence: such are heroes and exemplars—originals to imitate, paragons to emulate."

93. *EB* 329: "Is there a fatal flaw risked by this erotic sovereignty? This. Just in its glory it risks losing self in its affirming of itself, as glory turns to self-glorification, turning the circle of eros into a 'higher' autonomy that hiddenly is an autism of spirit, a solitude curved back into itself: freedom thankless, even though counting itself king of infinite possibility."

*EB* 339: "The tyrant is what one is, as willing all being to be for one, as willing the good as my good, as will willing itself as the absolute will, for which everything other serves. There is no service of the other in all this, and no true release of self."

94. *EB* 206: "Erotic sovereignty hides gratitude for the generosity of the gift. And the hiding can be double, either a denial or pushing aside, or something that, more shyly, will not coarsely claim as owned the gift of great powers."

*EB* 344: "The matter was not only a lack of nuanced mindfulness about the temptations of erotic sovereignty, but a clear minded choice for a sovereignty that refused or willed to exclude the divine gift, for every gift makes one other than absolutely autonomous."

95. *EB* 330: "Erotic self-transcending that comes to selve with a measure of sovereignty can retain its memory of the way the other has given one back to oneself."

96. *EB* 344: "It is only when our unease about the other as other has taken on conviction, that we seriously think about the abdication of erotic sovereignty. Abdication does not here mean an abject giving up, though there is a giving up; does not mean a lifeless surrender, though there is a surrender; does not mean a submission to impotence, though there is a consent to powerlessness. Abdication has to do with the reticence of power, and the reserve of the power of freedom beyond autonomy."

97. *EB* 347: "Erotic sovereignty seeks a freedom beyond autonomy, but it is still not released beyond its own self-mediation, and the will that wills its own glory. How might it be given over, give itself over more fully to this freeing beyond autonomy?"

*EB* 353: "Autonomy is not the sovereign it takes itself to be, but itself the issue of an origin or source, enigmatic just in its intimacy. Autonomy as self-transcendence opens into, or up to transcendence beyond autonomy."

*EB* 365: "Suppose one touches a measure of erotic sovereignty; there can be a fulfilling, but also a *new unrest.* Our infinite restlessness can only come to peace in a good itself infinite; we cannot be that good, though we have an infinite promise; and this our restlessness hearkens back to our first selving. It is impossible to rest with one's own fulfillment."

98. *BB* 453: "The agapeic self is centered beyond itself."

*CWSC* 41: "Agapeic selving is a being beyond self as willful and as willing itself; hence it implies a kind of unselving, if you like, but . . . with a willing beyond willfulness and beyond will to power, and indeed beyond good and evil, in so far as these are defined by a determinate human measure."

99. *BB* 408: The agapeic self is "doubly stressed in the between: between the excess of its own original power, and the willingness to suspend that power in the interests of the other . . . a middle between infinitudes."

*PU* 144: "The overdetermined power to be of selfhood is agapeic in these two ways: as *given to itself to be* out of an origin other to itself; and as the power to *give itself over to being* beyond itself in its own self-transcendence."

100. En 136: "Agape [is] a love out of surplus that gives to the other but not with the intent to secure a return to itself, but simply gives goodly for the good of the other as other."

*HG* 40: "A going towards the other but not from a lack in the lover but from an excess or surplus of good that gives from itself, gives beyond itself to the other. . . . It is beyond self-mediating love, affirming beyond proportionality, a disproportionate relation of being good for the other."

101. *EB* 217: "If erotic sovereignty is tempted to close the circle of desire, and make self both desiring and desired, by contrast, agapeic service cannot close any circle, for the desired is not the same as the desiring—when I desire I desire the good as other to my desire: the communal reference to the good as other is in the dynamism of our self-transcending. Desire itself is a primal openness to the other and the beyond."

102. *BB* 413: The agapeic self "is not lacking in interest; rather its interest is in the other for the other. . . . In fact, its very being is simply interest. Its *esse* is interest, *interesse,* where the stress is on the *inter.* In other words, *interesse* puts the self into the *inter,* puts it outside itself, beyond self-interest, makes it disinterested in that regard."

103. *PU* 119: "Agapeic mind expresses something that is both a regulative ideal and an ontological reality, somehow constitutive of our most intimate being."

*EB* 197: "Finite being is given for itself and given as good; it is given for nothing; but as being, it is the promise of agapeic self-becoming and self-transcendence, hence being in metaxological community. This promise reflects what we are and what we are to become. Relative to what we are to become, we come to understand *promise as command relative to inner exigence.*"

104. *BB* 199: "The freedom beyond self-determination is a gift, first *of* the other, then *for* the other."

CWSC 40: "There is an agapeic freedom that is released beyond the higher autonomy of erotic sovereignty. It is released in a being for the other that is for the other and not for any return to self."

105. *BB* 261: Agapeic being's "self-transcendence is truly self-transcending, since there is a kind of *releasing reversal* between self and other: the self is othered such that the other is given a freedom of being from the giving self.... The self-transcendence that is a reversal of self is a giving of genuine separateness to the other. Freedom is this separation."

*PU* 147: "Agapeic mind makes a welcome in the manner it *prepares the way* for the other to come to self-manifestation. Preparing a way is making a space in the middle, a space for the freedom of the other."

106. *DDO* 164, 167, 190; *CWSC* 41, 51; *EB* 169, 192, 217–18. *DDO* 164: "Goodwill may reveal a nonobjectifying recognition of otherness, which responds to the appeal of the other with a nonpossessive solicitude."

107. In a sense, the "return" of the other's giving to one precedes and enables one's giving. This complex interplay and enabling is more fully explicated in the section on community.

*EB* 161: "We are returned to the ethos in terms of its being *criss-crossed by the agapeic relation*, by its being from the origin the promise of the agapeic community which, given the internal complexity of its participants, is quickly stressed this way, that way, and indeed stressed into a distress where the agapeic relation becomes incredible. We need metaxological ethics to make sense of the service of the other in the agapeic relation."

108. *EB* 115: "There is an ethics of gratitude: a living out of the heed of deepest gratitude for the good of being. Gratitude to whom? The blue of the sky, the master of the ocean deeps, the voice of quiet and silence, thanks to God."

109. *EB* 168–69: "We are grateful for the generosity of the ground, and we respond to this with thanks, and with thanks lived as a form of existence. For it is not only the generosity of the giver that is important but the generosity of the receiver. We are the receivers, and, strangely, it is the generosity of the other that possibilizes our comportment of generosity towards the other. Generosity entails no servile reception or abjection before the other. In fact, the other's generosity does more than occasion our gratitude; it charges us with the living of generosity."

*EB* 217: "Affirming is consent to *gift*. Generosity is born of a primal gratitude. Ethics springs from gratitude. This is lived in ethical and religious service beyond autonomy. What is this service? It is a willingness beyond will, beyond will to power, beyond my will to power."

110. *EB* 354: "Agapeic self-transcendence arises from an overdetermined source of origination, and not from a deficient condition or a merely indefinite possibility. Its power is the very definite power of generosity, an excess of original being which is also the expression of the primal freedom of the self. Rather than being our assertion of power over against the valueless absurd, real creativity reveals the generosity of being, the free power to give itself to what is other to itself. Agapeic self-transcending is a giving of being to the other, and for the other. There is no insistence on a return to self."

111. *EB* 348: "I can say: 'I am at your service,' and mean by that my willingness to be there for the aid of the other, beyond any external imposition, but just because I have been freed beyond myself into another relation of generosity for the other."

*EB* 363–64: "There is asked a willingness beyond will; a willingness that is a new will in us, but a will that cannot be described as self-willing, or any kind of self-determining willing; it is a willingness beyond self-determining."

112. *EB* 351: "One would rather not be in any debt to another. This is the autonomy that finds it hard to say thanks. And what about self-mastery? Does this make sense beyond a certain point? Is one servant on one level, and master on another? What is one mastering when one masters oneself? Is it just one's base side, say one's body? But then just the so-called autonomy that is won is not at all free from the self that has been mastered. The autonomy of self-mastery is enslavement to oneself. Is there a freedom beyond self-mastery? What about the coherence of the notion of self-service?"

113. *EB* 362: "It is another 'freedom towards': there is a direction in its transcending not only to itself in its own self-becoming; its self-becoming moves it towards what it is not, and not what it will become, but what it would love, as a good that is itself and for itself, and not at all product of our self-becoming, and without which no self-becoming on our part would at all be possible. It is a freedom beyond self-determination, in which *proximately* we are released to being with others differently."

*EB* 508: "As there is an autonomy beyond servility, there is a service beyond autonomy and servility, and this service is releasing of freedom beyond autonomy and subjection, beyond the instrumental domination and subjection of serviceable disposability, beyond the self-affirming dominion of erotic sovereignty. This service is release into community in which we live from the good of the absolute other, and towards the good of ourselves and finite others as others, and again through them live towards the good of the absolute other."

114. *BB* 414: "[T]here is a kind of return to the first, because agapeic acting, willing, creating, doing are germinated in passion, suffering, imitation, patience. The passion of being that is always already spread out in the elemental I, returns in the end."

115. *EB* 367: It is "suffering that returns willing to an intimacy with the good deeper than its intimacy with itself."

116. *EB* 367: "It may well be the case that the new willing cannot become itself without some kind of askesis: not the askesis which simply denies or negates; more the suffering that wears away, strips the masks of false selving; the suffering that mediates self in its most elemental love, as well as loosing it to its being free beyond itself; suffering that returns willing to an intimacy with the good deeper than its intimacy with itself; embarking it on a voyage of love in which its harbor lies in the transcendent good beyond finite measure. Infinite depths, infinite restlessness: desire turned to the abyss of inwardness, desire turned to the height of transcendence."

117. *EB* 370: "If the idiocy of suffering brings us back to the origin, this means it is bound up with *the sacred*. Because suffering is thus idiotic as well as universal, philosophy does not always deal with it well, since philosophy's universals are often such as to shun the idiotic."

118. *EB* 365: "We must join the meaning of 'freedom from' and 'freedom towards.' The 'from' is from the origin as giver, but as freeing us, and into gratitude for the gift, even in suffering. This is not 'freedom from' the other which wants to be outside of community, but freedom given from the agapeic origin, and hence a 'from' that founds elemental community. And here too 'freedom towards' is beyond 'freedom to' be oneself, since in certain sufferings there is an excess to self-transcending that is freed beyond it-

self and towards the good as other. This 'freedom towards' has a vector that is ontologically intimate: both selfless and the deepest selving. One goes towards the good, sometimes sightlessly, in agapeic selving."

119. *EB* 365: "Can suffering be at the origin of a new willingness, breaking one open, asking one to understand the others who suffer (even tormented sovereigns)?"

*EB* 367: "The new willingness can be called will-less, if by will we mean the will that wills itself; but in truth it is a transformation of willing that is here at issue."

120. *PU* 151: "What is this compassion? It is a pluralized passion, or patience, or pathos. It is an undergoing, and a going out of self, and an inwardizing of the other's suffering. It is a community of passion, a community of suffering."

121. Desmond's understanding of suffering as the highest selving, as a selving that opens beyond selving toward community, *such that suffering is neither the primordial enabling gift nor the consummate communal end of our selving,* reflects Milbank's recognition (for all of his uneasiness regarding agape's apparent lack of reciprocity and participation) of the presence of agapeic suffering, of an always apparently unredeemed sacrifice in our present fallen world—a suffering that is enabled by a prior fullness. Marion (like Desmond here regarding the agapeic self but missing the broader enabling and teleological reciprocal community emphasized by Milbank and Desmond . . . in the next section), in seeing that the true lover "decides to love in advance," proposes in a manner parallel to Desmond that the willing giving of the agapeic self is a precondition to a kind of reciprocal gift-exchange. See Milbank, *Being Reconciled,* 155–57; Marion, *The Erotic Phenomenon,* passim.

122. *BB* 415: The process of ethical selving is "the unfolding of self from the elemental I of idiotic inwardness is thus from the aesthetic passion of immediacy, into the self-insistent I of self-will, through the self-mediation of ethical will, to the religious passion in which the I radically gives itself back to the between and its origin."

*EB* 377: "Ethics brings us to the limit of the ethical, as determined by autonomy and erotic sovereignty. At this limit a witness to something more is solicited."

123. *EB* 197: "Community with the good is not a subsequent construction; there is a primal community with the good that emerges into diverse articulation and more explicit formation of ethical community in the between."

*EB* 200: "There is a given community of self and other that grounds the doing of the good in the ethos. We do not first create metaxological community. It is given. What we are given in its given betweenness is the freedom to realize more fully the promise of agapeic transcending, in self-integrity and forms of community that concretize its truth in the world."

124. *EB* 416–17: "The commons I most want to consider now concerns the web of utility in the world of work. This web, delicate and entangling, is yet an interconnecting, driven by the exchange of instrumental goods and services. A dominion of use-values pervades the ethical milieu, and infiltrates all the levels of ethical intermediation. This dominion is unavoidable; but it is not finally sufficient, indeed it is pernicious when totalized relative to the ethos."

125. *BB* 434: "The community of distracted desire emerges from the frustration of any univocal formation of human self-transcendence."

*BB* 434: "Desire excites itself beyond univocal satisfaction, but perplexes itself in this self-activation."

126. *BB* 435: "What if we pluralize such restless beings? . . . All things serve desire's satisfaction, but since there is no real satisfaction, they really do not serve satisfaction but the endless arousal of dissatisfaction. Each member of this community is for-itself,

but for itself in a manner that does not really take the other as other into account, except insofar as the other is for the self."

127. *EB* 444: "To be sovereign is to approach the supreme and useless—beyond serviceable disposability. It is useless but as such more supremely useful: it gives use the self-justifying excellences the network of serviceable disposability lacks, and without which the whole seems finally pointless.... This worth beyond serviceable disposability can take different forms. Examples: the worth of a work of art, beyond the instrumental work ruled by a schema of means: there is something sovereign about the great artist or work."

128. *BB* 441: "Our self-relating sociability must win through to an achieved integrity of self in the between. There it is together with other selves, also engaged in the adventure of integrity. The community of erotic sovereignty is the community of such achieving wholes."

129. *BB* 440: The sovereign self "breathes freedom in the companionship of other such sovereigns. Self-assertion is not the point, nor is domination. A sovereign self is at home with itself and at home with other sovereign selves."

130. *BB* 439: "Self-transcending comes to rest on the others, and here comes to look at itself from the point of view of the other. Put differently, the other turns the self mindfully back to itself, offers it a way to be at home with itself.... Through the other I come to recognize myself; through the other's recognition I come to self-recognition."

131. *EB* 339: "Erotic sovereignty, qualified by openness to transcendence as higher than itself, can show us the glory of the world. In the upbuilding of communities of justice, sovereigns who have come into a maturity of self-possessed freedom, are essential. They are essential to show us something of the realized promise of immanent excellence: such are heroes and exemplars—originals to imitate, paragons to emulate."

132. *BB* 446: "In the most inclusive of communities, there will be no real other at all, only the absolute whole mediating with itself in its other, which is only *itself* again in its otherness."

*BB* 447: "The essential danger of dialectical totalism, we might say, is in giving a wrong priority to the notion of the whole over the excess of the infinite."

133. *EB* 481: "What cannot be absolutely incorporated into the power of the ascendant sovereign? At one extreme, there is the idiot self—the void, you might say sometimes, the indeterminate source of innerness that is never exhausted by any determination, though its determinate existence be in bondage to them. The idiot is not absolute solitude, but is intermediated prior to determinate mediation: God is in the immanence of the soul.... This idiot extreme points to the other religious extreme, namely, the community that tries to live in the between in light of its acknowledged metaxological relation to the divine: in light of the generous finitude of its being, given the goodness of the 'to be,' out of nothing and for nothing but the good of being. This is the religious community of agapeic service that enacts the intermediation of the good beyond erotic sovereignty and in ethically likening itself to the generosity of the agapeic origin. If at the first extreme, erotic sovereignty gives way to mystical consent, at the second extreme the festival of a community becomes a sacramental drama."

134. *BB* 490: "When sovereignty does not close on itself, its power can become releasing rather than domineering.... This is the fulfillment of the original power of being that reaches its richest truth to itself in the service of agapeic being."

135. *EB* 161: "We are returned to the ethos in terms of its being *criss-crossed by the agapeic relation*, by its being from the origin the promise of the agapeic community which, given the internal complexity of its participants, is quickly stressed this way, that

way, and indeed stressed into a distress where the agapeic relation becomes incredible. We need metaxological ethics to make sense of the service of the other in the agapeic relation."

136. *EB* 162: "The agapeic relation suggests [that] a promise already be at work in order for community, in a more overt, determinate sense, to be constituted. The ethos is the promise of the agape of being."

*HG* 181: "The spirit of agapeic community seeks to be true to the promise of the given goodness of being in creation and history."

137. *BB* 453: "Agapeic self-transcendence into the between is not a decentering so much as an *excentering* of self. For the self is still a center, even when it makes its original energy of being available for the other; it is centered eccentrically. Even within its own inward centering, it is eccentric, since the inward otherness points beyond the for-self towards the other origin. The agapeic self is centered beyond itself."

138. In this broader vision of agapeic community, Desmond provides resources to answer Badiou's critique of agape and ethical consideration of the "other" that he (Badiou) levels against a Levinasian position. Desmond provides an alternative account of singularity, difference, and relation in terms of a metaxological community of being as the promise of agapeic human community. See Badiou, *Ethics,* passim.

139. Milbank likewise sees charity as giving forth and letting be freedom and singularity—but also a sharing and blending in the midst of otherness—a relation in the midst of otherness. See Milbank, *Theology and Social Theory,* 422; Milbank, *Being Reconciled,* 121, 168.

140. *BB* 456: "Agapeic service is a certain love of singularity. We do not see singularity as the opposite of community. Instead love of the singular is the concrete enactment of agapeic community, which is a being together with the goodness of the *this,* this being as being, this being in its being for itself. Put otherwise, the community of agapeic service alone can do justice to the idiocy of selfhood. The latter signals the radical intimacy to singularity that is the infinite worth of the human self."

141. *EB* 217: "Generosity is born of a primal gratitude. Ethics springs from gratitude. This is lived in ethical and religious service beyond autonomy. What is this service? It is a willingness beyond will, beyond will to power, beyond my will to power."

*EB* 489: "A fundamental gratitude is resurrected, expressing itself in an ethics of generosity towards the frailty of beings in the between, human and nonhuman."

142. *EB* 509: "Double service: God service, religious service; neighbor service, ethical service. Service is the word for the enactment of this love. The word too quickly withers into sentimentality, or into cynicism under the leer of those grown old with jaded enlightenment. This is loss. Only love lives the agape of being."

143. *EB* 486: "Religious community binds together (*re-ligare*—Augustine) the human and divine, and out of this transforms the bonds holding humans together. The sources of social power undergo a transformation which carries human power to the edge of its humanness. We understand power as given all along, a gift from motiveless generosity, motiveless goodness beyond the goodness of the gift, rousing in community the vision of humans together living an ethics of generosity in finite image of the ultimate generosity."

144. *EB* 220: "The agape of being is first given to us, but we are called to an agapeic being which is the doing of living, in an ethics of gratitude to the origin, and of generosity to self and other. The agape of being intimates a fullness, but it is not being full of oneself. One does nothing to merit it, and no payment is exacted, for it offers itself

simply as the life of the good, a life we are to live. It has no reason, beyond itself, which is to be beyond itself, in being itself."

145. *EB* 217: "Is it possible for humans to sustain an ethics of agapeic service? Extremely hard. We are always drawn back into the being of selving as for-itself."

*EB* 219: "The life of agapeic service is impossible if we are alone, and without the sustaining power of the good as other. As I suggested before, the familiar word (and I think best word) for transcendence itself is God. The fullest community with the good is reflected in the openness of the metaxological way towards God as ultimate other."

*EB* 494: "Religious community is itself the appeal to the good for that help to be good. We cannot do it on our own, as we cannot free ourselves from bewitchment on our own. To ask to be free from the idols is to ask for the spiritual strength of a divine service."

146. *EB* 165: "What is intimated in the arche here becomes community in humanity, itself now called to be a concretion of agapeic community, and witness to the ultimate agapeic source. This end is participation in community with the arche, and hence itself a finite form of the community of agapeic service. This is the good we must seek to be, failing again and again, and beginning again and again, as we must."

*EB* 486: "We understand power as given all along, a gift from motiveless generosity, motiveless goodness beyond the goodness of the gift, rousing in community the vision of humans together living an ethics of generosity in finite image of the ultimate generosity."

On religious community as imaging the agapeic origin, see Milbank, *Theology and Social Theory,* 416; Marion, *Erotic Phenomenon,* 221–22.

147. *PO* 168: The agape feast is "the essence of human fellowship"—"the realized promise of the metaxological community of being."

*EB* 512: "Genuine feast days, days of festive being are hyperbolic gifts of the agapeic good. The consummate community is one of celebration, of our solidarity with the ultimate power, despite evil, in our own good in its many forms, in our struggle to be released from evils into which we fall, celebration of the sweet gift of life, as well as the peace we seek facing the terrors of death. Rebirth to the good of the elemental things is now celebrated."

148. See Marion, *Erotic Phenomenon,* passim.

149. See Pickstock, *After Writing,* passim; Milbank, *Being Reconciled,* 153.

150. See Milbank, *Theology and Social Theory,* 416; Milbank, "Can the Gift Be Given?" 137. See Marion, *Erotic Phenomenon,* passim.

151. Marion, *Erotic Phenomenon,* 220–21.

152. See Milbank, *Theology and Social Theory,* 408–409; Milbank, *Being Reconciled,* 148–49; Milbank, "Can the Gift Be Given?" 131, 145.

153. See Milbank, *Being Reconciled,* 46–7, 148, 152; Marion, *Erotic Phenomenon,* 204–205.

154. *PO* 160: "The ethical is an articulation of being as good, the charge of being in us that we become, actualize, the given promise of the good."

*PO* 161: "We value according to an ontological sense of being, the self-knowledge of which we often lack."

155. *NDR* 44: "One of the richest ways of speaking of [being] would be to say: it is hospitable to the gift of the good. It is enveloped by a light of worth. The metaphysical milieu, the ontological ethos of our philosophizing, requires reflection in terms of this, reflection on this hospitality of being to the good."

156. *EB* 269: "If the freedom that ferments in ethical selving is not univocal but plurivocal, it follows that there are different freedoms, corresponding to different formations of self-transcending."

157. *BB* 456: "Agapeic service is a certain love of singularity. We do not see singularity as the opposite of community. Instead love of the singular is the concrete enactment of agapeic community, which is a being together with the goodness of the this, this being as being, this being in its being for itself. Put otherwise, the community of agapeic service alone can do justice to the idiocy of selfhood. The latter signals the radical intimacy to singularity that is the infinite worth of the human self."

158. *EB* 217: "Is it possible for humans to sustain an ethics of agapeic service? Extremely hard. We are always drawn back into the being of selving as for-itself."

159. *BB* 453: "Agapeic self-transcendence into the between is not a decentering so much as an *excentering* of self. For the self is still a center, even when it makes its original energy of being available for the other; it is centered eccentrically. Even within its own inward centering, it is eccentric, since the inward otherness points beyond the for-self towards the other origin. The agapeic self is centered beyond itself."

160. *AE* 41, 121–22. Caputo cites the Augustine quote from Augustine's Commentary on the First Epistle of John, in Migne, *Patrologia Latina*, vol. 35, p. 2033.

161. *BB* 456: "Agapeic service is a certain love of singularity. We do not see singularity as the opposite of community. Instead love of the singular is the concrete enactment of agapeic community, which is a being together with the goodness of the this, this being as being, this being in its being for itself. Put otherwise, the community of agapeic service alone can do justice to the idiocy of selfhood. The latter signals the radical intimacy to singularity that is the infinite worth of the human self."

162. *EB* 161: "We are returned to the ethos in terms of its being *criss-crossed by the agapeic relation,* by its being from the origin the promise of the agapeic community which, given the internal complexity of its participants, is quickly stressed this way, that way, and indeed stressed into a distress where the agapeic relation becomes incredible. We need metaxological ethics to make sense of the service of the other in the agapeic relation."

163. *EB* 168–69: "We are grateful for the generosity of the ground, and we respond to this with thanks, and with thanks lived as a form of existence. For it is not only the generosity of the giver that is important but the generosity of the receiver. We are the receivers, and, strangely, it is the generosity of the other that possibilizes our comportment of generosity towards the other. Generosity entails no servile reception or abjection before the other. In fact, the other's generosity does more than occasion our gratitude; it charges us with the living of generosity."

*EB* 217: "Affirming is consent to *gift.* Generosity is born of a primal gratitude. Ethics springs from gratitude. This is lived in ethical and religious service beyond autonomy. What is this service? It is a willingness beyond will, beyond will to power, beyond my will to power."

164. *BB* 261: Agapeic being's "self-transcendence is truly self-transcending, since there is a kind of *releasing reversal* between self and other: the self is othered such that the other is given a freedom of being from the giving self.... The self-transcendence that is a reversal of self is a giving of genuine separateness to the other. Freedom is this separation."

*PU* 147: "Agapeic mind makes a welcome in the manner it *prepares the way* for the other to come to self-manifestation. Preparing a way is making a space in the middle, a space for the freedom of the other."

165. *BB* 415: The process of ethical selving in "the unfolding of self from the elemental I of idiotic inwardness is thus from the aesthetic passion of immediacy, into the self-insistent I of self-will, through the self-mediation of ethical will, to the religious passion in which the I radically gives itself back to the between and its origin."

*EB* 377: "Ethics brings us to the limit of the ethical, as determined by autonomy and erotic sovereignty. At this limit a witness to something more is solicited."

166. See chapter 2, part two, section III, §4.

167. See chapter 2, part two, section III, §4.

168. *EB* 200: "There is a given community of self and other that grounds the doing of the good in the ethos. We do not first create metaxological community. It is given. What we are given in its given betweenness is the freedom to realize more fully the promise of agapeic transcending, in self-integrity and forms of community that concretize its truth in the world."

### 4. God and Religion

1. AT 236: "Suppose such an ethos of 'neutralization' is itself an ontological contraction of the given milieu of being as saturated with value."

2. *PO* 228: "The order we make is grafted onto another order that we ourselves do not produce."

3. BDD 760: "The general spiritual ethos is pervasively pragmatic and oriented to instrumental problem-solving. We give our concern to things about which we can do something, where we seem able to will it and bring them under some control."

4. *EB* 41: "Modernity's shaping of the ethos grows out of distrust of equivocity, expressed in the univocalizing mentality of dualistic opposition that produces a devaluing objectification of being on one side, and a subjectification of value on the other."

5. See Milbank's understanding of the secular as a modern invention, as an invention of pure power with humanity functioning as a false double of God. Milbank, *Theology and Social Theory,* chap. 1 passim, pp. 13, 18.

6. *EB* 167: "The loss of the ethos takes the form of the so-called death of God. And this is correct in that this is the loss of the elemental good of being in the between. It is not primarily a matter of finding the arguments for God unconvincing, or finding oneself living fine without God, or indeed even of turning against God. It is a loss of the mindful attunement between the indeterminate openness of elemental expectation in us and the goodness of the source."

7. NDR 43–44: "Absolutize autonomy and you must relativize transcendence; but if transcendence cannot be so relativized, autonomy must itself be relativized."

*EB* 33: "Can one serve two masters as god? Is there not a certain *antinomy* of autonomy and transcendence? For both cannot be absolute together, in the terms proposed by the priority of autonomy. Absolutize the first, you relativize the second; absolutize the second, you relativize the first, and hence put a strain on the proposed priority of autonomy."

8. PR 109: "Can God be thus used? Have we taken a fateful or fatal step outside fitting reverence, when God is thus used? And is not the self-projection of our own power not then the superiority we project? Not God as the superior, but our selves as creating ourselves at a higher level as superior being."

9. *GB* 35: "Though we might feel we are as nothing, nevertheless we still participate in an elemental affirmation of being at all, in that we continue to be."

10. *BHD* 84–85: "Philosophy and religion are not necessarily and essentially instru-

mentalities. . . . Both are what I would call finalities or integrities: finalities, not in any sense of bringing the dunamis of mind or being to a dead closure, but modes of mindfulness that engage what is ultimate, ways of being mindful that themselves try to approximate ultimacy; integrities, as embodying something of the realized, yet open promise of human wholeness."

11. HT 24: "Surely, philosophy can think about anything; in principle, everything can be the occasion of thought, especially our most basic notions. This also entail[s] philosophy's willingness to reformulate its own characteristic ways of reflection under the impact of those dissident others, like religion and art, that contest and challenge it."

*AOO* 294: "Religion *reflected* in its truth is (metaxological) philosophy which understands that *to be is to be religious,* namely, to have one's being in the happening of the between by virtue of the ultimate giving of the agapeic origin."

12. *AOO* 290: "After long consideration, I see that religion has power that neither art or philosophy has: it is most intimate with the primal porosity, the *passio essendi,* and the urgency of ultimacy."

*HG* 187: "We need to reconsider the religious matrix in which philosophical thought is grown, and a new mindfulness of what that matrix communicates."

*BR* 211: "Religion is closer to the mother that makes us who we are."

13. *HG* 70: "*Intellectus* does not speculatively surpass *fides,* but rather finds that, in dialogue with religion, or perhaps in the secret communication between thinking and the divine source, it has to seek beyond itself, for the origin and ground of its own confidence, and this is a *con-fiding* from a source not itself the product of our thought. The confiding is a '*fides*' '*con*', a 'fidelity' 'with': our faithful thinking is 'with' (*con*) what it does not produce through thinking itself. This we find then: not that philosophy speculatively surpasses religion; but that philosophy must surpass its speculative idealistic form, just in its being true to the excess of religion."

*HG* 97–98: "It is not faith seeking understanding; it is faith after the effort to understand that does not now dispel the mystery but finds itself more wrapped in it than ever, more deeply struck into perplexity and praise and love at the being greater than the greatest of our thoughts."

14. *HG* 76: "What if there is a different poverty of philosophy: one where philosophy comes closer to a fulfillment, not at the point where knowing no longer goes beyond itself, but just the opposite—where knowing is called upon to an exodus beyond itself, above itself, into the darkness of the divine?"

15. *PO* 235: "The contemplative attitude epitomizes our highest freedom, the freedom to mind what is of ultimate worth."

16. *BHD* 81–82: "But one does not, one cannot cease, one will not cease to think speculatively. Philosophy's reasonable dream of the ultimate otherness renounces all totalizing hubris. In this renunciation, speculative philosophy is renewed as thought's restless exigency to still think otherwise what is other to thought, to think what we can hardly think: the absolute original as the absolute other."

17. *BHD* 136: "Philosophical mind negates our ascription of absoluteness to the relative yet it is on speculative watch for the appearances of the absolute in the relative. It detaches and distances the self, but in the distance it may involve mind deeper with the other. Its speculative watch is vigilant towards the togetherness of the self and the ultimate other. The speculative watch is the openness of mind to this togetherness."

18. HT 25: "Philosophy is just the thoughtful engagement of the sources of intelligibility immediately at work in the between."

19. *PU* 207: "Metaphysical metaphors are responsive to what Jaspers calls 'boundary questions.' Within the boundary, we make intelligible sense of things by means of determinate finite categories. But at the boundary, and relative to the boundary, no such finite determinate category will do. Here we ask about the ground of determinate categories that exceeds complete categorical determination."

20. *BB* 218–19: "Equivocal language may have to be *risked* if we want to affirm the absolute difference of the transcendent. Here the equivocity is that to speak the transcendent, equivocally or otherwise, is already to bring it out of its absolute difference, and so either not to name it, or to imply that there is no absolute difference. I think this equivocity has to be *lived with* dynamically; it cannot be resolved into a univocal or dialectical determination."

21. *PO* 134: "Do we not rob God of mystery, power, and transcendence? The name seems then to be the fundamental violence on otherness."

*PO* 135: "By directly naming the divine we objectify it, turn it into a finite object, turn it into something it is not."

22. *PO* 140: "No religion is free from the risk of idolatry, because none can continue without the sacred image."

23. *PO* 135: "If we name, we miss; if we do not name, we miss. . . . We must live in this tension, mindful of its stress."

24. *PO* 135: "We have to name otherness in a way that names our failure to name otherness."

*PU* 210: "The image images the original, it is not the original. No name is the name, and the best names name themselves as other than *the* name. The best name names its own necessary failure."

25. *HG* 127: "Iconic speech is needed which incarnates in itself just this confession of its own finitude, and its witness to what exceeds finiteness. Its doubleness is just its being on the boundary *between finitude and infinity*."

26. *BB* 219: "The equivocal is the *threshold of enigma,* a subverter of every claim to have encompassed the enigma of transcendence. It has, so to say, the guardianship of this threshold. It is a suitor in love with the ultimate beloved that it does not know."

*HG* 69: "If, as I think, the doubleness of the representation suggests rather an *imagistic hyperbole* in the finite that communicates *between* finitude itself and God, then for that representation to be true to God, and to be true to itself, it must always keep open the space of difference between itself and God."

27. *PU* 207: "One needs to speak also . . . of analogies, symbols, and hyperboles. My use of 'metaphor,' in the present instance, tends to telescope these different needs."

Thus, Desmond's use of "metaphor" is somewhere between indirection generally (above) and the more particular way of indirection that he comes to focus on, the hyperbolic (below).

28. *PU* 209: "The conjunction of the two meanings points to a sense of the 'beyond,' the 'more' as also moving in, and through, and between the middle. The metaphor carries us through the middle to a beyond that is not the mere beyond of a dualistic opposition. It is a 'more,' a plenitude as other to the middle, but with an otherness that marks a community, not an antithesis, with the middle. . . . The metaphor may bespeak some sense of the beyond in the between. It is an image that mediates an open sense of the 'more.'"

29. *DDO* 39: "Exploiting this double sense, we see that a metaphysical metaphor may not be a fully determinable concept in any limited, finite sense. Yet neither need it be

wholly indefinite. It is like an articulated image, which points to a meaning that cannot be pinned down or fixed absolutely, but which nevertheless manages to genuinely articulate what is more than any particularized determination."

*DDO* 182: "Metaphor may be a creative act of naming that stretches language beyond 'literal' univocal determinacy, yet at the same time always reserves the right to call itself into question and to dissolve any pretension to unsurpassable absoluteness regarding the name that it has uttered in the middle. This subversion of claims to mastery in the very act of articulation opens the space of irreducible difference once again."

30. *BB* 210: "The metaphorical 'is,' as I understand it, keeps itself open as an identification of otherness, hence is never the encapsulation of transcendence, but instead a vector towards and beyond the circle of self-thinking thought. . . . [M]etaphor is metaphysical and metaxological. It defines a complex mindful intermediation between us and what is ultimately other. It offers no direct possession of the ultimate. Rather its indirection is respect for the enigma of the ultimate, expressed in the openness on the metaphorical 'is' itself."

31. *BB* 209: "In living metaphor there is a certain identification of otherness."

*PU* 210: "Metaphysical metaphor must dissolve the pretension finally to have uttered the final word, for every word of our is in the middle, and hence carries the trace of inevitable untruth. . . . Metaphor, under the skeptical shadow of this speculative suspicion, rejects the seduction whereby a likeness is turned into an identity. Thus, it rejects the consolation of univocity, without losing all articulacy in nameless equivocity."

32. *BB* 218: "We are thrown towards transcendence by our being." Hyperbole "throws mindfulness into the *huper,* the beyond."

*BB* 256: "The way of transcendence is hyperbolic. Transcending thinking finds itself thrown upwards at an ultimate limit."

33. This should be contrasted with Deleuze's vision of a rejection of transcendence in order to affirm immanence. Desmond sees transcendence and immanence as interrelated such that immanence is not devalued by transcendence but is indeed valued in itself—this value bespeaks a broader community of the transcendent and the immanent. Ontologically speaking, the immanent is suspended in the transcendent. Phenomenologically speaking, the immanent hyperbolically refers in itself beyond itself to the transcendent. See *Radical Orthodoxy* on "Suspending the Material."

34. *BB* 218: "Excess is the way to *huperousia,* beyond being, above being, being above being. Being beyond being is a double saying: paradoxical language is unavoidable."

*BB* 219: "The equivocal is the *threshold of enigma,* a subverter of every claim to have encompassed the enigma of transcendence. It has, so to say, the guardianship of this threshold. It is a suitor in love with the ultimate beloved that it does not know."

*HG* 127: "Iconic speech is needed which incarnates in itself just this confession of its own finitude, and its witness to what exceeds finiteness. Its doubleness is just its being on the boundary *between finitude and infinity.*" In this way, "the asymmetrical difference is kept open."

35. *BB* 221: "Hyperbole offers a *via eminentiae,* in a metaxologically reformulated sense. The hyperbolic is a way of excess that throws beyond finitude. But this *via* is by way of agapeic mind; hence the point is not to proceed from lack to perfection, but from perfection and plenitude, indeed from perfection in the between to pluperfection in transcendence. Agapeic astonishment intimates the pluperfection that is always already more, always is and will be more, eternally more. The hyperbolic way will pile up perfection on perfection, knowing it will always not be enough to do justice to transcendence. This *via eminentiae* would be the hyperbole of praise."

36. *BB* 221: There is "a *reversal, relative to ultimacy itself.* We do not have its measure; the measure is beyond measure. The hyperbolic measure beyond our measure instead measures us. We are not going from perfection here to ultimacy there; but there is perfection here, because there is ultimacy. Perfection here is an image of an ultimacy whose perfection always exceeds immanence. There is a reversal into an asymmetry; finite perfection is a created image of ultimacy. There is no 'It is good' in the between, but for the ultimate 'It is good' that cannot be encompassed or mastered."

See here Milbank on the infinite shining through the finite and drawing the finite to itself, to the infinite. Milbank, *Being Reconciled,* 77.

37. *HG* 138: The hyperboles of being "point beyond themselves, not to a whole that includes them all, but to an ultimate power that is hyperbolic again to the creation as a happening of contingency."

*HG* 187–88: "When we return to the ontological matrix or ethos wherein being religious and philosophical come to articulation, we come on certain happenings that are 'too much,' certain hyperboles of being that occasion, on our part, deep reservations about claims made for holistic immanence as the last word or the ultimate horizon."

38. *EB* 219: "We do not understand the mystery of God. Metaxological mindfulness mulls over the signs of God in the between, alert to what comes to it from beyond itself. Traces of transcendence are communicated in many ways to the twilight or dawn of the middle."

39. *PU* 188: "I do not think we need to take God as an 'explanation,' if we mean some determinate univocal reason why things are thus and thus. God as a merely univocal explanation would be a ruse by which reason uses the idea of God to shirk the deeper ontological perplexity about God. Reason then uses God to allow itself to go back to sleep again. If God is an 'explanation,' there is a sense in which this answer is darker than the question it answers, because the answer involves a certain extraordinary complex *acknowledgement* of the mystery of the ultimate. This mystery is the answer, but this answer is no answer in the more normal sense of a relatively self-transparent, rational demonstration. God deepens our perplexity about being, makes mind sleepless."

40. *HG* 138: "Hyperboles of being . . . point beyond themselves, not to a whole that includes them all, but to an ultimate power that is hyperbolic again to the creation as a happening of contingency."

41. *AOO* 268: "The transcendence of *beings as other* in exteriority. The transcendence of such beings consists in their not being the product of our process of thinking; their otherness to us resists complete reduction to our categories, especially in so far as they simply are, or have being at all."

42. *BB* 207: The infinities of outward infinite succession (becoming) and inward intentional infinitude "suggest a more radical sense of the infinite that is in excess of either, and reducible to none, even as it gives them their being for themselves. The astonishing middle rouses the thinking of radical transcendence as itself an agapeic origin."

*BB* 506: "Finite transcending points beyond itself to the absolute origin as the primal giver of the promise of creation, and as the sustaining ground of its metaxological milieu. As giver and sustaining, the origin is immanent in the metaxological milieu."

43. *HG* 127: "Suppose creation . . . is what one might call a hyperbolic thought. Suppose creation were more like a *metaphysical hyperbole,* the thought of something hyperbolic, and in excess of finite, univocal determination, or our self-determination."

*AOO* 5: "The idea of God as creator suggests, by contrast, a more recalcitrant notion of origination. I call creation a hyperbolic thought, in that it exceeds all determinate intelligibilities."

44. *PO* 138: "Finite things have being but are not ultimate or absolute; they image in their intermediate being the ultimate ground. They shimmer in their lack of fixed self-subsistence and make a dance of symbols that tells of something other or more. In the finite we divine the infinite—the religious cipher is the middle agency spanning their divide."

45. *BB* 473: "*That they are at all*—this is the metaphysical splendor of simply being. This is excessive and occurs in a reference to the origin of being as creation."

*HG* 3: "I would say that there is something *hyperbolic* about the being given to be of beings: not what they are, but that they are at all. Hyperbolic in that the astonishment aroused by this givenness of being is not a determinate question seeking a determinate answer, but something exceeding determinate thinking."

46. *HG* 3: "What makes possible the possibility of their being at all? This is the metaphysical question: Why beings and not nothing? The possibility of a transcendence as other to their transcendence is raised by such a question. This is a major source of perplexity about God as the origin of being."

47. GEW 26: "The ontological perplexity concerning primal givenness concerns our appreciation of finitude not first as becoming, but as *coming to be:* not becoming this or that, but its coming to be at all. This is extremely difficult to approach, for it lies at the boundary of determinate knowing."

HT 34: "Coming to be is not identical with becoming. For in becoming, one becomes a *determinate something.* . . . Coming to be, by contrast, is prior to becoming this or that; for one must be, and have come to be, before one can become such and such. . . . In every finite being that becomes, which is all beings, there is intimated this prior coming to be which is not a finite becoming: 'that it is at all' is here in question, and that it has come to be this at all."

48. HT 39: "The notion of God as creator gives some articulation to this ontological dependency of finite being as a whole, even as it also tries to name something of the originative being of God, originative in a radical unique way."

49. *BB* 291: "Creation as universal impermanence is an immanent process of ontological transcendence that points beyond itself to its metaphysical ground in the origin itself, but the gap between the two, even in their community, is always kept open."

HT 38: "*Our sense of the whole seems to point beyond the whole.* For the coming to be and the passing out of being are *not events within the whole,* but the originary issuing of the between as the finite whole."

50. *DDO* 184: "The world, in the thereness of things, presents itself as something originated. As originated, it is not identical with its origin, even if it does image it."

51. *HG* 3: "I would say that there is something *hyperbolic* about the being given to be of beings: not what they are, but that they are at all. Hyperbolic in that the astonishment aroused by this givenness of being is not a determinate question seeking a determinate answer, but something exceeding determinate thinking. An approach to God via this hyperbole of being suggests a source not reducible to being in the sense of the whole of finite being."

*HG* 203: "One might argue that the finitude of creation, in its being given to be at all, points . . . to the reserved difference of divine infinitude as exceeding the terms of holistic immanence."

52. HT 34: "Coming to be is hyperbolic happening. What is suggested is an overdetermined source of origination out of which coming to be unfolds. To speak of 'creator,' I suggest, is a way of putting us in mind of this other source."

53. In resonance with this understanding of the givenness of being as hyperbolic,

Milbank sees faith as possible because (against Heidegger) the givenness of being can be read "as the trace of a real donation"—thus with wonder and gratitude. See Milbank, "Can a Gift Be Given?" 152.

54. *PU* 212: "Without this overfull, freely originating ground there would be no community of plurality. As originated from agapeic excess, the community of plurality does not collapse into the ground as into an absorbing god."

*DDO* 180: "Ground of plurality in the ultimate origin of real difference, a ground that supports and preserves plurality."

55. *BB* 263: "This metaxological community is not the ultimate, but rather is grounded in the ultimate origin that makes relations of true otherness possible in the middle, communities that absolve and release their members to their own freedom and relativity to others. In this real plurality there is both a community that allows a release of singularity, and a releasing of singularity into the promise of solidarity."

*PU* 238: "The plurality of finite entities comprise a metaxological community of being. The ground of that community as agapeic gives the other its irreducible otherness, but the metaxological interplay of self and other is ultimately grounded in the agapeic origin."

56. *BB* 356: "The notion of the agapeic origin suggests a ground of founding trust.... The agapeic origin incites thought to conceive the basis of ontological and epistemological trust in intelligibility as going all the way down and up in being."

*PU* 246: "Determinate reason cannot be completely self-mediating but points beyond itself to a ground of reason that is not determinate. This ground is what I am calling the agapeic origin."

57. *PU* 170: "The ultimate might be other than the grounded, it may in a certain sense unground the grounded. It may be an enigmatic abyss, relative to the mind in thrall to restricted categories of finitude. It may unsettle all self-satisfied finitude. But this would be an agapeic incommensurability, one that does not induce the slumber of mind, but energizes it into renewed restlessness."

58. HT 28–29: "What grounds determinate intelligibility? The answer cannot be *another* determinate intelligibility; for that too would be in question. If there is such a ground of determination, it must be *a determining in excess of determinate intelligibles.* I suggest we link creation to such an overdeterminate grounding. If, then, we call creation a hyperintelligible, this would be to say that it concerns the beyond of intelligibility that sources the possible intelligibility of the determinately intelligible."

59. *BB* 277: "In the elemental the trace of the agapeic origin is revealed in *matter as good for itself.* Sensuous being is charged with value. Its very being there is an ontological good."

60. *EB* 195: "Reverence: it is worthy in itself."

BR 226: "Reverence is a happening in which the worth and the being-there of the other are conjoined."

61. BR 221: "Reverence, properly understood, can give signs about the source. . . . These signs suggest that this source cannot be contained within the circle of thought that thinks itself; for again the release to a superior otherness of reverence is a granting that is not self-produced by us; it is a happening, in which we are as much gifted, as we are carried by a transcending beyond ourselves."

BR 229: "The wonder that is closer to reverence is inseparable from the good of being, and not only its intelligible order. This reverence is closer to the *deeming* of the goodness of being, which puts us in mind of God in Genesis, who consents to creation: It is good, it is very good."

62. *PU* 225: "How can we speak of such value as intrinsic to being? The language of 'creation' points in a direction which cannot stop short of metaphysics, indeed a certain theology. Creation is good because to be is to be a value; to be a value is to be so because one is valued; but who is the one that values the creation? The most radical answer is that the origin does."

*EB* 493: "What gives the goodness of being? What originates it? It is not self-grounding by the between itself. For the between as double is not absolutely self-originating. It too is involved in an intermediation with what is other to it. This is the source beyond it. This other is the origin. The ground of the goodness of the between is the origin that gives the between. This original ground must itself be good to give the goodness of the between."

63. *EB* 200: "The idiot self concretizes the infinite value in the ontological roots of human being as given to itself by the origin."

64. *EB* 138: "We sometimes speak of the infinite value of the person. But what could ground such an immeasurable value, an infinite worth? It exceeds every calculation, and there could be no way to objectify it. Were we to have a bank cheque of infinite value, there is no way we could cash it; for there is no bank with the resources to deal out what is needed to be on a par with it. What is this strange value? And what source could be on a par with making sense of its given reality? For it is a given reality; we do not produce or create this end; it is what we are, constitutive of our being."

*EB* 188: "How do we measure this worth? It seems there is *no finite measure,* since each is a singular infinite, and there is no common whole which would place each in its status relative to the others. The measure of the infinite must itself be infinite. The measure of the infinite value of self must itself be infinite, more than the infinite restlessness but actually infinite. This is not a human measure."

*EB* 190: "Without relation to a source of infinite worth other than the human, the infinite worth of the human hardly makes sense."

65. *EB* 201: "In the metaxological ethos, relativity to the origin as the ultimate other grounds the infinite value of self, but beyond the inadequacy of more usual dualistic categories. Original good is being agapeic, as giving the self its infinite value, out of which it becomes itself, with a freedom first given to the person, before directed and appropriated by that person."

66. En 138: "In the original idiot the seed of being in relation to God is there."

*HG* 190: "There is the overdetermination, the 'too much,' of the singularity in the recess of the intimacy of being. The soul is too much even for itself, but its too muchness is not only its own."

67. *BB* 408: "The metaxological space between self and other is a middle between infinitudes. As well as the self's inward infinitude, there is recognized the infinitude of the other. This other infinitude can be the infinite succession of external becoming, the universal impermanence; it can be the self-mediating infinitude of an other self; it can be the actual infinitude of the absolute origin."

68. *EB* 215: "The anomalous being of the human is revealed in this freedom of infinite desire. Infinite desire emerges in finite being—excess of being rises up in the human being as selving: transcending as more, and towards the more. This "more" means enigmatic otherness in inwardness itself: the very interiority of being is the coming to show of infinity, the transcending power of the being, the transcendence towards infinity of the human being."

69. *BB* 208: "Are we not driven to think about the origin whence, and the ground

wherefrom, and the matrix wherein, and the goal whither of the passage of self-transcendence."

*BB* 231: "Is this self-transcendence merely an anomalous overreaching into emptiness, or a genuine self-surpassing towards transcendence as other?"

70. *BB* 378: "The vector of self-transcendence in the human being opens universally, at least in promise, to all the community of being in its otherness, as the self-mediation of this being deepens beyond measure towards infinity. Put otherwise, infinite inwardness goes hand in hand with a certain promise of inexhaustible transcendence."

71. *BB* 540–41: "This hyperbole of the Unequal is echoed in the hyperbole of our self-transcending, the excess of our infinite desire that will not reach and end. For no end will ever match its reaching, except an infinite end; but an infinite end is beyond all determinate ends; precisely as infinite, it is beyond all determination, and hence, in another sense, it is something that we finite middles can never completely reach. We live in the light, or the shadow, of this never-to-be-dispelled enigma."

72. *PU* 204: "Our transcending being is unfolded as the quest of ultimacy. The field of being and our being in that field, both point beyond themselves. . . . Within the self-transcending urgency of desire, we find an opening to the ultimate other. We are the interior urgency of ultimacy, this other is ultimacy as the superior."

73. *EB* 212: "A restlessness emerges that testifies to an infinite dimension to human desire. We cannot force all desire into the mould of finite appetite. To live in terms of that forcing is to deform ourselves. The infinite restlessness must be given allowance to be itself. Allowing it so, however, risks futility on one side, our coming into something more transcendent, on the other."

74. *EB* 214: "An abyss breaks open within, bringing terror as well as excitement. What is this abyss? An infinite neediness gapes in our desire. . . . The abyss is beyond finite determination; the neediness is beyond finite alleviation. *It is not an infinite lacking that stands in need of itself.* For what would its neediness do to itself except close a circle of insufficiency, even though it presents the face of absolute self-sufficiency to the world? It stands in need of what is other, the good that is other: not this good or that good, but the good as other. The infinite need of the good as other seeks another good that, to meet the lack, must itself be infinite. Short of this our desire is a futile passion. Transcending would be our absurd overreaching into the void. Without an infinite good that comes into relation with our transcending, desire is an emptiness that must end in emptiness, a void that calls and must call to void."

75. *PO* 111: "The urgency of ultimacy reveals the self-transcending of human desire, as a restless intentional infinitude in search of actual infinitude in otherness itself"

*EB* 215: "The infinite restlessness throws us back upon finitude in a way that opens up the possibility of another sense of the infinite, an infinite not at all defined by the mediation of finitude and infinity in our self-mediation: an appearance of the infinite into the middle and in a relation of superiority relative to our infinite restlessness."

*EB* 365: "Our infinite restlessness can only come to peace in a good itself infinite; we cannot be that good, though we have an infinite promise; and this our restlessness hearkens back to our first selving. It is impossible to rest with one's own fulfillment."

76. *DDO* 152: Intentional infinitude and infinite succession "point to a more that is more absolutely original, relative to which they are to be seen as images, as ontologically derivative, despite the originative powers of being that they exhibit in their own right."

77. *BHD* 255: "Does thought thinking itself open to the strange thought of the unthinkable, the thought of the ultimate other? Does singular mediation of dialectical

mind open to the double mediation of metaxological mind, and philosophy become, not just thought thinking itself but thought trying to think the ultimate other that exceeds thought?"

*HG* 93: "In self-knowing, knowing knows an excess in its own immanence: something other to thought thinking itself that enables thought to think at all but is not completely determinable through itself, nor a matter of thought's own self-determination. This immanent otherness to thought thinking itself is strikingly communicated in the measure that the infinitude of selving strikes home: its excess to finite determinability and its own complete self-determination. This excess, or excess in immanence is hyperbolic, and perhaps also says something about the hyperbolic being of God beyond the whole."

78. *HG* 97: "In the primal porosity of the intimate communication between God and humans, there is no absolute *self*-elevation *we* determine; there is gift that elevates the self: a *passio* that lifts the soul, not a *conatus* in which it lifts itself."

79. *HG* 130: " 'Being given to be' here is gift: not self-determination. This 'being given to be' is a *passio essendi* before it is a *conatus essendi*. And this is not necessary, either with reference to its originating source, or in itself: it is but it might not be. To be as [*sic*?] this gift—this is contingency as created good. It is the good of the ultimate 'to be' that is at the source of this givenness as gift."

*AOO* 291: "We are *passio essendi* before we are *conatus essendi,* passion of being before striving to be. We are first created, before we create. If so, what is the more ultimate source of originality? The issue at bottom is the interpretation of originality and ultimacy in terms of human self-transcendence or in terms of transcendence as other, or the communication between these two."

80. *BB* 5: "Transcendence as other to us works along with human self-transcendence."

*HG* 203–204: "This *passio essendi* signifies our disproportion to ourselves, hence source of our infinite restlessness and inadequacy to complete self-possession. But that disproportion and inadequacy points us beyond ourselves, above ourselves to an other infinitude. Our infinite restlessness points above itself to this other infinitude whose difference cannot be abrogated speculatively."

81. *BB* 160: "In the abyss of its own inward otherness, it comes before itself and opens to a sense of the infinite that exceeds its own self-mediation. Yet in the tension between its own excess as transcendence and the transcendence of the other, it is being perfected, made whole, never closed even in the radical innerness."

*PU* 11: "The pursuit of the ultimate itself testifies to a positive power of being in the self; it cannot be mere lack that drives desire beyond lack; it is the original power of being that constitutes the self as openness to what is other to itself; the dunamis of eros reveals a self-transcending openness to transcendence as other to desire itself."

82. *EB* 218: "Transcending desire discovers that, in being fully itself, it is more than itself and called forth by transcendence as more than itself, transcendence as superior to it."

83. *BB* 414: "The name 'God' arises in the inward otherness of the deepest intimacy of our being."

*PU* 101: "Augustine said that God was *intimior intimo meo*. This is the intimacy of being beyond the ego, and beyond the intimacy of self. It is the idiocy of God. Of God we are made mindful in an idiot wisdom."

84. *BB* 447: "Man is not God, man is never identical with God; man and God may be together, but the space of transcendence is never obliterated, even in the most intimate

communion of the two. God is more inward to inwardness than inwardness is to itself; and yet this more intimate inwardness, this radical immanence of God, is God's absolute transcendence, since it is immeasurably more unmeasured that the unmeasured infinitude of inwardness itself."

*PU* 83: "In the beginning and in the end, the intimacy of 'being with' is inseparable from being religious. The word *religio* itself communicates this in its naming of a bond of relatedness and a tie of trust. The intimacy of sacred communion is in the depth of the idiocy of being. Were this depth entirely desecrated, the distinctive personal 'being with' of human community would wither at the roots."

*HG* 97: "In the primal porosity of the intimate communication between God and humans, there is no absolute *self*-elevation *we* determine; there is gift that elevates the self: a *passio* that lifts the soul, not a *conatus* in which it lifts itself."

85. *EB* 502–503: "What grounds the good? It is not nature simply: there is goodness to nature, and yet this is disproportionate to the good as we come to know it, both in human life, and in our response to all being. . . . Is the ground human freedom? It seems not. Our freedom is *already* in communion with the good, and is given to be as a good from a source other than itself. . . . If the human is a source of good, there is a more primordial source of good not human. . . . Since humans are endowed with the promise of freedom, this other source must be adequate to the pluralism of singulars without determinate number that constitutes the many humans that have come and passed away, and will yet come and pass away in lines of succeeding generations that are beyond all human ken. The ground of the good must be proportionate to, indeed in excess of this. The prospect staggers the mind, beggars the imagination. We either say there is no ground; there is nothing; and the between is the ultimately void space where humans come and go, brief flares of inexplicable life that inexplicably bind themselves to a sense of the good, as if it were absolute, and yet the flare is snuffed out, and the singular proven to be a nothing in the cosmic void. Or we say, there is a ground but it must be proportionate to the sense of the good we experience in the between. *If so, this ground must be disproportionate just to be proportionate.* . . . A ground less than the living God does not ground the exorbitant good that comes to manifestation in the between, does not do justice to what is communicated to being ethical in the between, does not itself enable communication between itself and that very between."

86. *PO* 159: "In being ethical we are constrained by ultimacy in relation to the other as a self of inviolable worth. Aesthetic and religious respect for otherness are wider than this, not so directly focused on the other self as moral."

87. *EB* 495: "What is the ground on which we are willing to enter in agapeic service with the earth and fellow humans? If this service, as a kind of piety of the between, lives in light of the good of the other, that goodness is not from us."

88. *EB* 481: "This is the religious community of agapeic service that enacts the intermediation of the good beyond erotic sovereignty and in ethically likening itself to the generosity of the agapeic origin."

*EB* 486: "Religious community binds together (*re-ligare*—Augustine) the human and divine, and out of this transforms the bonds holding humans together. The sources of social power undergo a transformation which carries human power to the edge of its humanness. We understand power as given all along, a gift from motiveless generosity, motiveless goodness beyond the goodness of the gift, rousing in community the vision of humans together living an ethics of generosity in finite image of the ultimate generosity."

89. *GB* 138–39: "*Is the intelligibility of finite intelligibility itself intelligible in finite terms? . . .* We have to appeal to the *huperintelligible* to throw light on the finitely intelligible."

90. *HG* 7: "In truth, there is nothing but deep water when we come to God. The question of God, for the philosopher as well as for the religious person, concerns our discrimination of the false doubles of God, that is, idols. No one escapes the need for finesse to tell the difference here."

91. *HG* 9: "Much hangs on whether there is any original to which reference can be made to sustain the claim to be true, or false. If there is no original, there is no counterfeit; there is not even an image, since any image, without an original, images nothing, hence is no image."

92. *HG* 8: "The problem of the counterfeit double is that the image will mimic as well as show the original, and mimic by presenting itself as the original."

*HG* 9: "A counterfeit double is an image that is almost exactly like the original, but something has been altered that vitiates its claim to be true."

93. *BHD* 102: "Idolatry is an ontological inversion that reduces the doubleness of the sacred middle to manipulable univocity. It cannot tolerate the constitutive ambiguity of sacred presence/absence, but substitutes a domineering univocity for what it sees as an intolerable equivocity."

*BHD* 103: "Instead of the festivity of participation in the excess of the sacred, idolatry reveals the will to totalitarian ascendancy over the infinite."

94. *BHD* 104: "The god of idolatry, whether the archaic fetishism of premodernity or the instrumentally enlightened fetishism of modernity, is a dead god. . . . Idolatry and sheer profanity thus come to the same thing. Both are related outcomes of the same collusion between an anthropocentric will to power over being's otherness and the will to univocalize being entirely. Both are indifferently different avenues to the same dead god, a god dead equally in time and in eternity, and dead whether we call this god, god or man."

95. Desmond expands greatly on univocal way of thinking of God in *GB* 49–72.

96. *DDO* 90: "Absoluteness, in fact, tends to be identified with immutability. . . . Time, because always becoming, amounts almost to a defective condition of being, an unreal succession of shadows, all without abiding substance. The philosopher, however seeks an abiding reality beyond time, a realm not cursed by change."

97. *PU* 200: "God as the ultimate is the univocal *Ens Realissimum* outside the openness of the dynamic middle. Here we find the idea of an eternal God who stands aloof from time, absolutely fixed, outside time, never in the midst of what is in process here and now. . . . The ultimate becomes the circular self-mediating absolute."

98. *PU* 202: "The idea of God as self-thinking thought, an idea in some respects the metaphysical and theological apotheosis of univocal logic. In God as self-thinking thought there would be no contradiction, only the absolutely pure self-consistency of mind at one with itself."

99. *PU* 188: "I do not think we need to take God as an 'explanation,' if we mean some determinate univocal reason why things are thus and thus. God as a merely univocal explanation would be a ruse by which reason uses the idea of God to shirk the deeper ontological perplexity about God. Reason then uses God to allow itself to go back to sleep again. If God is an 'explanation,' there is a sense in which this answer is darker than the question it answers, because the answer involves a certain extraordinary complex *acknowledgement* of the mystery of the ultimate."

100. *EB* 44: "We turn around the God who would be for us into a God that we make

to be for us, according to terms we dictate, terms not true to the fullness of the ethos. This instrumentalization means that God is not for us as an agapeic origin, but as a means by which we again secure ourselves in the world. This is an idolatrous use of God. Nor is God to be *used* to 'secure' ethics."

*PU* 171: "The dualistic opposition of time and eternity might seem to suggest a *univocal* eternity as a complete determinate answer for the equivocations of time."

101. *BB* 96: "The absolutization of this mathematical univocity leads eventually to the dissolution of God as the universal geometrical maker: the clock-making divinity of the clock-work world is made *redundant* with respect to the working of the made clock. The original dispenser of intelligibility is made dispensable with respect to determinate intelligibility, now taken as self-sufficient."

*EB* 42: "I think Descartes has use for God, but his use for God eventually made God useless. The use he had for God was as a necessary means to further his new project. He needed God to guarantee the ontological import of his cognitive powers."

*EB* 44: "God as useful becomes God as useless, once the circle of our self-generating power gets under way and works up enough steam. God as a means will be dispensed with for other means more useful. The self using God will now use itself, where before it used God."

102. *PU* 217: "The danger with any defense of eternity as time's other, which wants to preserve the real pluralism of the ultimate and finitude, is that it becomes entrenched in a dualistic opposition. This, in turn, tends to produce and equivocal difference between time and eternity without the possibility of mediation. This equivocity itself springs from thinking eternity in univocal terms. Eternity is the unsurpassable stasis of univocal being, beyond the equivocal mutability of time."

On the manner in which the univocal generates the equivocal (and undoes itself) see Pickstock's discussion of how Soctus's univocity of being in fact produces an unsurmountable *quantitative* difference between humans and God (God is brought onto our plane, but a billion miles away from us). See also Conor Cunningham's understanding of the logic of nihilism in which (alienating) dualism and (ultimately empty) monism are dialectically intertwined. Pickstock, *After Writing,* 122–23; Cunningham, *Genealogy of Nihilism,* passim.

103. Desmond expands greatly on this equivocal way of thinking of God in *GB* 73–90.

104. *EB* 24: Dualistic opposition "opens an abyss between creation and the good as ground. But if this abyss can only be defined by dualistic opposition, no *immanent mediation* of the presence of inherent good is communicated to creation. It is in this last line that the dualistic opposition of creation and God (as ground of good) is *reborn* in the human being, as itself in opposition to equivocal creation."

*EB* 25: "Simply put: if the dualistic transcendent God *is* ground of good, as opposing other it *cannot be* the ground of the good in creation."

105. *BB* 240: Dualistic thinking of transcendence "has the paradoxical result of making the transcendent *unavailable* for divination in the world of given being. The dualism sunders time and eternity, becoming and the origin. But the whole matter concerns the *interplay* of these two, not their mutual repulsion. This interplay requires a notion of each that goes beyond a reductive sense of their togetherness and an antagonistic sense of their difference. One must say that eternity as origin is here asserted purely in the mode of negation: eternity is what time is not; the 'not' speaks the gulf of difference and transcendence. . . . The negation produces, in fact, the *nonrelatedness* of origin and creation. For if the eternal origin is purely in and for itself, then its power to originate what is other, and its relativity to what is so originated as other, is undermined."

106. Desmond expands on this dialectical way of thinking of God in *GB* 91–115.

107. *BHD* 80: "Dualism begets an essentially oppositional relation between two terms or realities, and in the long run an oppositional relation generally tends to undercut itself."

*PU* 14: "Dualistic opposition and equivocal difference subvert themselves, as does mere univocity, if we think the matter through. The possible togetherness of the opposites, indeed the passing of one side into the other, is opened up by the dialectical sense."

108. *DDO* 28: The absorbing god entails "a principle of completion which, purporting to be absolute wholeness, subsumes all parts within itself and in this engulfment absorbs their distinctiveness."

109. *BB* 246: "The *exitus* of the origin into otherness will be seen rather as the middle term by which the initial origin, as indefinite, mediates its own indefiniteness, and hence mediates with itself. In this, and finally, the origin will be seen to return to itself in properly articulated self-relation. . . . The *reditus* of the production to the source is the self-mediation of the source, in which the source, in its reconstituted self-relativity, produces itself as absolute self-mediation, or as the self-mediation of the absolute."

110. *BB* 247: The erotic origin "denies plurality to be ultimately 'outside' the origin. If there is plurality 'outside' the origin, this 'outside' is only provisional. . . . Finally, there is no irreducible otherness."

111. This transcendence is "foundational" in the sense of a prior possibilizing origin. See below.

112. *DDO* 198: "The sublimity of the originative source of what is, the infinitude sensuously suggested by the overwhelming majesty of being, which towers above us by its transcendence of finitude."

113. *HG* 59: "If God is *the* superior (than which none greater can be conceived), the relation has an *asymmetry* built into it: the higher as above the lower relates to the lower differently from the way the lower relates to the higher."

114. *BHD* 177: "the reserve of the sacred other, its mystery beyond all conceptual encapsulation."

*HG* 200: "Transcendence is shown and reserved, and so it appears on, and forbears beyond, the unfixed boundary between mediation and mystery."

115. *BB* 502: "This hiddenness of the ultimate truth again invokes our need of images and metaphors, themselves both true and untrue, double. . . . This reserve is significant because it unequivocally reverses our anticipation that we can reduce the truth of the origin to our truth, be on a par with it in our conceptual mediations."

116. *BB* 330: "God thought metaxologically would be . . . the overdetermined excessive plenitude of the free original power of being."

117. *BB* 208: The between's "original ground is the transcendence that is too much, always more, always beyond, and always giving beyond itself as an agapeic origin."

118. HT 34: "What is suggested is an overdetermined source of origination out of which coming to be unfolds. To speak of 'creator,' I suggest, is a way of putting us in mind of this other source."

119. *DDO* 192: "As an originating whole, the absolute original is self-originating; as creative infinity, it is the ageless origin of the finite world."

*DDO* 196: "Between the absolute original and the originated world lies a discontinuity between the absolute original as its own whole and the world as freely created and other."

120. *DDO* 189: "The idea of infinity may help us make sense of its difference and its power of creation in relation to otherness."

*DDO* 195–96: "Even though we speak of the absolute original as whole and infinite, there is a sense in which the metaxological view means that a sense of the openness of infinity is more primordial than any form of wholeness."

121. *DDO* 192: Such would "falsely fix the boundary of the whole."

122. *DDO* 192: Such would "let being dissolve into a bad indefiniteness."

123. No other being possesses the characteristics of wholeness/absoluteness and infinitude/originality in this way. However, all being (T1, T2) possesses lesser, dependent analogues of these characteristics.

124. *BB* 263: "The agapeic origin is absolute by absolving the finite creation it gives. It absolved in freeing from itself. It never functions as an absorbing god, but as a God who releases finite otherness for itself, and as other to its own absolute otherness. So it retains its own otherness, even while in relation to the otherness of the finite creation."

125. *EB* 495: "We name that source in many ways, 'God' being one of the names, and in many ways the best. I call that source the agapeic origin."

126. *AOO* 6: "I am interested in the metaphysics of origination and the relations implied therein. Most basically, there is the *transcendence* of the divine: an *otherness* to the origin that cannot be assimilated to any worldly process of becoming. . . . There is the difference of origin as (one might say) creating as creating and the world as creation created, and the difference of origin and world not only names the otherness of the former, but releases the latter into its own being for itself."

127. HT 32: "If there is one absolute source, our major choice seems to be between holistic self-creation and creation from nothing, that is, if we are intent on affirming the One as absolute source."

128. HT 39: "The notion of God as creator . . . tries to name something of the originative being of God, originative in a radical unique way. . . . Creating is a name for that absolutely unique originating."

*HG* 129: "Creation as the act by which this God brings being to be points in this direction of unconditional origination."

129. *HG* 127: "Suppose creation . . . is what one might call a hyperbolic thought. Suppose creation were more like a *metaphysical hyperbole,* the thought of something hyperbolic, and in excess of finite, univocal determination, or our self-determination."

*AOO* 5: "The idea of God as creator suggests, by contrast, a more recalcitrant notion of origination. I call creation a hyperbolic thought, in that it exceeds all determinate intelligibilities."

On the hyperbolic thought of creation, see Milbank's understanding of creation in terms of an ontology of the impossible—of the excessive thought of creation (that anything exists outside of God), of its outcome exceeding its occasion. Milbank, *Being Reconciled,* 62–63, 70.

130. *BB* 262: "This 'not-being' God also means that the meaning of nothingness is not that of determinate negation. The nothingness between God and creation would not be a negation that would negate itself and so prove dialectically affirmative."

*HG* 136: "The nothing again names the qualitative difference of origin and creation, since this absolute absolving act is not creating itself in creating creation. The nothing names the hyperbolic asymmetry of the God who creates."

See Cunningham, *Genealogy of Nihilism,* passim.

131. *BB* 269: "Creation comes out of an origin, but that coming out suggests a double-

ness: at once a giving of the plentitude of being, for creation is there; and yet a coming out shadowed by nothingness. For creation would be nothing, were it not for the giving of the origin."

*HG* 130: "The originating is by God from nothing, in that the finite being is brought to be, and it would be nothing at all were it not brought to be. *The nothing is constitutive of its finite being, not by constituting it, but by qualifying the mode of its ontological constitution, such that, by its very being, it is not God and cannot be God.* The 'not' is not only between it and God, but is in it as its nothingness without the most radically intimate ontological origination that always now sustains it in being."

On this constitutive nothingness, see the vision presented by Milbank (et al.) of a participatory ontology—in which the finite exists inasmuch as it participates in the infinite—of the natural/immanent suspended in the supernatural/transcendent—suspended over the nothing, everything (save God) would be without God. Milbank, *Being Reconciled*, 179.

132. HT 24: "A creator as origin is not a *first being* whence other beings become: the ultimate source of coming to be cannot be a being in that derived determinate sense."

*HG* 128: "Creation has to do with *the coming to be* of finite being. How think, how can we think, the ultimate origin of coming to be? We cannot think it absolutely: as creations of the origin, we ourselves are derivative, hence not on a par with the origin."

133. *HG* 129: "Creation is not self-determination, but the giving to be of what is not the origin in itself: creation is the origination of the happening of being as the finite between; the happening of finitude is, but it might not be, were it not that it were given to be by the absolute original."

134. *BB* 336: "We might think of this primordial power as the *first possibilizing,* in contrast to the *second possibilizing,* which refers to the determinate realization of a particular possibility. This first power of the possible is a creative possibilizing."

*HG* 3: "Transcendence itself would be in excess of determinate beings, as their original ground; it would be in excess of our self-transcendence, as its most ultimate possibilizing source. It would be beyond the ordinary doublet of possibility/reality, as their possibility source; it could not be just a possibility, nor indeed a determinate realization of possibility."

135. *BB* 506: "Finite transcending points beyond itself to the absolute origin as the primal giver of the promise of creation, and as the sustaining ground of its metaxological milieu. As giver and sustaining, the origin is immanent in the metaxological milieu."

136. *BB* 255: The origin's " 'perfection' would be, so to say, a 'pluperfection.' It would be pluperfection, not just in the sense of always having been perfected, but pluperfect as now being, and as always being. Such pluperfection would not be reducible to any or all of the tenses of time. It would be the beyond of time as always already more than any process of becoming. It would be the surplus of eternity."

See Milbank on God's being more than God, on God's fullness, on God's goodness as prior to any evil as lack. Milbank, *Being Reconciled,* xii, passim.

137. *BB* 215: "There is an asymmetry in agapeic creation, but it is not the asymmetry of nonrelatedness. Agapeic asymmetry is asymmetry per se, in that the relation is for the other as other, and not for a return to self-relation."

138. *PU* 221: "Plurality itself becomes the generosity of creation, the irreducible gift of the agapeic origin.... The agapeic origin is thus the ground of a between that is genuinely nonreductive of plurality, even while it allows the intermediation between the one and the other."

139. *BB* 270: "The doubleness of creation then would seem to imply a tense coexis-

tence of independence and dependence. *Independence,* in that the outcome of origination is not the self-origination of the origin: the creation is other."

140. *BB* 270: "The doubleness of creation then would seem to imply a tense coexistence of independence and dependence. . . . *Dependence,* in that the creation is not absolutely self-supporting; it hovers over the nothingness out of which it was called into being, and to which again many of its forms of being, perhaps all of it, will eventually return."

*HT* 39: "The notion of God as creator gives some articulation to this ontological dependency of finite being as a whole."

141. *BB* 448: "The origin as agapeic gives creation its other-being for itself, for the goodness of creation, and not just mediately for itself as origin. This goodness of being-other for itself reaches its richest ontological expression in creation with the human being as an end of infinite worth."

*PU* 226: "It is as if the Creator, in giving being to the creation also gave it its value for itself. Anything we humans do subsequently follows in the train of this first absolute amen to the goodness of being. To comprehend the meaning of this amen is almost impossible for us."

142. *PU* 131: "An origin that from the beginning is articulated in terms of plenitude rather than lack simply, I call an agapeic origin. Such origination does not proceed simply from lack to plenitude, but from plenitude to plenitude, or from plenitude/lack to plenitude."

*HG* 135: "Agapeic origination is a way of speaking of this: 'bringing to be' from surplus good rather than from initial lack."

143. *HG* 136: "The agapeic origin does not produce itself in giving creation. It is always already itself—superplus power of origination, overdeterminate, not in 'need' of finite determination. Finitude is not its own determination, but is a released happening that if given its own promise of being creative. This God gives the being of creation."

144. On this excess, see Milbank's understanding of God's goodness as genuine and non-reactive—as an original plenitude. Milbank, *Being Reconciled,* 149.

145. *HG* 136: "God gives the being of creation."

146. *PU* 218: "Agapeic creation would be the giving of being to the other that lets that other-being be as other. Finite being is let be as irreducibly other."

147. *PU* 100: "The ultimate origin is an agapeic source that gives the finite other its being, not for the origin itself, but for the finite being as other in its own right. The finite entity is let be in its thisness as other and its own."

148. *HG* 138: "The agapeic One redoubles its giving, but it does not redouble itself here to give itself to itself, but frees the finite into its being for itself."

149. *PU* 221: "Plurality itself becomes the generosity of creation, the irreducible gift of the agapeic origin. . . . The agapeic origin is thus the ground of a between that is genuinely nonreductive of plurality, even whole it allows the intermediation between the one and the other."

*AOO* 293: "The agapeic origin sources the pluralism of creation."

150. *BHD* 116: "Agapeic creating is not a fall into self-division of the erotic One, but the overfull generosity of the original power of being that grants plurality."

*PU* 221: "Plurality itself becomes the generosity of creation, the irreducible gift of the agapeic origin. . . . The agapeic origin is thus the ground of a between that is genuinely nonreductive of plurality, even whole it allows the intermediation between the one and the other."

151. *BB* 184: "The singularity of the thing in its unique *that it is* is its nonequivalence

to anything other. . . . There are no univocal or dialectical equivalences for the singular sense of the *that it is* that exceeds every equivalence."

*BB* 187: "Only God is on the level of this absolute enigma of singularity: singularity as being at all by virtue of its being valued for itself in its singularity. . . . The singular being is the great art of God."

*BB* 294–95: "The fecundity of creation gives rises [sic] to the newness of the 'once' that is infinitely pluralized in the marvel of singularity. Such a pluralization is a repetition that never repeats itself, that never reiterates the univocal same. Creation is an ever-fresh, never-diminished origination of singularity."

152. *PU* 234: The agapeic origin is the "giver of the middle in its being; giver of the middle as the space of open being, keeping its openness open, and keeping its openness for good; keeping it open for the good of the other, as it dissolves its own 'dominance' of the beings within the relativity. This self-dissolving keeping is the agapeic renunciation of the origin's 'for-itself,' in order to let the 'for-itself' of the finite creation come into its own."

153. *PU* 212: "The agapeic ground as overfull grounds the community of finite others, in the sense of letting the community of others be as free. Without this overfull, freely originating ground there would be no community of plurality. As originated from agapeic excess, the community of plurality does not collapse into the ground as into an absorbing god."

154. See here Pickstock's understanding of God as ecstatically preoccupied, as displaced in his concern for the other—in creation situating sites. Pickstock, *After Writing*, 229.

155. *PU* 221: "The agapeic origin casts its bread but asks for nothing in return, constrains nothing, but lets it be, lets it be in its promise, loves it to be in its real otherness. Its cast of being is from its joy, flows forth from its agape."

*PU* 231: "God does nothing for Himself; everything is done for the other. There is a sense in which nothing is *for* God. God lets be, since everything given by God is for that thing, given for that thing itself."

*PU* 232: "A giving without the expectancy of return is beyond our measuring. This is pure gift. God demands nothing."

156. *HT* 41: "There is nothing jealous about agapeic origination. The image of *non-possessive dispensation* is more appropriate. . . . Like creation as hyperbolic generosity, agapeic dispensation transcends possession. Its richness is its own willing poverty, in willing to be nothing, that the genuine other may be endowed as something as good."

157. *BHD* 80: "Doubling, redoubling would be the creative generosity of the ultimate origin as an agapeic absolute."

*PU* 230: "This is the original meaning of the givenness of being: a generosity of being that gives for no reason beyond the goodness of giving being."

158. *BHD* 182: "The *directionality* of its giving of being out of excess or plenitude is all important."

*HG* 137: "If the first absolute relation we call creation is asymmetrical in radically giving being to be, it exceeds the economy of the interplay of beings in the finite between."

159. *PU* 221: "The metaphysical difficulty of thinking the agapeic origin stems from our disability of being, our own being as the living lack of agapeic generosity. We fail to understand an unconstrained gift. For us its excess is too much, something for nothing, purposive in its purposelessness beyond all our finite purposes."

*PU* 231: "Since our minds and being are so insistently erotic, such absolute agapeic being seems hardly conceivable, much less believable."

160. *BB* 264: "The releasing of creation is with the view to the unconditional gift of free being."

161. *BHD* 80: "Agapeic creation gives an irreducible otherness to the being of finite creatures. This is an ontological freedom that may always shatter the dialectical claims of a singular, totalized self-mediation."

AT 250: "The promise of freedom is a being free, but before that it is being freed. Being freed, we are free. The agapeic generosity of the origin frees us into the freedom of being for ourselves. But being free(d) is not originally the product of freedom but the gift of freedom. . . . This giving is not our own. This giving gives us to be ourselves."

162. *EB* 365: "This is not 'freedom from' the other which wants to be outside of community, but freedom given from the agapeic origin, and hence a 'from' that founds elemental community."

163. *BB* 263: "The agapeic origin absolves itself from its relativity to the creation in the sense that, while remaining in relation, it allows the creation for itself to absolve itself from the relation, even to the point of turning against the origin, such as we find in human evil. The agapeic origin is absolute by absolving the finite creation it gives. It absolves in freeing from itself."

164. BR 224: "We are in the gift of the agapeic origin that lets us be to be free in our own difference, even to the oblivion of mindfulness of the generosity of the source: loss of reverence goes with this oblivion."

En 150: "There can be no *necessary* redemption of the evil, this enemy. The *letting be* of evil, as free, is entailed by the agapeic love."

*PU* 249: "This patience is perplexing and horrifying. That is, the freedom of finitude given by the agapeic origin lets be even demonic possibility. The extremity of spiritual nihilism as a free possibility is allowed by the agapeic origin."

165. *PU* 221: "God's generosity is horrifying to our rational prudence; relative to our prudence it seems purposeless; there is no determinate purpose to being. . . . Ultimate generosity is 'purposeful' beyond every finite purpose."

*BB* 545: "It is *because* God exists, that everything is permitted, even radical evil. This does not mean that evil is loved. Freedom is loved, freedom to be the good, freedom as the good. Absolutely nothing is asked of us, yet absolutely everything is being asked of us. The hyperbolic asking in the face of the terror of divine permission resides in the fact that freedom of spirit alone can restore the freedom of being."

166. *PO* 348: The "defense of perversity as a defense of freedom might be turned into a 'proof' of God *from evil.*"

One can see a difference of emphasis here between Desmond and Milbank. Desmond focuses on how God lets the world be, is patient with evil, and thus lets be something like a "secular" realm—of that which has quit God. This though is not the deepest reality, for even evil is thoroughly dependent on the agapeic origin for is being. Agapeic creation is such that one given to be *can* turn to evil.

167. *PU* 135: "I call the Good the 'agapeic origin.' "

168. *BB* 71: "The good of creation for itself is given by this origin. We greet it in the primal agapeic astonishment, which is an echo of the primal 'It is good.' "

*BB* 448: "The origin as agapeic gives creation its other-being for itself, for the goodness of creation, and not just mediately for itself as origin. This goodness of being-other for itself reaches its richest ontological expression in creation with the human being as an end of infinite worth."

169. *BB* 512: "God's astonishing saying on beholding creation: It is good, it is very good. God does not say: I am good. God does not say: It is good for this purpose or that

purpose. Nor again does God say: It is good for this being or that being—say, the human being—who indeed is offered dominion by God. There is a prior original yes: It is good. It is not good for human beings; *It* is good, good for itself. The giving of being is itself the gift of being as good. There is no other reason for it, beyond the fact that creation as being is good."

*PU* 242: "God's 'It is very good' names the superlative worth of being, the issue of perfection from the pluperfect."

170. This can be compared to Badiou's understanding of being and value. True value, for Badiou, arises in relation to an event, not being-as-being. Desmond, however, sees value as indeed related to an event—but to the event of the origin of being, to creation. Thus, for Desmond, being is valuable, and there are not two orders: one of the subjective, of the Event, and one of the objective, of Being. See Badiou, *Being and Event,* passim; Hallward, *Badiou,* 78.

171. *PO* 285: "God simply loves being, but we do so on and off."

*HG* 140: "God's seeing [being as good] is sabbatical. God is looking with love on the creation as itself good, and good in itself, and for itself."

172. *PU* 241: "God lets the sun shine equally on the wicked and the righteous. . . . God does not hate the hateful; God loves the evil, the hateful, the enemy. From our moralistic standpoint the idea of God as agapeic is monstrous."

*PU* 242: "God's agape seems to be an insult to our justice, a reckless generosity exceeding the measure of our rational self-mediating morality."

173. *BB* 452: "True interest suggests a limitless expanse of metaxological mindfulness. In that regard, only God is truly interested in being, in community with being. Only God loves all being down to the ontological intimacy of singularity. We humans are not capable of that absolute pitch of interest, of being between."

174. *BB* 330: The agapeic origin is "reflected in the creation of unique singularity; the being of the thing is loved unrepeatably for itself, and hence has its being in this ontological generosity that is absolute—unconditionally for the singular thing itself, in the ontological worth of being."

*PU* 84: "God who is not an absorbing Moloch, but an agapeic absolute who does not dissolve the differences of creatures, but loves them in the singularity of their singularity."

175. *EB* 195: "The origin is the ultimate giver of the gift of the good of being in the between. Self and others are recipients of the gift in the between, and both in community by their being and called to realize the promise of community."

*EB* 220: "The agape of being is first given to us, but we are called to an agapeic being which is the doing of living, in an ethics of gratitude to the origin, and of generosity to self and other."

176. *EB* 476–77: "What if the power of God is not to be imaged on this sovereignty, this imperial power to command without controversion? What if there is a power higher than such sovereignty? God as the agapeic servant who does not determine but frees? I take Jesus as suggesting this, in his life and death, in parables like the prodigal son. The tension of the higher good and sovereignty can lead to a struggle between the 'prince of the world' and God. The prince of the world is the erotic sovereign thinking itself the last absolute, and hence having to stand over against God in spiritual agon."

177. *EB* 207: "But the divine, like the human, is not the good as self-sufficient perfection, but as generosity that exceeds itself . . . [This] is the God that enters into the midst of suffering and that comes to suffer with the despised others; that communicates the truth of the agapeic relation in the willingness to suffer with and for the other."

178. *HG* 194: "Re-creation involves the absolving offer, opening again a new beginning. And because of the rupture between the old and new creation, this 'being re-made' cannot be fully worked out in terms of self-creation, self-making."

179. *BB* 531: "As we cannot give the primal goodness, so we cannot give this renewal of ontological goodness; only a God can save us."

*PU* 245: "Who can bear the unbearable burden of evil? What power of good would not be crushed by evil? Not a human power; no human being can bear it without being crushed. Only a God. The agapeic origin means: bearing the infinitely crushing burden of evil, and yet not being crushed. How could *we* think this? How *dare* we think this?"

*EB* 115: "The crushing weight of evil is carried, and we cannot carry it. Who carries it, if not God? . . . We cannot completely answer extreme evil; the answer is other to us. The answer is the goodness of the good, a power of living good that exceeds us. If God does not somehow bear evil, the whole thing comes to nothing. Do we perish at the thought? (Why do you squirm?) If only God can redeem evil, then God too must die. The good must embrace its own most extreme opposite, and recreate its perverted power. This is the kenotic power of the good: as passing over, and passing away, it is a passing into finitude. God is passage of that good."

180. *HG* 194: "If there are continuities between creation and re-creation, it is the promise of the good of the 'to be' in the first instance that finds its promise renewed. This promise we do not first produce, though we do participate in its redemption or betrayal."

181. *EB* 218–19: "Hence our laying of ourselves as open seems like a constant striving, or like a pathway through a wilderness that often vanishes, making us think we had been fooling ourselves, only then to reappear suddenly further along, and hearten us that our faith in the good, faith without certitude, is not without unexpected fruit. The life of agapeic service is impossible if we are alone, and without the sustaining power of the good as other. As I suggested before, the familiar word (and I think best word) for transcendence itself is God."

182. *DDO* 174: "To gain goodwill, self-will would have to reverse its fall and leap upward; but this, ensnared as it is, it cannot do by itself. It requires the ingression of something from above, rain to water its droughted roots. We would never return home, be restored, unless we were called home, loved."

*EB* 363–64: "This release comes to one, it is given to one. One can await it, one can purify oneself in advance in hope. One can pray. One can struggle with one's demons, and the struggle is somehow the gift itself, as well as the preparation. One can will to enter the struggle, but the willing cannot make the gift be given. One can knock and knock on the door but the knock does not open the door, for the door is opened from the other side, and hence the opening comes to one, even though one has roused the night into noise that the gods themselves seem unable to ignore. The opening is a simple elemental gift that cannot be commanded. There is asked a willingness beyond will; a willingness that is a new will in us, but a will that cannot be described as self-willing, or any kind of self-determining willing; it is a willingness beyond self-determining."

183. *EB* 75: "God is the most secret partner, the most anonymous helper, the most intimate prompter, the good that asks nothing for itself, for its nature as the good is simply to broadcast the good to the other, broadcast itself to the other as other, sustaining that otherness."

184. *EB* 494: "Religious community is itself the appeal to the good for that help to be good. We cannot do it on our own, as we cannot free ourselves from bewitchment on our

own. To ask to be free from the idols is to ask for the spiritual strength of a divine service."

185. *EB* 486: "We understand power as given all along, a gift from motiveless generosity, motiveless goodness beyond the goodness of the gift, rousing in community the vision of humans together living an ethics of generosity in finite image of the ultimate generosity."

On God as agapeic sustainer, see Milbank's discussion of creation's participation in God. Milbank, *Theology and Social Theory*, 429–31.

186. See Section II, §5 above on the refiguring of the hyperboles in *GB*.

187. *AOO* 294: "Religion *lived* is our being in the porous happening of communication between ultimate transcendence (T3) and finite transcendences (T1, T2). Religion *reflected* in its truth is (metaxological) philosophy which understands that *to be is to be religious,* namely, to have one's being in the happening of the between by virtue of the ultimate giving of the agapeic origin."

188. *PO* 158: "Being religious, as recollected in the inwardness of the metaxologically open self, may help midwife the reemergence of sacramental earth. Out of that inwardness, it will issue its charge: renew reverence for being; recall a sense of the sacredness of life; reactivate a proper piety of being there."

189. *HG* 188: "Being religious has to do with a community of humans with the divine, but also with a certain singularity that is reserved to, in the sense of being more intimate than, any merely general relation to God. . . . This is an ontological intimacy to singularity that is, in truth, fulfilled in participation in community, and most of all community with God, but that community and singularity cannot be described in the standard dialectical languages of a more total inclusivity."

190. *AOO* 294: "Religion *lived* is our being in the porous happening of communication between ultimate transcendence (T3) and finite transcendences (T1, T2)."

191. *HG* 130: "'Being given to be' here is gift: not self-determination. This 'being given to be' is a *passio essendi* before it is a *conatus essendi*. And this is not necessary, either with reference to its originating source, or in itself: it is but it might not be. To be as this gift—this is contingency as created good. It is the good of the ultimate 'to be' that is at the source of this givenness as gift."

192. *PU* 83: "In the beginning and in the end, the intimacy of 'being with' is inseparable from being religious. The word *religio* itself communicates this in its naming of a bond of relatedness and a tie of trust. The intimacy of sacred communion is in the depth of the idiocy of being. Were this depth entirely desecrated, the distinctive personal 'being with' of human community would wither at the roots."

193. *HG* 140: "We humans are to live the 'It is good' also, relative to the finite, and also a hyperbolic life beyond holistic immanence, relative to God."

194. *HG* 140: "God's seeing [being as good] is sabbatical. God is looking with love on the creation as itself good, and good in itself, and for itself. . . . We are called to being as sabbatical, and to be as sabbatical."

195. *PU* 230: "The metaphor of the agapeic absolute would run: origin as excess plenitude, transcendence itself as other; creation as finite concreteness, but not for the return of the origin to itself; the 'exitus,' if we call it such at all, is for what is given as other in the middle; and while there may a different 'return' in the metaxological middle, this is not dictated by the logic of a circular erotic self-becoming; it is gratuitously emergent in the created order as itself trying to be agapeic being; 'return' is the cocreation of community by the finite other."

196. *BB* 408: The agapeic self is "doubly stressed in the between: between the excess of its own original power, and the willingness to suspend that power in the interests of the other. . . . a middle between infinitudes"

*PU* 144: "The overdetermined power to be of selfhood is agapeic in these two ways: as *given to itself to be* out of an origin other to itself; and as the power to *give itself over to being* beyond itself in its own self-transcendence."

197. *EB* 110: "Being blessed is an exalting gift; one is lifted up to the superior; but the exalting is often, perhaps always, matched by suffering. It is cursed by sorrow. The gift is too much, and to be up to it, we have to undergo breakdown, to let its breakthrough or inbreaking come. No breaking in, without breaking down."

198. *BB* 222: "This is the movement of agapeic mindfulness into radical humility before transcendence itself. It is also a movement of exaltation into the superior."

199. BR 225: "Reverence grants the worthiness of being."

*EB* 195: "Reverence: it is worthy in itself."

200. *PU* 163: "The question of the transfigurative power of agapeic mind concerns the transformation of self such that it can love the hateful."

201. *PO* 158: "Being religious, as recollected in the inwardness of the metaxologically open self, may help midwife the reemergence of sacramental earth. Out of that inwardness, it will issue its charge: renew reverence for being; recall a sense of the sacredness of life; reactivate a proper piety of being there."

202. *BHD* 17: "There is a speculative laughter that issues from the festive celebration of being by agapeic mindfulness. This speculative yes to the community of being in no way subordinates the otherness of being to any conceptual whole constructed by the philosopher's mind. The yes of this laughter is a festive gesture towards the metaxological openness of agapeic being."

203. *BB* 194: "We make thanks (*gratias agimus*). Thanking is a doing of being, a being agapeic, a saying yes to the other for its otherness."

204. *EB* 510–11: "Alternatively, we can live with this beyond of time with a thanks that does not always know whom it thanks, yet it knows it is under the need to give thanks. There is a thanks in excess of singulars who can be thanked, and the excess spills over into a life whose seedbed is thanks. One gives thanks to and for a giver one cannot name always, and yet an indeterminate thanks is asked by the goodness of what is come to us. Such thanks is like a religious trust which wakes to itself as entrusted with the gift of coming to be, entrusted by a giver it does not determinately know."

205. *HG* 55: "Thanksgiving which grants the excess generosity of divine transcendence, and the very asymmetry calls forth the ultimate gratitude."

206. One thinks here of Josef Pieper's book: *Leisure, The Basis of Culture*. "Leisure," in Pieper's sense, is a receptive/passive stance of appreciation, of affirming, the noninstrumental goodness of being. Leisure thus understood is closely linked with gratitude, festivity, worship, and generosity.

207. BR 216: "Reverence is beyond autonomy, but is not a form of affirmed integrity. Reverence is beyond autonomy, but is not a form of servitude: it is a freeing, a being free in relation to the superior other. It always has some relation to the superior in it"

BR 227: "Reverence already places us in this hyperbolic dimension of being: it is not the abject degrading that reduces us to the 'below.' It has everything to do with elevation and the dimension of height. When we revere truly we are carried by our love of the superior to a higher level. . . . reverence is a release, a being freed to the superior."

208. *BB* 41: "The transcendence of self involved in religious *worship* or *adoration* is

a placing of oneself before the ultimate, a *praise* of the other without demand, a joy in the glory of the divine. Again the closed circle of immanent selfhood and thinking dies; one is reborn to a different mindfulness in the space beyond self, the space of the middle between humanity and the divine."

*PU* 183: "The thought of God may cause to fade the pretense of all human thought. It fades, not always into nothing, but sometimes into praise."

*HG* 58–59: "Worship in a purer register might be said to free us of finite desire that seeks and grasps something from the other; to purify our sense of the divine as not needing anything from us, being a freer being; to purify the difference of its latent hostilities; to purify the communication of the sly temptation to dominion."

209. *HG* 138: Worship "is love in the dimension of the hyperbolic, where the God loved is absolutely other in absolute intimacy. Only in worship are absolute otherness and absolute intimacy at one."

Likewise, Pickstock sees liturgical space as being just this kind of *metaxu*—opening up a place of relation between ourselves and God that transfigures the worshiping community. (See below on worshiping community as image of the agapeic origin.) Pickstock, *After Writing*, 232.

210. *PU* 101: "Prayer may be the deepest enactment of the intimacy of being; for the praying self is the most idiotic. It is senseless and yet divines sense beyond sense. It is given over, yet it is the audacity of trust."

*HG* 198: "If praying is a love that knows God, or is known by God, then it lives a communicative porosity between God and us that could not be exhausted by a knowledge either fully determinate, or claiming to be fully self-determining. Such claims would falsify this religious knowing, this porosity, this loving, this praying. Prayer is the friend of a paradoxical poverty of philosophy that loves the reserve of the full."

211. *BHD* 95: "To worship is to celebrate the ground of the world: the festivity of cultus may be gratitude for the gift of being this ground gives."

212. *BHD* 96: "Worship . . . claims to return the human being to participation in the divine order of the cosmos."

*EB* 512: "The consummate community is one of celebration, of our solidarity with the ultimate power, despite evil, in our own good in its many forms, in our struggle to be released from evils into which we fall, celebration of the sweet gift of life, as well as the peace we seek facing the terrors of death. Rebirth to the good of the elemental things is now celebrated."

213. Milbank and Pickstock see in the Eucharist the paradigm of this agapeic feast, indeed of the gift as such, as gift-exchange. For in the Eucharist, we meet God's gift with surrender and reception—we offer, give ourselves as gift in return. See Milbank, *Being Reconciled*, 149, 161; Pickstock, *After Writing*, Part II.

214. *EB* 165: "What is intimated in the arche here becomes community in humanity, itself now called to be a concretion of agapeic community, and witness to the ultimate agapeic source. This end is participation in community with the arche, and hence itself a finite form of the community of agapeic service. This is the good we must seek to be, failing again and again, and beginning again and again, as we must."

This tracks with Pickstock's eucharistic theology in which we in worship, in offering to God, enter into the perpetual offering within the Trinitarian God—participating "in the self-giving flow of life between the persons of the Trinity." Pickstock, *After Writing*, 242–43.

*EB* 486: "We understand power as given all along, a gift from motiveless generosity, motiveless goodness beyond the goodness of the gift, rousing in community the vision of humans together living an ethics of generosity in finite image of the ultimate generosity."

215. *EB* 220: "The agape of being is first given to us, but we are called to an agapeic being which is the doing of living, in an ethics of gratitude to the origin, and of generosity to self and other. The agape of being intimates a fullness, but it is not being full of oneself. One does nothing to merit it, and no payment is exacted, for it offers itself simply as the life of the good, a life we are to live. It has no reason, beyond itself, which is to be beyond itself, in being itself."

216. *EB* 168–69: "We are grateful for the generosity of the ground, and we respond to this with thanks, and with thanks lived as a form of existence. For it is not only the generosity of the giver that is important but the generosity of the receiver. We are the receivers, and, strangely, it is the generosity of the other that possibilizes our comportment of generosity towards the other. Generosity entails no servile reception or abjection before the other. In fact, the other's generosity does more than occasion our gratitude; it charges us with the living of generosity."

*EB* 217: "Affirming is consent to *gift*. Generosity is born of a primal gratitude. Ethics springs from gratitude. This is lived in ethical and religious service beyond autonomy. What is this service? It is a willingness beyond will, beyond will to power, beyond my will to power."

217. *EB* 217: "We affirm the good as the source of this good: God. Affirming is consent to *gift*. Generosity is born of a primal gratitude. Ethics springs from gratitude."

CWSC 51: "An ethics of gratitude can be called forth, lived as a life of generous offering. Thanks is incarnated as a form of life."

Milbank likewise observes that the giving of oneself arises from a fullness, a "plenitude of vision" such that doxology and charity, the gift thankfully received and given, become inseparable. Yet it is the enabling gift of God and our grateful recognition of this gift that comes first—as Milbank writes: "Festival, first of all." The mirror image of this is the way in which suspicion disables the reception of the gift and therefore generosity. Here, Marion is in agreement, inasmuch as the priority of the question, "Does anyone love me?" holds it fundamental place. Milbank, *Being Reconciled*, 150, 157, 180–81; Milbank, "Can a Gift be Given?" 154; Marion, *Erotic Phenomenon*, passim.

218. In Pickstock's powerful analysis, receiving and returning are intimately intertwined. The gift is contagious, ever overflowing into more giving, into repeated nonidentical return. Ultimately, the gift (God's gift, our being) is truly received by being "offered humbly back" in gratitude and then "handed on" in generosity. Pickstock, *After Writing*, 246–48, 250.

219. *EB* 498: "How love God? By enacting in life the truth of the agape of being, and this most concretely in service of the neighbor."

CWSC 51: "The depth of generosity is sustained by humility in relation to the ultimate."

220. *BB* 536: "To give ourselves up means that we consent to the fact that our being and all of being is a gift. The gift is first a giving over by the agapeic origin. And when we give ourselves up, we liken ourselves to the origin in its ontological generosity."

221. *DDO* 167: Desire as goodwill "reveals that desire may be more than an erotic rush from lack to wholeness, that it may be an agapeic pouring forth from a wholeness already real."

222. *EB* 505: "And of course, you cannot separate the divine and the ethical service. Divine service is agapeic communication in relation to God; ethical service is agapeic communication in relation to creation and human others. There is not one without the

other, though there may be an ethical service that does not comprehend its ground in divine service, as there may be a love of God so caught up in this love that its *singular form* of ethical service is just to show to others the fruit of that love which is *holiness*."

223. *EB* 505: "Ethical service arises from God service, though it be often *incognito;* ethical service is enacted God service. God service itself is liturgical, in the sense that liturgy is a public service for the people, a feast in service. Moralities are ethical services that, so to say, suffer from amnesia about their liturgical origin. Without God service, ethical service becomes a moral ritual of duty without joy, like a festive drama that has lost the festivity."

224. *PU* 119: "Agapeic mind expresses something that is both a regulative ideal and an ontological reality, somehow constitutive of our most intimate being."

225. *BB* 536: "To give ourselves up means that we consent to the fact that our being and all of being is a gift. The gift is first a giving over by the agapeic origin. And when we give ourselves up, we liken ourselves to the origin in its ontological generosity."

*EB* 365: "We must join the meaning of 'freedom from' and 'freedom towards.' The 'from' is from the origin as giver, but as freeing us, and into gratitude for the gift, even in suffering. This is not 'freedom from' the other which wants to be outside of community, but freedom given from the agapeic origin, and hence a 'from' that founds elemental community. And here too 'freedom towards' is beyond 'freedom to' be oneself, since in certain sufferings there is an excess to self-transcending that is freed beyond itself and towards the good as other. This 'freedom towards' has a vector that is ontologically intimate: both selfless and the deepest selving. One goes towards the good, sometimes sightlessly, in agapeic selving."

226. *EB* 217: "Generosity is born of a primal gratitude. Ethics springs from gratitude. This is lived in ethical and religious service beyond autonomy. What is this service? It is a willingness beyond will, beyond will to power, beyond my will to power."

*EB* 489: "A fundamental gratitude is resurrected, expressing itself in an ethics of generosity towards the frailty of beings in the between, human and nonhuman."

Again, Pickstock, meditating on the Eucharist, sees this same agapeic being as ontological and regulative. Our giving is enabled by our receiving—not just our receiving some discrete gift to our selves, but our receiving *of ourselves* in our transformed humanity. This gift of transformed humanity in Christ enables us to offer gifts, yet it is only by giving that we truly receive our transformed humanity. Pickstock, *After Writing,* 240–45.

227. *PU* 163: "The question of the transfigurative power of agapeic mind concerns the transformation of self such that it can love the hateful."

228. *PU* 144: "Our being is itself the gift of the generosity of creation. To consent agapeically is to create beyond oneself out of this generosity."

*PU* 232: "The gift of agapeic being solicits in us the gift of agapeic being."

On agapeic mind as seeing the self's being as agapeic—the self as a gift that is given and for the giving—see Milbank's discussion of how reception, gratitude, and return constitute the creature itself. Milbank, "Can a Gift be Given?" 135.

229. *PU* 221: "The metaphysical difficulty of thinking the agapeic origin stems from our disability of being, our own being as the living lack of agapeic generosity. We fail to understand an unconstrained gift. For us its excess is too much, something for nothing, purposive in its purposelessness beyond all our finite purposes."

230. *EB* 220: "The agape of being is first given to us, but we are called to an agapeic being which is the doing of living, in an ethics of gratitude to the origin, and of generosity to self and other. The agape of being intimates a fullness, but it is not being full

of oneself. One does nothing to merit it, and no payment is exacted, for it offers itself simply as the life of the good, a life we are to live. It has no reason, beyond itself, which is to be beyond itself, in being itself."

231. GEW 27: "Within the immanent exigence of the ethical absolute, we find ourselves exceeded by the call of an absolute we do not produce ourselves."

232. GEW 26–27: "The call of the good is such that we can never be its master but are always called to an obedience to what is absolute. How make sense of this obedience? Only by thinking the source of the primal ethos: if the primal ethos indicates its truth through the power of the ethical, something about that source is communicated as inseparable from the good."

233. PU 227: "The confluence of ethics and metaphysics requires a metamorphosis in our thinking. . . . The value of being, and indirectly the value of the human being, has to be thought in relation to an other origin of value."

234. BB 33: "We reach out to what is other in self-transcendence, but there is in agapeic mind a transcendence different to that of erotic perplexity that wills finally and always to return to self."

BB 206: Agapeic mind is "the self-transcendence of mindfulness as it goes towards the other as other, and not just simply as a mirror of itself, or a means to mediate with its own self. It is genuinely self-transcending, for it is the thinking of the other in its otherness. . . . It thinks beyond itself, thinks in excess of its own self-mediation. And so such a communicative mindfulness is the living exemplification of a coming into the community of being."

235. BB 415: The process of ethical selving is "the unfolding of self from the elemental I of idiotic inwardness . . . from the aesthetic passion of immediacy, into the self-insistent I of self-will, through the self-mediation of ethical will, to the religious passion in which the I radically gives itself back to the between and its origin."

EB 377: "Ethics brings us to the limit of the ethical, as determined by autonomy and erotic sovereignty. At this limit a witness to something more is solicited."

236. EB 220: "The agape of being is first given to us, but we are called to an agapeic being which is the doing of living. . . . It has no reason, beyond itself, which is to be beyond itself, in being itself."

237. BB 408: The agapeic self is "doubly stressed in the between: between the excess of its own original power, and the willingness to suspend that power in the interests of the other. . . . a middle between infinitudes"

PU 144: "The overdetermined power to be of selfhood is agapeic in these two ways: as *given to itself to be* out of an origin other to itself; and as the power to *give itself over to being* beyond itself in its own self-transcendence."

238. BB 536: "To give ourselves up means that we consent to the fact that our being and all of being is a gift. The gift is first a giving over by the agapeic origin. And when we give ourselves up, we liken ourselves to the origin in its ontological generosity."

This selving beyond selving parallels Pickstock's understanding of the liturgical negotiation of identity—of the manner in which worship opens up and challenges, decenters one's identity—unselves in its selving. Pickstock, *After Writing*, 199.

239. EB 506: "In the double, redoubled service of agapeic community: the God service in which human service, neighbor service comes to be. Religious service comes to be ethical service. Beyond sovereign power this is living the life of gratitude and the ethics of a generosity that gives what good it has and is."

240. EB 486: "Religious community intermediates humans to the ultimate power, albeit imaged or represented in the available terms the human community has, terms that

are never the best, and often are mixed in with much that is idolatrous or potentially so. Religious community binds together (*re-ligare*—Augustine) the human and divine, and out of this transforms the bonds holding humans together."

241. *EB* 494: "Religious community is itself the appeal to the good for that help to be good. We cannot do it on our own, as we cannot free ourselves from bewitchment on our own. To ask to be free from the idols is to ask for the spiritual strength of a divine service."

242. *EB* 508: "This service is release into community in which we live from the good of the absolute other, and towards the good of ourselves and finite others as others, and again through them live towards the good of the absolute other."

243. *EB* 481: "This is the religious community of agapeic service that enacts the intermediation of the good beyond erotic sovereignty and in ethically likening itself to the generosity of the agapeic origin. If at the first extreme, erotic sovereignty gives way to mystical consent, at the second extreme the festival of a community becomes a sacramental drama."

244. *EB* 165: "What is intimated in the arche here becomes community in humanity, itself now called to be a concretion of agapeic community, and witness to the ultimate agapeic source. This end is participation in community with the arche, and hence itself a finite form of the community of agapeic service. This is the good we must seek to be, failing again and again, and beginning again and again, as we must."

*EB* 507: "That it is at all is ultimately a gift of the supergenerosity of the origin. Being as nothing brings us to an extreme where ethical service may image something of this giving. To treat the nothings with the love which affirms the good of their being is to image the generosity of the origin. This generosity is both before and points beyond the instrumentality of the network, and the dominion of the sovereign."

245. "If faith and theology understand themselves well, if they learn to speak of themselves and of God well . . . then they understand that they cannot, that they are structurally unable . . . to close the circle, finally and effectively to assure their own destination, truth, and validity" (*PT* 59).

"The faithful need to concede that they do not cognitively know what they believe in any epistemologically rigorous way" (*OR* 111).

246. *PU* 221: "Plurality itself becomes the generosity of creation, the irreducible gift of the agapeic origin. . . . The agapeic origin is thus the ground of a between that is genuinely nonreductive of plurality, even while it allows the intermediation between the one and the other."

247. *BB* 294–95: "The fecundity of creation gives rises [*sic*] to the newness of the 'once' that is infinitely pluralized in the marvel of singularity. Such a pluralization is a repetition that never repeats itself, that never reiterates the univocal same. Creation is an ever-fresh, never-diminished origination of singularity."

248. *PU* 188: "God as a merely univocal explanation would be a ruse by which reason uses the idea of God to shirk the deeper ontological perplexity about God. Reason then uses God to allow itself to go back to sleep again. If God is an 'explanation,' there is a sense in which this answer is darker than the question it answers, because the answer involves a certain extraordinary complex *acknowledgement* of the mystery of the ultimate."

249. *BB* 218–19: "Equivocal language may have to be *risked* if we want to affirm the absolute difference of the transcendent. Here the equivocity is that to speak the transcendent, equivocally or otherwise, is already to bring it out of its absolute difference, and so either not to name it, or to imply that there is no absolute difference. I think this

equivocity has to be *lived with* dynamically; it cannot be resolved into a univocal or dialectical determination."

250. *PU* 183: "God remains other to our thinking in our thinking of God."

*HG* 69: "If, as I think, the doubleness of the representation suggests rather an *imagistic hyperbole* in the finite that communicates *between* finitude itself and God, then for that representation to be true to God, and to be true to itself, it must always keep open the space of difference between itself and God."

251. *HT* 25: "Philosophy is just the thoughtful engagement of the sources of intelligibility immediately at work in the between."

252. *HT* 30: "We are naturally struck into astonishment before this being there at all, and wonder about its source. . . . Indeed, there is something astonishing in the fact that we have such hyperbolic thoughts at all, thoughts such as concern creation and nothing. They are clearly *disproportionate* to our finitude as things in nature."

*HG* 3: "I would say that there is something *hyperbolic* about the being given to be of beings: not what they are, but that they are at all. Hyperbolic in that the astonishment aroused by this givenness of being is not a determinate question seeking a determinate answer, but something exceeding determinate thinking."

253. *BB* 338: "Only with the agapeic origin as ground of possibility do we try to make sense of the other as other, and hence genuine plurality, and not just self-pluralization."

*PU* 212: "Without this overfull, freely originating ground there would be no community of plurality. As originated from agapeic excess, the community of plurality does not collapse into the ground as into an absorbing god."

*DDO* 180: "Ground of plurality in the ultimate origin of real difference, a ground that supports and preserves plurality."

254. *BB* 345: "Creation intimates an origin prior to the drawing of the line that makes it possible for us to think of the emergence of intelligibility"

*BB* 356: "The notion of the agapeic origin suggests a ground of founding trust. . . . The agapeic origin incites thought to conceive the basis of ontological and epistemological trust in intelligibility as going all the way down and up in being."

255. *BB* 513: "I want to say that the prior 'It is good' means a different understanding of *aesthetic value*. Aesthetic value means the worth of the thereness, as given in its sensuous manifestness. In this ontological meaning, aesthetic value is the show of the worth of being."

256. *EB* 200: "The idiot self concretizes the infinite value in the ontological roots of human being as given to itself by the origin."

257. *EB* 212: "A restlessness emerges that testifies to an infinite dimension to human desire. We cannot force all desire into the mould of finite appetite. To live in terms of that forcing is to deform ourselves. The infinite restlessness must be given allowance to be itself. Allowing it so, however, risks futility on one side, our coming into something more transcendent, on the other."

258. *HG* 97: "In the primal porosity of the intimate communication between God and humans, there is no absolute *self*-elevation *we* determine; there is gift that elevates the self: a *passio* that lifts the soul, not a *conatus* in which it lifts itself."

259. *PU* 204: "Our transcending being is unfolded as the quest of ultimacy. The field of being and our being in that field, both point beyond themselves. . . . Within the self-transcending urgency of desire, we find an opening to the ultimate other. We are the interior urgency of ultimacy, this other is ultimacy as the superior."

260. *BB* 160: "In the abyss of its own inward otherness, it comes before itself and opens to a sense of the infinite that exceeds its own self-mediation. Yet in the tension

between its own excess as transcendence and the transcendence of the other, it is being perfected, made whole, never closed even in the radical innerness."

261. *HG* 130: "'Being given to be' here is gift: not self-determination. This 'being given to be' is a *passio essendi* before it is a *conatus essendi*. And this is not necessary, either with reference to its originating source, or in itself: it is but in might not be. To be as this gift—this is contingency as created good. It is the good of the ultimate 'to be' that is at the source of this givenness as gift."

262. *HG* 97: "In the primal porosity of the intimate communication between God and humans, there is no absolute *self*-elevation *we* determine; there is gift that elevates the self: a *passio* that lifts the soul, not a *conatus* in which it lifts itself."

263. *BB* 218: "We are thrown towards transcendence by our being." Hyperbole "throws mindfulness into the *huper*, the beyond."

264. BR 227: "It is in the hyperbolic dimensions of disproportion that finesse is needed to read our place in being for signs of the ultimate excess, the unsurpassable beyond, beyond which nothing can be thought—God."

265. *DH* 210: "The *re-ligare* in Derrida, . . . Kierkegaard and Levinas . . . is the *ob-libare*, the bond of responsibility to the singularity of the 'wholly Other,' the bond of the one-on-one of the self to the Other."

266. *PT* 49: "The other is any other, God or someone or something else. So love means love the other as other, any other, any wholly other."

267. *PT* 201–202: "It is enough for 'God' to be the name of the absolutely other, a place holder for the *tout autre*"—this is "the work done by the name of God, the value of religious discourse and religious stories."

268. *BB* 218: "We are thrown towards transcendence by our being." Hyperbole "throws mindfulness into the *huper*, the beyond."

269. *EB* 498: "How love God? By enacting in life the truth of the agape of being, and this most concretely in service of the neighbor."

270. *BB* 536: "To give ourselves up means that we consent to the fact that our being and all of being is a gift. The gift is first a giving over by the agapeic origin. And when we give ourselves up, we liken ourselves to the origin in its ontological generosity."

271. *EB* 505: "Ethical service arises from God service, though it be often *incognito;* ethical service is enacted God service. God service itself is liturgical, in the sense that liturgy is a public service for the people, a feast in service. Moralities are ethical services that, so to say, suffer from amnesia about their liturgical origin. Without God service, ethical service becomes a moral ritual of duty without joy, like a festive drama that has lost the festivity."

272. GEW 26–27: "The call of the good is such that we can never be its master but are always called to an obedience to what is absolute. How make sense of this obedience? Only by thinking the source of the primal ethos: if the primal ethos indicates its truth through the power of the ethical, something about that source is communicated as inseparable from the good."

273. *PO* 353: "What is there, what 'is,' has no intrinsic worth; worth is merely an instrument of the projecting self, already set in opposition to being. The fact/value distinction is an expression of this ethical/ontological estrangement."

274. *EB* 167: "The loss of the [primal] ethos takes the form of the so-called death of God. And this is correct in that this is the loss of the elemental good of being in the between. It is not primarily a matter of finding the arguments for God unconvincing, or finding oneself living fine without God, or indeed even of turning against God. It is a

loss of the mindful attunement between the indeterminate openness of elemental expectation in us and the goodness of the source."

275. *HG* 130: "The originating is by God from nothing, in that the finite being is brought to be, and it would be nothing at all were it not brought to be. *The nothing is constitutive of its finite being, not by constituting it, but by qualifying the mode of its ontological constitution, such that, by its very being, it is not God and cannot be God.* The 'not' is not only between it and God, but is in it as its nothingness without the most radically intimate ontological origination that always now sustains it in being."

276. *PU* 221: "Plurality itself becomes the generosity of creation, the irreducible gift of the agapeic origin.... The agapeic origin is thus the ground of a between that is genuinely nonreductive of plurality, even whole it allows the intermediation between the one and the other."

*AOO* 293: "The agapeic origin sources the pluralism of creation."

277. *OR* 5: "How easily saying 'God is love' slides over into saying 'love is God.' This slippage is provocative and it provides us with an exceedingly important and provocative ambiguity, opening up a kind of endless substitutability and translatability between 'love' and 'God.' "

278. *BB* 452: "True interest suggests a limitless expanse of metaxological mindfulness. In that regard, only God is truly interested in being, in community with being. Only God loves all being down to the ontological intimacy of singularity. We humans are not capable of that absolute pitch of interest, of being between."

279. *BB* 536: "To give ourselves up means that we consent to the fact that our being and all of being is a gift. The gift is first a giving over by the agapeic origin. And when we give ourselves up, we liken ourselves to the origin in its ontological generosity."

280. *EB* 486: "Religious community intermediates humans to the ultimate power, albeit imaged or represented in the available terms the human community has, terms that are never the best, and often are mixed in with much that is idolatrous or potentially so. Religious community binds together (*re-ligare*—Augustine) the human and divine, and out of this transforms the bonds holding humans together."

281. *PU* 119: "Agapeic mind expresses something that is both a regulative ideal and an ontological reality, somehow constitutive of our most intimate being."

282. *EB* 510–11: "Alternatively, we can live with this beyond of time with a thanks that does not always know whom it thanks, yet it knows it is under the need to give thanks. There is a thanks in excess of singulars who can be thanked, and the excess spills over into a life whose seedbed is thanks. One gives thanks to and for a giver one cannot name always, and yet an indeterminate thanks is asked by the goodness of what is come to us. Such thanks is like a religious trust which wakes to itself as entrusted with the gift of coming to be, entrusted by a giver it does not determinately know."

283. *HG* 55: "Thanksgiving which grants the excess generosity of divine transcendence, and the very asymmetry calls forth the ultimate gratitude."

284. *EB* 138: "We sometimes speak of the infinite value of the person. But what could ground such an immeasurable value, an infinite worth? It exceeds every calculation, and there could be no way to objectify it. Were we to have a bank cheque of infinite value, there is no way we could cash it; for there is no bank with the resources to deal out what is needed to be on a par with it. What is this strange value? And what source could be on a par with making sense of its given reality? For it is a given reality; we do not produce or create this end; it is what we are, constitutive of our being."

285. *PU* 221: "The metaphysical difficulty of thinking the agapeic origin stems from

our disability of being, our own being as the living lack of agapeic generosity. We fail to understand an unconstrained gift. For us its excess is too much, something for nothing, purposive in its purposelessness beyond all our finite purposes."

*PU* 231: "Since our minds and being are so insistently erotic, such absolute agapeic being seems hardly conceivable, much less believable."

286. *EB* 218–19: "Hence our laying of ourselves as open seems like a constant striving, or like a pathway through a wilderness that often vanishes, making us think we had been fooling ourselves, only then to reappear suddenly further along, and hearten us that our faith in the good, faith without certitude, is not without unexpected fruit. The life of agapeic service is impossible if we are alone, and without the sustaining power of the good as other. As I suggested before, the familiar word (and I think best word) for transcendence itself is God."

287. *EB* 75: "God is the most secret partner, the most anonymous helper, the most intimate prompter, the good that asks nothing for itself, for its nature as the good is simply to broadcast the good to the other, broadcast itself to the other as other, sustaining that otherness."

Conclusion

1. *EB* 169–70: "There is a 'postmodernity' that, in all humility, seems to be coming around to a new insight into the patience of the human before God, and the active patience that is the ethics of generosity, and the life of service going with it. There is also a 'postmodernity,' and this seems the more frequent, which is an accentuation of the modern, an aggravation of the powers of self-determining, but now grown skeptical and bitter about themselves: wanting still to be absolute, insisting on themselves always, secretly now, overtly now; and yet knowing these cannot be absolute, for a presentiment of the other has made its way into the heart of humanity, puffing itself up as a project; the project is wounded by a shadow or a compassion or a terror or an abyss or . . . some indeterminate nothing."

2. Merold Westphal calls this "cognitive transubstantiation" (*Overcoming Onto-Theology*, 289).

# Bibliography

**William Desmond's Works**

*Art, Origins, Otherness.* Albany, N.Y.: SUNY Press, 2003.
"Autonomia Turannos." *Ethical Perspectives* 5:4 (1998).
*Being and the Between.* Albany, N.Y.: SUNY Press, 1995.
"Being, Determination, and Dialectic." *Review of Metaphysics* 48 (June 1995).
*Beyond Hegel and Dialectic.* Albany, N.Y.: SUNY Press, 1992.
"Caesar with the Soul of Christ." *Tijdschrift voor Filosofie* 61 (1999).
*Desire, Dialectic and Otherness.* New Haven, Conn.: Yale University Press, 1987.
*Ethics and the Between.* Albany, N.Y.: SUNY Press, 2001.
"Enemies." *Tijdschrift voor Filosofie* 63 (2001).
*God and the Between.* Oxford: Blackwell, 2008.
"God, Ethos, Ways." *International Journal of the Philosophy of Religion* 45 (1999).
*Hegel's God.* Aldershot: Ashgate, 2003.
"Hyperbolic Thoughts." In *Framing a Vision of the World,* ed. André Cloots and Santiago Sia. Leuven: Leuven University Press, 1999.
"Is There Metaphysics after Critique?" (2004) [unpublished].
"Neither Deconstruction nor Reconstruction." *International Philosophical Quarterly* 40:1:157 (March 2000).
"On the Betrayals of Reverence." *Irish Theological Quarterly* 65 (2000).
*Philosophy and Its Others.* Albany, N.Y.: SUNY Press, 1990.
"Philosophy of Religion." In *The Examined Life,* ed. Stanley Rosen. New York: Quality Paperback Book Club, 2000.
*Perplexity and Ultimacy.* Albany, N.Y.: SUNY Press, 1995.

**John D. Caputo's Works**

*After the Death of God.* Ed. Jeffery Robbins. New York: Columbia University Press, 2007.
*Against Ethics: Contributions to a Poetics of Obligation with Constant Reference to Deconstruction.* Bloomington: Indiana University Press, 1993.
"Beyond Aestheticism: Derrida's Responsible Anarchy." *Research in Phenomenology* 18 (1988).
*Blackwell Readings in Continental Philosophy: The Religious.* Ed. John D. Caputo. Oxford: Blackwell, 2001.
*Demythologizing Heidegger.* Bloomington: Indiana University Press, 1993.
"God and Anonymity: Prolegomena to an Ankhoral Religion." In *A Passion for the Impossible: John D. Caputo in Focus,* ed. Mark Dooley. Albany, N.Y.: SUNY Press, 2003.
"Heidegger, Kierkegaard and the Foundering of Metaphysics." In *International Kierkegaard Commentary,* Vol. 6: "Fear and Trembling" and "Repetition," ed. Robert Perkins. Macon, Ga.: Mercer University Press, 1993.
"Metanoetics: Elements of a Postmodern Christian Philosophy." In *Christian Philosophy Today.* New York: Fordham University Press, 1999.

*Modernity and Its Discontents.* New York: Fordham University Press, 1992.

*More Radical Hermeneutics: On Not Knowing Who We Are.* Bloomington: Indiana University Press, 2000.

"On Mystics, Magi, and Deconstructionists." In *Portraits of American Continental Philosophers,* ed. James Watson. Bloomington: Indiana University Press, 1999.

*On Religion.* London and New York: Routledge, 2001.

*Philosophy and Theology.* Nashville, Tenn.: Abingdon, 2006.

"Postmodernism and the Desire for God: An Email Conversation with Edith Wyschogrod." *Cross-Currents* 48:3 (Fall 1998).

*Radical Hermeneutics: Repetition, Deconstruction and the Hermeneutic Project.* Bloomington: Indiana University Press, 1987.

"The Good News about Alterity: Derrida and Theology." *Faith and Philosophy* 10 (1993).

*The Prayers and Tears of Jacques Derrida: Religion without Religion.* Bloomington: Indiana University Press, 1997.

*The Weakness of God: A Theology of the Event.* Bloomington: Indiana University Press, 2006.

"Without Sovereignty, Without Being: Unconditionality, the Coming God and Derrida's Democracy to Come." *JCRT* 4:3 (August 2003).


Other Works Cited

Badiou, Alain. *Being and Event.* Trans. Oliver Feltham. London: Continuum, 2005.

———. *Ethics: An Essay on the Understanding of Evil.* Trans. Peter Hallward. London: Verso, 2002.

Cunningham, Conor. *Genealogy of Nihilism.* London: Routledge, 2002.

Deleuze, Gilles. *Difference and Repetition.* Trans. Paul Patton. Columbia, 1995.

———. *The Logic of Sense.* Trans. Mark Lester. Columbia, 1990.

Hallward, Peter. *Badiou: A Subject to Truth.* Minneapolis: University of Minnesota Press, 2003.

Kelly, Thomas A. F., ed. *Between System and Poetics: William Desmond and Philosophy after Dialectic.* Aldershot: Ashgate, 2006.

Marion, Jean-Luc. *The Erotic Phenomenon.* Trans. Stephen E. Lewis. Chicago: University of Chicago, 2006.

Milbank, John. *Being Reconciled: Ontology and Pardon.* London: Routledge, 2003.

———. "Can the Gift Be Given? A Prolegomenon to a Future Trinitarian Metaphysics." *Modern Theology* 3:1 (1995).

———. *Theology and Social Theory.* 2nd ed. Oxford: Blackwell, 1990, 2006.

Pickstock, Catherine. *After Writing: On the Liturgical Consummation of Philosophy.* Oxford: Blackwell, 1998.

Pieper, Josef. *Leisure: The Basis of Culture.* Trans. Gerald Malsbary. South Bend, Ind.: St. Augustine's Press, 1998.

Westphal, Merold. *Overcoming Onto-Theology.* New York: Fordham University Press, 2001.

# Index

CPSIA information can be obtained
at www.ICGtesting.com
Printed in the USA
LVHW081603171218
600752LV00020B/1066/P